Oxford Studies in European Law

Series editors: Paul Craig and Gráinne de Búrca

THE EUROPEAN FUNDAMENTAL FREEDOMS

A Contextual Approach

OXFORD STUDIES IN EUROPEAN LAW

Series Editors: Paul Craig, Professor of English Law at St John's College, Oxford and Gráinne de Búrca, Professor of Law at New York University School of Law

The aim of this series is to publish important and original research on EU law. The focus is on scholarly monographs, with a particular emphasis on those which are interdisciplinary in nature. Edited collections of essays will also be included where they are appropriate. The series is wide in scope and aims to cover studies of particular areas of substantive and of institutional law, historical works, theoretical studies, and analyses of current debates, as well as questions of perennial interest such as the relationship between national and EU law and the novel forms of governance emerging in and beyond Europe. The fact that many of the works are interdisciplinary will make the series of interest to all those concerned with the governance and operation of the EU.

OTHER TITLES IN THIS SERIES

National Identity in EU Law
Elke Cloots

The Constitutional Foundations of European Contract Law
A Comparative Analysis
Kathleen Gutman

The Criminalization of European Cartel Enforcement
Theoretical, Legal, and Practical Challenges
Peter Whelan

Fundamental Rights in Europe
Challenges and Transformations in Comparative Perspective
Federico Fabbrini

The Principle of Loyalty in EU Law
Marcus Klamert

Constitutional Pluralism in the EU
Klemen Jaklic

EU Consumer Law and Human Rights
Iris Benöhr

The Principle of Mutual Recognition in EU Law
Christine Janssens

The Coherence of EU Free Movement Law
Constitutional Responsibility and the Court of Justice
Niamh Nic Shuibhne

European Law and New Health Technologies
Edited by Mark Flear, Anne-Maree Farrell, Tamara Hervey, and Thérèse Murphy

European Agencies
Law and Practices of Accountability
Madalina Busuioc

The Legal Effect of EU Agreements
Mario Mendez

The Foundations of European Union Competition Law
The Objective and Principles of Article 102
Renato Nazzini

The Emergence of EU Contract Law
Exploring Europeanization
Lucinda Miller

Participation in EU Rule-making
A Rights-Based Approach
Joana Mendes

Regulating Cartels in Europe
Second Edition
Christopher Harding, Julian Joshua

Religion and the Public Order of the European Union
Ronan McCrea

Governing Social Inclusion
Europeanization through Policy Coordination
Kenneth A. Armstrong

Judicial Control in the European Union
Reforming Jurisdiction in the Intergovernmental Pillars
Alicia Hinarejos

EU Counter-Terrorist Policies and Fundamental Rights
The Case of Individual Sanctions
Christina Eckes

From Dual to Cooperative Federalism
The Changing Structure of European Law
Robert Schütze

The European Fundamental Freedoms

A Contextual Approach

PEDRO CARO DE SOUSA

OXFORD
UNIVERSITY PRESS

OXFORD
UNIVERSITY PRESS

Great Clarendon Street, Oxford, OX2 6DP,
United Kingdom

Oxford University Press is a department of the University of Oxford. It furthers the University's objective of excellence in research, scholarship, and education by publishing worldwide. Oxford is a registered trade mark of Oxford University Press in the UK and in certain other countries

First Edition published in 2015

Published in the United States of America by Oxford University Press
198 Madison Avenue, New York, NY 10016, United States of America

British Library Cataloguing in Publication Data
Data available

Library of Congress Control Number: 2015934528

ISBN 978-0-19-872772-9

To family. To friends. Mas, especialmente, para o Avô.

SERIES EDITOR'S PREFACE

This is a book which deals with a well-known and much-analyzed subject, namely the internal market of the EU and its fundamental freedoms. However, the book seeks to bring a new perspective to the subject by arguing that traditional analytical approaches to appraising the development of the fundamental freedoms by the European Court of Justice are lacking. The author argues that they are lacking because they tend to focus exclusively on normative issues and omit adequate consideration of the institutional constraints and other extra-legal dimensions within which the Court operates and within which those fundamental freedoms apply.

Caro de Sousa argues that mainstream academic approaches to the four freedoms are generally de-contextualised, in that they seek to explain doctrinal developments by reference mainly or only to factors which are 'internal' to the law and the legal setting. By contrast, he argues that the development of the law on the four freedoms can be better understood in the light of disciplines 'external' to legal discourse. In particular he suggests that institutional and sociological factors, such as the interests of the stakeholders and litigants who are bringing cases, or the extra-legal constraints facing the court in trying to decide between different contested conceptions of single market rules, help to provide a more accurate account of EU free movement law as well as a more attractive theoretical framework for it. He points out that the interaction between the formal, internal legal doctrinal developments and these external factors are iterative, ongoing and two-way: law can create changes in the external environment, and the external environment can significantly influence the way the law develops.

The author illustrates his thesis by taking several key legal debates in the area of free movement law and demonstrating how external and internal factors interacted to produce particular shifts and developments in doctrine. More specifically, he points to external perspectives such as the interests of litigants who are in a position to sue, the choices faced by the court between various preferred conceptions of the internal market, and other institutional constraints on the court, to seek to explain peculiarities and sectoral divergences in doctrine as between different freedoms, such as the horizontal scope of the freedoms and the 'purely internal situation' limit.

In concluding the book, he argues that a 'normatively under-determined standard' should be adopted as the judicial test for identifying restrictions on free movement, so as to reflect the institutional realities of enforcement, as well as political fact of disagreement concerning the normative underpinnings of the internal market freedoms.

This is a clearly written and engaging book which offers a fresh and thoughtful perspective on a core area of EU law, namely the internal market and the fundamental freedoms. It should be of interest to students of law and political science alike who are concerned with questions of European integration and the role of the Court.

Paul Craig and Gráinne de Búrca

ACKNOWLEDGEMENTS

It is said it takes a village to raise a child. Not that this is in any way a fair comparison, but it took five large cities—Lisboa, Oxford, Firenze, London, and New York—to give birth to this book, which grew out of my DPhil dissertation at Oxford.

Without having lived in each of these places, this book would not be what it is; without having made the acquaintance of the people I met along the way, the experience of writing it would not have been half as enjoyable. Many people deserve thanks, and necessarily some names will be overlooked—I apologize in advance.

I must first acknowledge my supervisor, Stephen Weatherill, who provided constant support, helpful comments, and constructive criticism at every step of the way, without ever allowing his personal opinions to influence his assessment of my work—to this day, I'm still not quite sure what he thinks of the opinions I express in this book, and I mean this as a great compliment.

While at Oxford, and on the legal side, Raquel Barradas de Freitas, Vasiliki Brisimi, Ernesto Feliz, Maria Ioannidou, Insa Lee Koch, Pablo Marquez, Julian Nowag, and Anzhela Yevgenyeva provided me with much needed company, friendship and support. On the college side, particular thanks must go to Gordon Stevenson and James Reeve, who have learnt more about law than they ever wished to know. A number of other great friends I had the privilege to make—A.J., Ed Batrouney, Sourav Choudhouri, Jeremiah Dancy, Meg Edwards, Holly Morse, Charles Finch and Emily Popp, Jaya Gupta, Will Lawrence, Ana Isabel Lopez, James Ogg, Paulina Preciado, Natalie Sanderson, Julia Shanks, and Zinta Sommers, among others—also deserve to be mentioned. Thanks are also due to all the people at the Oxford Law Faculty and at Lady Margaret Hall who provided me with support and help. Lastly, I must express my gratitude to Ariel Ezrachi, Sionaidh Douglas-Scott and particularly to Angus Johnston and Jukka Snell, who provided extremely useful feedback on earlier versions of this book. I would also like to thank the two anonymous academic reviewers from OUP, who provided invaluable comments that led to this being a much better book.

During a period spent at the European University Institute, I had the privilege of thinking and learning in a fantastic scholarly environment. While I'd like to thank all the people I met there, the assistance and feedback I received from Miguel Poiares Maduro in particular, but also from Loic

Azoulai, Marise Cremona, Hans-Wolfgang Micklitz and Dennis Patterson were crucial. Particular thanks are due to Neil Komesar, who kindly agreed to comment on a very preliminary draft of this book. The great thing about the EUI, however, is not only its faculty but also its larger academic community, and concomitant possibilities for making good friends. In this respect, I must mention Luis Barroso, Goncalo Coelho, Johanna Croon, Fabiano de Andrade Correa, Juan Lamote de Grignon, Tiago Fidalgo de Freitas, Timo Hiller, Pedro Lomba, Mislav Mataija, Urska Petrovcic, Filipa Raimundo, Julien Topal, Guilherme Vilaca, and Visna Vukov to name just a few.

Back in London, I had the opportunity of becoming a member of the academic community at King's College, under the auspices of Piet Eeckhout and Andrea Biondi. It was another remarkable experience, and particular thanks are due to Egle Dagilyte, Katerina Maniadaki, and Stephanie Ripley for welcoming me into the fold.

In New York, thanks must go first to NYU's School of Law and to Prof. Weiler for taking me in. It was a memorable year, and I could not have asked for better roommates than Goncalo Coelho and Emillie Hunter. My experience would also not have been the same if I had not had been able to share it with fellow researchers at NYU, including Luigi Crema, Lisa Ginsborg, Lisa Kerr, Emily Kidd White, David Kosar, Rosio Lorca, Hillary Nye, Leonid Sirota, Arie Rosen, Neto Waite, and Vanessa Casado Perez. Particular thanks are due to Damian Chalmers and Ran Hirschl for reading and commenting on papers that I wrote while in New York, parts of which found their way into this book.

Lastly, I need to thank a number of people back home in Lisboa. This book would not have been possible if I had not been granted a four-years doctoral scholarship by FCT—Fundação para a Ciência e a Tecnologia. My friends at Linklaters—both in Lisboa and in London—proved invaluable in their support, and in keeping me grounded in the realities of practice even as I flew into the increasingly refined air of legal theory. Particular thanks in this regard are due to Carlos Pinto Correia, whose influence and personal friendship I cannot overstate, and to Linklaters LLP for giving me the time and support, first to undertake my doctoral studies, and, later, to convert my thesis into a book.

Naturally, my most wholehearted thanks are due to my closest friends and family—you know who you are, so you'll forgive me if I don't name you. In any event, while I expect some of you to try to read this book out of personal affection, there really is no need—just know that you are the reason I was able to write it in the first place.

CONTENTS

Table of Cases xv
Table of Statutes xxxiii
Table of Other Primary Legal Sources xxxv
List of Abbreviations xxxvii

Introduction 1

SECTION I. *The External and Internal Dimensions*

1. The External Dimension—Law, Courts, and the Court of Justice of the EU 9
   I. Introduction 9
   II. The Singular Nature of European Courts 10
   III. Extra-Legal Factors 16
   IV. Institutional Constraints and the Court of Justice 34
   V. Normative Implications 48
   VI. Conclusions 53

2. The Internal Dimension—The Fundamental Freedoms' Normative Foundations 55
   I. Introduction 55
   II. Normative Foundations Common to All Market Freedoms 55
   III. The Specific Normative Foundations of Individual Market Freedoms 63
   IV. European Citizenship 71
   V. Conclusion 83

SECTION II. *The Freedoms*

3. The Concept of Restriction on Free Movement—An Introduction 87

I. Introduction 87
II. A Bit of Legal History 87
III. Discriminatory Approaches 89
IV. Economic Due Process 99
V. Typological Approaches 103
VI. Access to Market 106
VII. Conclusion 114

4. Restricting Free Movement Rights—Unpacking the Normative Foundations 117

I. Introduction 117
II. What Do the Market Freedoms Do? 118
III. What Ought the Market Freedoms To Be Doing? 123
IV. Towards a Contextualized Perspective 124
V. Conclusion 135

5. Re-framing the Concept of Restriction 137

I. Introduction 137
II. Institutional Context and Free Movement Law 137
III. A More Comprehensive Description 146
IV. Normative Implications 166
V. Conclusion 172

6. The Fundamental Freedom's Scope—Beyond Restriction 175

I. Introduction 175
II. Cross-Border Movement 176
III. Economic Aim 188
IV. From Fundamental Freedoms to Rights of Free Movement—the Connecting Factor 193
V. Private Action and Free Movement—The Question of Horizontal Effect 200

VI. Some Normative Suggestions 214
VII. Conclusion 223

Conclusion 225

Bibliography 231
Index 255

TABLE OF CASES

Court of Justice of the European Union

Chronological and Numerical

2/73 Geddo v Ente [1973] E.C.R. 865 88
5/83 Rienks [1983] E.C.R 4233 141
6/64 Costa v ENEL [1964] E.C.R. 585 186
8/74 Dassonville [1974] E.C.R. 837 . . . . . 88, 99, 138, 140
13/76 Donà v Mantero [1976] E.C.R. 1333 . . . . . 201, 208, 212
14/83 von Colson [1984] E.C.R. 1891 206
15/74 Centrafarm v Sterling [1974] E.C.R. 1147 105
15/79 Groenveld [1979] E.C.R. 340 161–162
19/84 Pharmon v Hoechst [1985] E.C.R. 2281 . . . . . 203, 207
20/87 Gauchard [1987] E.C.R. 4879 178
20/85 Roviello [1988] E.C.R. 2805 119
33/74 van Binsbergen [1974] E.C.R. 1299 . . . . . 96, 106
33/88 Allué and Coonan [1989] E.C.R. 1591 94
34/79 Henn and Darby [1979] E.C.R. 3795 . . . . . 92, 191
35/76 Simmenthal [1976] E.C.R. 1871 . . . . . 105, 186, 206
35 and 36/82 Morson and Jhanjan [1982] E.C.R. 3723 . . . . . 58, 78, 196
36/74 Walrave [1974] E.C.R. 1405 . . . . . 62, 208, 211–212
39/75 Coenen [1975] E.C.R. 1547 92
39/86 Sylvie Lair [1988] E.C.R. 3161 78
41/84 Pinna [1986] E.C.R. 1 119
44/79 Hauer [1979] E.C.R. 3727 46
52/79 Debauve [1980] E.C.R. 833 185
55/80 and 57/80 Musik-Vertrieb [1981] E.C.R. 147 105
56 and 58/64 Consten and Grundig [1966] E.C.R. 299 211
58/80 Dansk Supermarked [1981] E.C.R. 181 . . . . . 203, 207
60/84 and 61/84 Cinéthèque [1985] E.C.R. 2605 . . . . . 100–101, 141
75/81 Blesgen [1982] E.C.R. 1211 101
76/86 Commission v Germany [1989] E.C.R. 121 128
78/70 Deutsche Grammophon [1971] E.C.R. 487 . . . . . 105, 211
80 and 81/77 Commissionnaires Réunis v Receveur des douanes [1978] E.C.R. 927 119
81/87 Daily Mail [1988] E.C.R. 5483 156–158
98/86 Mathot [1987] E.C.R. 809 . . . . . 85, 178
104/79 Foglia I [1980] E.C.R. 745 186

107/83 Klopp [1984] E.C.R. 2971 96
110/78 and C-111/78 Van Wesemael [1979] E.C.R. 35 . . . . . 92, 106, 140
115/78 Knoors [1979] E.C.R. 399 141
118/75 Watson and Belmann [1976] E.C.R. 1185 62
118/86 Nertsvoederfabriek Nederland [1987] E.C.R. 3883 162
120/78 Rewe-Zentral AG [1979] E.C.R. 649 . . . . . 88, 99, 126, 138–139
130/80 Kelderman [1981] E.C.R. 527 128
136/78 Auer [1979] E.C.R. 437 . . . . . 108, 141
143/87 Stanton [1988] E.C.R. 3877 . . . . . 68, 96, 153
145/88 Torfaen [1989] E.C.R. 765 . . . . . 60, 88, 101–103
148/85 Forest [1986] E.C.R. 3449 101
152/82 Forcheri [1983] E.C.R. 2323 56
154 and 155/87 Wolf and Dorchain [1988] E.C.R. 3897 . . . . . 68, 96
155/80 Oebel [1981] E.C.R. 1993 . . . . . 101, 161
172/82 Inter-Huiles [1983] E.C.R. 555 161
175/78 Saunders [1979] E.C.R. 1129 177
177 and 178/82 van de Haar [1984] E.C.R. 1797 . . . . . 203, 207
180/83 Moser [1984] E.C.R. 2539 180
186/87 Cowan [1989] E.C.R. 195 . . . . . 78, 193
187/80 Merck v Stephar [1981] E.C.R. 2063 . . . . . 105, 207
190/87 Moormann [1988] E.C.R. 4689 105
197/86 Malcolm Brown [1988] E.C.R. 3205 78
203/80 Casati [1981] E.C.R. 2595 . . . . . 60, 65
216/84 Commission v France [1988] E.C.R. 793 . . . . . 100, 128
222/86 Unectef v Heylens [1987] E.C.R. 4097 . . . . . 108, 142–143
237/82 Kaas [1984] E.C.R. 4025 161
240/83 ADBHU [1985] E.C.R. 531 57
244/80 Foglia II [1981] E.C.R. 3045 186
246/80 Broekmeulen [1981] E.C.R. 2311 141
263/86 Humbel [1988] E.C.R. 5365 190
265/87 Schräder [1989] E.C.R. 2237 48
271/82 Auer II [1983] E.C.R. 2727 . . . . . 108, 141
279/80 Webb [1981] E.C.R. 3305 106
286/81 Oosthoek's [1982] E.C.R. 4575 . . . . . 101, 161, 181
292/86 Gullung [1988] E.C.R. 111 141
294/83 Les Verts v Parliament [1986] E.C.R. 1339 11
311/85 Vlaamse Reisbureaus [1987] E.C.R. 3801 . . . . . 203, 207
314/81 to 316/81 and 83/82 Waterkeyn [1982] E.C.R. 4337 185
352/85 Bond van Adverteerders [1988] E.C.R. 20851 190
355/85 Driancourt v Cognet [1986] E.C.R. 3231 85
407/85 Drei Glocken [1988] E.C.R. 4233 185
434/85 Allen and Hanburys [1988] E.C.R. 1245 . . . . . 203, 207
C-265/88 Messner [1989] E.C.R. 4209 46

C-23/89 Quietlynn [1990] E.C.R. I-3059 101
C-54/88, C-91/88 and C-14/89 Nino [1990] E.C.R. I-3537 . . . . 178, 185
C-61/89 Bouchoucha [1990] E.C.R. I-3551 108
C-69/88 Krantz [1990] E.C.R. I-00583 101
C-106/89 Marleasing [1990] E.C.R. I-04135 206
C-175/88 Biehl [1990] E.C.R. I-1779. 147
C-331/88 *Ex Parte* Fedesa [1990] E.C.R. I-4023 . . . . 45, 48
C-362/88 GB-INNO-BM [1990] E.C.R. I-667 70
C-41/90 Höfner and Elser [1991] E.C.R. I-1979 . . . . 180, 185, 188, 190, 202
C-76/90 Säger [1991] E.C.R. I-4221 . . . . 88, 107, 143
C-154/89 Tourist Guides France [1991] E.C.R. I-00659. . . . . 97, 107, 143
C-159/90 Grogan [1991] E.C.R. I-4685 192
C-180/89 Tourist Guides Italy [1991] E.C.R. I-00709. 107
C-198/89 Tourist Guides Greece [1991] E.C.R. I-00727 . . . . 97, 107, 143, 178
C-339/89 Alsthom Atlantique [1991] E.C.R. I-00107 161
C-312/89 Conforama [1991] E.C.R. I-00997 . . . . 88, 101
C-332/89 Marchandise [1991] E.C.R. I-1027 . . . . 88, 101
C-340/89 Vlassopoulou [1991] E.C.R. I-2357 . . . . 88, 108, 142–143
C-349/87 Paraschi [1991] E.C.R. I-4501. 94
C-363/89 Roux [1991] E.C.R. I-00273 . . . . 60, 62, 68
C-2/90 Walloon Waste [1992] ECR I-4431 . . . . 191, 221
C-47/90 Delhaize frères [1992] E.C.R. I-3669. 162
C-60/91 Morais [1992] E.C.R. I-2085 178
C-104/91 Borrell [1992] E.C.R. I-3003. 142
C-106/91 Ramrath [1992] E.C.R. I-3351 . . . . 62, 68
C-169/91 Stoke and Norwich v B&Q [1992] E.C.R. I-6635 . . . . 46, 88
C-332/90 Steen [1992] E.C.R. I-341 185
C-351/90 Commission v Luxembourg [1992] E.C.R. I-3945. 96
C-369/90 Micheletti [1992] E.C.R. I-4239 74
C-370/90 Singh [1992] E.C.R. I-4265. . . . . 68, 193–194
C-19/92 Kraus [1993] E.C.R. I-1663 . . . . 57, 62, 88, 108, 143
C-109/92 Wirth [1993] E.C.R. I-64 190
C-112/91 Werner [1993] E.C.R. I-00429 196
C-157/92 Banchero [1993] E.C.R. I-1085 187
C-159/91 and C-160/91 Poucet and Pistre [1993] E.C.R. I-637 189
C-168/91 Konstantinidis [1993] E.C.R. I-1191. 197
C-259/91, C-331/91 and C-332/91 Allué and Coonen and others [1993] E.C.R. I-4309. 94
C-267/91 and 268/91 Keck and Mithouard [1993] E.C.R. I-6097. . . . . . 60, 88, 91, 104, 109–110, 144
C-272/92 Spotti [1993] E.C.R. I-5185. 94
C-292/92 Hünermund [1993] E.C.R. I-6787 . . . . 102–103, 110

C-18/93 Corsica Ferries Italia [1994] E.C.R. I-178 187
C-91/92 Faccini Dori [1994] E.C.R. I-03325 206
C-280/93 Germany v Council [1994] E.C.R. I-497. 73
C-315/92 Estée Lauder [1994] E.C.R. I-00317 105
C-319/92 Haim [1994] E.C.R. I-00425. 142
C-323/93 Crespelle [1994] E.C.R. I-5077 106
C-363/93, C-407/93, C-408/93, C-409/93, C-410/93 and C-411/93
Lancry [1994] E.C.R. I-3957 178
C-364/92 Eurocontrol [1994] E.C.R. I-0043 . . . . 189, 202
C-375/92 Commission v Spain [1994] E.C.R. I-0923 . . . . 107, 142–143
C-379/92 Peralta [1994] E.C.R. I-3453 185
C-55/94 Gebhard [1995] E.C.R. I-4165 142
C-80/94 Wielockx [1995] E.C.R. I-2493 148–149
C-96/94 Spedizioni Marittima del Golfo [1995] E.C.R. I-2883 202
C-107/94 Asscher [1996] E.C.R. I-3089 . . . . .68, 148
C-152/94 Buynder [1995] E.C.R. I-3981. 178
C-279/93 Schumaker [1995] E.C.R. I-0225 148–149
C-384/93 Alpine Investments [1995] E.C.R. I-1141. . . . 88, 109–110, 114, 162, 181
C-412/93 Leclerc-Siplec [1995] E.C.R. I-0179. . . . . 93, 104, 106, 114
C-415/03 Bosman [1995] E.C.R. I-4921 . . . . .88, 110, 114, 172, 201, 211–212
C-9/94, C-10/94, C-11/94, C-14/94, C-15/94, C-23/94, C-24/94 and
C-332/94 Semeraro and Others [1996] E.C.R. I-2975 60
C-53/95 Kemmler [1996] E.C.R. I-0703. 153
C-84/94 UK v Council [1996] E.C.R. I-5755. 48
C-193/94 Skanavi and Chryssanthakopoulos [1996] E.C.R. I-0929. . . . . . . .46, 77
C-237/94 John O'Flynn [1996] E.C.R. I-2617 94–95
C-267/95 and C-268/95 Beecham Group v Europharm [1996]
E.C.R. I-6285 207
C-278/94 Commission v Belgium [1996] E.C.R. I-4307 .95
C-470/93 Mars [1996] E.C.R. I-1923 105
C-29/95 Pastoors [1997] E.C.R. I-285 46
C-34/95 to 36/95 De Agostini [1997] E.C.R. I-3843 . . . . 93, 105
C-64/96 and C-65/96 Uecker and Jacquet [1997] E.C.R. I-3171 178
C-105/94 Ditta A. Celestini [1997] E.C.R. I-2971. 106
C-114/96 Kieffer and Thill [1997] E.C.R. I-3629 106
C-189/95 Franzén [1997] E.C.R. I-5909. 106
C-250/95 Futura [1997] E.C.R. I-2417 150
C-265/95 Commission v France [1997] E.C.R. I-6959 . . . . 57, 106, 209, 212
C-299/95 Kremzow [1997] E.C.R. I-2629 180
C-316/95 Generics [1997] E.C.R. I-3929 . . . . .203, 207
C-321/94 to C-324/94 Pistre [1997] E.C.R I-2343 179
C-337/95 Evora [1997] E.C.R. I-6013 106

C-343/95 Cali & Figli [1997] E.C.R. I-1547 .202
C-358/95 Morellato [1997] E.C.R. I-1431 .106
C-368/95 Familiapress [1997] E.C.R. I-3689 .105
C-35/96 Commission v Italy [1998] E.C.R. I-3851 .202
C-85/96 Martínez Sala [1998] E.C.R. I-2691 .72–73, 208
C-120/95 Nicolas Decker [1998] E.C.R. I-1831 .154
C-158/96 Kohll [1998] E.C.R. I-1931 .154
C-200/96 Metronome [1998] E.C.R. I-01953 .70
C-266/96 Corsica Ferries France [1998] E.C.R. I-3949 57, 162
C-274/96 Bickel and Franz [1998] E.C.R. I-7637 .62, 76, 194
C-336/96 Gilly [1998] E.C.R. I-2793 148, 151
C-375/96 Zaninotto [1998] E.C.R. I-6629 .48
C-67/96 Albany [1999] E.C.R. I-5751 .202
C-108/98 RI.SAN. [1999] E.C.R. I-5219 .181
C-115/97 to C-117/97 Brentjens' [1999] E.C.R. I-6025 .202
C-212/97 Centros [1999] E.C.R. I-1459 .158
C-294/97 Eurowings [1999] E.C.R. I-7447 .147
C-307/97 Saint-Gobain [1999] E.C.R. I-6161 150–151
C-350/97 Wilfried Monsees [1999] E.C.R. I-2921 106, 162
C-378/97 Wijsenbeek [1999] E.C.R. I-6207 .46, 77
C-391/97 Gschwind [1999] E.C.R. I-5451 .148
C-412/97 ED v Fenocchio [1999] E.C.R. I-3845 161–162
C-34/98 Commission v France [2000] E.C.R. I-995 .57
C-51/96 and C-191/97 Deliège [2000] E.C.R. I-2549 181, 201, 212
C-135/99 Ursula Elsen [2000] E.C.R. I-10409 .62, 76
C-176/96 Lethonen [2000] E.C.R. I-2681 .113
C-180/98 to C-184/98 Pavlov [2000] E.C.R. I-6451 .189
C-190/98 Graf [2000] E.C.R. I-00493 114, 172
C-228/98 Dounias [2000] E.C.R. I-00577 .57
C-238/98 Hocsman [2000] E.C.R. I-6623 .142
C-254/98 TK-Heimdienst [2000] E.C.R. I-00151 93, 105
C-281/98 Angonese [2000] E.C.R. I-4139 95, 213
C-355/98 Commission v Belgium [2000] E.C.R. I-1221 .106
C-376/98 Tobacco Advertising I [2000] ECR I-8419 .121
C-448/98 Guimont [2000] E.C.R. I-10663 179, 182, 184
C-17/00 De Coster [2001] E.C.R. I-9445 147, 150
C-157/99 Smits & Peerbooms [2001] E.C.R. I-5473 .190
C-162/99 Commission v Italy [2001] E.C.R. I-00541 95, 143
C-184/99 Grzelczyk [2001] E.C.R. I-6193 .73
C-368/98 Vanbraekel [2001] E.C.R. I-5363 155, 190
C-379/98 PreussenElektra [2001] E.C.R. I-2099 180, 221
C-405/98 Gourmet International [2001] E.C.R. I-1795 105, 181

Case C-491/01 British American Tobacco [2002] ECR I-11543 . . . . .48, 121
C-60/00 Carpenter [2002] E.C.R. I-6279 194–195
C-100/01 Oteiza Olazabal [2002] E.C.R. I-10981 77
C-136/00 Danner [2002] E.C.R. I-8147 147
C-159/00 Sapod Audic [2002] E.C.R. I-5031 . . . . .203, 207
C-208/00 Überseering [2002] E.C.R. I-9919. 157–158
C-224/98 D'Hoop [2002] E.C.R. I-6191 76
C-309/99 Wouters [2002] E.C.R. I-1577 . . . . 201, 212
C-324/00 Lankhorst-Hohorst [2002] E.C.R. I-11779 150
C-385/00 de Groot [2002] E.C.R. I-11819 150–151
C-390/99 Canal Satélite Digital [2002] E.C.R. I-00607 . . . . .60, 62, 64
C-393/99 and C-394/99 INASTI [2002] E.C.R. I-2829 153
C-413/99 Baumbast [2002] E.C.R. I-7091 . . . . .72, 208
C-436/00 X and Y [2002] E.C.R. I-10829. . . . . .97, 150
C-483/99 Commission v France [2002] E.C.R. I-4871 57
C-515/99, C-519/99 to C-524/99, and C-526/99 to C-540/99 Reisch [2002] E.C.R. I-2157 . . . . 177, 180
C-6/01 Anomar [2003] E.C.R. I-8261 . . . . .180, 186
C-42/02 Lindman [2003] E.C.R. I-13519 . . . . 147, 150
C-92/01 Stylianakis [2003] E.C.R. I-1291 77
C-92/02 Kristiansen [2003] E.C.R. I-14597 154
C-109/01 Akrich [2003] E.C.R. I-9607. 196
C-112/00 Schmidberger [2003] E.C.R. I-5659 . . . . 57, 70, 209, 212, 218
C-167/01 Inspire Art [2003] E.C.R. I-10155 158
C-168/01 Bosal [2003] E.C.R. I-9409. 150
C-232/01 van Lent [2003] E.C.R. I-11525 97
C-234/01 Gerritse [2003] E.C.R. I-5933. . . . . 147–148, 151
C-313/01 Morgenbesser [2003] E.C.R. I-13467 142
C-318/00 Bacardi-Martini [2003] E.C.R. I-0905. 187
C-322/01 DocMorris [2003] E.C.R. I-14887 . . . . .93, 105
C-355/00 Freskot [2003] E.C.R. I-5263. . . . . 181, 190
C-385/99 Müller-Fauré [2003] E.C.R. I-4509 . . . . 57, 155
C-8/02 Leichtle [2004] E.C.R. I-2641 155
C-36/02 Omega [2004] E.C.R. I-9609 . . . . 70, 181, 218
C-72/03 Carbonati Apuani [2004] E.C.R. I-8027 178
C-210/03 Swedish Match [2004] E.C.R. I-11893 121
C-239/02 Douwe Egberts [2004] E.C.R. I-7007 105
C-293/03 Gregorio My [2004] E.C.R. I-12013. 196
C-442/02 CaixaBank [2004] E.C.R. I-8961 . . . . 88, 110, 113–114
C-456/02 Trojani [2004] E.C.R. I-7573 62
C-39/04 Fournier [2005] E.C.R. I-2057 147
C-151/04 and C-152/04 Nadin [2005] E.C.R. I-11203 68
C-209/03 Bidar [2005] E.C.R. I-2119 78

C-215/03 Oulane [2005] E.C.R. I-01215 181
C-250/03 Mauri [2005] E.C.R. I-1267 180
C-293/02 Jersey Produce [2005] E.C.R. I-9543 . . . . 163, 178
C-376/03 D. [2005] E.C.R. I-2421. . . . . 148, 150
C-403/03 Schempp [2005] E.C.R. I-6421 150
C-411/03 SEVIC [2005] E.C.R. I-10805 159
C-446/03 Marks & Spencer [2005] E.C.R. I-10837. 150
C-94/04 and C-202/04 Cipolla [2006] E.C.R. I-2107 113
C-152/03 Ritter-Coulais [2006] E.C.R. I-1711 . . . . 180, 196
C-158/04 and C-159/04 Alfa Vita Vassilopoulos [2006]
E.C.R. I-8135 . . . . 77, 79, 105
C-192/05 Tas-Hagen [2006] E.C.R. I-10451 72
C-205/03 P FENIN [2006] E.C.R. I-6295. 188–189
C-345/05 Commission v Portugal [2006] E.C.R. I-10633 77
C-374/04 Test Claimants [2006] E.C.R. I-11673 153
C-380/03 Tobacco Advertising II [2006] E.C.R. I-11573 120–121
C-410/04 ANAV [2006] E.C.R. I-3303. 181
C-452/04 Fidium Finanz [2006] E.C.R. I-8135 61
C-493/04 Piatkowski [2006] E.C.R. I-2369 154
C-513/03 van Hilten-van der Heijden [2006] E.C.R. I-10653 . . . . 178, 191
C-513/04 Kerckhaert and Morris [2006] ECR I-10967 151
C-519/04 P Meca-Medina [2006] E.C.R. I-6991 188–189
C-520/04 Turpeinen [2006] E.C.R. I-10685 . . . . 148, 151
C-1/05 Jia [2007] E.C.R. I-001 196
C-11/06 and C-12/06 Morgan and Bucher [2007]
E.C.R. I-9161 77
C-40/05 Lyyski [2007] E.C.R. I-0099 89
C-134/05 Commission v Italy [2007] E.C.R. I-6251 113
C-157/05 Holböck [2007] E.C.R. I-4051 61
C-182/06 Lakebrink [2007] E.C.R. I-6705. 148
C-208/05 ITC [2007] E.C.R. I-181. 77
C-284/04 T-Mobile Austria [2007] E.C.R. I-05189. 188
C-291/05 Eind [2007] E.C.R. I-10719 194
C-329/05 Meindl [2007] E.C.R. I-1107. 148
C-332/05 Cellozi [2007] E.C.R. I-0056 95
C-341/05 Laval [2007] E.C.R. I-11767 . . . . 89, 219
C-392/05 Alevizos [2007] E.C.R. I-3505 . . . . .96, 152
C-438/05 Viking [2007] E.C.R. I-10779 . . . . 118, 208–209, 213, 222
C-444/05 Stamatelaki [2007] E.C.R. I-3185 155
C-464/05 Geurts [2007] E.C.R. I-9325 196
C-94/07 Raccanelli [2008] E.C.R. I-5939. . . . . 213, 219
C-127/08 Metock [2008] ECR I-6241. 196
C-141/07 Commission v Germany [2008] E.C.R. I-06935 . . . . .93, 105

C-152/05 Commission v Germany [2008] E.C.R. I-00039 196
C-205/07 Gysbrechts and Santurel Inter [2008] E.C.R. I-09947 161–162
C-210/06 Cartesio [2008] E.C.R. I-9641 160–161
C-212/06 Government of Communauté française and Gouvernement wallon [2008] E.C.R. I-1683. . . . . 185, 196
C-228/07 Petersen [2008] E.C.R. I-6989 153
C-282/07 Truck Center [2008] E.C.R. I-10767 96
C-330/07 Vermögensverwaltungs-Gesellschaft [2008] E.C.R. I-9099. 147
Case C-389/05 Commission v France [2008] E.C.R. I-5337 113
C-402/05 P and C-415/05 P Kadi [2008] E.C.R. I-06351 218
C-527/06 Renneberg [2008] E.C.R. I-7735. . . . . .96, 148, 196
C-110/05 Commission v Italy [2009] ECR I-00519 . . . . 88, 111
C-142/05 Mickelsson and Roos [2009] E.C.R. I-04273. . . . . 111, 172
C-171/07 and C-172/07 Apothekerkammer des Saarlandes [2009] E.C.R. I-04171. 113
C-208/07 Chamier-Glisczinski [2009] E.C.R. I-06095 .119
C-269/07 Commission v Germany [2009] E.C.R. I-07811 97
C-314/08 Filipiak [2009] E.C.R. I-11049 . . . . .98, 147
C-318/07 Hein Persche [2009] E.C.R. I-00359 191
C-345/08 Peśla [2009] E.C.R. I-11677 142
C-81/09 Idrima Tipou [2010] E.C.R. I-10161 113
C-96/08 CIBA [2010] E.C.R. I-2911. 151
C-108/09 Ker-Optika [2010] E.C.R. I-12213 113
C-173/09 Elchinov [2010] E.C.R. I-08889 155
C-211/08 Commission v Spain [2010] E.C.R. I-5267. 155
C-311/08 SGI [2010] E.C.R. I-487 89
C-325/08 Olympique Lyonnais [2010] E.C.R. I-02177 113
C-384/08 Attanasio [2010] E.C.R. I-02055. 113
C-421/09 Humanplasma [2010] E.C.R. I-12869 57
C-510/08 Mattner [2010] E.C.R. I-3553 148
C-512/08 Commission v France [2010] E.C.R. I-08833 155
C-543/08 Commission v Portugal [2010] E.C.R. I-11241 109
C-25/10 Missionswerk [2011] E.C.R. I-00497 191
C-34/09 Zambrano [2011] I-01177 . . . . 75, 82, 178, 208, 216
C-161/09 Kakavetsos-Fragkopoulos [2011] I-00915 163
C-212/09 Commission v Portugal [2011] I-10889 113
C-255/09 Commission v Portugal [2011] I-10547. 155
C-256/11 Dereci [2011] I-11315. . . . . .76, 178, 208
C-284/09 Commission v Germany [2011] I-09879 151
C-434/09 McCarthy [2011] I-03375 . . . . 75, 178
C-378/10 Vale [2012] 161
C-617/10 Åkerberg Fransson [2013] 200
C-48/13 Nordea Bank Danmark [2014] 150

C-204 to C-208/12 Essent Belgium [2014] 221–222
C-254/13 *Orgacom* [2014] 178
C-326/12 van Caster [2014] 150
C-390/12 Pfleger [2014] 200
C-457/12 S and G [2014] 195
C-573/12 Ålands vindkraft AB [2014] 221

Chronological and Alphabetical

Costa v ENEL (Case 6/64) [1964] E.C.R. 585 186
Consten and Grundig (Joined Cases 56 and 58/64) [1966] E.C.R. 299 211
Deutsche Grammophon (Case 78/70) [1971] E.C.R. 487 . . . . 105, 211
Geddo v Ente (Case 2/73) [1973] E.C.R. 865 88
Centrafarm v Sterling (Case 15/74) [1974] E.C.R. 1147 105
Dassonville (Case 8/74) [1974] E.C.R. 837 . . . . 88, 99, 138, 140
van Binsbergen (Case 33/74) [1974] E.C.R. 1299 . . . . 96, 106
Walrave (Case 36/74) [1974] E.C.R. 1405 . . . . 62, 208, 211–212
Coenen (Case 39/75) [1975] E.C.R. 1547 92
Donà v Mantero (Case 13/76) [1976] E.C.R. 1333 . . . . 201, 208, 212
Simmenthal (Case 35/76) [1976] E.C.R. 1871 . . . . 105, 186, 206
Watson and Belmann (Case 118/75) [1976] E.C.R. 1185 62
Commissionnaires Réunis v Receveur des douanes
(Joined Cases 80 and 81/77) [1978] E.C.R. 927 119
Auer (Case 136/78) [1979] E.C.R. 437 . . . . 108, 141
Groenveld (Case 15/79) [1979] E.C.R. 3409 161–162
Hauer (Case 44/79) [1979] E.C.R. 3727 46
Henn and Darby (Case 34/79) [1979] E.C.R. 3795 . . . . 92, 191
Knoors (Case 115/78) [1979] E.C.R. 399 141
Rewe-Zentral AG (Case 120/78) [1979] E.C.R. 649 . . . . 88, 99, 126, 138–139
Saunders (Case 175/78) [1979] E.C.R.1129 177
Van Wesemael (Joined Cases C-110/78 and C-111/78) [1979]
E.C.R. 35 . . . . 92, 106, 140
Debauve (Case 52/79) [1980] E.C.R. 833 185
Foglia I (Case 104/79) [1980] E.C.R. 745 186
Broekmeulen (Case 246/80) [1981] E.C.R. 2311 141
Casati (Case 203/80) [1981] E.C.R. 2595 . . . . 60, 65
Dansk Supermarked (Case 58/80) [1981] E.C.R. 181 . . . . 203, 207
Foglia II (Case 244/80) [1981] E.C.R. 3045 186
Kelderman (Case 130/80) [1981] E.C.R. 527 128
Merck v Stephar (Case 187/80) [1981] E.C.R. 2063 . . . . 105, 207
Musik-Vertrieb (Joined Cases 55/80 and 57/80) [1981] E.C.R. 147 105
Oebel (Case 155/80) [1981] E.C.R. 1993 . . . . 101, 161
Webb (Case 279/80) [1981] E.C.R. 3305 106

Blesgen (Case 75/81) [1982] E.C.R. 1211 101
Morson and Jhanjan (Joined Cases 35 and 36/82) [1982] E.C.R. 3723 . . . 58, 78, 196
Oosthoek's (Case 286/81) [1982] E.C.R. 4575 . . . . . 101, 161, 181
Waterkeyn (Joined Cases 314/81 to 316/81 and 83/82) [1982] E.C.R. 4337 185
Auer II (Case 271/82) [1983] E.C.R. 2727 . . . . . 108, 141
Forcheri (Case 152/82) [1983] E.C.R. 2323 56
Inter-Huiles (Case 172/82) [1983] E.C.R. 555 161
Rienks (Case 5/83) [1983] E.C.R 4233 141
Kaas (Case 237/82) [1984] E.C.R. 4025 161
Klopp (Case 107/83) [1984] E.C.R. 2971 96
Moser (Case 180/83) [1984] E.C.R. 2539 180
van de Haar (Joined Cases 177 and 178/82) [1984] E.C.R. 1797 . . . . . 203, 207
von Colson (Case 14/83) [1984] E.C.R. 1891 206
ADBHU (Case 240/83) [1985] E.C.R. 531 57
Cinéthèque (Joined Cases 60/84 and 61/84) [1985] E.C.R. 2605 . . . . 100–101, 141
Pharmon v Hoechst (Case 19/84) [1985] E.C.R. 2281 . . . . . 203, 207
Commission v France (Case 270/83) [1986] E.C.R. 273 147
Driancourt v Cognet (Case 355/85) [1986] E.C.R. 323 85
Forest (Case 148/85) [1986] E.C.R. 3449 101
Les Verts v Parliament (Case 294/83) [1986] E.C.R. 1339 11
Pinna (Case 41/84) [1986] E.C.R. 1 119
Commission v Germany (Case 178/84) [1987] E.C.R. 1227 47
Gauchard (Case 20/87) [1987] E.C.R. 4879 178
Mathot (Case 98/86) [1987] E.C.R. 809 . . . . . 85, 178
Nertsvoederfabriek Nederland (Case 118/86) [1987] E.C.R. 3883 162
Unectef v Heylens (Case 222/86) [1987] E.C.R. 4097 . . . . . 108, 142–143
Vlaamse Reisbureaus (Case 311/85) [1987] E.C.R. 3801 . . . . . 202, 207
Allen and Hanburys (Case 434/85) [1988] E.C.R. 1245 . . . . . 203, 207
Bond van Adverteerders (Case 352/85) [1988] E.C.R. 2085 190
Commission v France (Case 216/84) [1988] E.C.R. 793 . . . . . 100, 128
Daily Mail (Case 81/87) [1988] E.C.R. 5483 156–158
Drei Glocken (Case 407/85) [1988] E.C.R. 4233 181
Gullung (Case 292/86) [1988] E.C.R. 111 141
Humbel (Case 263/86) [1988] E.C.R. 5365 190
Malcolm Brown (Case 197/86) [1988] E.C.R. 3205 78
Moormann (Case 190/87) [1988] E.C.R. 4689 105
Roviello (Case 20/85) [1988] E.C.R. 2805 119
Stanton (Case 143/87) [1988] E.C.R. 3877 . . . . . 68, 96, 153
Sylvie Lair (Case 39/86) [1988] E.C.R. 3161 78
Wolf and Dorchain (Joined Cases 154 and 155/87) [1988] E.C.R. 3897 . . . . . 68, 96
Allué and Coonan (Case 33/88) [1989] E.C.R. 1591 94
Commission v Germany (Case 76/86) [1989] E.C.R. 121 128
Cowan (Case 186/87) [1989] E.C.R. 195 . . . . . 78, 193

Messner (Case C-265/88) [1989] E.C.R. 4209 46
Schräder (Case 265/87) [1989] E.C.R. 2237 48
Torfaen (Case 145/88) [1989] E.C.R. 765 . . . . 60, 88, 101–103
Biehl (Case C-175/88) [1990] E.C.R. I-1779 147
Bouchoucha (Case C-61/89) [1990] E.C.R. I-3551 108
Ex Parte Fedesa (Case C-331/88) [1990] E.C.R. I-4023 . . . . .45, 48
GB-INNO-BM (Case C-362/88) [1990] E.C.R. I-667 70
Krantz (Case C-69/88) [1990] E.C.R. I-00583. 101
Marleasing (Case C-106/89) [1990] E.C.R. I-04135. 206
Nino (Joined Cases C-54/88, C-91/88 and C-14/89) [1990]
E.C.R. I-3537. . . . . 178, 185
Quietlynn (Case C-23/89) [1990] E.C.R. I-3059 101
Alsthom Atlantique (Case C-339/89) [1991] E.C.R. I-00107. 161
Conforama (Case C-312/89) [1991] E.C.R. I-00997 . . . . 88, 101
Grogan (Case C-159/90) [1991] E.C.R. I-4685 192
Höfner and Elser (Case C-41/90) [1991] E.C.R. I-1979. . . . 180, 185, 188, 190, 202
Marchandise (Case C-332/89) [1991] E.C.R. I-1027 . . . . 88, 101
Paraschi (Case C-349/87) [1991] E.C.R. I-4501 94
Roux (Case C-363/89) [1991] E.C.R. I-00273. . . . . .60, 62, 68
Säger (Case C-76/90) [1991] E.C.R. I-4221 . . . . 88, 107, 143
Tourist Guides France (Case C-154/89) [1991] E.C.R. I-00659 . . . . . . 97, 107, 143
Tourist Guides Greece (Case C-198/89) [1991] E.C.R. I-00727 . . .97, 107, 143, 178
Tourist Guides Italy (Case C-180/89) [1991] E.C.R. I-00709 107
Vlassopoulou (Case C-340/89) [1991] E.C.R. I-2357. . . . . 88, 108, 142–143
Borrell (Case C-104/91) [1992] E.C.R. I-3003 142
Commission v Luxembourg (Case C-351/90) [1992] E.C.R. I-3945 96
Delhaize frères (Case C-47/90) [1992] E.C.R. I-366 162
Micheletti (Case C-369/90) [1992] E.C.R. I-4239 74
Morais (Case C-60/91) [1992] E.C.R. I-2085 178
Ramrath (Case C-106/91) [1992] E.C.R. I-3351 . . . . .62, 68
Singh (Case C-370/90) [1992] E.C.R. I-4265 . . . . 68, 193–194
Steen (Case C-332/90) [1992] E.C.R. I-341 185
Stoke and Norwich v B&Q (Case C-169/91) [1992] E.C.R. I-6635. . . . . .46, 88
Walloon Waste (Case C-2/90) [1992] E.C.R. I-4431 . . . . 191, 221
Allué and Coonen and others (Joined cases C-259/91, C-331/91 and
C-332/91) [1993] E.C.R. I-4309 94
Banchero (Case C-157/92) [1993] E.C.R. I-1085 187
Hünermund (Case C-292/92) [1993] E.C.R. I-6787 . . . . 102–103, 110
Keck and Mithouard (Joined Cases C-267/91 and 268/91)
[1993] E.C.R. I-6097. . . . . 60, 88, 91, 104, 109–110, 144
Konstantinidis (Case C-168/91) [1993] E.C.R. I-1191 197
Kraus (Case C-19/92) [1993] E.C.R. I-1663 . . . . 57, 62, 88, 108, 143
Poucet and Pistre (C-159/91 and C-160/91) [1993] E.C.R. I-637. 189
Spotti (Case C-272/92) [1993] E.C.R. I-5185 94

Werner (Case C-112/91) [1993] E.C.R. I-00429 196
Wirth (Case C-109/92) [1993] E.C.R. I-6447 190
Commission v Spain (Case C-375/92) [1994] E.C.R. I-0923 .... 107, 142–143
Corsica Ferries Italia (Case C-18/93) [1994] E.C.R. I-1783.................187
Crespelle (Case C-323/93) [1994] E.C.R. I-5077 106
Estée Lauder (Case C-315/92) [1994] E.C.R. I-00317 105
Eurocontrol (Case C-364/92) [1994] E.C.R. I-0043 ....189, 202
Faccini Dori (Case C-91/92) [1994] E.C.R. I-03325 206
Germany v Council (Case C-280/93) [1994] E.C.R. I-4973 73
Haim (Case C-319/92) [1994] E.C.R. I-00425 142
Lancry (Joined Cases C-363/93, C-407/93, C-408/93, C-409/93,
C-410/93 and C-411/93) [1994] E.C.R. I-3957 178
Peralta (Case C-379/92) [1994] E.C.R. I-3453 185
Alpine Investments (Case C-384/93) [1995] E.C.R. I-1141 .... 88, 109–110,
114, 162, 181
Bosman (Case C-415/03) [1995] E.C.R. I-4921 ....88, 110, 114, 172, 201, 211–212
Buynder (Case C-152/94) [1995] E.C.R. I-3981 178
Gebhard (Case C-55/94) [1995] E.C.R. I-4165............................142
Leclerc-Siplec (Case C-412/93) [1995] E.C.R. I-0179 .... 93, 104, 106, 114
Schumaker (Case C-279/93) [1995] E.C.R. I-0225....................148–149
Spedizioni Marittima del Golfo (Case C-96/94) [1995] E.C.R. I-2883 202
Wielockx (Case C-80/94) [1995] E.C.R. I-2493......................148–149
Asscher (Case C-107/94) [1996] E.C.R. I-3089 ....68, 148
Beecham Group v Europharm (Joined Cases C-267/95 and C-268/95)
[1996] E.C.R. I-6285...207
Commission v Belgium (Case C-278/94) [1996] E.C.R. I-4307 95
John O'Flynn (Case C-237/94) [1996] E.C.R. I-2617....................94–95
Kemmler (Case C-53/95) [1996] E.C.R. I-0703 153
Mars (Case C-470/93) [1996] E.C.R. I-1923.............................105
Semeraro and Others (Joined Cases C-418/93 to C-420/93, C-421/93,
C-460/93, C-461/93, C-462/93, C-464/93, C-9/94, C-10/94,
C-11/94, C-14/94, C-15/94, C-23/94, C-24/94 and C-332/94)
[1996] E.C.R. I-2975...60
Skanavi and Chryssanthakopoulos (Case C-193/94) [1996]
E.C.R. I-0929 ....46, 77
UK v Council (Case C-84/94) [1996] E.C.R. I-5755 48
Cali & Figli (Case C-343/95) [1997] E.C.R. I-1547 202
Commission v France (Case C-265/95) [1997] E.C.R. I-6959.... 57, 106, 209, 212
De Agostini (Joined Cases C-34/95 to 36/95) [1997] E.C.R. I-3843· 93, 105
Ditta A. Celestini (Case C-105/94) [1997] E.C.R. I-2971 106
Evora (Case C-337/95) [1997] E.C.R. I-6013 106
Familiapress (Case C-368/95) [1997] E.C.R. I-3689 105
Franzén (Case C-189/95) [1997] E.C.R. I-5909 106

Futura (Case C-250/95) [1997] E.C.R. I-2417 150
Generics (Case C-316/95) [1997] E.C.R. I-3929. . . . . 203, 207
Kieffer and Thill (Case C-114/96) [1997] E.C.R. I-3629. 106
Kremzow (Case C-299/95) [1997] E.C.R. I-2629. 180
Morellato (Case C-358/95) [1997] E.C.R. I-1431 106
Pastoors (Case C-29/95) [1997] E.C.R. I-285. 46
Pistre (Joined Cases C-321/94 to C-324/94) [1997] E.C.R I-2343 179
Uecker and Jacquet (Joined Cases C-64/96 and C-65/96) [1997]
E.C.R. I-3171. 178
Bickel and Franz (Case C-274/96) [1998] E.C.R. I-7637 . . . . .62, 76, 194
Commission v Italy (Case C-35/96) [1998] E.C.R. I-3851 202
Corsica Ferries France (Case C-266/96) [1998] E.C.R. I-3949 . . . . 57, 162
Gilly (Case C-336/96) [1998] E.C.R. I-2793. . . . . 148, 151
Kohll (Case C-158/96) [1998] E.C.R. I-1931 154
Martínez Sala (Case C-85/96) [1998] E.C.R. I-2691 . . . . .72–73, 208
Metronome (Case C-200/96) [1998] E.C.R. I-01953 70
Nicolas Decker (Case C-120/95) [1998] E.C.R. I-1831 154
Zaninotto (Case C-375/96) E.C.R. I-6629 48
Albany (Case C-67/96) [1999] E.C.R. I-5751 202
Brentjens' (Joined Cases C-115/97 to C-117/97) [1999]
E.C.R. I-6025 202
Centros (Case C-212/97) [1999] E.C.R. I-1459 158
ED v Fenocchio (Case C-412/97) E.C.R. I-3845 161–162
Eurowings (Case C-294/97) [1999] E.C.R. I-7447. 147
Gschwind (Case C-391/97) [1999] E.C.R. I-5451. 148
RI.SAN. (Case C-108/98) [1999] E.C.R. I-5219. 181
Saint-Gobain (Case C-307/97) [1999] E.C.R. I-6161. 150–151
Wijsenbeek (Case C-378/97) [1999] E.C.R. I-6207 . . . . .46, 77
Wilfried Monsees (Case C-350/97) [1999] E.C.R. I-2921 . . . . 106, 162
Angonese (Case C-281/98) [2000] E.C.R. I-4139 . . . . 95, 213
Commission v Belgium (Case C-355/98) [2000] E.C.R. I-1221. 106,
Commission v France (Case C-34/98) [2000] E.C.R. I-995 57
Deliège (Joined Cases C-51/96 and C-191/97) [2000]
E.C.R. I-2549 . . . . 181, 201, 212
Dounias (Case C-228/98) [2000] E.C.R. I-00577 57
Graf (Case C-190/98) [2000] E.C.R. I-493. . . . . 114, 172
Guimont (Case C-448/98) [2000] E.C.R. I-10663. . . . . 179, 182, 184
Hocsman (Case C-238/98) E.C.R. I-6623 142
Lethonen (Case C-176/96) [2000] E.C.R. I-2681. 113
Pavlov (Joined Cases C-180/98 to C-184/98) [2000] E.C.R. I-6451. 189
TK-Heimdienst (Case C-254/98) [2000] E.C.R. I-151 . . . . 93, 105
Tobacco Advertising I (Case C-376/98) [2000] ECR I-8419. 121
Ursula Elsen (Case C-135/99) [2000] E.C.R. I-10409 .62, 76

Commission v Italy (Case C-162/99) [2001] E.C.R. I-541 . . . . 95, 143
De Coster (Case C-17/00) [2001] E.C.R. I-9445 . . . . 147, 151
Gourmet International (Case C-405/98) E.C.R. I-1795 . . . . 105, 181
Grzelczyk (Case C-184/99) [2001] E.C.R. I-6193 73
PreussenElektra (Case C-379/98) [2001] E.C.R. I-2099 . . . . 180, 221
Smits & Peerbooms (Case C-157/99) [2001] E.C.R. I-5473. 190
Vanbraekel (Case C-368/98) [2001] E.C.R. I-5363. 155, 190
Baumbast (Case C-413/99) [2002] E.C.R. I-7091. . . . . .72, 208
British American Tobacco (Case C-491/01) [2002] ECR I-11543 . . . . .48, 121
Canal Satélite Digital (Case C-390/99) [2002] E.C.R. I-00607 . . . . .60, 62, 64
Carpenter (Case C-60/00) [2002] E.C.R. I-6279. 194–195
Commission v France (Case C-483/99) [2002] E.C.R. I-4871 57
D'Hoop (Case C-224/98) [2002] E.C.R. I-6191 76
Danner (Case C-136/00) [2002] E.C.R. I-8147 147
de Groot (Case C-385/00) [2002] E.C.R. I-11819. 150–151
INASTI (Joined cases C-393/99 and C-394/99) [2002] E.C.R. I-2829 153
Lankhorst-Hohorst (Case C-324/00) [2002] E.C.R. I-11779. 150
Oteiza Olazabal (Case C-100/01) [2002] E.C.R. I-10981. 77
Reisch (Joined Cases C-515/99, C-519/99 to C-524/99 and C-526/99 to C-540/99) [2002] E.C.R. I-2157 . . . . 177, 180
Sapod Audic (Case C-159/00) [2002] E.C.R. I-5031. . . . . .203, 207
Überseering (Case C-208/00) [2002] E.C.R. I-9919 157–158
Wouters (Case C-309/99) [2002] E.C.R. I-1577. . . . . 201, 212
X and Y (Case C-436/00) [2002] E.C.R. I-10829 . . . . .97, 150
Akrich (Case C-109/01) [2003] E.C.R. I-9607 196
Anomar (Case C-6/01) [2003] E.C.R. I-8261 . . . . .180, 186
Bacardi-Martini (Case C-318/00) [2003] E.C.R. I-905 .187
Bosal (Case C-168/01) [2003] E.C.R. I-9409 150
DocMorris (Case C-322/01) [2003] E.C.R. I-14887. .93, 105
Freskot (Case C-355/00) [2003] E.C.R. I-5263 . . . . 181, 190
Gerritse (Case C-234/01) [2003] E.C.R. I-5933 . . . . 147–148, 151
Inspire Art (Case C-167/01) [2003] E.C.R. I-10155 158
Kristiansen (Case C-92/02) [2003] E.C.R. I-14597 154
Lindman (Case C-42/02) [2003] E.C.R. I-13519 . . . . 147, 150
Morgenbesser (Case C-313/01) [2003] E.C.R. I-13467 .142
Müller-Fauré (Case C-385/99) [2003] E.C.R. I-4509. 57, 155
Schmidberger (Case C-112/00) [2003] E.C.R. I-5659 . . . . 57, 70, 209, 212, 218
Stylianakis (Case C-92/01) [2003] E.C.R. I-1291 77
van Lent (Case C-232/01) [2003] E.C.R. I-11525 97
CaixaBank (Case C-442/02) [2004] E.C.R. I- 8961 . . . . 88, 110, 113–114
Carbonati Apuani (Case C-72/03) [2004] E.C.R. I-8027. 178
Douwe Egberts (Case C-239/02) [2004] E.C.R. I-7007 .105
Gregorio My (Case C-293/03) [2004] E.C.R. I-12013 196

Leichtle (Case C-8/02) [2004] E.C.R. I-2641 155
Omega (Case C-36/02) [2004] E.C.R. I-9609 .... 70, 181, 218
Swedish Match (Case C-210/03) E.C.R. I-11893 121
Trojani (Case C-456/02) [2004] E.C.R. I-7573 62
Bidar (Case C-209/03) [2005] E.C.R. I-2119 78
D. (Case C-376/03) [2005] E.C.R. I-2421 .... 148, 150
Fournier (Case C-39/04) [2005] E.C.R. I-2057 147
Jersey Produce (Case C-293/02) [2005] E.C.R. I-9543 .... 163, 178
Marks & Spencer (Case C-446/03) [2005] E.C.R. I-10837 150
Mauri (Case C-250/03) [2005] E.C.R. I-1267 181
Nadin (Joined cases C-151/04 and C-152/04) [2005] E.C.R. I-11203 68
Oulane (Case C-215/03) [2005] E.C.R. I-01215 181
Schempp (Case C-403/03) [2005] E.C.R. I-6421 150
SEVIC (Case C-411/03) [2005] E.C.R. I-10805 159
Alfa Vita Vassilopoulos (Joined Cases C-158/04 and C-159/04) [2006] E.C.R. I-8135 .... 77, 79, 105
ANAV (Case C-410/04) [2006] E.C.R. I-3303 181
Cipolla (Joined Cases C-94/04 and C-202/04) [2006] E.C.R. I-2107 113
Commission v Portugal (Case C-345/05) [2006] E.C.R. I-10633 77
FENIN (Case C-205/03 P) [2006] E.C.R. I-6295 188–189
Fidium Finanz (Case C-452/04) [2006] E.C.R. I-8135 61
Kerckhaert and Morris (Case C-513/04) [2006] ECR I-10967 151
Meca-Medina (Case C-519/04 P) [2006] E.C.R. I-6991 188–189
Piatkowski (Case C-493/04) [2006] E.C.R. I-2369 154
Ritter-Coulais (Case C-152/03) [2006] E.C.R. I-1711 .... 180, 196
Tas-Hagen (Case C-192/05) [2006] E.C.R. I-10451 72
Test Claimants (Case C-374/04) [2006] E.C.R. I-11673 151
Tobacco Advertising II (Case C-380/03) [2006] E.C.R. I-11573 120–121
Turpeinen (Case C-520/04) [2006] E.C.R. I-10685 .... 148, 151
van Hilten-van der Heijden (Case C-513/03) [2006] E.C.R. I-10653 .... 178, 191
Alevizos (Case C-392/05) [2007] E.C.R. I-3505 .... 96, 152
Cellozi (Case C-332/05) [2007] E.C.R. I-563 95
Commission v Italy (Case C-134/05) [2007] E.C.R. I-6251 62
Eind (Case C-291/05) [2007] E.C.R. I-10719 194
Geurts (Case C-464/05) [2007] E.C.R. I-9325 196
Holböck (Case C-157/05) [2007] E.C.R. I-4051 61
ITC (Case C-208/05) [2007] E.C.R. I-181 77
Jia (Case C-1/05) [2007] E.C.R. I-001 196
Lakebrink (Case C-182/06) [2007] E.C.R. I-6705 148
Laval (Case C-341/05) [2007] E.C.R. I-11767 .... 89, 219
Lyyski (Case C-40/05) [2007] E.C.R. I-0099 89
Meindl (Case C-329/05) [2007] E.C.R. I-1107 148

Morgan and Bucher (Joined Cases C-11/06 and C-12/06) [2007] E.C.R. I-9161 ... 77
Stamatelaki (Case C-444/05) [2007] E.C.R. I-3185 ... 155
T-Mobile Austria (Case C-284/04) E.C.R. I-05189 ... 188
Viking (Case C-438/05) [2007] E.C.R. I-10779 ... 118, 208–209, 213, 222
Cartesio (Case C-210/06) [2008] E.C.R. I-964 ... 160–161
Commission v France (Case C-389/05) [2008] E.C.R. I-5337 ... 113
Commission v Germany (Case C-141/07) [2008] E.C.R. I-06935 ... 93, 105
Commission v Germany (C-152/05) [2008] E.C.R. I-00039 ... 196
Government of Communauté française and Gouvernement wallon (Case C-212/06) [2008] E.C.R. I-1683 ... 185, 196
Gysbrechts and Santurel Inter (Case C-205/07) [2008] E.C.R. I-09947 ... 161–162
Kadi (Joined Cases C-402/05 P and C-415/05 P) [2008] E.C.R. I-06351 ... 218
Metock (Case C-127/08) [2008] ECR I-6241 ... 196
Petersen (Case C-228/07) [2008] E.C.R. I-6989 ... 153
Raccanelli (Case C-94/07) [2008] E.C.R. I-5939 ... 213, 219
Renneberg (Case C-527/06) [2008] E.C.R. I-7735 ... 96, 148, 196
Truck Center (Case C-282/07) [2008] E.C.R. I-10767 ... 96
Vermögensverwaltungs-Gesellschaft (Case C-330/07) [2008] E.C.R. I-9099 ... 147
Apothekerkammer des Saarlandes (Joined Cases C-171/07 and C-172/07) [2009] E.C.R. I-04171 ... 113
Chamier-Glisczinski (Case C-208/07) [2009] E.C.R. I-06095 ... 119
Commission v Germany (Case C-269/07) [2009] E.C.R. I-07811 ... 97
Commission v Italy (Case C-110/05) [2009] ECR I-00519 ... 88, 111
Filipiak (Case C-314/08) [2009] E.C.R. I-11049 ... 98, 147
Hein Persche (Case C-318/07) [2009] ECR I-00359 ... 191
Mickelsson and Roos (Case C-142/05) [2009] E.C.R. I-04273 ... 111, 172
Peśla (Case C-345/08) [2009] E.C.R. I-11677 ... 142
Attanasio (Case C-384/08) [2010] E.C.R. I-02055 ... 113
CIBA (Case C-96/08) [2010] E.C.R. I-2911 ... 151
Commission v France (Case C-512/08) [2010] E.C.R. I-08833 ... 155
Commission v Portugal (Case C-543/08) [2010] E.C.R. I-11241 ... 109
Commission v Spain (Case C-211/08) [2010] E.C.R. I-5267 ... 155
Elchinov (Case C-173/09) [2010] E.C.R. I-08889 ... 155
Humanplasma (Case C-421/09) [2010] E.C.R. I-12869 ... 57
Idrima Tipou (Case C-81/09) [2010] E.C.R. I-10161 ... 113
Ker-Optika (Case C-108/09) [2010] E.C.R. I-12213 ... 113
Mattner (Case C-510/08) [2010] E.C.R. I-3553 ... 148
Olympique Lyonnais (Case C-325/08) [2010] E.C.R. I-02177 ... 113
SGI (Case C-311/08) [2010] E.C.R. I-0487 ... 89
Commission v Germany (Case C-284/09) [2011] I-09879 ... 151
Commission v Portugal (Case C-212/09) [2011] I-10889 ... 113
Commission v Portugal (Case C-255/09) [2011] I-10547 ... 155

Dereci (Case C-256/11) [2011] I-11315 . . . . 76, 178, 208
Kakavetsos-Fragkopoulos (Case C-161/09) [2011] I-00915 163
McCarthy (Case C-434/09) [2011] I-03375. . . . . 75, 178
Missionswerk (Case C-25/10) [2011] E.C.R. I-00497 191
Zambrano (Case C-34/09) [2011] I-01177. . . . . 75, 82, 178, 208, 216
Vale (Case C-378/10) [2012]. 161
Åkerberg Fransson (Case C-617/10) [2013]. 200
Nordea Bank Danmark (Case C-48/13) [2014]. 150
Ålands vindkraft AB (Case C-573/12) [2014] 221
Essent Belgium (Joined Cases C-204 to C-208/12) [2014] 221–222
Orgacom (Case C-254/13) [2014] 178
Pfleger (Case C-390/12) [2014] 200
S and G (Case C-457/12) [2014] 195
van Caster (Case C-326/12) [2014] 150
General Court of the European Union
T-155/04 Selex [2006] E.C.R. II-4797 189
European Court of Human Rights
Belgian Linguistic case (No 2) [1968] 1 EHRR 252 205

Germany

Lüth (Judgement of 15 January 1958) BVerfGE 7 198
(Bundesverfassungsgericht) 204
Solange I (Judgment of 29 May 1974) BVerfGE 271
(Bundesverfassungsgericht) 13
Solange II (Judgment of 22 October 1986) BVerfGE 339
(Bundesverfassungsgericht) 13
Maastricht (Judgement of 12 October 1993) BVerfGE 155
(Bundesverfassungsgericht) 13
Lisbon Treaty (Judgements of 30 June 2009) BvE 2/08, 2 BvE 5/08,
2 BvR 1010/08, 2 BvR 1022/08, 2 BvR 1259/08, 2 BvR 182/09
(Bundesverfassungsgericht) 13

United States

Edwards v. California [1941] 314 U.S. 160 (Supreme Court). 69

TABLE OF STATUTES

European Union

Commission Directive 70/50/EEC of 22 December 1969 based on the provisions of Article 33 (7), on the abolition of measures which have an effect equivalent to quantitative restrictions on imports and are not covered by other provisions adopted in pursuance of the EEC Treaty OJ L 13, 126
Regulation No 1408/71 of the Council on the Application of Social Security Schemes to Employed Persons and Their Families Moving Within the Communities OJ L 149 OF 152
Council Directive 73/148/EEC on the abolition of restrictions on movement and residence within the Community for nationals of Member States with regard to establishment and the provision of services OJ 1973 L 172 195
Council Directive 77/799/EEC of 19 December 1977 concerning mutual assistance by the competent authorities of the Member States in the field of direct taxation OJ 1977 L 336 149
Council Directive 79/112/EEC relating to the labelling, presentation and advertisement for foodstuffs for sale to the ultimate consumer OJ L33/01 128
Council Directive 88/361/EEC of 24 June 1988 for the implementation of Article 67 of the Treaty OJ L 178 . . . . 66, 191
Council Directive 89/48/EEC on a general system for the recognition of higher-education diplomas awarded on completion of professional education and training of at least three years' duration OJ L 19, 16–23 . . . 108
Council Directive 90/364/EEC of 28 June 1990 on the right of residence [1990] OJ L 180 71
Council Directive 90/365/EEC of 28 June 1990 on the right of residence for employees and self-employed persons who have ceased their occupational activity OJ L 180 71
Council Directive 92/51/EEC on a second general system for the recognition of professional education and training to supplement Directive 89/48/EEC OJ L 209, 25–45 108
Council Directive 93/96/EEC of 29 October 1993 on the right of residence for students OJ L 317 71
Council Regulation (EC) No 2157/2001 of 8 October 2001 on the Statute for a European Company (SE) OJ L 294 159
Directive 2004/38/EC of the European Parliament and of the Council of 29 April 2004 on the right of citizens of the Union and their family

members to move and reside freely within the territory of the Member States OJ L 158. . . . . .73, 195
Regulation (EC) No 883/2004 of the European Parliament and of the Council of 29 April 2004 on the coordination of social security systems OJ L 166. 152
Directive 2005/36/EC of the European Parliament and of the Council of 7 September 2005 on the recognition of professional qualifications OJ L255/22 108
Directive 2005/56/EC of the European Parliament and of the Council of 26 October 2005 on cross-border mergers of limited liability companies OJ L 310 159

TABLE OF OTHER PRIMARY LEGAL SOURCES

The Brussels Report on the General Common Market (Spaak Report) [1956] 56
Communication from the Commission concerning the consequences of the Judgment given by the Court of Justice on 20 February 1979 in Case 120/78 (Cassis de Dijon) 126, 145
Commission's White Paper on 'Completing the Internal Market' 145
Communication from the Commission to the European Parliament, the Council, the European Economic and Social Committee and the Committee of the Regions Accompanying the Communication on 'A single market for 21st century Europe' Services of general interest, including social services of general interest: a new European Commitment COM 2007 725 Final 188

LIST OF ABBREVIATIONS

AJIL	American Journal of International Law
AmEconRev	American Economic Review
AmJCompL	American Journal of Comparative Law
AmJSoc	American Journal of Sociology
AmPolitSciRev	American Political Science Review
AmSociolRev	American Sociological Review
ArizJInt'l&CompL	Arizona Journal of International and Comparative Law
ArizStLJ	Arizona State Law Journal
Auckland UL Rev	Auckland University Law Review
BTR	British Tax Review
BULRev	Boston University Law Review
CDE	Cahiers de Droit Européen
ChiJInt'lL	Chicago Journal of International Law
CLJ	Cambridge Law Journal
CLR	California Law Review
ColumLRev	Columbia Law Review
ColumJEurL	Columbia Journal of European Law
ColumJTransnat'lL	Columbia Journal of Transnational Law
CML Rev	Common Market Law Review
Commission	Commission of the European Communities
Cornell LRev	Cornell Law Review
Court or Court of Justice	Court of Justice of the European Union
Creighton LRev	Creighton Law Review
CYELS	Cambridge Yearbook of European Legal Studies
CYELP	Croatian Yearbook of European Law and Policy
DULJ	Dublin University Law Journal
Duke LJ	Duke Law Journal
DVBl	Deutsches Verwaltungsblatt
EBLRev	European Business Law Review
EEA	European Economic Area
EJIL	European Journal of International Law
EJLS	European Journal of Legal Studies
ELJ	European Law Journal
ELRev	European Law Review
EmoryLJ	Emory Law Journal
EPL	European Public Law

EUConst	European Constitutional Law Review
EUR	EuropaRecht
EurCoL	European Company Law
EurJLawEcon	European Journal of Law and Economics
EWS	Europäisches Wirtschafts- & Steurrecht
EuZW	Europäische Zeitschrift für Wirtschaftsrect
Fordham Int'l L.J.	Fordham International Law Journal
GeoLJ	Georgetown Law Journal
GeoWashLRev	George Washington Law Review
GLJ	German Law Journal
HanseLR	Hanse Law Review
HarvLRev	Harvard Law Review
Hastings LJ	Hastings Law Journal
HRLRev	Human Rights Law Review
ICLQ	International Comparative Law Quarterly
I•CON	International Journal of Constitutional Law
ILJ	Industrial Law Journal
IndLJ	Indiana Law Review
IowaLRev	Iowa Law Review
IrJEurL	Irish Journal of European Law
JCMS	Journal of Common Market Studies
JEPP	Journal of European Public Policy
JIEL	Journal of International Economic Law
JILP	Journal of International Law and Politics
JL&Relig	Journal of Law and Religion
JLS	Journal of Legal Studies
JPE	Journal of Public Economics
JSSL	Journal of Social Security Law
L.& Soc.Inquiry	Law & Social Inquiry
Law&Phil	Law and Philosophy
LIEI	Legal Issues of European Economic Integration
Loy.L.Rev.	Loyola Law Review
LS	Legal Studies
MdLRev	Maryland Law Review
MichLRev	Michigan Law Review
MinnLRev	Minnesota Law Review
MJ	Maastricht Journal of European and Comparative Law
MLR	Modern Law Review
Notre Dame LRev	Notre Dame Law Review
NYULRev	New York University Law Review
Penn St Int'l LRev	Penn State International Law Review
PolSciQ	Political Science Quarterly

PolTheo	Political Theory
RIDC	Revue internationale de droit comparé
RTDeur	Revue tremestrielle de droit européen
RivDirEur	Rivista di Diritto Europeo
San Diego LRev	San Diego Law Review
Scientia Jur	Scientia Juridica
SocForces	Social Forces
StanLRev	Stanford Law Review
StanL & Pol'y Rev	Stanford Law and Policy Review
TexLRev	Texas Law Review
TheoInqL	Theoretical Inquiries in Law
UChiLRev	University of Chicago Law Review
UHawLRev	University of Hawai'i Law Review
VaJInt'l L	Virginia Journal of International Law
VaLRev	Virginia Law Review
WestPolQ	The Western Political Quarterly
WmMitchell LRev	William Mitchell Law Review
WTR	World Trade Review
Yale LJ	Yale Law Journal
YEL	Yearbook of European Law
ZaöRV	Zeitschrift für ausländisches öffentliches Recht und Völkerrecht

Our meddling intellect/Mis-shapes the beauteous forms of things:/We murder to dissect.

William Woodsworth, The Tables Turned

La grammaire, avec son mélange de règle logique et d'usage arbitraire, propose au jeune esprit un avant-goût de ce que lui offriront plus tard les sciences de la conduite humaine, le droit ou la morale, tous les systèmes où l'homme a codifié son expérience instinctive.

Marguerite Yourcenar, Memoires d'Hadrian

The growth of knowledge, particularly specialized knowledge, is a very slow process. Far from being merely additive or cumulative, the growth of knowledge is a process of selective accumulation, displacement, rearrangement, and insistence within what has been called a research consensus... My principal operating principles were—and continue to be—that fields of learning, as much as the works of even the most eccentric artists, are constrained and acted upon by societies, by cultural traditions, by worldly circumstance, and by stabilising influences like schools, libraries and governments; moreover, that both learned and imaginative writing are never free, but are limited in their imagery, assumptions and intentions; and finally, that advances in a 'science'... are less objectively true than we often like to think.

Edward W. Said, Orientalism

Every philosopher, in addition to the formal system he offers to the world, has another, much simpler, of which he may be quite unaware. If he is aware of it, he probably realizes it won't quite do; he therefore conceals it, and sets forth something more sophisticated, which he believes because it is like his crude system, but which he asks others to accept because he thinks he has made it such as cannot be disproved.

Bertrand Russell, History of Western Philosophy

In every system of morality, which I have hitherto met with, I have always remark'd, that the author proceeds for some time in the ordinary ways of reasoning, and establishes the being of a God, or makes observations concerning human affairs; when all of a sudden I am surpriz'd to find, that instead of the usual copulations of propositions, is, and is not, I meet with no proposition that is not connected with an ought, or an ought not. This change is imperceptible; but is however, of the last consequence. For as this ought, or ought not, expresses some new relation or affirmation, 'tis necessary that it shou'd be observ'd and explain'd; and at the same time that a reason should be given; for what seems altogether inconceivable, how this new relation can be a deduction from others, which are entirely different from it.

David Hume, A Treatise of Human Nature (1739), Book III, Part I, Section I

Introduction

The fundamental freedoms are the 'original' constitutional rights of the EU.[1] As open constitutional provisions, they are 'arenas' where different models of integration fight for preponderance. The outcome of specific decisions in this field push the law in directions which trigger a number of (political) reactions from a variety of different entities—political, social, economic—and thereby condition the development of European integration and the interpretation of the fundamental freedoms alike. They raise serious normative issues as to the model of EU integration, but they also pose questions of institutional choice and of separation of powers in the EU.

For heuristic purposes, one can distinguish between academic literature adopting legal and extra-legal approaches to the fundamental freedoms. Literature focusing on 'legal matters' can be said to focus on rationalizing the case law on, and developing normative theories about, the nature of the fundamental freedoms. This literature focuses on the following kinds of question: Are the market freedoms anti-protectionist devices or economic due-process clauses? Should the fundamental freedoms only bind public authorities? Do the market freedoms share common normative goals, and should they be subject to the same interpretation? What does European Citizenship entail?, etc. Literature on 'extra-legal matters' focuses instead on matters concerning the adjudicative process and institutional comparative choice, and looks into questions such as: Will an extension in the scope of the fundamental freedoms lead to an increase in the competences of the EU? Will such an extension increase the power of the Court of Justice vis-à-vis

[1] These include the market freedoms—the free movement of goods, right of establishment, the free provision of services, the free movement of workers and the free movement of capital—and European Citizenship.

other EU institutions? Would this be desirable, or do we prefer to limit the power of the Court of Justice and protect that of other institutions? What is the effect of a decision extending the scope of the fundamental freedoms on the Court of Justice's docket control and its ability to correctly manage and decide cases?

In reality, it is rare for legal scholarship not to touch on extra-legal issues. However, extra-legal considerations are usually not addressed explicitly in the legal literature, but are treated instead as implicit or as merely incidental. This book bridges this gap between the legal and extra-legal perspectives by focusing expressly and systematically on the interplay between the different normative concerns behind the EU fundamental freedoms identified in traditional legal discourse—as results mainly from court decisions and academic debates—and the institutional environment in which that legal discourse takes place—as analysed and evidenced in studies about the law in general, and EU law and the Court of Justice in particular. In doing so, this book develops a framework for the 'internalization' of extra-legal factors into legal discourse regarding the fundamental freedoms. For ease of reference, such a framework will be referred to as being 'contextual' throughout this book.

The existence of extra-legal elements that are relevant to the 'legal' discourse of the EU legal community is, to a certain extent, uncontroversial, constituting a 'tacit dimension' of legal practice—a set of propositions and opinions shared by the legal community deemed to be so obvious that they are never fully articulated or systematized.[2] The tacit dimension of EU constitutional law and constitutionalism is not dissimilar to that of national constitutional orders. However, as the Court of Justice has stated, and the Member States have explicitly or implicitly admitted, the EU is a new legal order. Instead of a unitary State or a Federal entity, the EU embodies a new type of political entity that consists of a supranational structure superimposed on a number of historically settled and culturally diverse sovereign nation-States. With the failure of the European Constitution, it is not now foreseeable that a (written) constitution will provide the fundamental political ands legal underpinning for the Union, as it does for most of the Member States. The EU nonetheless possesses a constitution within the context of the philosophical theories, legal documents, and political praxis of constitutionalism—EU law allocates public powers between different bodies, protects

[2] Michael Polanyi and Amartya Sen, *The Tacit Dimension* (University of Chicago Press 2009).

the rights of its citizens through the judiciary, and promotes a number of values traditionally associated with the constitutionalist tradition such as the rule of law, the separation of powers, and democracy.[3]

The *sui generis* character of this constitution does not dispense with constitutionalism, but neither is it fully compatible with the traditional theories of constitutionalism developed for modern nation-States.[4] A different type of polity requires a different type of constitution; more importantly, it also requires a different way of thinking, a new constitutionalism able to address the relevant descriptive and normative questions facing it.[5] This new constitutionalism may borrow the language of traditional constitutionalism, but it must take care that such language is translated carefully, and that it develops a new vocabulary as necessary.[6]

The main obstacle to the development of EU constitutionalism to the same level of sophistication as that of a nation-State is not that the EU falls outside traditional political forms, but that the EU is effectively still determining what kind of polity it wants to be.[7] A good example of this can be found in the provisions regulating the fundamental freedoms. In these provisions, and in debates concerning them, questions about which model of integration the EU should follow and about what kind of *polis* the EU should become bubble underneath a veneer of technical legal discourse. The fundamental freedoms are accordingly a good prism through which one can analyse how this new constitutionalism is developing and try to understand the role that the EU's 'constitutional' court plays in this.

While the Court of Justice's treatment of the fundamental freedoms has been strikingly innovative, its approach has tended to be understood in terms of traditional international and constitutional law theories, ignoring the constraints resulting from the very specific institutional setting in which these freedoms are applied. In particular, the Court of Justice's decisions are accepted in the Member States not as a result of a hierarchical imposition,

[3] Joseph Weiler, *The Constitution of Europe* (Cambridge University Press 1999); Sergio Dellavalle, 'Constitutionalism beyond the Constitution: The Treaty of Lisbon in Light of Post-National Public Law' [2009] Jean Monnet Working Paper 03/09, 31.

[4] Joseph Weiler, 'In Defence of the Status Quo: Europe's Constitutional Sonderweg' in J.H.H. Weiler and Marlene Wind (eds), *European Constitutionalism Beyond the State* (Cambridge University Press 2003), 18–19.

[5] Critically, Martin Loughlin, 'What is Constitutionalisation?' in Petra Dobner and Martin Loughlin (eds), *The Twilight of Constitutionalism?* (OUP 2010), 65–66.

[6] Neil Walker, 'The Idea of Constitutional Pluralism' (2002) 65 MLR 317, 322.

[7] On the contested purpose of EU integration, see Jan Komárek, 'Judicial Law Making and Precedent in Supreme Courts' [2011] LSE Law, Society and Economy Working Papers 4/2011, 29.

as is typical of decisions adopted by higher courts in national legal orders, but as a result of continuous mutual (constitutional) tolerance between distinct legal orders.[8] In other words, European constitutionalism has specific normative underpinnings that arise from the particular political nature and institutional structure of the EU, even if those underpinnings are to a large extent borrowed from and shared by the constitutional traditions of the Member States.

EU constitutional law cannot be fully understood through a decontextualized, purely legal lens. On the contrary, EU constitutional law arises from the interplay between legal and extra-legal elements that can be better perceived by reference to the findings of some disciplines 'external' to legal discourse such as economics, philosophy, and political science. A contextual approach that incorporates insights arising from these 'external' disciplines into the traditional modes of legal discourse and analysis of the EU fundamental freedoms—in effect, the internalization into EU legal discourse of these 'external' elements—can provide both a more accurate descriptive framework of EU free movement law and more attractive normative theories concerning it.

Furthermore, as will be shown, the inclusion of these 'external' considerations may also help to explain the evolution and change of the normative underpinnings of the law, and how this change in intellectual environment can in turn lead to modifications in the institutional context in which the law is applied. There is no simple chain of causation to be found here: on the contrary, there is a constant feedback loop between the legal and extra-legal dimensions. What is more, since this process is iterative, interactive, and dynamic, extra-legal constraints can lead to developments in the law, while the law may in turn cause changes to the relevant institutional environment. In acknowledging this, the present book also reflects on the nature and role of EU scholarship and practice, and develops a meta-theory regarding the impact of EU scholarship and practice on EU law and its development.

To understand the interplay between legal and extra-legal elements, however, one must first flesh out both the legal and extra-legal dimensions. Facts and norms are mediated through modes of legal reasoning; but such mediation can only be understood if the relevant facts and norms are previously known themselves. Accordingly, this book is divided into two different sections.

[8] Weiler, 'In Defence of the Status Quo: Europe's Constitutional Sonderweg', 21. But see the discussion on pluralism in Chapter 1, Section II below.

The first section will identify the relevant extra-legal and legal elements for our analysis. The first chapter focuses on extra-legal factors. In the light of the fact that this book is concerned with the EU's fundamental freedoms, which is an area of mainly court-made law, the 'external' elements used in this thesis are findings in jurisprudence, economics, sociology and political science concerning legal adjudication, judicial law-making and the institutional constraints facing courts, and in particular the Court of Justice. The second chapter then pursues an analysis of the classic 'decontextualized' normative theories accepted in EU legal circles as underpinning the fundamental freedoms. This analysis will begin by reviewing the normative foundations that are generally held to be common to all fundamental freedoms, before reviewing those normative positions said to apply to specific freedoms. This will allow for a review of the full gamut of normative positions found in the literature.

The book will then move on to a second section that analyses the interaction between legal and extra-legal elements in specific areas of EU free movement law. In areas where the law is the same for all fundamental freedoms, one can reasonably assume that the same normative inputs and institutional constraints are at play.[9] On the other hand, in areas where it is arguable that the fundamental freedoms diverge, it is a reasonable hypothesis that specific normative concerns and/or institutional constraints exist, and that it is the existence of these specific normative and institutional inputs that explains the differences between the freedoms. This means that the areas where the law on the fundamental freedoms diverge provide ideal grounds for mapping out the interaction between normative concerns and institutional constraints in the development of the law. An added benefit of this approach is that it allows one to assess the attractiveness of subjecting the fundamental freedoms to a single integrated and multi-disciplinary analytical framework.

As such, chapters in the second section will focus on areas where it is generally accepted that there is no common approach applicable to all the freedoms, particularly regarding their scope. Chapters III to V focus on the concept of restriction on free movement: Chapter III reviews traditional 'decontextualized' debates on what constitutes a restriction on free movement and the appropriate judicial tests to identify such a restriction; Chapter IV attempts to unpack the normative foundations underlying these debates; and Chapter V

[9] This is not to deny the possibility that different normative inputs and institutional constraints may lead to similar outcomes in different situations, but this is unlikely and, more importantly, much harder to test.

exemplifies how a contextual approach that takes into account institutional elements, in addition to those considerations deemed relevant in traditional legal discourse, helps make better descriptive and normative sense of the law and related academic controversies. Chapter VI will then deal with other areas of the law on the scope of the fundamental freedoms where there is no common approach to all freedoms.

In short, it will be demonstrated that a contextual approach that adds extra-legal elements to traditional legal approaches allows for better descriptive theories of EU free movement law and its development. Normatively, it will be argued that contextual approaches to the fundamental freedoms should be more attractive to the legal community than those not taking extra-legal considerations into account. An incidental result of this will be that, by the end of this book, a general theory on the fundamental freedoms will have been sketched.

SECTION I

The External and Internal Dimensions

For the sake of clarity, a distinction needs to be made between the 'internal' and the 'external' dimensions of legal discourse. The 'internal' dimension consists of the official justificatory discourse supporting legal decisions—expressed through legal reasoning and the application of legal methodologies. What can be included in the internal dimension will vary from place to place, but it traditionally consists of the outcome of efforts by lawyers to rationalize and systematize the law, and to develop normative theories on how the law should develop. The 'external' dimension, on the other hand, is usually unearthed as the result of efforts of disciples that look at the law from the outside as the subject of sociological, economic, or philosophical analysis.

This section will look into the relevant elements of the 'internal' and 'external' dimensions affecting the fundamental freedoms. The first chapter will focus on the external dimension—i.e. the extra-legal elements relevant for the understanding of the EU fundamental freedoms—while the second chapter will focus on the internal dimension—i.e. the different normative positions and reasons that are identified in legal discourse as underpinning those freedoms.

1

The External Dimension—Law, Courts, and the Court of Justice of the EU

I. Introduction

The EU fundamental freedoms were developed primarily through case law, which means that the 'external' elements relevant for their development are those related to the activity of courts—and the Court of Justice, in particular. As such, this chapter will begin by first looking into the similarities and differences between the Court of Justice and national courts. It will then review, in the light of findings in the areas of jurisprudence, economics, sociology, and political science, a number of non-legal factors that affect the activity of courts in general—including the individual preferences of judges, the institutional and political context in which courts operate, the strictures imposed by precedent, and concerns about the perceived legitimacy of courts' decision-making practices. However, these external constraints do not exercise their power directly, but are mediated instead by the accepted parameters of legal reasoning, which will also be reviewed. The chapter will then look into how the external dimension affects the Court of Justice's decision-making practice in particular, before submitting that, in the light of the descriptive relevance of extra-legal elements, normative approaches that take the external dimension into account are more attractive than purely legal/internal ones.[1]

[1] The more detailed analysis of the relevance of extra-legal elements in the development of specific areas of the law will be pursued in Section II.

II. The Singular Nature of European Courts

The role of the Court of Justice in the creation of the EU was so atypical that it has been described as a fairy tale:

Tucked away in the fairyland Duchy of Luxembourg and blessed, until recently, with benign neglect by the powers that be and the mass media, the Court of Justice of the European Communities has fashioned a constitutional framework for a federal type structure in Europe.[2]

Political science and legal studies have extolled its importance to the development of EU law to such an extent that the Court of Justice has become arguably the most important subject of both legal and political science literature on EU integration.[3] This focus should, however, be understood in the context of perceptions about the contemporary role of the judiciary, which have changed from regarding courts as merely finding and applying the law to recognizing that courts are also law-makers.[4] It is also generally agreed that the scope of judicial power has been increasing steadily, be that due to the growth of administrative and constitutional law, to an increase in social and economic regulation, or to the adoption of constitutions that have given judges the power to control the contents of laws.[5] This last development lies at the origin of judicial review and the 'judicialization' of politics through the transfer of decision-making powers from legislatures and executives to courts.[6] An overview of constitutional practices in Europe indicates that two main modes of constitutional review have been adopted: abstract review, whereby a specialized judicial body is asked to review the constitutionality of a measure in the absence of litigation; and concrete review, whereby a

[2] Eric Stein, 'Lawyers, Judges and the Making of a Transnational Constitution' (1981) 75 AJIL 1, 1.

[3] See ibid; Joseph Weiler, 'The Transformation of Europe' (1991) 1000 Yale LJ 2403; Alec Stone Sweet, *The Judicial Construction of Europe* (OUP 2004).

[4] Joseph Raz, *The Authority of Law—Essays on Law and Morality* (OUP 1979), 176; H.L.A. Hart, Penelope A. Bulloch and Joseph Raz, *The Concept of Law* (2nd edn, Clarendon Press 1994), 124 ff.

[5] C. Neal Tate and Torbjörn Vallinder, *The Global Expansion of Judicial Power* (New York University Press 1995); Tom Ginsburg, 'The Global Spread of Judicial Review' in Gregory A. Caldeira, R. Daniel Kelemen and Keith E. Whittington (eds), *The Oxford Handbook of Law and Politics* (OUP 2008); A.E. Dick Howard, 'A Traveler from an Antique Land: The Modern Renaissance of Comparative Constitutionalism' (2009) 50 VaJInt'l L 3, 21–25.

[6] Torbjörn Vallinder, 'When the Courts Go Marching In' in C. Neal Tate and Torbjörn Vallinder (eds), *The Global Expansion of Judicial Power* (New York University Press 1995), 13–15.

constitutional court answers questions posed by a non-specialized judicial court on constitutional matters.[7] These modes of judicial review are analogous to some of the actions which can be brought before the Court: abstract review is comparable to the action for failure of a Member State to fulfil its obligations and to the action for annulment prescribed in Articles 258 and 263 TFEU, while concrete review is similar to the preliminary reference mechanism provided for by Article 267 TFEU. In effect, the Court of Justice has a number of characteristics usually associated with constitutional courts, such as having the power to review the conformity of democratically enacted legislation with a 'higher' law, adjudicate on the powers of EU organs, and rule on the vertical division of competences between the EU and its Member States.[8]

The 'constitutionalization' of Europe, and the development of the EU's own brand of constitutionalism, flowed from the Court of Justice's decisions, which endowed EU law with constitutional effects and led to the adoption of a constitutional discourse regarding European integration.[9] This is clear, for example, from the development by the Court of Justice of a number of constitutional doctrines such as supremacy, direct effect, and implied powers; from the 'subjectivation' of the Treaty; and from the limits EU law was found to impose on the exercise of national powers.[10] However, it is also clear that not all classical 'constitutional' concepts and categories are relevant to EU law. Even though the analytical categories that have shaped much of the scholarly and political debate about the EU originated from

[7] Alec Stone Sweet, 'Why Europe Rejected American Judicial Review and Why It May Not Matter' (2003) 101 MichLRev 2744, 2771. On the existent variants in Europe, see Mauro Cappelletti and others, *Methods, Tools and Institutions. Book 1. A Political, Legal and Economic Overview* (Walter de Gruyter 1986), 273–278.

[8] Takis Tridimas, 'The Court of Justice and Judicial Activism' (2006) 21 ELRev 199, 206.

[9] See Weiler, 'The Transformation of Europe'; Weiler, *The Constitution of Europe*; Sweet, *The Judicial Construction of Europe*; Robert Schütze, *Fom Dual to Cooperative Federalism* (OUP 2009), 49–50; and Case 294/83 *Les Verts v Parliament* [1986] E.C.R. 1339.

[10] José Luis da Cruz Vilaça and Nuno Piçarra, 'Y a-t-il des Limites Matériélles à la Revision des Traites Instituant les Communautés Européennes?' [1993] CDE 3, 10–13; Norbert Reich, 'A European Constitution for Citizens' (1997) 3 ELJ 131, 132; Miguel Poiares Maduro, *We, the Court—The European Court of Justice and the European Economic Constitution—A Critical Reading of Article 30 of the EC Treaty* (Hart Publishing 1998), 8–9; Weiler, *The Constitution of Europe*, 19–25; Alec Stone Sweet and James Caporaso, 'From Free Trade to Supranational Polity: European Court and Integration' in Wayne Sandholtz and Alec Stone Sweet (eds), *European Integration and Supranational Governance* (OUP 1998), 102; Paul Craig, 'Constitutions, Constitutionalism, and the European Union' (2001) 7 ELJ 125, 128–139; Julio Baquero Cruz, *Between Competition and Free Movement* (Hart Publishing 2002), 2.

intellectual traditions devoted to the study of national constitutional polities and international organizations,[11] the EU is not a typical international law entity, and, more importantly, it is not a classical State-based constitutional polity either.[12]

The role of the Court of Justice in developing the enforcement mechanisms of EU law fits with general functional theories of federalism, according to which judicial review can operate as a mechanism for dealing with collective action issues arising from the implementation of a free trade system in an area where there are multiple legislatures with incentives to set up protectionist barriers.[13] The main peculiarity of EU law in this respect is that the effectiveness of its judicial review mechanism depends primarily on the acceptance by national courts and administrations of decisions adopted by the Court of Justice. The fact that these national courts and administrations may find that their loyalties lie with the national legislature that set up those protectionist barriers in the first place creates both opportunities and risks for the Court of Justice.[14] If national courts are empowered to challenge national rules by the supremacy and direct effect doctrines, and thereby act as the 'sword' that fosters integration and forces policy change on reluctant governments,[15] EU law can nonetheless be denied its full practical effect by those same national courts should they decide that national sovereignty should be protected. This is the case particularly with national supreme or constitutional courts, which tend to see themselves as defenders of the integrity of national systems, and to refuse the supremacy doctrine as postulated by the Court of Justice.

To negotiate this tension, the Court of Justice seems to have entered into an indirect dialogue with national courts, with each party agreeing to

[11] Schütze, *Fom Dual to Cooperative Federalism*, 3–4, 51. A third option is to see the EU through an administrative law prism. See Peter L. Lindseth, 'Democratic Legitimacy and the Administrative Character of Supranationalism: The Example of the European Community' (1994) 99 ColumLRev 628, 654.

[12] Pavlos Eleftheriadis, 'Aspects of European Constitutionalism' (1996) 21 ELRev 32, 42.

[13] For the USA, see Martin Shapiro, 'Federalism, the Race to the Bottom and the Regulation-averse Enterpreneur' in H. Scheiber (ed.), *North-American and Comparative Federalism* (Institute of Governmental Studies Press 1992), 328.

[14] Imelda Maher, 'National Courts as European Community Courts' (1994) 14 LS 226; Wayne Sandholtz and Alec Stone Sweet, 'Integration, Supranational Governance, and the Institutionalization of the European Polity' in Wayne Sandholtz and Alec Stone Sweet (eds), *European Integration and Supranational Governance* (OUP 1998), 18.

[15] Andreas J. Obermaier, 'The National Judiciary as Sword of European Court of Justice Rulings: The Example of the *Kohll/Decker* Jurisprudence' (2008) 6 ELJ 735; Weiler, *The Constitution of Europe*, 194.

disagree: while the Court of Justice states that the European legal order is hierarchically superior to national legal orders, national supreme and constitutional courts have insisted on their own role as guardians of fundamental rights and resisted further transfers of the main core of Member States' sovereignty from the national to the European level.[16] This dichotomy led to the emergence and increasing popularity of constitutional pluralism, a descriptive endeavour with several variants that attempts to conceptualize the conflicting pretensions of legal supremacy[17] as leading to interactive rather than hierarchical relations between legal orders.[18] It should be noted

[16] The main role in this saga was taken by the German Federal Constitutional Court, which in its Solange decisions—*Solange I* BVerfGE 271; *Solange II* BVerfGE 339; *Maastricht* BVerfGE 155; J2 BvE 2/08, 2 BvE 5/08, 2 BvR 1010/08, 2 BvR 1022/08, 2 BvR 1259/08, 2 BvR 182/09, 9 *Lisbon Treaty*—developed a doctrine which was adopted by most of the other Member States' supreme courts. On this, see Neil MacCormick, 'The Maastricht-Urteil: Sovereignty Now' (1995) 1 ELJ 259, 259–260, 609; Ernst-Ulrich Petersmann, 'Judging Judges: From "Principal-Agent" Theory to "Constitutional Justice" in Multilevel "Judicial Governance" of Economic Cooperation Among Citizens' (2008) 11 JIEL 827, 857; Ernst-Ulrich Petersmann, 'Do Judges Meet their Constitutional Obligation to Settle Disputes in Conformity with 'Principles of Justice and International Law'?' (2007) 1 EJLS, 23 ff; Giacinto della Cananea, 'The Italian Constitutional Court and the European Court of Justice: From Separation to Interaction' (2008) 14 EPL 523; Xavier Groussot, 'European Rights and Dialogues in the Context of Constitutional Pluralism' in M. Avbelj and J. Komárek (eds), *Constitutional Pluralism in the EU and Beyond* (Hart Publishing, 2012), 19; Florence Giorgi and Nicolas Triart, 'National Judges, Community Judges: Invitation to a Journey through the Looking-glass—On the Need for Jurisdictions to Rethink the Inter-systemic Relations beyond the Hierarchical Principle' (2008) 14 ELJ 693.

[17] In other words, each claim to legal supremacy is valid from the internal point of view of each of the opposing systems.

[18] The roots of this theory in the EU context can be traced back to the *Maastricht-Urteil* and to Neil McCormick, in particular both Neil MacCormick, 'Beyond the Sovereign State' (1993) 56 MLR 1, MacCormick, 'The Maastricht-Urteil: Sovereignty now', and Neil MacCormick, *Questioning Sovereignty: Law, State, and Nation in the European Commonwealth* (OUP 1999). A number of different pluralist theories have been put forth, not only for the EU but for other supranational organizations as well: see, for example, Miguel Poiares Maduro, 'Contrapunctual Law: Europe's Constitutional Pluralism in Action' in Neil Walker (ed.), *Sovereignty in Transition—Essays in European Law* (Hart 2006), 501; Miguel Poiares Maduro, 'Courts and Pluralism: Essay on a Theory of Judicial Adjudication in the Context of Legal and Constitutional Pluralism' in M Avbelj and J Komárek (eds), Constitutional Pluralism in the EU and Beyond (Hart Publishing 2012); Mattias Kumm, 'Who is the Arbiter of Constitutionality in Europe?' (1999) 36 CML Rev 351; Petersmann, 'Judging Judges', particularly at pages 866–867 and 877–878; Nikolais Lavranos, 'Regulating Competing Jurisdictions Among International Courts and Tribunals' (2008) 68 ZaöRV 575, 612–621; Groussot, 'European Rights', 9, 15; Neil Walker, 'The EU and the WTO: Constitutionalism in a New Key' in Gráinne de Burca and Joanne Scott (eds), *The EU and the WTO—Legal and Constitutional Issues* (Hart Publishing 2001), 34–41.

that constitutional pluralism is not unanimously accepted, at least from a normative perspective;[19] nonetheless, resistance is much frailer concerning its descriptive force in explaining how different legal systems making contradictory claims of authority on issues of constitutional relevance such as fundamental rights, institutional autonomy, and allocation of competences, can operate hand-in-hand.[20] In practice, national courts act as if belonging to the EU legal system when applying EU law, while the relevant national and European courts and institutions manage potential conflicts regarding supremacy in such a way as to avoid their escalation.[21] As a result, the principle of supremacy of EU law is recognized and applied in practice, even if its normative-legal grounds are not as securely embedded in national constitutional frameworks as the Court of Justice might demand.[22]

The issue of constitutional pluralism falls outside the scope of the present book, but is brought up because it brings to the forefront the fact that the Court of Justice exists in an environment of institutional bargaining where not every legal problem can be solved legally. It illustrates how an approach based exclusively on an internal perspective of the law—particularly one that views judicial decisions as resulting from a strictly deductive approach to the law and the Treaties—will not do. To understand EU law, one must take into account not only the text of the law, or even the legal formulas adopted in the Court of Justice's decisions, but also other extra-legal elements latent in (but external to) traditional legal analysis. Among these extra-legal elements are included a number of constraints that condition how courts in general, and the Court of Justice in particular, operate: these will be henceforth referred to as 'institutional constraints'.[23] Concerning the concept of institution itself—as the source of the relevant

[19] Julio Baquero Cruz, 'The Legacy of the Maastricht-Urteil and the Pluralist Movement' [2008] 14 ELJ 389; Julie Dickson, *How Many Legal Systems? Some Puzzles Regarding the Identity Conditions of, and Relations between, Legal Systems in the European Union* (SSRN 2008), 12.

[20] Daniel Sarmiento, 'The Silent Lamb and the Deaf Wolves—Constitutional Pluralism, Preliminary References and the Role of Silent Judgments in EU Law' in M Avbelj and J Komárek (eds), *Constitutional Pluralism in the EU and Beyond* (Hart Publishing 2012), 4.

[21] Miguel Poiares Maduro, *A Crise Existencial da Constituição Europeia* (FDUNL 1999), 16.

[22] Katja Ziegler, 'International Law and EU Law: Between Asymmetric Constitutionalisation and Fragmentation' in Alexander Orakhelashvili (ed.), *Research Handbook on the Theory of International Law* (Elgar 2011), 269, 278–279.

[23] This choice derives from the usefulness of the concept in relating data to each other and in orienting research to profitable modes of gathering and organizing the data. See Howard B. Kaplan, 'The Concept of Institution: A Review, Evaluation, and Suggested Research Procedure' (1960) 29 SocForces 176.

constraints—I will follow the vocabulary used by Stone Sweet, Sandholtz, and Fliegstein.[24] They distinguish between:

- rule-systems, or institutions *per se*, which include formal rules, such as constitutions, statutes, common law, regulations, and even contracts. Also included are informal rules, such as '*(1) extensions, elaborations and modifications of formal rules, (2) socially sanctioned norms of behaviour, and (3) internally enforced standards of conduct*'.[25] Informal rules tend to be disregarded in legal discussions, but they are arguably as important, if not more so, as formal rules. Local cultures are made up of informal rules that are reflected in shared cognitive frameworks. These shared cognitive frameworks allow, among other things, for the definition of social relationships and for the existence of interpretative frameworks that allow one to render meaningful the actions of others and to understand one's own position in social relationships.[26] In other words, shared cognitive frameworks provide the structure within which social interaction occurs and make purposive action possible by providing individuals with a framework of shared expectations[27]—and they cannot be made sense of without taking informal rules into account.
- organizations, meaning groups of individuals, more or less formally constituted in specific times and places, who pursue a set of collective purposes. Organizations mediate between individual actors and the rule-setting in which they operate.
- actors, meaning individuals acting purposefully within a specific institutional framework.

[24] Alec Stone Sweet, Wayne Sandholtz, and Neil Fligstein, *The Institutionalization of Europe* (OUP 2001), 6–8.

[25] Douglass C North, *Institutions, Institutional Change and Economic Performance* (Cambridge University Press 1990), 40. Similarly, Neil Fligstein, 'Markets as Politics' (1996) 61 AmSociolRev 656, 658.

[26] Neil Fligstein, *The Architecture of Markets: An Economic Sociology of Twenty-First-Century Capitalist Societies* (Princeton University Press 2001), 15.

[27] Edward L. Rubin, 'The New Legal Process, the Synthesis of Discourse, and the Microanalysis of Institutions' (1996) 109 HarvLRev 1393, 1414. On the concept of cognitive frameworks as interpretive systems through which individuals process information and make sense of their experiences, see Karl E. Weick, *Making Sense of the Organization* (Blackwell Business 2001). For a review of current research on this topic, see Judith A. Howard and Daniel G. Renfrow, 'Social Cognition' in John Delamater (ed.), *Handbook of Social Psychology* (Springer 2006), 262–269.

Section III will be devoted to identifying some extra-legal factors that are relevant for courts in general. The subsequent section will then focus on how these elements are relevant to better descriptions of the Court of Justice's decision-making practices.

III. Extra-Legal Factors

A. A basic typology

a. Personal preferences

The personal preferences of judges are the first extra-legal factor that one should take into account when trying to explain a judicial decision. That judges may have personal policy preferences that affect their decisions may seem obvious, but while there is a long tradition in the United States of studying this,[28] it was only recently—and mainly through North-American scholars—that the issue has started to be studied in Europe.[29]

A number of models have been developed regarding the impact that the preferences of judges may have on their decisions. The simpler one is the attitudinal model, according to which the preferences of judges (and, in some cases, the preferences of those appointing them) will determine the outcome of judicial proceedings.[30] Other models take into account other variables, such as the impact of collegial decision-making or other institutional factors in the expressed preferences of judges.[31] An additional element that may have to be taken into account is the existence of a particular professional *ethos*, which may be further reinforced if the participants in the legal process share a common socio-cultural background.[32] In any event, what all these models have in common is that they assume that behind the legal 'veil of objectivity'

[28] Particularly as a result of the work of the legal realists, on which see Brian Leiter, 'Rethinking Legal Realism—Towards a Naturalised Jurisprudence' (1997) TexLRev, 267.

[29] See, famously, Alec Stone Sweet, *The Birth of Judicial Politics in France: The Constitutional Council in Comparative Perspective* (OUP 1992).

[30] This model has been developed mainly by reference to the US Supreme Court—see Jeffrey Allan Segal and Harold J. Spaeth, *The Supreme Court and the Attitudinal Model Revisited* (Cambridge University Press 2002), 44–114—but the insights it provides are also relevant for understanding other high courts.

[31] On this and other models, see A Dyevre, '*Making Sense of Judicial Lawmaking: A Theory of Theories of Adjudication*' (EUI, 2008/09), <http://cadmus.eui.eu/dspace/bitstream/1814/8510/1/MWP_2008_09.pdf>.

[32] Gunnar Beck, *The Legal Reasoning of the Court of Justice of the EU* (Hart 2013), 37–42.

hides a person with her own preferences and biases, which will unavoidably be reflected in her decisions.[33]

b. Institutional context and popular opinion

Even if courts are generally able to constrain the activities of other political entities, not even the most powerful national courts have the power of the 'purse' or 'sword'. It is a staple of political science that courts' limited institutional resources mean that they are dependent on the goodwill of other branches of government for support as regards the enforcement of, and compliance with, judicial decisions.[34]

Judges face *de facto* informal constraints arising from their inability to enforce their own rulings, which may translate into a tendency to adopt decisions that are in line with the preferences of other branches of government or public opinion.[35] A related point is that courts are usually part of a judicial hierarchy—which means that judges are likely to take into account not only the position of their colleagues when members of a collegial court, but also the possibility that their decisions may be overturned by higher courts.[36] Further, other political institutions may also overrule judicial decisions, which means that the odds of such a political overrule occurring are relevant to the discretion judges have—or think they have—when deciding certain issues. These political constraints also mean that popular opinion may be a hidden consideration when courts decide, not only because of concerns about the likelihood of a decision being enforced or the legitimacy of the court being affected, but also because of the pressure it may put on political institutions, which are more sensitive to public opinion, to change the law and negate the effects of judicial decisions.

c. The need for precedent and its implications

Precedent can be seen as a reaction to the tension between judges' law-making role and the need for certainty and law-obeisance: it arises as an inherently legal constraint on discretion and law-making, while also allowing judges

[33] Ibid, 42.

[34] James L. Gibson, Gregory A. Caldeira and Vanessa A. Baird, 'On the Legitimacy of National High Courts' (1998) 92 AmPolitSciRev 343. On the limited impact of judicial decisions on policy settings, and on how the impact of such decisions depends on external context, see L. Connant, *Justice Contained—Law and Politics in the European Union* (Cornell University 2002), particularly 15–39.

[35] Beck, *The Legal Reasoning of the Court of Justice of the EU* , 37–38.

[36] On the other hand, it is also possible for higher courts to take into account the preferences of judges on the judicial hierarchy's lower rungs.

to portray their decisions as self-evident, redundant deductive extensions of pre-existing law.[37] Simultaneously, precedent effectively entrenches the powers or jurisdiction a court may have claimed in previous decisions by both providing a reason for such powers and restricting the reasons which can be used by its opponents.[38] When a process of case-by-case adjudication is adopted, something akin to precedent must of necessity develop so that courts are able to comply with the imperative of treating factually similar situations alike.[39] The existence of law-making elements in legal interpretation means that, even in civil systems, judicial decisions are relevant to the development of the law;[40] this is expressly so in common law systems that embrace *stare decisis*.

Precedent flows from the requirements of legal reasoning and is simultaneously instrumental to, and the goal of efforts to, categorize and rationalize prior case law. It is thus relevant for both the stabilization and the development of law. A consequence of this is that informal rules of precedent and legal reasoning, operating in the context of a specific common legal culture, effectively constrain the development of the law.

North has provided a general theory on institutional change and development, which is also a good heuristic device to explain how legal change occurs incrementally, with even discontinuous changes being constrained by the embeddedness of informal rules such as established customs, traditions, codes, and conducts.[41] Under this heuristic, taking into account cultural constraints is crucial to understanding the path of historical change, and how organizations and rules-settings interact and mutually constrain one another.

In particular, organizations have to operate under the existing rule setting, and thus have to navigate the options that such an institutional setting provides. Simultaneously, organizations are major agents of institutional change: as organizations evolve and adapt, they alter the rule-setting in which they operate as well. In particular, incremental change arises from the perceptions of individuals, and political and economic organizations, that

[37] Sweet, *The Judicial Construction of Europe*, 10.

[38] In the US context, see Barry Friedman and Erin F. Delaney, 'Becoming Supreme: The Federal Foundation of Judicial Supremacy' (2011) 111 ColumLRev 1137, 1188–1192.

[39] G. Christie, *Philosopher Kings?* (OUP 2011), 132.

[40] See, in particular and with great detail, K. Larenz, *Methodenlehre der Rechtswissenchaft* (J Lamego tr) (Springer-Verlag 1991).

[41] North, *Institutions, Institutional Change and Economic Performance*. It should be noted that the author's argument is very much focused on showing that institutional change need not be economically efficient, which in no way undermines the use of this theory here.

they could do better by altering the existent institutional framework at the margin, and from their pursuit of such changes. On the other hand, those individuals and organizations' perceptions are usually framed by incomplete information processed through mental constructs, which leads to institutional developments not being strictly those envisaged by the individuals and organizations advancing them. In other words, the path of institutional change is shaped by both the lock-in and path-dependency that arise from the symbiotic relationship between institutions and organizations, and the feedback process by which people perceive and react to the existing choice-set facing them.

This is particularly the case with legal systems, namely those that are precedent-based:

past decisions become embedded in the structure of the law, which changes marginally as new cases arise involving new, or at least in terms of past cases unforeseen issues; when decided these become in turn, a part of the legal framework. The judicial decisions reflect the subjective processing of information in the context of the historical construction of the legal framework. (...) However we account for the judicial process, the institutional framework is continuously but incrementally modified by the purposive activities of organizations bringing cases before the courts.[42]

In other words, history matters: the selection of a prior path determines current behaviour. Precedents are part of the cognitive framework in which courts operate, generating adaptive expectations that constrain litigants to argue within the bounds of existing precedent and law, even when attempting to push the law further.[43] On the one hand, this means that the idea of precedent stabilizes the law. On the other, this cognitive framework sets in place a number of specific institutional dynamics, which, through path-dependence, lead to three distinct, if interconnected, phenomena.[44]

The first phenomenon is non-ergodicity, meaning that the development of the case law is not necessarily incremental, and that not all developments are equally likely. Instead, small early events can have a disproportionate impact

[42] Ibid, 97. On the suitability of this framework for the Court of Justice see Adrienne Héritier, 'Overt and Covert Institutionalization in Europe' in Alec Stone Sweet, Wayne Sandholtz, and Neil Fligstein (eds), *The Institutionalization of Europe* (OUP 2001), 159.

[43] Oona A. Hathaway, 'Path Dependence in the Law: The Course and Pattern of Legal Change in a Common Law System' 86 IowaLRev 601, 627–630. On the role of litigants in shaping the development of EU law, see Mitchel Lasser, *Judicial Deliberations: A Comparative Analysis of Judicial Transparency and Legitimacy* (OUP 2004), 109–110; more specifically for their role in developing the European economic freedoms, see Maduro, *We, the Court*, 25 ff.

[44] I here follow Hathaway, 630–634.

on the eventual direction the case law takes—apparently irrelevant decisions may have large, unexpected consequences. The second effect is lock-in, or inflexibility: once a court has taken a decision on a legal question, precedent and other informal rules lock in that decision and the underlying legal rule. It should also be pointed out that there are legitimate ways for judges to eschew precedent within the cognitive framework in which they operate, such as relying on different precedents, on linguistic imprecisions, or on factual distinctions.[45] However, this can be costly or impossible to the extent that courts and the actors with whom they interact have invested resources, and adapted their routines, expectations, and relationships in step with how the law has evolved.[46] The third consequence is indeterminacy of outcome, as a decision choosing between different solutions that were possible at an initial stage will have been adopted on the basis of imperfect information as to its consequences, and may end up affecting the subsequent development of the law in unexpected, and even surprising, ways. This indeterminacy of outcome is also relevant to the identification of the normative underpinnings of the law. In particular, it may occur that, through their efforts to explain and rationalize the case law, legal operators may divine normative reasons which were previously absent, or conclude that normative concerns which were originally present in the law have ceased to be relevant, even though that was not foreseen or intended by the relevant decision-makers. These normative developments may then have unexpected implications of their own on how the case law further evolves, which exemplifies how unintended consequences flow from human thought no less than from human action.[47]

d. Legitimate judicial decision-making

A particular concern for courts is how to ensure obedience to their decisions, since they rely on other branches of government for their enforcement. As such, a court will usually seek to have its decisions perceived as legitimate, in order to ensure that they are implemented.

However, legitimacy is an elusive concept. It is normally given three different meanings: the first takes legitimacy as addressing the conformity of certain behaviours to the existing legal rules (legal legitimacy, or procedural legitimacy); the second looks into whether what the law prescribes is

[45] Clayton P. Gillette, 'Lock-In Effects in Law and Norms' (1998) 78 BULRev 813, particularly 824–825; Hathaway, 624–625.

[46] Stone Sweet, Sandholtz, and Fligstein, *The Institutionalization of Europe*, 20.

[47] Albert O. Hirschman, *The Passions and the Interests: Political Arguments for Capitalism Before its Triumph* (Princeton University Press 1997), 41.

normatively justified according to rationally defensible principles (moral or substantive legitimacy);[48] lastly, legitimacy can be seen as the existence of non-coerced consent to authority by its subjects. In the light of problems with measuring subjective adherence to a given system, some social scientists prefer to talk of consensus, as a measure of empirically demonstrable acceptance of authority by its subjects, rather than of subjective consent. Regardless, both consent and consensus vary along a continuum from active participation to passive acceptance to sullen obedience, and with them varies also the level of sociological legitimacy.[49]

Some literature drifts uncertainly between legitimacy as normative input and as behavioural output,[50] but these are different beasts: the difference lies in the distinction between the existence of empirically verifiable sociological legitimacy and the normative grounds upon which the belief of the existence of a legitimate authority rests. Normative approaches to legitimacy search for a truth that is logically independent from the strictly empirical question of whether law's subjects share a belief in the legitimacy of legal decisions. Normative theories are usually unitary and exclusionary, while it is quite possible for multiple theories of normative legitimacy to coexist as foundations of sociological legitimacy. It is true that normative arguments may change the beliefs of the relevant people and thus undermine the sociological legitimacy of political systems, but to mix these dimensions of legitimacy would constitute a normative fallacy.[51]

Weber famously tried to map the relationship between normative and sociological legitimacy: he identified a number of normative grounds for legitimacy—the rational-legal, traditional, and charismatic principles of authority—and then proceeded to conclude that in the modern State the relevant normative ground was the rational-legal, meaning that procedural

[48] David Beetham, *The Legitimation of Power* (Peter Jones and Albert Weale eds) (MacMillan 1991), 3–6.

[49] Dolf Sternberger, 'Legitimacy' in David L. Sills (ed.), *International Encyclopedia of the Social Sciences*, vol IX (Macmillan 1968), 244; P. H. Partridge, *Consent and Consensus* in Leonard Schapiro (ed.) (Pall Mall 1971), 71; Joseph Rothschild, 'Observations on Political Legitimacy in Contemporary Europe' (1977) 92 PolSciQ 487, 498; Beetham, *The Legitimation of Power*, 3–20; David Beetham and Christopher Lord, *Legitimacy and the EU* in Kenneth Dyson and Kevin Featherstone (eds) (Longman 1998), 12; R. Stryber, 'Legitimacy' in Neil J. Smelser and Paul B. Bates (eds), *International Encyclopedia of the Social & Behavioural Sciences*, vol XIII (Elsevier 2001), 8700–8701; Mattei Dogan, 'Conceptions of Legitimacy' in Mary Hawkesworth and Maurice Kogan (eds), *Encyclopedia of Government and Politics* vol I (2nd edn, Routledge 2003), 110.

[50] Ian Clark, *International Legitimacy and World Society* (OUP 2007), 17.

[51] Arie Rosen, 'The Normative Fallacy Regarding Law's Authority' in Will Walluchow and Steffan Sciaraffa (eds.), *The Nature of Law* (OUP, 2013), 75.

legitimacy would lead to sociological legitimacy.[52] This approach is at least still partially shared by some authors, who consider that the logic of argumentation inherent in legal discourse imposes a measure of procedural rationality that legitimizes both legal procedures and democratic legislation.[53] The dominant contemporary view, however, is that the normative grounds of legitimacy in modern States are mixed and fluid. In the face of the relationship between people's belief in legitimacy and the normative justification for such beliefs, on the one hand, and the evolution and variance of such normative justifications, on the other, sociological legitimacy is best understood as arising wherever a tolerable consensus is achieved between different normative foundations, with the weight of each remaining largely indeterminate.[54]

In Western liberal democracies, the normative grounds for sociological legitimacy are usually deemed to comprise a mix of substantive and formal sources, but the most commonly identified source of legitimacy is the perception that a government is operating under democratic principles and is subject to the will of the people who regularly express their consent, mainly through organized elections.[55] Democracy is a concept whose meaning can be lost amidst a cacophony of competing interpretations, but in the Western World it can be understood as referring to a number of different principles such as the need for elected officials, universal, equal, secret, and regular suffrage, freedom of expression, the right to engage in political activities, and the concomitant need to create a space for continuous debate between opposing social forces, interests, and ideas, inter alia.[56]

Other sources of sociological legitimacy, however, can and usually do exert pressure in an anti-democratic direction. Constitutionalism fits this

[52] See Max Weber, *Economy and Society: An Outline of Interpretive Sociology* (Bedminster Press 1968). See also Habermas, 'Law and Morality', 220–228; Stryber, 8700.

[53] J. Habermas, 'Law and Morality' in S.M. McMurrin (ed), TheTanner Lectures on Human Values, vol. VIII (Universit of Utah 1988, 229–280.

[54] Dogan, 'Conceptions of Legitimacy', 118; Beetham, *The Legitimation of Power*, 24–25; Ian Clark, *Legitimacy in International Society* (OUP 2007), 20, 226; Clark, *International Legitimacy and World Society*, 13.

[55] For the EU, see Articles 6 and 7 TEU.

[56] Giovanni Sartori, 'Democracy' in David L. Sills (ed.), *International Encyclopaedia of the Social Sciences*, vol IV (Macmillan 1968), 112; Nanette Neuwahl and Steven Wheatley, 'The EU and Democracy—Lawful and Legitimate Intervention in the Domestic Affairs of States?' in Anthony Arnull and Daniel Wincott (eds), *Accountability and Legitimacy in the European Union* (OUP 2002), 223; T.D. Christiano, 'Democracy: Normative Theory' in Neil J. Smelser and Paul B. Bates (eds), *International Encyclopedia of the Social & Behavioral Sciences*, vol V (Elsevier 2001), 3413; Beetham and Lord, *Legitimacy and the EU*, 6, 9; R.A. Dahl, 'Democracy' in Neil J. Smelser and Paul B. Bates (eds), *International Encyclopedia of the Social & Behavioral Sciences*, vol

bill, as it implies the adoption of a value-order protected by fundamental rights beyond the reach of democratic decisions. Another non-democratic source of sociological legitimacy is technocratic, namely the existence of scientific grounds which provide normative justifications for the adoption of certain rules.[57] Yet another source of sociological legitimacy is efficiency. In a noted essay, Lipset distinguished between economic efficiency, which was instrumental to the sustainability of a democratic system, and the normative underpinnings that had to be commonly accepted for democracy to emerge.[58] It is nowadays generally accepted that the performance of a system forms a necessary component of its legitimacy, and that political legitimacy usually requires both a morally authoritative source for government power and an ability to satisfy the ends that justify holding power. Accordingly, in addition to formal and substantive sources, we can also identify input (normative) and output (performance) sources of sociological legitimacy.[59]

The sophisticated machinery of modern democratic States reflects, among other things, a concern with the fact that the legitimacy of courts depends on their ability to meet the public's conception of the proper role of courts; and this conception can, in turn, be said to rely on a number of common, basic, assumptions. One assumption is that the judicial process is pursued by fair-minded and intelligent people, and will ultimately lead to fair and impartial decisions through adherence to a number of procedural requirements concerning the right to counsel, right to a fair hearing, rules on evidence, *inter alia*. Another assumption is that the law is previously known (or at least knowable) by the people staffing the adjudicatory process, and dictates the appropriate resolution of the relevant disputes brought before courts. This in turn requires the assumption that law is, at least for the most part, out there to be discovered by a trained judiciary in a quasi-mechanical way.[60] In other words,

V (Elsenier 2001), 3406–3408; Robert Dahl, *On Democracy* (Yale University Press 1998) 84–86; Jeremy Waldron, 'Can There Be a Democratic Jurisprudence?' (2009) 58 Emory LJ 675, 680. On the importance of the Charter of Paris to a New Europe of 1990 in summing up the essence of Western democratic practice, see Clark, *International Legitimacy and World Society*, 159.

[57] Beetham, *The Legitimation of Power*, 71–75; Clark, *Legitimacy in International Society*, 135–138. Paradoxically, the increased reliance on scientific-technical expertise by political and legal authorities can have the effect of increasing the politicization of this type of expertise and delegitimizing legal processes and institutions: see Stryber, 'Legitimacy', 8703.

[58] Seymour Martin Lipset, 'Some Social Requisites of Democracy: Economic Development and Political Legitimacy' (1959) 53 AmPolitSciRev 69, 86.

[59] Beetham, *The Legitimation of Power*, 137; Fritz Wilhelm Scharpf, *Governing in Europe: Effective and Democratic?* (OUP 1999), 6 ff.

[60] Christie, *Philosopher Kings?*, 77, 124.

the legitimacy of courts, and in particular of politically engaged courts, is to a great degree dependent on them being seen to act in accordance with a certain conception of judicial activity—which, in turn, means that the type of legitimacy courts will tend to be most concerned about is procedural legitimacy.

B. Internalizing extra-legal considerations

a. The institutional logic of legal reasoning

In the light of courts' concerns with making sure that their decisions are perceived as legitimate, how can extra-legal factors be translated into judicial decisions? The answer builds on the insight that courts are mainly concerned with rational-legal, procedural legitimacy, which is usually assessed with respect to whether courts followed the relevant procedure and whether their legal reasoning follows the accepted legal canons. Thus, one way through which extra-legal factors are translated into legitimate judicial decisions is through the adoption of legitimate modes of legal reasoning, which identification will in turn depend on the specific institutional and cognitive frameworks in which individual courts operate.

In other words, extra-legal considerations are, like background principles and values, mediated into legal discourse through a cognitive framework that makes sense of the existent institutional setting. For example, it has been said about the Court of Justice that:

> *Skilled social actors are crucial to institutional change because of their ability to generate or manipulate frames that make sense of institutional or policy problems and offer persuasive solutions. Frames can help mobilize cooperation among diverse actors by linking their interests and identities to a set of ideas—symbols, theories, models—that allow for further institutional development. We see skilled action, and sometimes new frames, in many situations, such as [for example when] the Court finds principles of mutual recognition in the Rome Treaty.*[61]

This description of the Court of Justice challenges purely internal legal perspectives and distinctions between pure political and judicial domains, according to which courts are supposed merely to apply the law.[62] Nonetheless, and even within the narrow confines of legal literature, the

[61] Stone Sweet, Sandholtz, and Fligstein, *The Institutionalization of Europe*, 12.

[62] According to which the judge 'est la bouche qui prononce les paroles de la loi'—Charles de Secondat Montesquieu, David Wallace Carrithers and Thomas Nugent, *The Spirit of Law: A Compendium of the First English Edition* (University of California Press 1977), Livre XI, chapitre VI. See also Sweet, 'Why Europe Rejected American Judicial Review and Why It May Not Matter', 2746.

perception of the role of judges has moved on from this traditional separation of powers' approach.

Judicial review, inasmuch as it requires the protection of rights by courts on constitutional grounds, conflicts with traditional conceptions of parliamentary democracy and strict separation of powers, but it is nonetheless a common feature of contemporary public law systems.[63] Also, while the task of judges still consists primarily of the independent and impartial interpretation, clarification, and protection of the rule of law, it is now generally acknowledged that every judgement of a new situation adds to the meaning of a rule or to the resolution of lacunae: the existence of lacunae in the legal system, when combined with the *non liquet* prohibition, leads to judges having to solve issues not foreseen by previous rules. Similarly, it is now commonly accepted that there are limits to the guidance that general language can provide due to its open texture: canons of interpretation can diminish, but not eliminate, interpretative uncertainties. These uncertainties can be syntactical, arising from the way words are organized in a sentence, or lexical, arising from: (a) the polysemy of words; (b) vagueness concerning their extension; and (c) the open texture which allows the precise extension of a given meaning to change over time.[64]

All legal systems compromise between the need for certain, simple rules which can be applied by the average citizen, and the need to deal with issues which may only be appreciated and settled by expert choice when they arise in a specific case.[65] Judges must sometimes face situations where there are different legitimate answers. In these situations, judges are still expected to invoke only those reasons which are recognized by law,[66] but courts nonetheless have to determine what the correct answer is based on criteria other than those used in a pure adjudicatory setting.[67] Legal reasoning with

[63] A M Bickel, *The Least Dangerous Branch: The Supreme Court at the Bar of Politics* (1962), 16–17; Alec Stone Sweet, 'Constitutional Courts and Parliamentary Democracy' (2002) 25 West European Politics 77, 78–79.

[64] Carlos Santiago Nino, *Introducción al análisis del derecho* (2nd edn, Editorial Astrea 1988), 260–268; Elina Paunio and Susanna Lindroos-Hovinheimo, 'Taking Language Seriously: An Analysis of Linguistic Reasoning and Its Implications in EU Law' (2010) 16 ELJ 395, 397–399.

[65] Hart, Bulloch and Raz, *The Concept of Law*, 126–130; Raz, *The Authority of Law*, 78.

[66] Raz, *The Authority of Law*, 200 and 208; Jeremy Waldron, 'Representative Lawmaking' (2009) 89 BULRev 335, 336.

[67] Raz, *The Authority of Law*, 182, notes that law itself may rule out several options as inappropriate and give some guidance as to how to choose between the remaining possible answers. Against this, arguing that only one right solution exists for each legal system, see Ronald Dworkin, *Taking Rights Seriously* (Harvard University Press 1977), 68–71 and 81–130.

law-making consequences is usually similar to, and continuous with, decisions interpreting and applying law[68] but, as we have seen in the previous section, extra-legal considerations may act in the shadows.[69]

This post-modern approach to adjudication, recognizing the pervasiveness of extra-legal considerations, should not however lead us to conclude that adjudication is a purely arbitrary operation. It is a common understanding of a shared 'story' about the contents and existence of a legal order which makes such order authoritative within a community.[70] Similarly, it is the obeisance to social practices and shared understandings by a legal community, which are in turn in accordance with a common understanding of what is legitimate law, that determines what judges can legitimately decide.[71] While courts, and particularly high courts, can generate and manipulate the institutional frameworks in which they operate, the fact remains that such exercises are effectively constrained by the pre-existing institutional framework. Judicial decisions are not valid because they are issued by a judge, but because they are issued by a judge within a specific setting in a duly reasoned manner.[72]

The point to be taken from the above discussion is that, in the institutional and cognitive setting in which legal officers in the Western world

[68] Larenz, *Methodenlehre der Rechtswissenchaft*, 519.

[69] Barry Friedman, 'The Politics of Judicial Review' (2005) 84 TexLRev 257.

[70] It should be noted that this insight is coherent with one of the main theoretical accounts of why people obey rules. From an evolutionary psychological perspective, rule obeisance is the result of cognitive, intuitive and emotional abilities that allow for the organization of behaviour around genetically grounded, yet culturally transmitted rules—see Richard Alexander, 'The Evolution of Social Behavior' (1974) 5 Annual Review of Ecology and Systematics 325; Michael Owren and Jo-Anne Bachorowski, 'The Evolution of Emotional Expression: A 'Selfish-Gene' Account of Smiling and Laughter in Early Hominids and Humans' in Tracy Mayne and George A. Bonanno (eds), *Emotions: Current Issues and Future Directions* (Guilford Press 2001), 239; Robert Trivers, 'The Evolution of Reciprocal Altruism' (1971) 46 Quarterly Review of Biology 35; and Robert Trivers, *Social Evolution* (Benjamin/Cummings 1985). For similar findings regarding other primates, see F.B.M de Waal, *Chimpanzee Politics: Power and Sex Among Apes* (Johns Hopkins University Press 1989); Dorothy L. Cheney and Robert M. Seyfarth, *Baboon Metaphysics: The Evolution of a Social Mind* (University of Chicago Press 2007). More generally, see Paul Seabright, *The Company of Strangers: A Natural History of Economic Life* (Princeton University Press 2010), 65–90 and Francis Fukuyama, *The Origins of Political Order* (Profile 2011).

[71] Robert Cover, 'Foreword: Nomos and Narrative' (1982) 97 HarvLRev 1; Gerald Postema, 'Implicit Law' (1994) 13 Law&Phil 361, 369–371.

[72] Adjudication is thus a device giving formal and institutional expression to reasoned argument—Lon L. Fuller, 'The Forms and Limits of Adjudication' (1978) 92 HarvLRev 353, 366.

operate, judicial activism has to mask itself as the discovery of law, even when it verges into law-making and politics; and, importantly, that this masking has serious consequences for how courts decide cases. Legal reasoning is in effect constrained by rules, even if some of those rules are merely informal. For courts to operate at all, every agent and organization participating in judicial processes must, in order for such participation to make sense, share in a common legal culture that frames and constrains the different cognitive frameworks available to them. This cognitive framework usually goes unremarked because it is unremarkable; it is part of what has been called the 'tacit dimension', meaning that it includes propositions and opinions shared by a group and deemed so obvious that they are never fully articulated or systematized.[73] For example, the cognitive framework shared by most, if not all, European legal orders requires that, when interpreting law, it is the language of the accepted law sources that is to be taken into account. Even if the meaning of the relevant provisions or authorities is uncertain, the limits of uncertainty of language are the boundaries of certainty of language as well: interpretation cannot go beyond what language itself allows. Another common assumption is the imperative of treating similar situations similarly: this imposes coherence and consistency requirements on legal systems, which underpin systemic imperatives and the impulse to generalize rules developed in individual cases. Such assumptions and imperatives are, in turn, related to the pursuit of legal certainty, the creation of a rule of law, and the removal of purely arbitrary decisions.[74]

In short, extra-legal considerations are translated into 'official' legal discourse through a cognitive setting that reflects a common 'culture' of legal reasoning. Such a culture imposes standards by which the correctness of legal interpretation is to be judged. Under the cognitive framework in place for most, if not all Western legal orders, decisions are arrived at through deliberation and analogical reasoning, and presented as relatively redundant, self-evident, incremental extensions of available legal materials. Control of whether the relevant parameters of legal reasoning have been complied with in a legal decision is ensured by the interactive nature of law practice: *ex ante* because cases are brought and argued before courts by lawyers trained and imbued in the spirit and grammar of a specific legal community; and *ex post* through systems of appeal and the criticism from an interpretive community

[73] Polanyi and Sen, *The Tacit Dimension*.

[74] Claus-Wilhem Canaris, *Systemdenken und Systembegriff in der Jurisprudenz* (A. Menezes Cordeiro tr) (2nd edn, Duncker und Humblot 1983), §1 (2).

recognizing as authoritative a number of commonly accepted parameters as to the correctness of interpretation.[75]

b. An example—balancing

A good example of how extra-legal considerations can be mediated into legal discourse is balancing, a technique for solving conflicts between individual rights, between individual rights and public interests, and between conflicting public interests, which in the European context is traditionally associated with the principle of proportionality.[76] Balancing plays an important role in the case law of many constitutional courts under different guises, including the Court of Justice.[77] Its most complete treatment in the European setting is probably by Alexy, who draws and builds on Dworkin's conceptual distinction between rules and principles.[78] According to Dworkin, while rules are applicable in an all-or-nothing fashion, principles can conflict, having a weight that provides non-conclusive reasons for deciding a case one way or another. Both principles and rules are norms, with principles being more general, abstract, indeterminate, and foundational than rules. The distinction, however, is not merely quantitative but also qualitative: a norm is either a principle or a rule depending on whether it provides a definitive reason for

[75] Gerald Postema, '"Protestant" Interpretation and Social Practices' (1987) 72 Law&Phil 283, 310–312. On the EU, see Ham Schepel and Rein Wesseling, 'The Legal Community: Judges, Lawyers, Officials and Clerks in the Writing of Europe' (1997) 3 ELJ 165. On the constitutive nature of such a grammar, if focusing on public law generally, Martin Loughlin, *Foundations of Public Law* (OUP 2010), 178–180.

[76] On its origins, see J. J. Gomes Canotilho, *Direito Constitucional e Teoria da Constituição* (3rd edn, Almedina 1998), 262 ff.

[77] Donald H. Regan, '*The Supreme Court and State Protectionism: Making Sense of the Dormant Commerce Clause*' (1985–1986) 84 MichLRev 1091, 1101–1108, describes a number of different balancing tests in the American context. Maduro, *We, the Court*, 54–58, does the same in the European context. For an analysis of the potential differences between balancing and proportionality, see Moshe Cohen-Eliya and Iddo Porat, 'American Balancing and German Proportionality: The Historical Origins' (2010) 8 I•CON 263, 268–270. Mapping the adoption of proportionality throughout the world, see Alec Stone Sweet and Jud Mathews, 'Proportionality, Balancing and Global Constitutionalism' (2008) 47 ColumJTransnat'lL 72.

[78] But the theories are distinct on a number of points: Alexy allows for the existence of multiple possible solutions, while Dworkin famously does not; constitutional rights for Dworkin are rules, while for Alexy they are, at least in some cases, principles; Dworkin expressly considers that balancing is not acceptable when individual rights are at stake, while Alexy builds his whole theory around the idea that the balancing of individual constitutional rights is unavoidable; and to Dworkin principles are not optimization requirements for policies and rights alike, as they are to Alexy, but mere standards providing reasons for individual rights.

action or not.[79] While a collision of rules can only be resolved by either the invalidation of one of the rules or the stipulation of an exception, a conflict of principles—i.e. a conflict of non-conclusive norms—must be solved by balancing the relative weight of each.[80] Alexy goes beyond this and considers that principles are not only standards of relatively high generality providing non-conclusive reasons for deontic decisions which may be displaced by other principles, but also optimization requirements demanding that something be realized to the greatest extent possible given the existing factual and legal possibilities. In other words, to Alexy, principles are value-claims with mere *prima facie* force, and balancing is inherent to them: when principles collide, unlike rules, the situation cannot be solved by declaring that one of the principles is invalid or by building exceptions into it.[81] His solution is to create a conditional relation of precedence for the balancing of principles in the light of the specific facts of the case.[82] To achieve this, Alexy proposes a 'Law of Balancing', which can be divided into three stages: first, establishing the degree of non-satisfaction of a first principle; second, establishing the importance of the competing principle; and third, establishing the relationship between the first two elements.[83]

This technique is supposed to create the appearance that law and legal decisions yield purely objective results and that law is not so much made as found. For this appearance to be true, an axiological unity of values in the legal system, allowing for the discovery of a single rational right answer, would be required.[84] This would require all legal solutions to be compatible and fit into a single whole, meaning that an objective order of values both has to exist and be epistemologically accessible.[85] Since truths cannot be logically incompatible, and since reason is common to all men, a right solution would then be acceptable to all rational persons.[86] However, without

[79] Dworkin, *Taking Rights Seriously*, 23–26. This distinction is similar to that between rules and standards: see Kathleen Sullivan, 'Foreword: The Justices of Rules and Standards' (1992) 106 HarvLRev 22, 57 ff.

[80] Dworkin, *Taking Rights Seriously*, 27.

[81] Robert Alexy, *A Theory of Constitutional Rights* (Julian Rivers tr) (OUP 2001), 66; Raz, *The Authority of Law*, 228.

[82] Alexy, *A Theory of Constitutional Rights*, 50–54, Sullivan, 'Foreword', 59.

[83] Groussot, 'European Rights', 4.

[84] See Canaris, *Systemdenken und Systembegriff in der Jurisprudenz*, in particular 204–208; Larenz, *Methodenlehre der Rechtswissenchaft*, 675–686.

[85] Isaiah Berlin, *Four Essays on Liberty* (OUP 1969), 145–147; Alexy, *A Theory of Constitutional Rights*, 94.

[86] Berlin, *Four Essays on Liberty*, lv.

an *a priori* demonstration that a total harmony of values is somewhere to be found, either through the reduction of the concept of good to a common measure or by creating a comprehensive hierarchy among goods, we have no reason to suppose that all ends and values can be harmonized.[87] Some values may be incommensurable, which will occur when the relevant goods cannot be aligned along a single metric without doing violence to our considered judgements about how these goods are best characterized.[88]

Even if one does not accept theories that claim universal validity for the highest values or goods, balancing still plays a role in the search for a *modus vivendi* among forms of life that are irreconcilable, or mediating claims which can never be solved.[89] On the other hand, if theories about universal validity were accepted, they would imply that a hierarchical solution would be available, in which case there would seem to be no need for balancing in the first place. The consequence of this is that balancing does not seem apt to arrive at definite, 'correct' solutions: when goods are not instrumental but intrinsic and no metric is available, no balancing is possible and choices must be made. Reasons run out,[90] which is why balancing can potentially be co-extensive with discretion.[91] Moral pluralism, the existence of a multitude of incompatible but morally valuable forms of life, and value pluralism, the existence of incompatible virtues which are

[87] William A. Galston, *Liberal Pluralism: The Implications of Value Pluralism for Political Theory and Practice* (Cambridge University Press 2002), 6.

[88] Raz, *The Morality of Freedom*, 325, mainly regarding failures of transitivity; Galston, *Liberal Pluralism*, 29 ff; Sunstein, 'Incommensurability and Valuation in Law', 796; Neil MacCormick, *Practical Reason in Law and Morality* (OUP 2008), 37. On the (legal) debate on incommensurability, see the overview provided in Brian Bix, *Law, Language and Legal Determinacy* (Clarendon Press 1993), 96–104.

[89] Berlin, *Four Essays on Liberty*, 167–171; John Gray, *Enlightenment's Wake: Politics and Culture at the Close of the Modern Age* (Routledge 2007), 13; Galston, *Liberal Pluralism*, 32–33. A discussion on modes of conciliating values in a pluralist environment can be found in Frank Michelman, 'The Supreme Court 1985 Term—Foreword: Traces of Self-Government' (1986) 100 HarvLRev 4, 31–33. He identifies three tendencies on modes of conciliation: procedural conditions of normative conversation (Habermas), pragmatic concerns with contingent and temporarily accepted premises which suffice for the purposes of conciliating values at a given time and space (Rorthy, Gadamer), and conditions based on the intersubjective and social formation of the self (Minow, the feminist movement). See also Cass Sunstein, 'Incommensurability and Valuation in Law' (1994) 92 MichLRev 779.

[90] Raz, *The Morality of Freedom*, 353; Habermas, *Between Facts and Norms*, 160.

[91] Julian Rivers, 'Proportionality and Discretion in International and European Law' in Nicholas Tsagourias (ed.), *Transnational Constitutionalism* (Cambridge University Press 2007), 107; Sunstein, 804; Jeremy Waldron, 'Fake Incomensurability: A Response to Professor Schauer' (1994) 45 Hastings LJ 813, 816.

not completely ranked by some impersonal criteria of moral worth, seem to be the rule instead.[92]

As much is acknowledged by Alexy himself, who refuses the existence of an order of values or principles determining the content of adjudication and expressly admits that balancing does not lead to a single 'right' solution in each case. Nonetheless, Alexy still contends that, while substantive answers to all morality questions are not possible, procedural moral theories formulating rules or conditions for rational practical argument are.[93] This may lead to the argument that balancing operates at a purely formal level, with its correctness merely a matter of discourse and of relative coherence rather than of any external, substantive standards. Nonetheless, this 'procedural' test requires the injection of significant elements of value[94] at least in two moments of the balancing assessment: in determining the relative 'weight' of the principles involved; and in carrying out the final balancing exercise, as the outcome which is considered to be best may depend on the concept of efficiency used or even on the specific balancing test that is adopted. Thus, while the focus is on the procedural dimension, this does not mean that balancing is substantively neutral.[95]

It should be noted that these concerns do not apply to judicial balancing alone: they also apply to political decisions by other bodies.[96] In effect,

[92] Raz, *The Morality of Freedom*, 133, 396–397. This line of thought equates values—and the current philosophical discussion on their incommensurability—with legal principles. Even though different in that values have an axiological character while principles are deontic value claims, both principles and values have essentially the same conceptual structure inasmuch as both have to do with the logic of applying norms and require balancing to solve conflicts between them—see Alexy, *A Theory of Constitutional Rights*, 93; J. Habermas, *Between Facts and Norms* (Polity Press 1996), 233.

[93] Alexy, *A Theory of Constitutional Rights*, 99, 365–370. See also Rivers, 'Proportionality and Discretion', 119; Gustavo Zagrebelsky, *Il diritto mite* (Einaudi 1992), 170. A similar process-based theory has been advanced by Habermas, 'Law and Morality', <http://www.tannerlectures.utah.edu/lectures/documents/habermas88.pdf>.

[94] Conway, 'Levels of Generality', 787. On how Habermas and other theorists fail to answer this question, see Thomas McCarthy, 'Practical Discourse: On the Relation of Morality to Politics' in Craig Calhoun (ed.), *Habermas and the Public Sphere* (MIT 1992), 51.

[95] Ben Schueler, 'Methods of Application of the Proportionality Principle in Environmental Law' (2008) 35 LIEI 231, 231; Groussot, 'European Rights', 8; Fiedrich Müller, *Die Einheit der Verfassung—Kritik des juristischen Holismus* (Dunken & Humblot 1979), particularly 199. Alexy considers this problem to be inherent to any practical reason discourse: see Alexy, *A Theory of Legal Argumentation*, 206–208, 288.

[96] Waldron, 'Fake Incomensurability: A Response to Professor Schauer', 822.

different orderings of value cannot always co-exist, in which case the political system must tilt one way or the other.[97] As Post has noted:

> *Politics and law are ... two distinct ways of managing the inevitable social facts of agreement and disagreement. As social practices, politics and law are both independent and interdependent. They are independent in the sense that they are incompatible. To submit a political controversy to legal resolution is to remove it from the political domain; to submit a legal controversy to political resolution is to undermine the law. Yet they are interdependent in the sense that law requires politics to produce the shared norms that law enforces, whereas politics requires law to stabilize and entrench the shared values that politics strives to achieve.*[98]

In other words, whatever institution is forced to choose between different values will need to make substantively charged decisions. Balancing, like most techniques of legal reasoning, is neither a purely formalistic or arbitrary operation. It provides courts with a commonly accepted procedural form for adopting politically charged decisions, while granting them a cover of neutrality that simultaneously acknowledges that legal interpretation is bounded, limited, and relative, and that its results cannot be found to be 'true' or 'false'.[99] Inasmuch as the law is silent or incomplete, recourse to extra-legal considerations will be necessary in order for courts to reach decisions. Balancing, like other forms of legal reasoning, is able to constrain the impact of extra-legal considerations through a series of rules and interpretative practices arising from a shared cognitive framework that distinguishes between legitimate and illegitimate decisions, while simultaneously allowing for various legitimate outcomes and protecting the (procedural) legitimacy of courts.

c. Legal reasoning and legal formulas

In the light of the above, legal reasoning is best understood as a discursive practice restricted by a series of conditions undertaken by, and within the

[97] Galston, *Liberal Pluralism*, 59.

[98] Robert Post, 'Theorizing Disagreement: Reconceiving the Relationship between Law and Politics' (2010) 98 CLR 1319, 1343.

[99] Bounded rationality is a term first proposed by Herbert Simon and used in economics to identify situations where people may not look for fully rational choices because of their inability to be sufficiently focused, or adequately steadfast or alert enough in seeking the information necessary to make a fully rational decision—see Herbert Simon, 'A Behavioral Model of Rational Choice' (1955) Quarterly Journal of Economics 69, and *Models of Thought* (Yale University Press 1979).

context of, a specific (legal) community with the purpose of putting forward rules which are of such limited normative content that individuals with different normative backgrounds may agree to them, but also strong enough for any discussion abiding by them to be acknowledged as rational and therefore legitimate by the ideal (legal) audience.[100] As Hart said, even though in some cases it cannot be demonstrated that a decision is uniquely correct, it may be made acceptable as a reasoned product of informed impartial choice.[101] One way to ensure this acceptance is to focus on the outcome of particular cases. In particular, courts may seek to find solutions that are acceptable on results and on low-level principles without taking sides in large-scale controversies, producing 'incompletely theorised agreements on particular outcomes'.[102]

While such an approach has advantages regarding the impartiality of courts and the legitimacy of their decisions, it is not without institutional implications. For purposes of access to and rationalization of the case law, participants in a legal community will tend to develop propositions that will serve as classificatory frameworks with the simultaneous goal of uncovering the underlying logic of previous case law and predicting the outcome of hypothetical future cases.[103] These classificatory frameworks can be framed within a continuum from bright-line rules to high-generality standards.[104]

In complex situations, judges may want to adopt standards which ensure greater flexibility to deal with specific issues and allow them to pursue the law's normative goals. Standards thus act as a reserve, implicitly granting competence to courts to decide a greater number of cases on the facts. The problem with standards is that the amount and complexity of litigation they

[100] Owen Fiss, 'Objectivity and Interpretation' (1982) 34 StanLRev 739, 743–745; Alexy, *A Theory of Legal Argumentation*, 19 and 288; Connant, *Justice* , 218; Jeremy Waldron, 'The Core of the Case Against Judicial Review' (2006) 115 Yale LJ 1346, 1381.

[101] Hart, Bulloch and Raz, *The Concept of Law*, 200.

[102] Cass R. Sunstein, *Legal Reasoning and Political Conflict* (OUP 1996), 4–5; Connant, *Justice Contained*, 51–52.

[103] Christie, *Philosopher Kings?*, 133–134.

[104] Frederick Schauer, 'Rules and the Rule of Law' (1991) 14 Harv JL & Pub Pol'y 645, 648–651; Louis Kaplow, 'Rules versus Standards: An Economic Analysis' (1992) 42 Duke LJ 557, 608–611. It should be noted, as these authors do, that the difference between standards and rules is merely one of degree. Rules and standards are not qualitatively distinct, but are shorthand for the different levels of discretion granted to adjudicatory bodies, and should therefore be understood as useful analytical tools—Sullivan, 'Foreword', 57–62. For heuristic purposes, rules and standards will be referred to as if one were comparing pure types, a practice common in legal theory, even though legal commands mix the two to varying degrees—see Frederick Schauer, 'The Convergence of Rules and Standards' [2003] NZLRev 303, 306–309.

can generate can lead to their overextension, which may in turn lead to an increase in strategic litigation and the surfacing of concerns about courts' physical capacity and docket control. Furthermore, a court may face specific issues concerning its legitimacy under a standard-based approach, as it may face highly politicized value-choices where no best solution is available, and risk ceding the impartial adjudicatory role that traditionally ensures the acceptance of a court's decisions by those to whom they are addressed.[105]

This creates incentives for courts to limit standards through the development of rules. Rules may be defended on grounds of fairness—since they treat *prima facie* similar cases similarly—legal certainty, saving time and costs in adjudication, and of restraining the discretion of courts.[106] They reduce uncertainty, facilitate settlement, and allow courts to allocate decision-making elsewhere. Rules tend, however, to be both over- and under-inclusive in relation to their normative underpinning. Judges may well want greater flexibility to deal with specific situations and thereby decrease errors of under- and over-inclusiveness.[107] This may, in turn, push courts back towards standards.

As the complexity and number of cases increase, all alternative solutions become imperfect, which may lead to cycling between rules and standards as a least-bad situation is attained, leading to a tension between the flexibility courts might obtain through the adoption of standards, and the reduction in litigation and allocation of cases to other organizations that simple rules allow.[108]

IV. Institutional Constraints and the Court of Justice

A. *A preliminary point: the legitimacy of EU law*

Among the various extra-legal factors that affect the Court of Justice's decision-making practice, concerns about the legitimacy of EU law must stand foremost.

[105] Waldron, 'Representative Lawmaking', 336.

[106] Sullivan, 'Foreword', 62–65.

[107] This includes considerations of fairness—taking into account similarities and differences which are suppressed by rules—preventing the exploitation of rules when knowledge or access to information is distributed unequally, and expressing the balancing exercise which is merely implicit in rules. Ibid, 66–69.

[108] Neil K. Komesar, *Law's Limits: The Rule of Law and the Supply and Demand of Rights* (Cambridge University Press 2001), 159–160.

As we have seen above, assessments of sociological legitimacy require the identification of the various relevant normative sources of sociological legitimacy and how they interact. A legitimacy deficit can be said to arise when constitutional structures, the substantive content of rules, or their adequacy to resolve problems of government performance do not conform sufficiently to accepted beliefs about the proper source of authority.[109] In the case of the EU, the balance between democracy, constitutionalism, technocratic options, and efficiency tends to boil down to the *vexata quaestio* of the Union's democratic deficit.

On this topic, it has been argued that EU law needs output legitimacy alone. In particular, Scharpf has argued that input legitimacy must be borrowed from the national level; output legitimacy, on the other hand, can be achieved at the European level by the EU's institutions sticking to the limited competences attributed to them in the Treaties and pursuing consensual technocratic solutions with low political visibility that increase economic efficiency.[110] Along the same lines, Majone submits that the EU is a regulatory State which can be legitimized without recourse to input legitimacy as long as it pursues only efficiency-enhancing policies that lead to Pareto-efficiencies, and redistribution and politically charged choices are avoided.[111] As Moravcsik has noted, a common element in these approaches is the view that the EU's activities should be restricted to its limited competences in technical areas of low political relevance.[112] The gist of the argument is that the EU is not a State, and, as such, the traditional balance between input and output legitimacy for nation-States does not apply. From this perspective, EU law is akin to administrative law: not susceptible to being legitimized by democratic means in light of the absence of a European polity and *demos*, but legitimate as long as it pursues its limited goals within the framework of competences attributed to it by democratically elected national bodies.

[109] Beetham, *The Legitimation of Power*, 75, 149, 208. 'Democratic deficit' is a concept which knows multiple formulations beyond this one: see Giandomenico Majone and Pio Baake, *Dilemmas of European Integration: The Ambiguities and Pitfalls of Integration by Stealth* (OUP 2005), 37; Andreas Follesdal and Simon Hix, 'Why There is a Democratic Deficit in the EU: A Response to Majone and Moravcsik' (2006) 44 JCMS 533, 534–537.

[110] Scharpf, *Governing in Europe: Effective and Democratic?*

[111] Giandomenico Majone and Pio Baake, *Regulating Europe* (Routledge 1996), 287–296; Giandomenico Majone and Pio Baake, 'Europe's "Democratic Deficit": The Question of Standards' (1998) 4 ELJ 5, 28.

[112] A. Moravcsik, 'In Defence of the "Democratic Deficit": Reassessing the Legitimacy of the European Union' (2002) 40 JCMS 603, 613–619.

Whatever legitimacy the EU is able to generate will have to arise from increased economic efficiency and the EU's ability to deal with transnational issues which national States and their majoritarian institutions are unable to address on their own. Thus, according to these authors, the democratic deficit is non-existent or limited to a few specific areas where the EU's actions go beyond its technocratic and efficiency-enhancing role.[113]

Another proposed non-democratic normative source of legitimacy at EU level relates to constitutionalism and to the protection of individual rights, including, in some formulations, the protection of individual economic freedoms against interferences from public powers. This approach draws from both ordo-liberal and Kantian legal theories,[114] with market freedoms legitimizing market integration and non-discriminatory competition by increasing individual autonomy, controlling abuses of government, and maximizing economic welfare.[115] An offshoot of this approach goes further and argues that individual freedoms are crucial to democratic consensus by ensuring the rule of law in pluralistic societies, understood as a minimal 'overlapping consensus' of reasonably diverse moral, religious, and political conceptions that is likely to endure over time in democratic societies.[116] A closely related approach is the 'transnationalist' one,[117] which sees EU law, and particularly the fundamental freedoms, as improving the democratic practices of the Member States. Transnationalists argue that institutional malfunctions can arise from 'national failures', in particular the parochial and selfish nature of national democratic systems. The concept of ideal democracy implicit in this approach focuses on the existence of a public domain of free discussion where all interests are taken into account

[113] This is a view usually associated with inter-governmentalism.

[114] E-J. von Mestmäcker, 'On the Legitimacy of European Law' (1994) 58 RabelsZ 617, 619, 626 ff; Ernst-Ulrich Petersmann, 'European and International Constitutional Law: Time for Promoting "Cosmopolitan Democracy" in the WTO' in Gráinne de Burca and Joanne Scott (eds), *The EU and the WTO—Legal and Constitutional Issues* (Hart Publishing 2001), 81–82.

[115] Miguel Poiares Maduro, 'Reforming the Market or the State? Article 30 and the European Constitution: Economic Freedom and Political Rights' (1997) 3 ELJ 55, 55–56; Petersmann, 'European and International Constitutional Law, 82. On ordo-liberalism, see David J. Gerber, 'Constitutionalizing the Economy: German Neo-Liberalism, Competition Law and the "New" Europe' (1994) 42 AmJCompL 25.

[116] Petersmann, 'Do Judges Meet their Constitutional Obligation to Settle Disputes?', 37; Petersmann, 'Judging Judges', 850.

[117] Anupam Chander, 'Globalization and Distrust' (2005) 114 Yale LJ 1197, 2000; Alexander Somek, 'The Argument from Transnational Effects I: Representing Outsiders through Freedom of Movement' (2010) 16 ELJ 315, 317–321. On the origins of this approach, see John Hart Ely, *Democracy and Distrust: a Theory of Judicial Review* (Harvard University Press 1980).

before decisions are made, instead of on the existence of majority rule applied to political decisions. Supranational institutions, and in particular free movement rights, are accordingly perceived as improving democracy by giving representation status to non-nationals in the political process of the Member States, thereby forcing them to take into account out-of-State interests.[118] Some authors have coupled this approach with the argument that the EU benefits from output legitimacy, and have gone on to argue that, as a result, the EU benefits from both input and output legitimacy, even if differently from nation states.[119]

All these theses assume that normative sources of legitimacy are able to add to the EU's sociological legitimacy, rather than test this empirically. But the richness of normative sources of legitimacy identified above, when coupled with the existence of formal legitimacy arising from the Treaties, indicates that, if there is a European legitimacy deficit, it is not so much a normative as a sociological one.

Traditionally, three types of consideration are put forth to justify decision-making by democratically unelected bodies: first, the mechanisms of electoral accountability are thought to be unsuited for the pursuit of certain goals and for addressing certain questions; secondly, achieving these goals and addressing these questions tends to require highly technical solutions, and the best way to pursue, critique, and control these solutions is thought to be to delegate this task to a specialized professional community; lastly, if decisions adopted go against broad majorities, elected bodies should be able to override the experts' options.[120] From this perspective, the main problem with EU law is that it is insufficiently democratic in relation to expected standards.[121] Since EU institutions are not subject to direct democratic control, this requirement of technocratic legitimacy is absent, leading to potentially serious de-legitimation consequences. In particular, the issue is that democratic processes are still mainly restricted to national units, while an ever-increasing number of decisions are adopted at EU level. This leads to

[118] Maduro, *We, the Court*; Maduro, 'Reforming the Market or the State?', 73–76; Christian Joerges and Jurgen Neyer, 'From Intergovernmental Bargaining to Deliberative Political Processes: The Constitutionalisation of Comitology' (1997) 3 ELJ 273, 294–295.

[119] Anand Menon and Stephen Weatherill, 'Legitimacy, Accountability and Delegation in the European Union' in Anthony Arnull and Daniel Wincott (eds), *Accountability and Legitimacy in the European Union* (OUP 2002), 120–131.

[120] Scharpf, *Governing in Europe: Effective and Democratic?* 16, 22.

[121] Weiler, *The Constitution of Europe*, 84.

European citizens having no effective means of debating European decisions or influencing European decision-making.[122]

The democratic deficit in Europe therefore seems to relate to the absence of a common polity where the majority principle can apply: there is not a European *demos*, no European-wide policy discourse and no European-wide institutional arrangements assuring the political accountability of European office holders.[123] The problem appears to be that people only accept that the majoritarian principle applies to them within a polity which they see themselves as belonging to. Democracy requires a previous polity in which a minority can accept being compelled by a majority.[124] Even though some authors have debated the ideal conditions for the creation of a European polity,[125] the fact remains that its creation, and even the creation of a 'thin identity'[126] with elements common to all Europeans, depends on very long-term factors, such as social, cultural, linguistic, and historical affinity. It may well be that it is only through a shared history that the acceptance of similar normative, civilizing, and liberal values across the EU can be given a durable social existence.[127]

The democratic deficit becomes particularly acute when one combines the impact of the supremacy principle, the extension of EU political competences, and the possibility of a significant number of national rules being subject to review by the European courts under the fundamental freedoms. In the light of the present impossibility of grounding the EU's legitimacy in a manner similar to that of Member States, particularly regarding its democratic credentials, it is not surprising that authors have scrambled to ground the EU's legitimacy on the normative sources identified above, or

[122] Jürgen Habermas, 'Citizenship and National Identity: Some Reflections on the Future of Europe' in Ronald Beiner (ed.), *Theorising Citizenship* (State University of New York 1995), 265–267; Brigid Laffan, 'The Politics of Identity and Political Order in Europe' (1996) 34 JCMS 81, 93–94. This also appears to be the position of the German Federal Constitutional Court: see *Lisbon Treaty*, para. 262–264.

[123] Scharpf, *Governing in Europe: Effective and Democratic?*, 187; Angus Johnston, 'Democracy in the European System: Towards a Critical Approach' (1998) 9 European Law Students Association Selected Papers in European Law 77.

[124] Weiler, *The Constitution of Europe*, 83, 337; Beetham and Lord, *Legitimacy and the EU*, 29, 33.

[125] See Habermas, 'Citizenship and National Identity'.

[126] Beetham and Lord, *Legitimacy and the EU*, 45–47, 58.

[127] Lindseth, 'Democratic Legitimacy and the Administrative Character of Supranationalism', 681.

on a combination of them.[128] However, as long as political identity clings to the nation-State, issues of democratic legitimacy will continue to surface in the EU. This is an empirical, sociological reality that cannot be theorized away,[129] and which poses particular obstacles to the Court of Justice in making sure that its decisions are followed and accepted as legitimate by their addressees. This concern may in turn be reflected in the way the Court of Justice acts and tries to present its actions.

B. The Court of Justice and its institutional context

The rules and procedures of the EU make up the framework of constraints and opportunities that are faced by actors who want to enhance their social, economic, or political positions within the EU.[130] Those actors may prefer to refer to courts instead of other organizations to further their ends, with the result that domestic courts can be routinely prompted by savvy litigants to take account of and interpret European law in otherwise mundane litigation.[131] The ease with which these litigants can refer to European law in situations where potential gains might be obtained depends, however, on the Court of Justice's own case law. No less importantly, the Court of Justice is simultaneously empowered and constrained by both formal (the Treaties, the specific procedural rules by which it must abide, etc.) and informal rules (e.g. the parameters of correct judicial discourse identified above). To begin with, like other courts, the Court of Justice consists:

> *of highly diverse people, who have a weak democratic pedigree and limited fact-finding capacity, and who must render many decisions, live together, avoid error to the extent possible, and show respect to each other, to the people who come before them, and to those affected by their decisions.*[132]

The Court of Justice was set up as the authoritative interpreter of EU law in the Treaties, many provisions of which were loosely worded in order to enable political agreement. The Court of Justice was thus empowered

[128] Agustin José Menéndez, 'The European Democratic Challenge: The Forging of a Supranational *Volonté Générale*' (2009) 15 ELJ 277, 282–284.

[129] Lindseth, 'Democratic Legitimacy and the Administrative Character of Supramatnationalism', 736.

[130] Stone Sweet, Sandholtz, and Fligstein, *The Institutionalization of Europe*, 10.

[131] An empirical analysis of this phenomenon can be found, among others, in Alec Stone Sweet and Neil Fligstein, 'Institutionalizing the Treaty of Rome' in Alec Stone Sweet, Wayne Sandholtz, and Neil Fligstein (eds), *The Institutionalization of Europe* (OUP 2001).

[132] Sunstein, *Legal Reasoning and Political Conflict*, 6.

judicially to clarify Treaty rules *ex post*.[133] Furthermore, for a long time the Court of Justice operated in an environment where EU rules had to be adopted by unanimity. Even today, the reversal by political means of the Court of Justice's interpretation of Treaty articles is primarily to be achieved by Treaty amendment, allowing the Court to interpret Treaty provisions, and particularly the fundamental freedoms, in such a way that their study is now for the most part the study of the relevant case law.[134] This rule governing the reversal of the Court of Justice's interpretations of the Treaty is a weak form of control favouring the Court's dominance over the constitutional development of the EU, particularly in the light of the limited threat from other court-curbing mechanisms.[135]

On the other hand, the Court of Justice is constrained by the fact that its decisions have to be applied by national courts and administrations. As we have seen, it is a common understanding of a shared 'story' about the contents and existence of a legal order that makes such order authoritative within a community; and it is the conformity with social practices and shared understandings about what is legitimate law that determines what judges can legitimately decide.[136] In the Western legal tradition, the legitimacy of courts derives to a large extent from courts performing the technical role of legal adjudicators in an impartial manner. While there is a degree of consensus among scholars that diffuse support for courts is an attitude that evolves over time through the slow accretion of positive messages about courts and the law,[137] courts are nonetheless expected to rely on much more than their ancient existence to be seen as legitimate. The Court of Justice, in particular, plays a political role that may become very visible when it addresses politically controversial issues, and which can thereby seriously impact its legitimacy.[138] One should thereby

[133] Tridimas, 'The Court of Justice and Judicial Activism', 204; Petersmann, 'Do Judges Meet their Constitutional Obligation to Settle Disputes in Conformity with "Principles of Justice and International Law"?', 4; Petersmann, 'Judging Judges', 840.

[134] Fritz Scharpf, 'Legitimacy in the Multi-Level European Polity' in Martin Loughlin and Petra Dobner (eds), *The Twilight of of Constitutionalism?* (OUP 2010), 93.

[135] Such as withdrawing resources, jurisdiction stripping, court packing, and judicial selection and reappointment, which all face the same difficulties as those inherent to overriding Court decisions—see R. Daniel Kelemen, 'The Political Foundations of Judicial Independence in the European Union' (2012) 19 JEPP 43.

[136] Postema, 'Implicit Law', 369–371.

[137] Gibson, Caldeira and Baird, 'On the Legitimacy of National High Courts', 345.

[138] See Michael O'Neill, 'Democracy and the EU: Legal Perspectives on the Political Debate' (1995) 4 IrJEurL 48, 63–64; Jukka Snell, *Goods and Services in EC Law: A Study of the Relationship between the Freedoms* (OUP 2002), 71–72; Lindseth, 'Democratic Legitimacy and the Administrative Character of Supranationalism', 699.

expect to see legitimacy concerns reflected in decisions with serious constitutional and political implications that may be fiercely resisted by their addressees, but can nonetheless only be overturned by Treaty revision. Since it is the Court of Justice's legitimacy, and that of EU law, that generally ensures the cooperation of national courts and administrations—alongside the empowering effect EU law has on lower courts that are granted a *prima facie* legitimate tool with which to contradict higher courts and national legislatures—such concerns feed into the institutional incentives for the Court of Justice strictly to abide by the commonly accepted precepts of legal reasoning.[139]

These are the main institutional constraints identified in the literature—the Court of Justice's need to operate within the accepted frameworks of legal reasoning, the empowering of national courts against national governments, and the institutional barriers to the overturning of the Court' of Justice's decisions— as interacting to determine the institutional ability of the Court's adjudicative process.[140] The fact that to a large extent the Court of Justice creates EU law, is able to regulate litigants' access to it, and its decisions are subject to only a weak form of political control creates a 'zone of discretion' for the Court.[141] But even in this zone, the Court of Justice must operate within a specific strategic environment that limits its discretion through formal and informal constraints, such as the fact that the Court must operate under the 'mask of law'.[142]

This accounts for the Court of Justice's incentive to develop its case law through a number of incompletely theorized decisions focusing on the specific facts of the case, instead of proposing fully fledged normative theories. This is an apt strategy for producing stability and acceptance in the midst of social disagreement and pluralism—and may even be virtuous from a democratic perspective, as it leaves fundamental principles to be discussed in democratic arenas, and recognizes the institutional limitations of ability and capacity which plague courts. It also recognizes that silence may

[139] Karen Alter, *Establishing the Supremacy of European Law* (OUP 2003). This is not to say that all that motivates lower courts is legitimate legal reasoning and concern for the law: there are a number of empirical studies pointing to lower courts referring preliminary questions when they wish to reverse national rules and refusing to do so when they wish to shield national systems: see Connant, *Justice Contained*, 86–87.

[140] Connant, *Justice Contained*, 38–45.

[141] Sweet, *The Judicial Construction of Europe*, 23–26.

[142] Walter Mattli and Anne-Marie Slaughter, 'Constructing the European Community Legal System from the Ground Up: the Role of Individual Litigants and National Courts' [1996] Jean Monnet Working Paper 6/96, Alec Stone Sweet, 'The Politics of Constitutional Review in France and Europe' (2007) 5 I•CON 69, 79.

help the present to learn from the future.[143] Such incomplete theorization of decisions leads to a case-by-case adjudicative strategy that has the advantage of assuaging misgivings about giving too much discretion to courts, while hiding and minimizing the impact of the exercise of that discretion. On the other hand, this type of judicial reasoning is also seemingly inherent to the Court of Justice's peculiar system of collegial decision-making. This system does not allow for majority and dissenting opinions, and can thus be expected to lead to a clipped form of reasoning that hides personal inclinations and skims over disagreements and underlying tensions, while reflecting the possible consensus within particular groups of judges.[144]

The case law's incomplete theorization can, on the other hand, lead to divergent lines of case law, particularly in the light of the system of chambers currently in place at the Court of Justice.[145] Legal discourse—both by litigants, courts, and in the literature—traces decisions back to the Court of Justice even when cases are decided in different chambers. This is a useful fiction when rationalizing the law; but the prevailing cognitive framework means that courts, litigants, and legal commentators will try to rationalize and extract useful categories from the case law *ex post* by trying to explain how judicial decisions, which were developed within a normatively indeterminate background, are either normatively coherent or 'wrong'. The results of such an exercise may vary; but more often than not a fiction that the normative foundations of the case law are, and always have been, something that can explain the whole of the case law at any given moment will be adopted, without any acknowledgment of how the law and its normative underpinnings have effectively changed, or of the constitutive role that legal practice plays in the development of normative ideas.

This illustrates how incompletely theorized decisions may, when coupled with the lack of a European democratic space, the strictures of legal

[143] Sunstein, *Legal Reasoning and Political Conflict*, 39.

[144] Lasser, *Judicial Deliberations*, 105–106; Vlad Perju, 'Reason and Authority in the European Court of Justice' (2009) 42 VaJInt'l L 307, 310–311, 331–332. That the existence of judges with different preferences leads to different judicial outcomes in cases decided by the Court of Justice has been first studied, and established, by Michael Malecki, 'Do ECJ Judges All Speak with the Same Voice? Evidence of Divergent Preferences from the Judgments of Chambers' (2012) 19 JEPP 59, particularly at 67.

[145] To understand the impact of this one need only realize that by the mid-nineties less than 20 per cent of all decisions were made by the full Court. See Malecki, 'Do ECJ Judges All Speak With the Same Voice?, 63, who also found evidence of systemic variation of outcomes attributable to chamber composition, and thus to individual judges—at 61.

reasoning, and the specific context in which the Court of Justice operates, lead down an unexpected path which is then hard to reverse. As with other judicial bodies, for the Court of Justice's role to be effective, legal actors must be able to identify the applicable legal rules and the consequences of their application. The Court of Justice's case law and its *ex post* rationalization creates a cognitive framework that allows for this, while simultaneously empowering a number of societal actors who pick up on the Court's case law.[146] Even in the absence of a formal *stare decisis* rule,[147] legal principles laid down by the Court of Justice seem to be given full effect only in decisions following those in which they were first identified, thereby grounding them in something akin to settled precedent.[148]. The existence of precedent, when coupled with this cognitive framework—which is shared by the European legal community, and influences the way litigants and referring courts frame their pleadings and questions—creates path-dependence.[149] This may, in turn, lead to the above-mentioned phenomena of non-ergodicity, lock-in, and indeterminacy of outcome.[150]

Even if a certain line of case law has been kick-started by accident, as a result of work pressure, lack of communication between different chambers, or of genuine disagreements within the Court of Justice, path-dependence and lock-in are still bound to kick in. The path adopted, moreover, will depend on the type of questions reaching the Court, and this will in turn depend on who the litigants are and on what questions the referring courts decide to send to Luxembourg. Such litigants will usually be those who can prospectively benefit from the case law and possess sufficient resources to spend in litigation. As a result, it is to be expected that the existence of different rates of participation and representation of interests in litigation will push the case law in a direction that benefits repeat players who have both the means and the incentives to participate in it. In this regard, it has been noted that the Court of Justice serves as a battleground for States, corporate

[146] Sweet, *The Judicial Construction of Europe*, 35.

[147] On how the Court of Justice, even though not *de iure* bound by precedent, still acts as if it was so bound in practice, see Anthony Arnull, *The European Union and its Court of Justice* (2nd edn, OUP 2006), 627; Lasser, *Judicial Deliberations*, 107–111.

[148] Maduro, *We, the Court*, 10, 20.

[149] Martin Shapiro, 'The European Court of Justice' in P Craig and G de Burca (eds), *The Evolution of EU Law* (OUP 1999), 328.

[150] Susanne K. Schmidt, 'Who Cares About Nationality? The Path-Dependent Case Law of the ECJ from Goods to Citizens' (2012) 19 JEPP 8, 10. Whether this is indeed the case will be tested in Chapters III to VI.

actors (particularly the wealthier industry players), and societal interest organizations—i.e. those entities who have the resources and organizational capacity to pursue litigation and obtain information on EU law.[151]

The Court of Justice's decision-making practice must also be understood in the context of an environment where the Court is required to follow the prevailing canon for legal reasoning, judicial methodology, and logics of presentation.[152] For example, when lacunae are identified, the Court of Justice has recourse to teleological interpretation in line with Article 31 of the Vienna Convention on the Law of Treaties,[153] namely through the use of broad systemic values such as the effectiveness and unity of EU law.[154] In addition to the Treaties, the Court of Justice draws on the ECHR and other international treaties to which the Member States are parties, on EU secondary legislation, and on general principles derived from national legal orders.[155] In particular, the Court of Justice can be said to search for common standards accepted by the Member States: this diminishes the risk of the Court of Justice going beyond what is acceptable to the various Member States, tries to avoid the perception that the Court is second-guessing national legislatures, and helps generate the requisite impression that the Court of Justice is finding law instead of merely creating it—thereby ensuring that national courts follow its decisions.[156] While the existing requirements of judicial accountability and control for the Court of Justice require judges to provide reasons for choosing one interpretative path over another,

[151] Connant, *Justice Contained*, 21, 28–29.

[152] Hart, Bulloch and Raz, *The Concept of Law*, 123.

[153] This is somewhat contentious, since that Article also provides, as elements of interpretation, the usual meaning of the words and the context, and there is no consensus as to whether there is a hierarchy between them.

[154] Pierre Pescatore, 'Le recours, dans la jurisprudence de la Cour de justice des Communautés européennes, à des normes déduites de la comparaison des droits des Etats membres' (1980) 32 RIDC 337; Thijmen Koopmans, 'The Birth of European Law at the Crossroads of Legal Traditions' (1991) 39 AmJCompL 493, 496–505; Koen Lenaerts, 'Interlocking Legal Orders in the European Union and Comparative Law' (2003) 52 ICLQ 873; Mitchel Lasser, 'Anticipating Three Models of Judicial Control, Debate and Legitimacy: The European Court of Justice, the Cour de Cassation and the United States Supreme Court' [2003] Jean Monnet Working Paper 1/03, 44–47. This may result in policy issues being dealt with as merely technical questions—see Lasser, 'Anticipating Three Models of Judicial Control, Debate and Legitimacy', 52.

[155] On the role of this legislation in determining the majority opinion at European level, see Maduro, *We, the Court*, 74–76.

[156] Lenaerts, 'Interlocking Legal Orders in the European Union and Comparative Law', 879–880.

traditional ideas about legal reasoning, concerns about the legitimacy of the Court, and the requirement that judges arrive at collegial decisions, all point towards a mode of reasoning which ignores the existence of serious interpretive and normative conflicts. On the other hand, the publication of Advocates General's Opinions ensures that the Court of Justice has engaged in an informed judicial debate between high-ranking judicial professionals, while allowing critiques by the Advocates General and legal commentators to play an influential dialogical role in the Court of Justice's decisions, thereby ensuring the legitimacy of the decision-making procedure in the eyes of a potentially critical legal community.[157]

C. *An example—proportionality*

A good example of a mode of legal reasoning along the lines described above, which hides important political decisions behind a patina of legal reasoning, is proportionality, a variant of balancing that has been imported by the Court of Justice from German administrative and constitutional law.[158] In German constitutional practice, proportionality addresses the question of: (i) whether a measure is adequate to the pursuit of the relevant public interest (*Geeignetheit*); (ii) whether a measure is necessary, in the sense of there being the possibility of a less restrictive measure being adopted (*Erforderlichkeit*); and finally, (iii) whether a measure is strictly proportional, in the sense of the costs imposed by the measure not being excessive in relation to its envisaged benefits (*Verhältnismässigkeit*).[159] Proportionality thus described is similar to the three different 'reasonableness' tests identified in international economic law literature, particularly at WTO level:[160] (a) means/ends

[157] Lasser, *Judicial Deliberations*, 316–317. See, more directly on the impact of the academic literature on the Court, and particularly the AG's Opinions, ibid, 122–133.

[158] Gráinne de Búrca, 'The Principle of Proportionality and its Application in EC Law' (1993) 13 YEL 105, 114. See also Maduro, *We, the Court*, 57; Giuseppe Federico Mancini, 'Crosscurrents and the Tide at the European Court of Justice' (1995) 4 IrJEurL 120, 123; Rivers, 'Proportionality and Discretion', 112. On balancing, see above, Section. III. B (b).

[159] Canotilho, *Direito Constitucional e Teoria da Constituição*, 264–265; Alexy, *A Theory of Constitutional Rights*, 66. In the EU context, see for example, Case C-331/88 *Ex Parte Fedesa* [1990] E.C.R. I-4023. This is akin to the proportionality test as used in most constitutional jurisdictions around the world. It should also be noted that this test can be preceded by an assessment of whether the goal pursued by a measure is legitimate to begin with: see Sweet and Mathews, 'Proportionality, Balancing and Global Constitutionalism', 76.

[160] Where a necessity test is usually applied to Articles XX GATT and XIV GATS, even though a fuller version of proportionality appear to be making inroads: see Kenneth A. Bamberger and Andrew T. Guzman, 'Keeping Imports Safe: A Proposal for Discriminatory Regulation of International Trade' (2008) 98 CLR 1405, 1440–1441; Petersmann, 'Judging

or suitability test; (b) cost-effectiveness or necessity test; and (c) cost/benefit or proportionality test. These three tests constitute an ascending series in terms of the intensity and intrusiveness of the review of national regulation. While strict proportionality calls for value assessments which may not be empirically testable, the necessity test is seen as merely delving into the factual efficiency of a given measure, without implying any balancing of values or imposing any limits to the level of State intervention. In international economic law, the necessity test acts as an anti-protectionist device, indicating whether there was a 'regulatory capture' of local political processes by the beneficiaries of protectionist measures, and forcing States to internalize the costs of their actions and to take into account out-of-State interests.[161]

The Court of Justice can be seen to follow two different formulations of proportionality. One resembles the necessity test, as it only ascertains whether the means employed are causally suitable to achieve the envisaged purpose and whether such means do not go beyond what is necessary to achieve that objective. The other version adds to these requirements the possibility of applying proportionality *stricto sensu*, but sensibly the Court of Justice only applies it rarely,[162] as this requirement is the one that most seriously impinges on the separation of powers and on Member State's value-choices.[163]

Judges', 838; Peter Van den Bossche, 'Looking for Proportionality in WTO Law' (2008) 35 LIEI 283, 292; Ben McGrady, 'Necessity Exceptions in WTO Law: Retreaded Tyres, Regulatory Purpose and Cumulative Regulatory Measures' (2009) 12 JIEL 153, 160; Donald H. Regan, 'The Meaning of "Necessary" in GATT Article XX and GATS Article XIV: The Myth of Cost-Benefit Balancing' (2007) 6 WTR 347.

[161] Alexy, *A Theory of Constitutional Rights*, 67, Rivers, 'Proportionality and Discretion', 115–117; Federico Ortino, 'From 'Non-Discrimination' to 'Reasonableness': A Paradigm Shift in International Economic Law?' [2005] Jean Monnet Working Paper 01/05, 33–34; McGrady, 'Necessity Exceptions in WTO Law', 154; Alan O. Sykes, 'Regulatory Protectionism and the Law of International Trade' (1999) 66 UChiLRev 1, 21; Regan, 'The Supreme Court and State Protectionism: Making Sense of the Dormant Commerce Clause', 1105–1107; Mark P. Gergen, 'The Selfish State and the Market' (1988) 66 TexLRev 1097, 1111.

[162] See Case 44/79 *Hauer* [1979] E.C.R. 3727, para. 23; Case C-265/88 *Messner* [1989] E.C.R. 4209, para. 9–12; Case C-169/91 *Stoke and Norwich v B&Q* [1992] E.C.R. I-6635, para. 12–15; Case C-193/94 *Skanavi and Chryssanthakopoulos* [1996] E.C.R. I-0929, para. 36; Case C-29/95 *Pastoors* [1997] E.C.R. I-285, para. 26; Case C-378/97 *Wijsenbeek* [1999] E.C.R. I-6207, para. 44.

[163] de Búrca, 'The Principle of Proportionality and its Application in EC Law', 113; Francis Jacobs, 'Recent Developments in the Principle of Proportionality in EC Law' in Evelyn Ellis (ed.), *The Principle of Proportionality in the Laws of Europe* (Hart Publishing 1999), 1; Walter van Gerven, 'The Effect of Proportionality on the Actions of Member States of the European Community: National Viewpoints from Continental Europe' in Evelyn Ellis (ed.), *The*

Like other forms of balancing, proportionality gives the appearance of being a merely formalistic exercise, but at least in the EU context even recourse to the necessity test does not wholly avoid the concerns raised by strict proportionality. For example, the construction of the regulatory goal by the Court of Justice is relevant, as the more narrowly the goal is construed the less likely it is that a less restrictive approach can be found. Under mutual recognition, it has been argued that goods can be lawfully marketed in a Member State when the rules in the producing State meet the overall objectives, if not the precise detail, of national law. But much depends on this choice between overall objective and precise detail. For example, substituting labelling requirements for rules on the composition of foodstuffs may be acceptable under an overall objective approach, but it will hardly meet the requirements of 'precise detail' in the host-State rule.[164] Besides, in the EU context even the necessity test is not value-neutral when applied to the fundamental freedoms: for example, when determining whether derogations from the fundamental freedoms not provided for in the Treaty are legitimate, the Court of Justice is second-guessing the *prima facie* legitimacy of Member States' value-choices.[165]

This illustrates how the Court of Justice adopts value-charged political decisions under a veneer of legal reasoning. The creation of constitutional rights by the Treaty, to be enforced and protected by the judiciary, does not remove them from political strife, but merely leads to a greater role for the courts.[166] Recourse to proportionality has the effect of both assigning to the Court of Justice the power to determine what institution—including itself—is best suited to decide certain questions, and to control the extent to which such institutions may exercise their discretion. This means that the intensity of review under proportionality or any other balancing test can vary depending on a

Principle of Proportionality in the Laws of Europe (Hart Publishing 1999), 37–42; Takis Tridimas, 'Proportionality in Community Law: Searching for the Appropriate Standard of Scrutiny' in Evelyn Ellis (ed.), *The Principle of Proportionality in the Laws of Europe* (Hart Publishing 1999), 68; Jan Jans, 'Proportionality Revisited' (2000) 27 LIEI 239, 240–248; Sacha Prechal, 'Free Movement and Procedural Requirements: Proportionality Reconsidered' (2008) 35 LIEI 201, 201.

[164] See, for example, Case 178/84 *Commission v Germany* [1987] E.C.R. 1227. Also Stephen Weatherill, 'Consumer Safety Legislation in the United Kingdom and Article 30 EEC' (1988) 12 ELRev 87, 91; Maduro, *We, the Court*, 56.

[165] Roel de Lange, 'Paradoxes of European Citizenship' in Peter Fitzpatrick (ed.), *Nationalism, Racism and the Rule of Law* (Dartmouth 1995), 103; McGrady, 'Necessity Exceptions in WTO Law', 157–162; Regan, 'The Meaning of "Necessary" in GATT Article XX and GATS Article XIV', 90.

[166] Raz, *The Morality of Freedom*, 257–260.

number of institutional factors, and we should expect to find a relationship between the intensity of review under the proportionality test and the amount of discretion available to a given institution depending on the nature of the original decision-making authority, the nature of the acts to be assessed, the importance and variety of the interests involved, the technicality of the measure, or even the urgency of the situation.[167] This seems to be borne out by the fact that the nature of the Court of Justice's scrutiny can be influenced by the type of act subject to challenge:[168] the Court of Justice adopts a test of variable intensity when reviewing Member States' measures depending on the nature of the subject matter, the expertise of the first-instance decision-maker, and the specificity of the jurisdictional condition.[169] For example, in exceptions to the fundamental freedoms concerning public morality, public policy, or national security, the Court of Justice tends to defer to the Member States' assessment.[170] When fundamental rights are at issue, or the case falls into harmonized areas where the Member States' discretion is curtailed, a more rigorous proportionality test is applied.[171] Concerning EU measures, the Court of Justice applies a 'manifestly inappropriate' test when reviewing EU acts which are adopted within the context of wide policy discretion, while applying a stricter standard when there is no such discretion.[172]

V. Normative Implications

What an organization should do is effectively limited by what it can do. A descriptive assessment can review not only what is being done but also what

[167] de Búrca, 'The Principle of Proportionality', 111; Gerven, 'The Effect of Proportionality on the Actions of Member States of the European Community', 61; Tridimas, 'Proportionality in Community Law'.

[168] Petersmann, 'Judging Judges', 869, fn. 125.

[169] Alexander Fritzsche, 'Discretion, Scope of Judicial Review and Institutional Balance in European Law' (2010) 47 CML Rev 361, 367–381.

[170] de Búrca, 'The Principle of Proportionality', 132.

[171] Schueler, 'Methods of Application of the Proportionality Principle in Environmental Law', 325–236; de Búrca, 'The Principle of Proportionality', 126 and 138; Xavier Groussot, 'Rock the KaZaA: Another Clash of Fundamental Rights' (2008) 45 CML Rev 1745, 1762.

[172] de Búrca, 'The Principle of Proportionality', 116–123; Aland Dashwood and Derrick Wyatt, *Wyatt and Dashwood's European Union Law* (6th edn, Sweet & Maxwell 2011), 123–124; Jacobs, 'Recent Developments in the Principle of Proportionality in EC Law', 3; Tridimas, 'Proportionality in Community Law', 66. See also cases Case 265/87 *Schräder* [1989] E.C.R. 2237, *Ex Parte Fedesa*, Case C-375/96 *Zaninotto* [1998] E.C.R. I-6629, Case C-84/94 *UK v Council* [1996] E.C.R. I-5755, Case C-491/01 *British American Tobacco* [2002] ECR I-11543.

can be done within a specific institutional setting, which in turn sets the limits of any question as to what ought to be done—assuming one would keep normative assessments pursued under practical reason within the realm of what is possible. In other words, evaluative and prescriptive research on courts and judges can only be fruitful if informed by a correct descriptive understanding of what courts and judges do.[173] There are thus normative implications to concluding that the Court of Justice is merely one among a variety of other political institutions with decision-making powers.

This chapter has described a world where a plurality of institutions with law-making powers co-exist, and where it is impossible to determine correct outcomes *a priori* even within strict formal requirements for decision-making such as those imposed by proportionality and balancing assessments—i.e. a world of divided powers, imperfect decision-makers, and value pluralism. In this context, different but *prima facie* equally valid normative frameworks may lead to different answers. Thus, the question is not merely whether a decision was wrong or right in accordance with a certain 'evaluative' normative framework, but also which entity should decide in certain circumstances, and how that decision should be adopted. In other words, preliminary to the substantive evaluation of potential solutions to a given question, the entity that is best placed to decide that question must be identified. This raises a comparative institutional question, whose answer depends on the context and specific institutional environment in which the relevant decision-makers operate, and for which the institutional elements analysed above are of the utmost importance.[174]

To evaluate whether a certain entity is the best decision-maker in a given context, one must take into account its organizational qualities, those of alternative decision-makers, and the institutional environment in which it operates. As a logically antecedent step, one can pose a similar question regarding which entity is best placed to determine who should make the relevant institutional comparative choice—and we can pursue this logical exercise *ad infinitum*. This is avoided in the real world by constitutional instruments allocating competences, usually to representative bodies on the basis of their perceived legitimacy. Even if these instruments are rarely complete and unambiguous, they tend to grant some organizations the power to either decide a certain issue themselves or to delegate the decision to other organizations—requiring an (implicit) comparative institutional analysis on

[173] Dyevre, *Making Sense of Judicial Lawmaking*, 46.

[174] Similarly, but in the US context, Rubin, 'The New Legal Process, the Synthesis of Discourse, and the Microanalysis of Institutions', 1403.

the part of the entity which was granted original competence. As regards the Court of Justice, its selection as the relevant decision-maker is usually mediated through the scope of its jurisdiction.

When the Treaties grant decision-making powers to the Court of Justice, implied in this is a comparative institutional choice in favour of the Court as opposed to other possible decision-makers. Recently, there has been a tendency for legislative bodies of the EU to increasingly choose the Court of Justice as the relevant decision-maker, the reason for which appears to be that regulation at EU level occurs:

> *in the context of a highly fragmented regulatory state with a powerful judicial system and a weak administrative apparatus. The vertical fragmentation between the EU and the member states and the horizontal fragmentation of power between institutions at the EU level (i.e., the Council, the Parliament, and the Commission) generate principal-agent problems that encourage the adoption of laws with strict, judicially enforceable goals, deadlines, and transparent procedural requirements. Also, given the EU's extremely limited implementation and enforcement capacities, EU lawmakers have an incentive to create justiciable rights and to empower private parties to serve as the enforcers of EU law.*[175]

The Member States and the EU political process are the institutions originally empowered to decide which organization is best suited to decide certain issues, and have implicitly assumed that the Court of Justice is the best comparative option. The Court of Justice, however, also has powers of its own to determine which organizations are the best decision-makers, a good example of which can be found in its interpretation of the Treaties, and in particular of the fundamental freedoms. If, on the one hand, the Treaties chose the Court of Justice as the relevant decision-maker as regards negative integration, the Court can nonetheless, through its control of the scope of the fundamental freedoms—which act as gatekeepers to the relevant balancing exercises and to the Court of Justice's jurisdiction—still exercise a certain amount of discretion in allocating decision-making powers between itself and other organizations.

In the light of this, it is clear that the institutional constraints identified above are relevant for normative discussions about the scope of the fundamental freedoms, and about the corresponding comparative institutional choice of the Court of Justice as the relevant decision-maker regarding the extent of such scope. Naturally, questions of comparative institutional choice

[175] R. Daniel Kelemen, *Eurolegalism: The Transformation of Law and Regulation in the European Union* (Harvard University Press 2011), 8.

do not preclude analyses of how the Court of Justice is supposed to adjudicate the questions coming before it but such analyses should also take these institutional elements into account, as they are demonstrably relevant to the outcome of the relevant decision-making processes. In other words, not only scholars, but also the Court of Justice itself should incorporate institutional considerations into its interpretative practices.[176]

For example, discussions about the legitimacy of proportionality tests by the Court of Justice would benefit from the insight that the pursuit of such a test fits into the operative and cognitive framework of legitimate judicial intervention, and will only take place following a comparative institutional choice having been made. It is true that courts face specific structural limitations which can make them unsuitable to undertake the role implicit in proportionality assessments: they often lack expertise and have high administrative costs, are subject to information biases in favour of those sufficiently organized to participate in the judicial process, may decide issues without hearing some of the affected interests, and do not have the advantage of being able to choose when to tackle politically charged decisions. But concluding from this that courts should not pursue proportionality assessments because such assessments are subjective, as some do, is objecting not to the decision-making practice but to the institutional choice of having courts decide the issue in the first place.

We cannot *a priori* assume that a court is superior or inferior to legislatures or governments in reaching good solutions, as both are institutional options with advantages and costs. The typical trade-off will be between political processes with more information but subject to both majoritarian and minoritarian biases, and an adjudicatory process with less information but that suppresses some of those biases, particularly through the independence of judges.[177] Accordingly, referring to a court's institutional limitations is not *per se* sufficient to demonstrate that it is not the best-suited organization to decide on a given issue—that might be the case or not, depending on the situation. A reason why having courts pursue proportionality assessments may be preferred to other legal decision-making practices is that, even if proportionality leaves a wide margin for subjectivity, it also acknowledges

[176] See similarly, for constitutional adjudication in the US, Cass R. Sunstein and Adrian Vermeule, 'Interpretation and Institutions' (2003) 101 Mich L Rev 885, 938.

[177] Maduro, 'Courts and Pluralism', 20; Neil Komesar, *Imperfect Alternatives—Choosing Institutions in Law, Economics, and Public Policy* (The University of Chicago Press 1994); Komesar, *Law's Limits*, 38.

the existence of clashes of rights and recognizes that there is no ready-made answer to them.[178] What is more, proportionality provides discursive structures that allow litigants to plead their interests and engage with their opponents' arguments, as well as a measure of predictability in how courts frame their decisions. Proportionality can be seen as a regulated argumentative framework within which the Court of Justice may accommodate conflicting values in a particular case in a way that is acceptable to all participants. This may lead to uncertainty, but it has the advantage of preventing, or at least allowing for the control of arbitrary and purely subjective decisions, and of improving the (bounded) rationality of judgements.[179] It also allows interested parties to participate in the legal theatre, reconstructing and accepting controversial, politically charged decisions as natural, unproblematic developments of previous legal practice. As has been noted:

Under conditions of supremacy (given a steady case load), fidelity on the part of the court to a particular framework will entrench that mode of argumentation as constitutional doctrine. To the extent that arguing outside of the framework is ineffective, skilled legal actors will use the framework, thereby reproducing and legitimizing it.[180]

This may well be deemed a comparative institutional advantage of courts over other institutions—democratic and representative, or not—as decision-making *loci*. From a practical perspective, it might be preferable that subjectivity occurs under conditions that are subject to rational control and criticism: legal reasoning aspires to objectivity,[181] and submitting subjective decisions to a discursive practice restricted by a series of conditions, such as respect for the law, precedent, and rules established in process codes, may lead to a good-enough approximation to that ideal.[182] Practical reason, for all its limitations, may be the best we can envision.[183] What is more, courts will usually be able to decide on the basis of the particular facts of the case without needing to engage with the large-scale societal questions that may underlie it: they may enlist silence as a device for producing convergence despite disagreement and uncertainty by adopting an incompletely

[178] Groussot, 'Rock the KaZaA', 1762.

[179] Alexy, *A Theory of Constitutional Rights*, 107, 387.

[180] Sweet and Mathews, 'Proportionality, Balancing and Global Constitutionalism', 89.

[181] MacCormick, *Practical Reason in Law and Morality*, 192.

[182] Alexy, *A Theory of Constitutional Rights*, 370–387.

[183] Zagrebelsky, *Il diritto mite*, 168 ff; Waldron, 'Fake Incomensurability', 823. On the relevance of practical reason to legal reasoning, see also Sunstein, 'Incommensurability and Valuation in Law', 859.

theorized outcome that may more accurately reflect the amount of societal consensus behind the adoption of a given rule. This mechanism is an important source of social stability, since it allows the participants to be clear on a result without having to agree on what theory or value accounts for it, and is well suited to a pluralist society.[184] It is the judicial equivalent to the legislative technique of using purposefully vague provisions to accommodate different normative theories and values.

VI. Conclusions

This chapter sought to demonstrate how, as the Court of Justice exists in an environment of institutional bargaining where not every legal problem can be solved legally, one must look beyond the purely 'internal' perspective. Instead, to understand its case law one must take into account not only the official legal discourse but also other elements latent in (but external to) traditional legal analysis, including those elements which constrain the actions of courts in general, and the Court of Justice in particular.

As relevant examples of institutional constraints on courts in general, we identified the individual preferences of judges, the institutional and political context in which courts operate, the strictures imposed by precedent, and concerns about the perceived legitimacy of courts' decision-making practices. It was also explained how these external constraints are translated into 'official' legal discourse through a shared cognitive setting that imposes certain standards of legal reasoning, and creates mechanisms of control of those standards *ex ante* by making sure that cases are brought and argued before courts by lawyers trained and imbued in the spirit and grammar of a specific legal community, and *ex post* through systems of appeal and criticism from an interpretive community that recognizes as authoritative a number of commonly accepted parameters regarding the correctness of legal reasoning.

We then looked specifically at the main institutional constraints that determine the institutional ability of the Court of Justice's adjudicative process. In particular, it was noticed that the institutional barriers to the overturning of the Court of Justice's decisions are strong, thereby favouring

[184] Sunstein, *Legal Reasoning and Political Conflict*, 5, 44.

the Court's dominance over the constitutional development of the EU, and that EU law empowers referring national courts against their governments and other courts higher in their national judicial hierarchies. On the other hand, EU law suffers from issues of (sociological) democratic legitimacy—a concern compounded by the fact that the Court of Justice's decisions have to be applied by national courts and administrative bodies—which creates incentives for the Court of Justice to focus on making sure that its decisions are followed and accepted as legitimate.

The Court of Justice's institutional ability thereby grants it a 'zone of discretion', but it also creates institutional incentives for the Court strictly to abide by commonly accepted precepts of legal reasoning and to adopt a case-by-case adjudicative strategy that eschews grand theoretical formulas. However, these incentives also create the potential for path-dependence and lock-in of the case law, particularly regarding highly visible or significant judicial decisions that were not normatively thought through. As such, one should expect to see the case law develop in a direction that benefits repeat players who have both the means and the incentives to participate in litigation and push the limits of the law.

This chapter then looked into the relevance of extra-legal elements for the development of normative approaches to EU law. It was explained that normative approaches to the law would be richer if they took into account insights arising from this 'external' dimension, because evaluative and prescriptive research on courts and judges can only be fruitful if informed by a correct descriptive understanding of what courts and judges (can) do. It was also suggested that, in a world of divided law-making powers, imperfect decision-makers, and value pluralism, in the absence of a 'right' decision to be found, the first question to be asked should be who is best placed to decide: a question for whose answer institutional considerations are of the utmost relevance. Furthermore, when, in a subsequent stage, one assesses individual decisions on their own merits, institutional considerations are also relevant in order to frame the possible 'good' outcomes within the specific institutional setting in which the chosen decision-maker operates. In short, institutional considerations are relevant for the development of evaluative or prescriptive assessments because they allow us to understand and map the boundaries for 'good' decision-making within the realms of the physical and legally possible, and therefore help us achieve a better fit between the ideal and what is achievable.

2

The Internal Dimension—The Fundamental Freedoms' Normative Foundations

I. Introduction

The previous chapter identified a number of elements 'external' to traditional EU legal discourse that, it was argued, should be taken into account when analysing the fundamental freedoms. Also essential to the analysis of the fundamental freedoms, and to understanding the relevance of those 'external' elements in the development of the law, is the identification of the freedoms' normative underpinnings. This will be the focus of this chapter, which will describe the main normative theories regarding the fundamental freedoms as usually found in the legal literature. A first section will look into those normative foundations said to be common to all market freedoms. A second section will review a set of normative positions said to apply to individual freedoms alone, which thus argue against a common approach being adopted. Lastly, we will review a number of normative theories regarding European Citizenship and its impact on the market freedoms.

II. Normative Foundations Common to All Market Freedoms

A. Market freedoms and constitutional rights

Any analysis of the market freedoms *in totum* must start by explaining why they should be subject to joint treatment. German legal circles were, and arguably still are, the *loci* where this question is most debated.[1] In these circles, there seems to be a consensus that the market freedoms are 'subjective public rights',[2] i.e. rights originating from public law that pursue both general and individual interests, and impose on public authorities a duty to behave in a certain way which can be procedurally enforced by individuals.[3] Among the various subjective public rights identified in the literature are included fundamental rights. The reason for this is that all subjective public rights—including fundamental rights—embody objective values that must be protected against State interference, and contain a corresponding subjective element entitling individuals to judicial protection against such interference.[4] In other words, market freedoms are part of a wider set of protection rights that can be invoked in court against acts or omissions by the State whenever there is a public law goal imposing upon that State an administrative duty to behave in a certain way in order to protect individual rights.

Some have gone as far as to argue that the market freedoms are fundamental rights themselves.[5] This position can find some support in the case law: since 1983, the Court of Justice has occasionally referred to the free movement of workers as a fundamental right,[6] even if that honour has only rarely been

[1] Thorsten Kingreen, 'Fundamental Freedoms' in Armin von Bogdandy and Jürgen Bast (eds), *Principles of European Constitutional Law* (Hart Publishing 2006), 550–552. See in particular Peter Behrens, 'Die Konvergenz der wirtschaftlichen Freiheiten im europäischen Gemeinschaftrecht' (1992) 27 EuR 145.

[2] Thorsten Kingreen and Reainer Störmer, 'Die subjektiv-öffentlichen Rechte des primären Gemeinschaftsrechts' [1998] EuR 263, 266; Norbert Reich, *Bürgerrechte in der Europäischen Union* (Nomos 1999), 450–451. Some authors argue that the fundamental freedoms are also subjective private rights, since they can be invoked against both State and private persons: see Josef Drexl, 'Competition Law as Part of the European Constitutions' in Armin von Bogdandy and Jürgen Bast (eds), *Principles of European Constitutional Law* (Hart Publishing 2006), 659. This relates to the question of the horizontal direct effect of the fundamental freedoms, which is analysed in Chapter 6.

[3] Sven Hölscheidt, 'Abschied vom subjecktif-öffentlichen Recht?' [2001] EuR 376, 379.

[4] Canotilho, *Direito Constitucional e Teoria da Constituição*, 273, 376; Dirk André Stoppel, 'Grundfreiheitliche Schutzpflichten der Mitgliedstaaten im Europäischen Gemeinschaftsrecht' (Heinrich-Heine-Universität Düsseldorf 2003), 41–42; Dirck Ehlers, 'General Principles' in Dick Ehlers (ed.), *European Fundamental Rights and Freedoms* (de Gruyter 2007), 193.

[5] Mainly from an ordo-liberal perspective (as economic fundamental rights)—see Albert Bleckman, 'Die Freiheiten des Gemeinsamen als Grundrechte' in Roland Bieber and Dietmar Nickel (eds), *Das Europa der zweiten Generation—Gedächtnisshrift für Christoph Sasse*, vol II (N. P. Engel Verlag 1981), 665 ff—but also from a trans-nationalist perspective as political fundamental rights—see Maduro, 'Reforming the Market or the State?', 73.

[6] Case 152/82 *Forcheri* [1983] E.C.R. 2323, para. 11.

bestowed on the free movement of goods.[7] The prevailing view, however, is that the market freedoms are different from fundamental rights. The main argument for differentiation is that, while the market freedoms are instrumental to the realization of a market without internal frontiers,[8] the fundamental rights' *telos* is to protect essential areas of freedom intrinsic to human dignity.[9] Regardless of one's particular position on this debate, there seems to be a consensus that both market freedoms and fundamental rights operate as constitutional rights of a fundamental nature, granting direct rights to individuals against Member States and the EU;[10] use the same analytical framework based on the identification of a *prima facie* restriction followed by the application of a proportionality assessment;[11] and are multi-level norms, regulating the interaction between Member States and the EU by determining the vertical allocation of competences between them, while simultaneously limiting the substantive scope of both EU and Member States' powers.[12]

In this formalistic sense, at least, the market freedoms seem to share the same underpinnings as other fundamental constitutional rights. These underpinnings are thin, however—they may require courts to protect certain interests against the desires of elected majorities, but they do not tell us what these interests might be. Accordingly, it is important to understand exactly what the relevant normative foundations of the market freedoms *qua* market freedoms are, as opposed to other constitutional rights.

[7] Peter Oliver and Wulf-Henning Roth, 'The Internal Market and the Four Freedoms' (2004) 41 CML Rev 407, 407. See Case C-228/98 *Dounias* [2000] E.C.R. I-00577, paras 64–65; Case C-421/09 *Humanplasma* [2010] E.C.R. I-12869, para. 25. On the free movement of goods as an element of the right to trade, see Case 240/83 *ADBHU* [1985] E.C.R. 531, para. 9.

[8] Case C-265/95 *Commission v France* [1997] E.C.R. I-6959, para. 30.

[9] See Walter Frenz, 'Grundfreiheiten und Grundrechte' [2002] EuR 603, and Kingreen, 'Fundamental Freedoms', 567–571.

[10] Situations where the Court referenced the fundamental nature of Treaty freedoms are various: see Case C-266/96 *Corsica Ferries France* [1998] E.C.R. I-3949, para. 8; Case C-34/98 *Commission v France* [2000] E.C.R. I-995, para. 49 (all four freedoms); Case C-19/92 *Kraus* [1993] E.C.R. I-1663, para. 28 (workers and establishment); Case C-385/99 *Müller-Fauré* [2003] E.C.R. I-4509, para. 72 (services); Case C-112/00 *Schmidberger* [2003] E.C.R. I-5659, para. 50, 51 and 74 (goods); and Case C-483/99 *Commission v France* [2002] E.C.R. I-4871, para. 45 and 48 (capital).

[11] Frenz, 'Grundfreiheiten und Grundrechte', 610–612.

[12] Kingreen, 'Fundamental Freedoms', 562–565; Michael Schillig, 'The Interpretation of European Private Law in the Light of Market Freedoms and EU Fundamental Rights' (2008) 15 MJ 285, 287. On the conception of human rights as rights with the particularity of setting limits to sovereignty, Joseph Raz, *Human Rights Without Foundations* (SSRN 2007), 14.

B. Common normative foundations

a. The Treaties

Market freedoms are usually distinguished from other constitutional rights by reference to their instrumentality to the internal market. This might suggest that the market freedoms should be subject to a uniform approach, but it is clear from a superficial reading of the Treaties that such an approach is not expressly adopted there. Different provisions create different freedoms, with different wordings pointing to both different issues being addressed and different solutions being used to tackle them.[13] The freedoms' scope *ratione materiae* and *personae* differ; even the scope *ratione locus* is not identical, since the free movement of capital extends to third countries while the other freedoms' effects are restricted to the European internal market.[14]

Arguments for a common approach can nonetheless be gleaned from the Treaty. From an historical perspective, the reason for the existence of different freedoms appears to be that it was easier to write four sets of provisions instead of one, particularly because the Member States originally wanted to be able to have a stricter control on the free movement of capital than on the other freedoms.[15] Furthermore, all freedoms were based on the same provisions of the Treaty, in particular Article 3(1) (c) EC, which established as a goal of the EC the creation of '*an internal market characterised by the abolition, as between Member States, of obstacles to the free movement of goods, persons, services and capital*'. With entry into force of the Treaty of Lisbon, Art. 26 TFEU now sets out that the '*Union shall adopt measures with the aim of establishing or ensuring the functioning of the internal market*', meaning '*an area without internal frontiers in which the free movement of goods, persons, services and capital is ensured*'. Such commonality of purpose between the freedoms was reflected in the case law of the Court of Justice from early on, with the Court holding that the goal of the free movement provisions, prior to Maastricht, was to assist in the '*abolition of all obstacles to the establishment of a common market in which the nationals of the Member States may move freely within the territory of those States in order to pursue their economic activities*'.[16] The systemic argument for the unity of the market freedoms is further reinforced by the Treaty giving regulatory

[13] Snell, *Goods and Services in EC Law*, 22.

[14] Peter Oliver and Stefan Enchelmaier, 'Free Movement of Goods: Recent Developments in the Case Law' (2007) 44 CML Rev 649.

[15] Snell, *Goods and Services in EC Law*, 22–23.

[16] Joined Cases 35 and 36/82 *Morson and Jhanjan* [1982] E.C.R. 3723.

competence to the Union concerning all the fundamental freedoms in a single provision, Article 114 TFEU, even if this is somewhat contradicted by the need for different majorities depending on the relevant freedom.

b. Theories of economic integration

The economic and common market theories that would appear to underpin the concept of the internal market classify labour, entrepreneurship, and capital as production factors, while identifying goods and services as material and non-material products, respectively.[17] While the free movement of products alone may be sufficient for free trade areas and customs unions, the benefits of the creation of a common market can only be fully attained if both products and productive factors are allowed to circulate freely.[18] If the goal of the market freedoms is to create a common market, then all market freedoms form part of the same economic unit and their basic function is to remove (unjustified) barriers to cross-border economic transactions.[19] There is thus no *prima facie* reason to allow different degrees of protectionism with regard to the various economic factors, nor is it normatively justified to distinguish between inbound and outbound movements, since from an economic perspective it is irrelevant which State erects the barrier to trade.[20]

c. Systemic coherence and legal certainty

Other arguments for a common approach to all market freedoms focus on systemic coherence and the need for legal certainty. These arguments start

[17] As far back as 1933, in Bertil Gotthard Ohlin, *Interregional and International Trade* (Harvard University Press 1933), 68 and 163, a distinction between goods—commodities and services—and factors of production—labour, capital, and land, to which the author adds risk taking—was considered to be classical. It was also noted how certain goods can be factors of production: see 148.

[18] These benefits include increases in the variety of goods available, gains in the allocation of goods through price equalization, productive efficiency, economies of scale, and other gains via competition: see Jacques Pelkmans and Alan Winters, *Europe's Domestic Market* (Routledge 1988), 16–25.

[19] Maureen Mackintosh, Vivienne Brown, and Neil Costello, *Economics and Changing Economies* (Open University Press 1996), 458–460, 47; Theodore Hitiris, *European Community Economics: A Modern Introduction* (Harvester Wheatsheaf 1988), 2–5, 36–37; Alasdair I. MacBean and P. N. Snowden, *International Institutions in Trade and Finance* (Allen & Unwin 1981), 145–147; Jean-François Deniau, *The Common Market* (4th revised edn, Barrie & Rockliff 1967), 60–65, 74.

[20] Axel Cordewener, 'The Prohibitions of Discrimination and Restriction within the Framework of the Fully Integrated Internal Market' in Frans Vanistendael (ed.), *EU Freedoms and Taxation* (IBDF 2006), 4–10.

from the descriptive reality that different market freedoms may be applicable to the same situation, and that, in these cases, there is great confusion concerning the rules determining which freedom, if any, should prevail.[21]

It is clear that goods and services may at times overlap,[22] that a particular situation regarding the free movement of persons may be subject to common assessment under the free movement of workers, the right of establishment, or the free provision of services,[23] that the exercise of any of the freedoms may require the cross-border movement of capital for their payment,[24] and that the free movement of people across borders may entail the movement across borders of goods and capital as well.[25] Even taking into account their different scopes, there are potential overlaps between all the freedoms. This potential is more pronounced in respect of some combinations of freedoms, but it is nonetheless possible as regards every freedom in relation to every other freedom. What is more, the broader the concept of restriction used for each freedom, the higher the odds that an overlap will occur.[26]

If there were serious concerns during the drafting of the Treaty concerning the market freedoms' different normative foundations, one would expect that there would be some rules to determine when to apply one freedom instead of another—but none are to be found in the Treaties, other than the now revoked rule that the free provision of services should apply subsidiarily to the other freedoms. Even though this rule seemed to assume the possibility of overlaps between different freedoms—at least regarding the free provision of services—and to establish a hierarchy whereby the free provision of services would be subordinate to the other market freedoms, the Court of Justice did not seem to follow this approach. Instead, the Court of Justice read the Treaty as using the notion of 'services' to cover situations

[21] Vassilis Hatzopoulos, 'Recent Developments of the Case Law of the ECJ in the Field of Services' (2000) 37 CML Rev 43, 54–55.

[22] Case C-390/99 *Canal Satélite Digital* [2002] E.C.R. I-00607.

[23] Case C-363/89 *Roux* [1991] E.C.R. I-00273.

[24] Case 203/80 *Casati* [1981] E.C.R. 2595, para. 8.

[25] Peter Oliver, *Free Movement of Goods in the European Union* (5th edn, Sweet and Maxwell 2010), 39. See also Advocate General Kokott's Opinion in *N*, paras 37–38.

[26] See, for example, Joined Cases C-418/93 to C-420/93, C-421/93, C-460/93, C-461/93, C-462/93, C-464/93, C-9/94, C-10/94, C-11/94, C-14/94, C-15/94, C-23/94, C-24/94, and C-332/94 *Semeraro and Others* [1996] E.C.R. I-2975, where the same case that had been pleaded under the free movement of goods in Case 145/88 *Torfaen* [1989] E.C.R. 765 was pleaded under the right of establishment and the free provision of services. This occurred after the scope of the free movement of goods had been restricted in Joined Cases C-267/91 and 268/91 *Keck and Mithouard* [1993] E.C.R. I-6097 and as the scope of the provisions on the free movement of persons was being expanded.

not governed by the other freedoms, in order to ensure that all economic activity fell within the scope of the market freedoms.[27] Thus, different market freedoms may apply to the same situations, and this is not deemed problematic: for the Court of Justice, it is more important that all restrictions on economic activity 'fall within the scope of the fundamental freedoms', regardless of the individual freedom that is engaged. This implies the existence of a common 'residual' category, and implicitly indicates that a common rationale that justifies a common approach to all market freedoms exists.[28]

The apparent absence of concern about which specific freedom is engaged in particular situations may be further demonstrated by the Court of Justice never having developed a coherent approach on how to address these overlaps between different market freedoms. The Court of Justice's approach can perhaps be described, in broad strokes, as including the following steps:[29]

(i) *Determine the scope of each freedom.* If it is able, the Court will try to distinguish between the parts of a situation that are affected by each freedom, and seek to apply the relevant provisions autonomously.

(ii) *Pursue subsidiary distinctions.* If the Court of Justice is unable or unwilling to determine whether a specific situation falls within the scope of one freedom and not another, the Court of Justice may choose the freedom it considers to be predominantly affected, try to identify what is the purpose of the legislation at issue, or try to determine whether the transaction in question primarily relates to goods, persons, services, or capital, as the case may be.[30] This last option is not available in infringement procedures, however, since whenever the Commission files an action against a State under Article 258 TFEU, the Court of Justice has to perform an abstract assessment of a national measure which is detached from the potential facts of a case.

(iii) *Accept the underlying identity of different freedoms.* Lastly, the Court of Justice may argue that no distinction is possible and no individual freedom is prevalent, in which case it may apply all the relevant

[27] Case C-452/04 *Fidium Finanz* [2006] E.C.R. I-8135, paras 32–33. Eventually this rule was removed from the Treaties, so that now the free provision of services has equal standing to the other freedoms.

[28] Snell, *Goods and Services in EC L*, 22–23; Behrens, 'Die Konvergenz der wirtschaftlichen Freiheiten', 146–147.

[29] It is possible that this step-by-step analysis is too kind on the Court of Justice's practice, which may very well be intuitive, maybe even arbitrary in some cases.

[30] Oliver and Enchelmaier, 'Free Movement of Goods', 668; Hatzopoulos, 'Recent Developments of the Case Law of the ECJ in the Field of Services', 54–55; Case C-157/05 *Holböck* [20070 E.C.R. I-4051, para. 22.

> market freedoms jointly.[31] The Court of Justice may have greater incentives to adopt this option in infringement proceedings, where no facts exist that could engage a specific freedom to the detriment of others, than in preliminary references. Furthermore, the Court of Justice has started to decide a variety of cases without determining which specific freedom is applicable. This is particularly the case regarding the free movement of workers, the free provision of services, and the right of establishment, which the Court of Justice often applies jointly under the banner of the free movement of persons.[32] This may be the result of difficulties in determining which the predominant activity is in the case at hand: a person's status is sometimes a hybrid, since people can be employed and self-employed at the same time,[33] which may lead to a decision being justified by recourse to different freedoms simultaneously. For example, in cases concerning direct taxation the same rule can be assessed under different freedoms depending on the status of the taxpayer.[34] Nevertheless, it cannot be denied that a unitary approach to the free movement of persons appears to have been adopted in the Court of Justice's language.[35]

To summarize, the systemic and legal certainty argument for a common approach to the market freedoms is that, since different market freedoms may apply to the same situations, it would be arbitrary to treat situations differently based on very technical and obscure decisions regarding which freedom is to be applied or is prevalently affected in a given case—particularly when no good reason capable of justifying such differentiation seems to exist. To this can be added that coherence and doctrinal clarity are beneficial to both justice, which requires courts to treat similar situations alike, and to

[31] For services and goods, see *Canal Satélite Digital*; for services, establishment, and workers, as they are held to concern the free movement of persons, see Case C-106/91 *Ramrath* [1992] E.C.R. I-3351 and *Kraus*; for cases concerning these freedoms and European Citizenship, see Case C-274/96 *Bickel and Franz* [1998] E.C.R. I-7637 and Case C-135/99 *Ursula Elsen* [2000] E.C.R. I-10409.

[32] See for example, *Roux*. Other examples include *Kraus*, where this occurred for establishment and workers; Case 36/74 *Walrave* [1974] E.C.R. 1405 and Case 118/75 *Watson and Belmann* [1976] E.C.R. 1185, for workers and services; and Case C-162/99 *Commission v Italy* [2001] E.C.R. I-541, for services and establishment.

[33] Paras 27-28 of Advocate General Geelhoed's Opinion in Case C-456/02 *Trojani* [2004] E.C.R. I-7573.

[34] Martha O'Brien, '*Fidium Finanz* Case Note' (2007) 44 CML Rev 1483, 1497.

[35] Hatzopoulos, 'Recent Developments of the Case Law of the ECJ in the Field of Services', 70.

the legitimacy of the law-enforcing bodies. In short, the argument here is that factual differences between cases falling under the market freedoms should be accommodated at the level of justification and proportionality, while the scope of application of the market freedoms should have a uniform structure.[36]

III. The Specific Normative Foundations of Individual Market Freedoms

Arguments for a common approach to all market freedoms seem to require a normative unity between those freedoms. Arguments against such an approach, on the other hand, tend to be freedom-specific: if it can be shown that specific normative concerns apply only to an individual freedom, then it follows that a common approach to all the freedoms is not desirable even if a thinner common normative substratum can be identified.[37] This requires a review of the main arguments for treating the market freedoms differently.[38]

A. Should we treat material and non-material products differently?

A number of objections have been levelled at the common treatment of goods and services. One line of argument is based on the different modes of supply of tangible and intangible products. The immateriality of services means that they are not susceptible to changing hands in a series of different transactions

[36] Snell, *Goods and Services in ECL*, 23; Cordewener, 'The Prohibitions of Discrimination and Restriction within the Framework of the Fully Integrated Internal Market', 4–10 and 39–41; Cruz, *Between Competition and Free Movement*, 94–96, arguing however that the free movement of workers calls for a different approach.

[37] It has also been held that a common approach has not been followed by the Court of Justice and that such a discrepancy did not hinder the creation of a common market—Hatzopoulos, 'Recent Developments of the Case Law of the ECJ in the Field of Services', 66–70; Jukka Snell, 'And Then There Were Two: Products and Citizens in Community Law' in Takis Tridimas (ed.), *European Law for the Twenty-First Century*, vol II (Hart Publishing 2004), 50–67. Regardless of the descriptive accuracy of such analysis, this does not constitute a normative argument for or against a common approach.

[38] These arguments seem to map out perceived differences in the treatment of the market freedoms, i.e. they seem to arise from *ex post* attempts to rationalize the case law, particularly as regards the lack of direct effect of the Treaty provisions on the free movement of capital until 1995, and the different treatment of goods and services in the post-*Dassonville* and then post-*Keck* worlds. This is also arguably the case concerning the free movement of persons, even if here legal commentators seem to be more pro-active in trying to bring about a desired change. In any event, the analysis of the relevant normative conceptions in this chapter is conceptually unrelated to, and completely independent of, whether they are descriptively accurate.

and may need to be produced at the place where they are provided, which might in turn require the movement of production factors in ways which are unnecessary for the free movement of goods.[39] This argument has been challenged on the grounds that differences in modes of production do not change the underlying economic calculus, and that, in the absence of restrictions on the free movement of production factors in the EU, different modes of supply do not constitute valid grounds to approach products differently based on their corporeality or lack of it.[40] Another line of argument invokes differences regarding the level and kind of regulation to which goods and services are subject. It is not only argued that services tend to be much more heavily regulated than goods, but that regulation concerning them usually targets the service provider, while the regulation of goods usually targets the product itself.[41] Against this, it has been held that this is a distinction of degree, not kind: the prevalence of regulation concerning the producer in services does not mean that such a technique cannot be adopted for goods, any more than the prevalence of the regulation of corporeal products would prevent such a technique being used for services. A similar argument holds for the existence of more extensive regulation of services than goods.[42] The prevailing view, accordingly, is that the provisions on the free movement of services and goods share the same normative background and should be treated similarly. The Court of Justice itself has recognized the similarity of these freedoms and ruled that the principles governing the justification of restrictions on the free movement of goods and the free provision of services are essentially the same.[43] Furthermore, it is common in Federal systems for the same provision to be used to regulate both goods and services, and there seems to be no good reason for the EU to depart from this practice.[44]

[39] Apostolos Gkoutzinis, 'Free Provision of Services in the EC Treaty and the Law of Contractual Obligations Relating to Banking and Financial Services' (2004) 41 CML Rev 119, 129–130.

[40] See Piet Eeckhout, 'Constitutional Concepts for Free Trade in Services' in Gráinne de Burca and Joanne Scott (eds), *The EU and the WTO—Legal and Constitutional Issues* (Hart Publishing 2001), 215, 220; Snell, *Goods and Services in EC Law*, 16–17.

[41] Eeckhout, 'Constitutional Concepts for Free Trade in Services', 221.

[42] Snell, *Goods and Services in EC Law*, 17–19.

[43] Oliver and Enchelmaier, 'Free Movement of Goods', 670. See also *Canal Satélite Digital*, para. 32.

[44] See, for example, the USA's Commerce Clause and Article 92 of the Australian Constitution.

B. *Should we distinguish between products and production factors?*

Once we accept that products should be treated similarly, regardless of whether they are tangible or intangible, the question that is left from an economic perspective is whether production factors should be treated differently from products. This would make sense if the EU were a free trade area or a customs union, since in that case production factors would face limited mobility when compared to products. As the EU is a common market, there appears to be no good economic reason to distinguish on these grounds. In economic terms, common markets depend on the free movement of both products and production factors. Furthermore, where goods and services cannot be traded, the free movement of capital, labour,[45] and technology can act as substitutes for them, and vice-versa.[46] Thus, there seems to be no good normative justification for such a distinction, and the Treaty itself does not pursue it.

C. *Should capital be treated differently?*

Another relevant question is whether there are good normative reasons to treat the free movement of capital differently from the other freedoms. While the Spaak Report addressed the free movement of capital in terms similar to those of the other freedoms, it admitted that the creation of a common market depended on the maintenance of a balance of payments' equilibrium, which was at the time ensured within the Bretton Woods system.[47] While means of payment had to be liberalized at the same rate as the free movement of other products or production factors—which, since means of payment fall within the definition of capital, meant that its free movement was a pre-condition for the fulfilment of the other freedoms[48]—the situation of purely financial movement of capital was deemed to be distinct. The Spaak Report emphasized the impact that the liberalization of purely

[45] Sometimes 'labour' is substituted by 'persons' in the economic literature; see Hitiris, *European Community Economics*, 36; MacBean and Snowden, *International Institutions in Trade and Finance*, 145.

[46] Ohlin, *Interregional and International Trade*, 167–170.

[47] Whereby some world currencies were pegged to the dollar, and the US promised to anchor its value by offering to redeem dollars held by foreign governments and central banks for gold at the rate of $35 per ounce. See Richard Syllar, 'Political Economy of Supplying Money to a Growing Economy: Monetary Regimes and the Search for an Anchor to Stabilize the Value of Money' (2010) 11 TheoInqL 1, 24.

[48] *Casati*, para. 8.

financial capital movements could have on monetary policies, particularly as a result of speculative outbreaks or of capital flight to laxer regulatory regimes. The nature of capital itself pointed to a different, more flexible, integration strategy than for the other freedoms. Greater discretion and technical knowledge would have to be applied at each stage in the creation of conditions for a common market for capital movements. Safeguard clauses would probably remain necessary even after the transition period in the absence of a common budget and monetary policy.[49]

The main example of this different integration strategy is how long it took for the free movement of capital to acquire direct effect and how dependent this was on secondary legislation—direct effect was only granted at the end of the deadline for transposing Directive 88/361 on 1 July 1990, and the Directive's Annex I is still the main instrument to identify which situations fall within the scope of the free movement of capital.[50] Underlying this different integration strategy may well be the well-known fact that a Member State can achieve at most two out of three political economy objectives: a fixed-exchanged rate; free movement of capital; and an independent monetary policy.[51] Thus, if Member States were to retain their independent monetary policies within a system of stable exchange rates—which was the dominant system under the gold standard, then the Bretton Woods system, later under the European Exchange Mechanism, and finally as a result of the adoption of the Euro—capital movement would have to be kept in check. Accordingly, even after the free movement of capital was granted direct effect, Directive 88/361 still included a safeguard for national unilateral action.[52]

Another example of the specificities of capital can be found in the vicissitudes of creating a market in financial services. The creation of such a market required capital liberalization, the removal of regulatory obstacles to cross-border financial transactions, and the concomitant deregulation of capital markets. In the 1980s, the idea that short-term economic gains and stability could lead to long-term distortions, and to a corresponding impact on long-term economic growth, gained credence. It was only then, as this long-term view became mainstream and was adopted as national policy by the Member States,

[49] *Spaak Report* [1956], 93–96.

[50] Council Directive 88/361/EEC. The exception was Art. 106 EEC, which had direct effect and applied to current payments related to other freedoms.

[51] Maurice Obstfeld, *Models of Currency Crises with Self-Fulfilling Features* (Centre for Economic Policy Research 1996); Niall Ferguson, *The Cash Nexus* (Penguin Books, London 2001), p. 332–340.

[52] Behrens, 'Die Konvergenz der wirtschaftlichen Freiheiten', 155.

that indirect instruments that tried to control credit expansion through price mechanisms such as interest rates replaced direct intervention in capital markets. Only after this intellectual environment favourable to deregulation came about was the internal market in financial services created. Even in this environment, however, the internal market in financial services was implemented through a number of Directives, and not through the granting of direct effect to Treaty provisions by judicial *fiat*.[53]

A last, but important, example of this different strategy concerns the extension of the scope of the *ratione loci* of the free movement of capital to States that are not members of the EU. If capital is unique among production factors in that it raises concerns for Member States about how to control exchange rates and international movements of capital, particularly speculative ones,[54] these concerns are aggravated by Article 63 TFEU, which promotes capital movement not only intra-Union but also between Member States and third countries, thereby extending certain benefits and rights to residents and citizens of countries not members to the EU without requiring any reciprocity on their part.[55] This third-country dimension was introduced by the Maastricht Treaty, with the apparent purpose of supporting the Euro as an international reserve currency and reassuring money markets regarding its external movement and availability. Nonetheless, this third-country dimension must be understood within a context where movement of capital already had been substantially liberalized and regulated between Member States and third countries by the OECD Code of Liberalisation of Capital Movements.[56] What is more, this peculiarity justifies provisions such as Article 64 TFEU allowing for restrictions on the movement of capital from third countries as long as such a restriction formed part of a Member State's legal order continuously from 31 December 1993. Furthermore, it explains why, when applying the proportionality test to capital, the Court accepts that justifications not valid for intra-Union movement of capital may be acceptable regarding third countries.[57]

[53] Mads Andenas, 'The Interplay of the Commission and the Court of Justice in Giving Effect to the Right to Provide Financial Services' in Paul Craig and Carol Harlow (eds), *Lawmaking in the European Union* (Kluwer 1998), 333–335.

[54] Deniau, *The CommonMarket*, 77.

[55] O'Brien, 'Taxation and the Third Country Dimension of Free Movement of Capital in EU Law: the ECJ's Rulings and Unresolved Issues' [2008] 6 BTR 628. See Advocate General Kokott's Opinion in Case C-282/07 *Truck Center* [2008] E.C.R. I-10767.

[56] Usher, J., 'Monetary Movements and the Internal Market' in N.N. Shuibhne (ed), *Regulating the Internal Market* (Edward Elgar 2006), 193.

[57] O'Brien, 'Taxation and the Third Country Dimension of Free Movement of Capital in EU Law', 663.

In the light of all of this, it has sometimes been held that capital deserves a different treatment from the other freedoms, particularly because Member States' control of movements of capital is an essential element of national economic and monetary policy. Substantial differences between the free movement of capital and the other freedoms can arguably be found even in the Treaty. On the other hand, the free circulation of capital is still an essential element of any common market, and in that sense it can be said to share the same basic normative foundations of the other market freedoms, particularly in countries that now belong to the same currency union.

D. *Is the free movement of persons different?*

The different Treaty provisions on the economic free movement of people can arguably be seen as complementary to a more general freedom for the movement of individuals and legal persons within the EU.[58] This is reflected in the Court of Justice's case law, which holds that the different Treaty provisions on the free movement of persons are based on the same principles as regards entry into, residence, and pursuit of an economic activity in the territory of the Member States by persons covered by EU law, while also prohibiting all discrimination against these people on grounds of nationality.[59] These provisions benefit from the same level of legal protection[60] and are intended to facilitate the pursuit of occupational activities of all kinds throughout the Union, precluding national legislation that might place persons at a disadvantage when they wish to extend their activities beyond the territory of a single Member State.[61]

It is hard to deny that a unitary approach to the free movement of persons appears to have been adopted in the Court of Justice's language.[62] However, determining whether the provisions on the free movement of persons should

[58] Dieter H. Scheuing, 'Freizügigkeit als Unionsbürgerrecht' [2003] EuR 744, 753; Stephen Weatherill, 'Discrimination on Grounds of Nationality in Sport' (1989) 9 YEL 55, 59; Snell, *Goods and Services in EC Law*, 9; Patrick Dollat, *Libre circulation des personnes et citoyenneté: enjeux et perspectives* (Bruylant 1998), 26. Arguing that services should be treated differently from establishment and workers, as the former can be regulated by the home-State and requires a lesser degree of integration in the host-State, see Luigi Daniele, 'Non-discriminatory Restrictions to the Free movement of Persons' (1997) 22 ELRev 191, 195–198.

[59] *Ramrath*, para. 17; Case C-107/94 *Asscher* [1996] E.C.R. I-3089, para. 29.

[60] *Roux*, Case C-151/04 and C-152/04 *Nadin* [2005] E.C.R. I-11203.

[61] Case 143/87 *Stanton* [1988] E.C.R. 3877, para. 13; Joined Cases 154 and 155/87 *Wolf and Dorchain* [1988] E.C.R. 3897, para. 13; Case C-370/90 *Singh* [1992] E.C.R. I-4265, para. 16.

[62] Hatzopoulos, 'Recent Developments in the Case Law of the ECJ in the Field of Services', 70.

be treated similarly is distinct from assessing whether they should in turn be treated differently from freedoms not involving such movement. This is the main issue addressed in the literature—does the right of persons to move freely from State to State in the Union occupy a more protected position than does the movement of cattle, fruit, steel, capital, and coal across State lines?[63] Underlying this question lurks the insight that the EU is more than an internal market; it is intended to become a politically and socially integrated polity. The most serious arguments for a distinctive approach to the free movement of persons relate to its nature as a fundamental (human) right and to European Citizenship.

Proponents of the view that the provisions on the free movement of persons reflect fundamental rights argue that persons, and particularly workers, are not viewed merely as a source of labour by the EU, but as human beings. They have also argued that the free movement of workers has a social element that distinguishes it from the other market freedoms, and that the Treaty itself views the free movement of persons as more than a merely economic freedom.[64] Lastly, they hold that the free movement of persons, as opposed to the other freedoms—which merely grant market or economic rights—reflects fundamental rights and goes beyond the aim of creating and maintaining a common market, and thereby deserves a higher level of protection.[65]

Against this position, it has been argued that, while it is clear that the right of establishment and the free movement of workers require effective cross-border movement by persons to occur, under the free provision of services increasingly the service travels but not its provider or recipient.[66] Similarly, while the free movement of goods and capital have traditionally been read as not prohibiting obstacles to the free movement of traders or financiers, but merely to the free movement of goods and capital themselves,[67] it is also apparent that even market freedoms that are not held

[63] As the question was put in the US by Justice Douglas in *Edwards v California* [1941] 314 U.S. 160, at 177.

[64] A. Arnull, D. Wyatt, and A. Dashwoodk, *Wyatt and Dashwood's European Union Law* (6th edn, Sweet & Maxwell 2011), 498–500; Snell, 'And Then There Were Two', 69–70.

[65] Chris Hilson, 'Discrimination in Community Free Movement Law ' (1999) 24 ELRev 445, 453; Oliver and Enchelmaier, 'Free Movement of Goods', 666.

[66] Catherine Barnard, 'Fitting the Remaining Pieces into the Goods and Persons Jigsaw?' (2001) 26 ELRev 35, 40.

[67] Alina Tryfonidou, 'Further Steps on the Road to Convergence among the Market Freedoms' (2010) 35 ELRev 36, 38–39.

by the Treaty as being concerned with the free movement of persons may imply exactly such a movement: the free movement of goods may require persons to cross borders as suppliers or as consumers, and the free movement of capital might overlap with the free movement of persons.[68] Additionally, even though it is easier to consider that the free movement of persons is a fundamental right than the free movement of goods or the free movement of capital,[69] these latter freedoms can also be seen as a reflection of the fundamental rights to conduct a business and to property (as recognized in the case law[70] and Articles 16 and 17 of the Charter of Fundamental Rights).[71] As we have seen, some authors even consider that all the fundamental freedoms are fundamental rights.[72] It is also argued that the market freedoms are constitutional rights on a par with fundamental rights, and that more important than whether they are fundamental or not is their importance in the scheme of the Treaty.[73] This is a position that appears to be adopted in the case law, inasmuch as, when the Court must decide between protecting the market freedoms or fundamental rights, it does not seem that the free movement of goods suffers from being considered less fundamental than the free movement of persons.[74]

The argument that the market freedoms on the free movement of individuals are 'fundamental rights' has at times been merged with arguments regarding the impact of European Citizenship on the market freedoms. It is, however, of crucial importance to distinguish these arguments. Fundamental rights and European Citizenship provide independent, if related, normative inputs to the market freedoms. The argument that the free movement of persons is fundamental, while the other market freedoms are not, faces the problem of being wholly dependent on controversial *a priori* assumptions as to what rights are fundamental. European Citizenship, on the other hand, apart from being able to extend the scope of EU law and thereby increase

[68] See Snell, *Goods and Services in EC Law*, 25, on the possibility of the people crossing a border to promote goods. See also Case C-362/88 *GB-INNO-BM* [1990] E.C.R. I-667, para. 8.

[69] Peter Oliver, 'Competition and Free Movement: Their Place in the Treaty' in T Tridimas and P Nebbia (eds), *European Law for the Twenty-First Century*, vol. II (Hart Publishing 2004).

[70] Case C-280/93 *Germany v Council* [1994] E.C.R. I-4973, para. 78, and Case C-200/96 *Metronome* [1998] E.C.R. I-01953, para. 21.

[71] Frenz, 'Grundfreiheiten und Grundrechte', 606–607; Oliver and Roth, 'The Internal Market and the Four Freedoms'; Oliver, 'Competition and Free Movement', 164.

[72] Bleckman, 'Die Freiheiten des Gemeinsamen asl Grundrechte', 665 ff; Maduro, 'Reforming the Market or the State?', 73.

[73] Oliver, 'Competition and Free Movement', 166.

[74] See, for example, *Schmidberger* and Case C-36/02 *Omega* [2004] E.C.R. I-9609.

the number of situations where EU fundamental rights protection can intervene, is able to provide normative justifications for arguments in favour of the precedence of free movement of persons, unsupported by and unrelated to any fundamental rights discourse. As a result, European Citizenship may have deep normative implications of its own and deserves a more detailed review.

IV. European Citizenship

For clarity's sake, this analysis will be subdivided into three subsections: first an introduction to European Citizenship; then an attempt to understand its normative underpinnings; and lastly a description of the impact that European Citizenship can have on the market freedoms and free movement law more generally. The latter description will focus on two possible types of impact: European Citizenship either (a) provides a basis for a wider interpretation of the provisions on the economic free movement of persons than for the other economic free movement provisions; or (b) it constitutes a broader basis for individual free movement which is nonetheless autonomous and separate from the market freedoms.

A. An introduction to European citizenship

European Citizenship grants a bundle of rights to citizens of a Member State in addition to those arising from national citizenship. At the time of the Maastricht Treaty, when European Citizenship was introduced, various categories of individuals—namely economically active nationals under the market freedoms and, through the three residence Directives adopted in 1990, non-economically active students, retired people, and those who were not economically active but had comprehensive medical insurance and sufficient resources not to become a burden on the welfare system of the host-State[75]—already possessed a number of rights of free movement and residence. As it was originally perceived, European Citizenship merely

[75] Council Directive 90/364/EEC [1990] OJ L 180 on the right of residence, 26; Council Directive 90/365/EEC [1990] OJ L 180 on the right of residence for employees and self-employed persons who have ceased their occupational activity, 28; and Council Directive 93/96/EEC [1993] OJ L 317 on the right of residence for students.

welded these rights together in a single provision of primary law that left the limitations to which those rights were subject untouched.[76]

Shortly afterwards, however, a different perspective on European Citizenship started to develop. From this point of view, European Citizenship was an autonomous Treaty provision that expanded free movement rights to all European citizens, regardless of whether they fell within the scope of existing legal provisions.[77] The basic idea was one of additionality: European Citizenship would only operate in addition to national citizenship, and where no more specific rights, such as those arising from the market freedoms and the residence Directives, applied.[78] This position was progressively adopted by a number of Advocates-General,[79] and, in *Baumbast*, the Court of Justice settled this specific debate by holding that the right to move to and reside within the territory of the Member States was not dependent on the existence of prior Treaty provisions or secondary legislation, but was instead conferred directly on every citizen of the Union by a clear and precise provision of the EC Treaty—namely, the provision establishing European Citizenship, Art. 21 (1) TFEU.[80] Also in accordance with this perspective, European Citizenship's personal

[76] Robert Kovar and Denys Simon, 'La Citoyenneté Européenne' [1993] CDE 285, 298; Hans d'Oliveira, 'European Citizenship: Its Meaning, Its Potential' in Renaud Dehousse (ed.), *Europe After Maastricht: An Ever Closer Union?* (LBE 1994), 135–141; Siofra O'Leary, 'The Relationship between Community Citizenship and the Protection of Fundamental Rights in Community Law' (1995) 32 CML Rev 519, 519; Sionaidh Douglas-Scott, 'In Search of European Citizenship' (1998) 18 YEL 29, 37; Dollat, *Libre circulation des personnes et citoyenneté: enjeux et perspectives*, 133.

[77] See, for a defence of this position, para. 19 of Advocate General La Pergola's Opinion in Case C-85/96 *Martínez Sala* [1998] E.C.R. I-2691.

[78] Carlos Closa, 'The Concept of Citizenship in the Treaty on the European Union' (1992) 29 CML Rev 1137, 1160

[79] Advocate General Geelhoed's Opinion in Case C-413/99 *Baumbast* [2002] E.C.R. I-7091; Advocate General Kokott's Opinion in Case C-192/05 *Tas-Hagen* [2006] E.C.R. I-10451. See also Yuri Borgmann-Prebil, 'The Rule of Reason in European Citizenship' 14 ELJ 328, 338; Stefano Giubboni, 'Free Movement of Persons and European Solidarity' (2007) 13 ELJ 360, 370.

[80] *Baumbast*, para. 78, 81–84. Sharing this interpretation, see Michael Dougan and Eleanor Spaventa, 'Educating Rudy and the Non-English Patient: A Double-Bill on Residency Rights under Article 18 EC' (2003) 28 ELRev 699; Chris Hilson, 'What's in a Right? The Relationship between Community, Fundamental and Citizenship Rights in EU law' (2004) 29 ELRev 636, 640; Alexander Somek, 'Solidarity Decomposed: Being and Time in European Citizenship' (2007) 32 ELRev 787, 794; Stephan Wernicke, 'Au Nom de Qui? The European Court of Justice between Member States, Civil Society and Union Citizens' (2007) 13 ELJ 380, 396; Francis Jacobs, 'Citizenship of the European Union—A Legal Analysis' (2007) 13 ELJ 591 596. Against this interpretation, see James Mather, 'The Court of Justice and the Union Citizen' (2005) 11 ELJ 722, 727–728.

scope was extended to include all citizens of a Member State.[81] It seemed indeed that:

Union citizenship is destined to be the fundamental status of nationals of the Member States, enabling those who find themselves in the same situation to enjoy the same treatment in law irrespective of their nationality, subject to such exceptions as are expressly provided for.[82]

B. The normative underpinnings of European citizenship

The above debate did not address the question of what European Citizenship entails. 'Citizenship' is such a wide concept that it can be used to propose virtually any normative approach—from the minimalist approach according to which European Citizenship is merely a symbolic ornament, which was explicitly rejected by the Court of Justice, to a maximalist one stating that European Citizenship completely changed the nature of the EU.[83] A uniform legal analysis of European Citizenship is not possible unless one is prepared, from the outset, to measure it against a pre-defined vision of the role of citizens in Europe.[84]

At its lowest level of definition—and, hence, at its most consensual—citizenship can be said to relate to a certain bundle of rights and duties which are attributed in terms of equality[85] to an individual as a result of belonging to a certain community.[86] Such a community is nowadays generally understood to be the State, but, except for a short period of time following the French

[81] *Martínez Sala*. This scope was further defined by secondary law in Directive 2004/38/EC [2004] OJ L 158 on the right of citizens of the Union and their family members to move and reside freely within the territory of the Member States. See also Somek, 'Solidarity Decomposed', 790–791; Jean-Yves Carlier, 'Le devenir de la libre circulation des personnes dans l'Union Européenne: regard sur la directive 2004/38' [2006] CDE 13, 23–27.

[82] Case C-184/99 *Grzelczyk* [2001] E.C.R. I-6193, para. 31.

[83] Dora Kostakopoulou, 'Ideas, Norms and European Citizenship: Explaining Institutional Change' 68 MLJ 233, 234–235.

[84] Stephan Kadelbach, 'Union Citizenship' in Armin von Bogdandy (ed.), *Principles of European Constitutional Law* (Hart Publishing 2006), 484.

[85] That this was the ideal is already apparent in Aristotle, *Politics* (Dover 2000), which however, excluded most of humanity from this condition: see J.G.A. Pocock, 'The Ideal of Citizenship since Classical Times' in Ronald Beiner (ed.), *Theorising Citizenship* (State University of New York 1995), 31.

[86] Michael Walzer, 'Citizenship' in Terence Ball, James Farr, and Russell L. Hanson (eds), *Political Innovation and Conceptual Change* (Cambridge University Press 1989), 211; David Held, 'Between State and Civil Society: Citizenship' in Geoff Andrews (ed.), *Citizenship* (Lawrence & Wishart 1991), 19; Josephine Shaw, 'Citizenship of the Union: Towards Post-National Membership?' [1997] Jean Monnet Working Paper 06/97; Closa, 'The Concept of Citizenship in the Treaty on the European Union', 1138.

Revolution, citizenship was not functionally tied to national identity.[87] The concept of citizenship predates the nation-State by a few millennia, and with the advent of the EU it can be said to post-date it too.[88] Although, in its original formulation, citizenship related essentially to rights of political participation, with the increase in size of political organizations citizenship became akin to a legal status of passive recipients of rights.[89] This can be said to be the dominant element of citizenship nowadays, even if liberal democracies also entitle citizens to participate in political life in an attempt to conciliate the instrumental elements of citizenship adopted in the liberal perspective springing from the Stoics and Locke, and the communitarian and ethical elements of citizenship identified by thinkers like Aristotle and Rousseau.[90]

In its complexity, citizenship can be said to combine the public and social dimensions of political life with its individual aspects.[91] Being a very malleable concept, its specific content is not set *a priori*, but seems to depend instead on specific socio-historical conditions. For example, European Citizenship is dependent on an individual being a citizen of a Member State, a *status* which is at the discretion of the Member States themselves.[92] European Citizenship is a historically, geographically, and culturally contingent institution that can only be fully understood by reference both to broader theories of citizenship and to situation-specific ideas about European integration that stress the dynamic, open-ended nature of that process. This under-determination of the normative contents of European Citizenship comes across very clearly in Advocate General Sharpston's Opinion in *Zambrano*, where she asks:

Is Union citizenship merely the non-economic version of the same generic kind of free movement rights as have long existed for the economically active and for persons of independent

[87] Habermas, 'Citizenship and National Identity', 259.

[88] Walker, 'The EU and the WTO', 47; Carlos Closa, 'Citizenship of the Union and Nationality of Member States' (1995) 32 CML Rev 487, 491–494; Ulrich K. Preuss, 'Problems of a Concept of European Citizenship' (1995) 1 ELJ 267, 280; Dollat, *Libre circulation des personnes et citoyenneté: enjeux et perspectives*, 405; Derek Heater, *What is Citizenship?* (Polity Press 1999), 149.

[89] This is visible in Aristotle, *Politics*, for example, but also in Benjamin Constant's distinction between the liberty of the ancients and that of the moderns in Livre XVI of Benjamin Constant, *Principes de politique: Applicables à tous les gouvernements* (Hachette Littératures 2006).

[90] Walzer, 'Citizenship', 215–216; Pocock, 'The Ideal of Citizenship since Classical Times', 43; Habermas, 'Citizenship and National Identity', 261; Heater, *What is Citizenship?*, 44–51.

[91] Held, 'Between State and Civil Society', 21; Preuss, 'Problems of a Concept of European Citizenship', 270.

[92] Even if cumulated with a double nationality of a non-Member State. See Case C-369/90 *Micheletti* [1992] E.C.R. I-4239.

means? Or does it mean something more radical: true citizenship, carrying with it a uniform set of rights and obligations, in a Union under the rule of law in which respect for fundamental rights must necessarily play an integral part?[93]

The Advocate General here identifies a number of relevant questions that European Citizenship currently raises: does European Citizenship grant a combined right to move to another Member State and then reside there? Or a sequential right to move to another Member State and, having moved there at some stage in the past, then to reside there? Or does European Citizenship grant two autonomous rights, the right to move to another Member State and the right to reside in any Member State, including the State of one's own nationality?[94] And, if this latter option is adopted, are there any 'purely internal situations' exempt from the scope of European Citizenship and concomitant protection of fundamental rights at EU level?

On this last issue, a number of developments have been observed recently. In *Zambrano*, the Court of Justice decided that European Citizenship: '*precludes national measures which have the effect of depriving citizens of the Union of the genuine enjoyment of the substance of the rights conferred by virtue of their status as citizens of the Union*'.[95] In the light of this, the Court of Justice held that dependent Belgian children who had never left Belgium would see the genuine enjoyment of the substance of their rights infringed by the deportation of their Colombian parents back to Colombia. This judgment could have been read as implying that the scope of European Citizenship extended to 'purely internal' situations. However, shortly afterwards, in *McCarthy*, the Court held that a United Kingdom/Irish national who had never left the UK was not able to rely on EU law when her Jamaican husband faced deportation, because her situation was purely internal.[96] This apparent contradiction was clarified in *Dereci*, a case concerning a refusal by the Austrian authorities to grant permission to third-country nationals to live with family members who were European citizens residing in, and nationals of, Austria but who had never exercised their right to free movement. Reiterating the formula developed in *Zambrano*, the Court of Justice went on to hold that there is a denial of the genuine enjoyment of the substance of European Citizenship rights when a European citizen is forced to leave the territory of the Union as a result of a Member State's refusal to grant a right of residence to a family member, but that the European citizen

93 Opinion in Case C-34/09 *Zambrano* [2011] E.C.R. I-01177, para. 3.
94 Ibid, para. 80 of the Opinion. 95 Ibid, para. 42.
96 Case C-434/09 *McCarthy* [2011] E.C.R. I-03375.

simply wanting to have third-country national family members live with her '*for economic reasons or in order to keep his family together in the territory of the Union*' is not enough for the Court of Justice to find that this would force a European citizen to leave the territory of the Union.[97] Even if this somewhat clarifies the scope of the intrusion of European Citizenship into purely internal situations, it still leaves serious questions to be addressed, particularly concerning how to identify which situations force a European citizen to leave the territory of the Union, what the '*substance of the rights conferred by virtue of their status as citizens of the Union*' may be in other contexts, and what the normative justifications for the creation of this specially protected status are.[98] What this also demonstrates very clearly is how 'fuzzy' and undetermined the concept of European Citizenship still is 20 years after it was first adopted.[99]

C. *The normative impact of European citizenship on the market freedoms*

Like the market freedoms, directly effective European Citizenship rights are subjective public rights. From a methodological perspective, the Court of Justice has applied European Citizenship and the market freedoms in an analogous way since its decision in *D'Hoop*.[100] The Court of Justice first tries to determine whether a national measure restricts the relevant freedom, and, secondly, it assesses whether that measure is justified.[101] There are also some areas of substantive overlap, which have led the Court of Justice sometimes to conflate the economic free movement of persons and European Citizenship. In *Bickel and Franz*, the Court of Justice considered that the prohibition of discrimination on the grounds of nationality set out in Article 18 TFEU applied equally to the free provision of services and to European Citizenship, while in *Ursula Elsen* the Court decided a case

[97] Case C-256/11 *Dereci* [2011] E.C.R. I-11315, paras 64–69.

[98] Kay Hailbronner and Daniel Thym, '*Zambrano* Case Opinion' (2011) 48 CML Rev 1253; Peter Van Elsuwege, 'Shifting the Boundaries? European Citizenship and the Scope of Application of EU Law' (2011) 38 LIEI 263; and Alicia Hinarejos, 'Extending Citizenship and the Scope of EU Law' (2011) 70 CLJ 309.

[99] See Niamh Nic Shuibhne, '(Some of) the Kids are All Right: Comment on *McCarthy* and *Dereci*' (2012) 49 CML Rev 349, 379, arguing that current developments on the 'the substance of rights granted by European Citizenship' make this an area of law which is virtually impossible to explain, teach, or advise on.

[100] Case C-224/98 *D'Hoop* [2002] E.C.R. I-6191. See Scheuing, 'Freizügigkeit als Unionsbüurgerrecht', 778–780.

[101] This is in effect typical of constitutional rights' adjudication—see Somek, 'Solidarity Decomposed', 794.

without determining whether a situation fell within the scope of the free movement of workers or European Citizenship.[102]

These similarities do not imply that European Citizenship must have an impact on the market freedoms, but they have lent support to normative arguments that the instrumental nature of the economic freedoms in the creation of the common market has been replaced by a wider rationale centred on the idea of European Citizenship and of a political Union going well beyond market integration. According to these arguments, the ideal of the economically active citizen that can be gleaned from the market freedoms—the market citizen—has been replaced by a broader 'citizen-focused' conception that may turn all free movement provisions into something akin to civil rights for citizenship purposes.[103] This approach found favour with a number of Advocates General,[104] and eventually found its way into decisions of the Court of Justice.[105] Even if the case law still gives priority to citizens pursuing an economic activity in relation to non-economically active migrants,[106] with Article 21 TFEU operating as a safety net when the traditional categories cannot apply,[107] European Citizenship is now held to be *lex generalis*, defining the core to which other freedoms give more specific expression as *lex specialis*.[108]

This approach naturally leads to European Citizenship being relevant in construing the market freedoms, and in particular to the expansion of their scope.[109] Such an expansion is in certain cases easily justified independently

[102] *Bickel and Franz*, para. 15; *Ursula Elsen*, para. 35–36.

[103] Shaw, 'Citizenship of the Union'; Wolfgang Streeck, 'From Market Making to State Building? Reflections on the Political Economy of European Social Policy' in Stephan Leibfried and Paul Pierson (eds), *European Social Policy—Between Fragmentation and Integration* (The Brookings Institution 1995), 399.

[104] Advocate General Cosmas in *Wijsenbeek*, Advocate General Jarabo-Colomer in Joined Cases C-11/06 and C-12/06 *Morgan and Bucher* [2007] E.C.R. I-9161, and Advocate General Maduro in Joined Cases C-158/04 and C-159/04 *Alfa Vita Vassilopoulos* [2006] E.C.R. I-8135.

[105] See, for example, Case C-345/05 *Commission v Portugal* [2006] E.C.R. I-10633 paras 13–14. For expressions of this case law on the economic fundamental freedoms, see: on right of establishment, *Skanavi and Chryssanthakopoulos*, para. 22; on freedom of movement for workers, see Case C-100/01 *Oteiza Olazabal* [2002] E.C.R. I-10981, para. 26; and on freedom to provide services, see Case C-92/01 *Stylianakis* [2003] E.C.R. I-1291, para. 18; on both free movement of workers and free provision of services, Case C-208/05 *ITC* [2007] E.C.R. I-181, paras 64–65.

[106] Charlotte O'Brien, 'Social Blind Spots and Monocular Policy Making: The ECJ's Migrant Worker Model' (2009) 46 CML Rev 1107, 1112.

[107] Ibid, 1109. [108] Scheuing, 'Freizügigkeit als Unionsbürgerrect', 764.

[109] Jacobs, 'Citizenship of the European Union—A Legal Analysis', 595; Síofra O'Leary, 'Developing an Ever Closer Union between the Peoples of Europe? A Reappraisal of the Case Law of the Court of Justice on the Free Movement of Persons and EU Citizenship' (2008) 27 YEL 167, 182–183.

of particular normative considerations. For example, in *Bidar*,[110] a case on European Citizenship, the Court of Justice extended the scope *ratione materiae* of the Treaty regarding maintenance grants attributed to students beyond what had been previously accepted for the free movement of workers or provided for in secondary legislation.[111] From a systematic perspective, if the autonomous function of European Citizenship is to protect those who are not encompassed by the economic fundamental freedoms, it would not make sense to protect non-workers more than workers, which is what would have happened had the material scope of the relevant market freedoms not been extended.

Other developments, however, seem to require a change in the normative foundations of the market freedoms. Even though the origins of this case law may be found prior to the introduction of European Citizenship into the Treaties,[112] it is arguable that the Court of Justice in certain cases interpreted the *telos* of the economic free movement provisions not as allowing nationals of the Member States to '*move freely within the territory of those States in order to pursue their economic activities*',[113] but as protecting the rights of all economically active persons whose personal situation has a cross-border dimension.[114] The *rationale* for these cases, rather than being connected to the internal market, seems to revolve around the creation of a meaningful status for European citizens centred on fundamental rights, and the fundamental right to a family life in particular. Arguably, the Court is protecting certain human rights of all moving Union citizens, without the kind of movement involved, or the relationship between the human rights' protection and the person's cross-border movement, being significant.[115]

In conclusion, it is clear that the Court of Justice has chosen to look at European Citizenship as being relevant to the way in which the market freedoms are construed.[116] In particular, European Citizenship is being used

[110] Case C-209/03 *Bidar* [2005] E.C.R. I-2119, paras 32–36.

[111] See Case 39/86 *Sylvie Lair* [1988] E.C.R. 3161, and Case 197/86 *Malcolm Brown* [1988] E.C.R. 3205.

[112] Case 186/87 *Cowan* [1989] E.C.R. 195.

[113] *Morson and Jhanjan*.

[114] Alina Tryfonidou, 'In Search of the Aim of the EC Free Movement of Persons Provisions: Has the Court of Justice Missed the Point?' (2009) 46 CML Rev 1591.

[115] Christophe Schiltz, '*Akrich:* A Clear Delimitation Without Limits' (2005) 12 MJ 241, 252; Alina Tryfonidou, 'Family Reunification Rights of (Migrant) Union Citizens: Towards a More Liberal Approach' (2009) 15 ELJ 634. See, in more detail, Chapter 4, Section IV below.

[116] See, for a somewhat similar analysis, Niamh Nic Shuibhne, 'The Resilience of EU Market Citizenship' (2010) 47 CML Rev 1597.

to expand the scope of the free movement provisions while imposing an even stricter interpretation of any derogation.[117] While originally the provisions on free movement were instrumental to the goal of allowing the cross-border pursuit of economic activities,[118] with European Citizenship the internal market recedes as a normative foundation and the existence of individual rights to free movement becomes more prominent. Thus, the argument from European Citizenship is usually made to defend a more important status for the free movement of persons within the economic freedoms.[119] Some authors have argued that European Citizenship may normatively justify extending the scope of the free movement of person provisions beyond discrimination into a rule of reason,[120] or extending the scope of European law to purely internal situations and thereby to ensure true equality between individuals through EU law.[121] It has also been argued that European Citizenship requires the Court to protect the human rights of any free moving European citizen,[122] and some go as far as to argue that European Citizenship calls for a transposition of solidarity from the national to the European level.[123] A trend which runs through this literature is the argument that European Citizenship should perhaps be used to interpret all free movement provisions in line with a fundamental rights discourse detached from market integration, with the concomitant replacement of national by EU fundamental rights protection. As such, these readings propose or justify the reinforcement of the powers of the EU and national

[117] Eleanor Spaventa, *Free Movement of Persons in the European Union* (Kluwer Law International 2007), 137–138.

[118] Scheuing, 'Freizügigkeit als Unionsbürgerrecht', 746. This is only the main, consensually accepted normative goal. As we have seen above, there are arguably other normative concerns for particular freedoms.

[119] Shaw, 'Citizenship of the Union'; Streeck, 'From Market Making to State Building?', 399; Snell, 'And Then There Were Two', 68–69; Spaventa, *Free Movement of Persons in the European Union*; Ferdinand Wollenschläger, 'A New Fundamental Freedom beyond Market Integration: Union Citizenship and its Dynamics for Shifting the Economic Paradigm of European Integration' (2011) 17 ELJ 1, 5–7; Jacobs, 'Citizenship of the European Union—A Legal Analysis', 595; O'Leary, 'Developing an Ever Closer Union between the Peoples of Europe?', 182–183. A notable exception is Advocate General Maduro's Opinion in *Alfa Vita Vassilopoulos*, para. 50.

[120] Spaventa, *Free Movement of Persons in the European Union*, 143–148.

[121] Eleanor Spaventa, 'Seeing the Wood Despite the Trees? On the Scope of Union Citizenship and its Constitutional Effects' (2008) 45 CML Rev 13, 36–39, for a purely internal situation, 41 for indirect review.

[122] Ibid, 39–44; Peter Neussl, 'European Citizenship and Human Rights: An Interactive European Concept' (1997) 24 LIEI 47.

[123] Somek, 'Solidarity Decomposed', 789.

courts, as well as an overlap between the competences of the Court of Justice and the European Court of Human Rights.[124]

These normative approaches, which seem predominant in the literature, have nonetheless been contested in some quarters. It has been noted that the creation of European Citizenship has not turned the EU into a State, transferred the citizens' allegiances from their State of nationality to the European level, or created solidarity bonds between European citizens equivalent to those between citizens of the same Member State. Even if one agrees that European Citizenship was originally intended to have the political function of easing the identification with the Union of its citizens, and that it performs a number of roles usually attributed to national citizenship—such as granting civil rights, political rights, and even, in certain circumstances, rights to social benefits—it is nonetheless arguable that European Citizenship corresponds to a thin conception of citizenship that grants an innovative legal status to individuals but is detached from any ethic of participation. Furthermore, from a drafting perspective, there is no indication in the Treaties that European Citizenship altered the goals of the market freedoms, and thus it is arguable that their goal is still to enable Member State nationals to move between Member States for economic purposes, instrumentally to the creation of a common market.

It is true that, whenever a situation concerns individual movement across borders and the taking up of residence in another Member State, it will fall under the scope of European Citizenship, and that, in some cases, that same situation will fall within the scope of a market freedom as well, without this overlap leading to any difference in the particular outcome of the case. However, it does not follow from this that the market freedoms should be extended to encompass more situations than what their *telos* requires; instead, this merely means that, when the market freedoms do not apply, European Citizenship, with its broader scope, will.[125] This argument can be further reinforced by reference to the recent development of the test according to which European Citizenship is infringed by national measures that have the effect of depriving citizens of the Union of the genuine enjoyment of the substance of the rights conferred by virtue of their status as citizens of

[124] Michael Dougan, 'The Constitutional Dimension to the Case Law on Union Citizenship' (2006) 31 ELRev 613, 625–626; Spaventa, 'Seeing the Wood Despite the Trees?', 39–44.

[125] Kadelbach, 'Union Citizenship', 465; Tryfonidou, 'In Search of the Aim of the EC Free Movement of Persons Provisions', 1612.

the Union.[126] Even though structurally similar to the existence of threshold tests for the market freedoms—reflecting their common status as judicially enforceable constitutional rights—and seemingly constituting a test which is more difficult to meet than those thresholds, it should be remembered that this formulation effectively builds on, and is accordingly more expansive than, the thresholds applicable to the market freedoms.

The argument that European Citizenship requires a more exalted status for the free movement of persons within the economic freedoms may also be contested by noting that all market freedoms entail, to a greater or lesser extent, the possibility of people crossing borders, with the result that it is arbitrary to distinguish between the market freedoms on this basis. From this perspective, European Citizenship, unlike what is commonly argued, actually poses problems for the idea that the provisions on the economic free movement of persons should be treated differently from the other market freedoms. If European Citizenship requires that the Court of Justice give priority to the economic movement of individuals, since only physical persons may rely on Article 21 TFEU,[127] this would mean that different approaches would need to be adopted within specific freedoms depending on whether the free movement of European citizens was at stake.[128] This would lead to the creation of two sets of rules within each freedom, particularly for the free provision of services and the right of establishment.

A final argument against an extensive effect of European Citizenship on the market freedoms focuses on the former's normative under-conceptualization, and the resulting under-theorization of what its impact on the market freedoms should be. To regulate situations that should fall exclusively within the scope of European Citizenship under the banner of market freedoms merely leads to confusion as to what the relevant normative underpinnings of European Citizenship and the market freedoms are, and where their dividing lines lie. The consequences of such normative confusion may be pernicious. If the goal of the free movement of persons is now to protect the human rights of all economically active persons whose personal situation has a cross-border dimension, this will require an extension of the scope of the market freedoms, and of the Court of Justice's duty to balance them with fundamental rights. This extension can, *in extremis*, lead to all situations

[126] See, in this chapter, fn. 95 to 99 above.

[127] Alongside Art. 45 TFEU: see Laenerts, K and Bernardeau, L, 'L'encadrement communautaire de la fiscalité directe' (2007) 43 CDE 19, 52.

[128] As also noted by Snell, 'And Then There Were Two', 70, fn. 111.

where someone who has had any kind of economic relationship with any foreign good or service at any time in the past falling within the scope of the market freedoms, in effect turning the Court of Justice into a last-resort appeal instance for virtually any dispute involving a European citizen. The question would then turn on how the protection of human rights by the Court of Justice relates to that same protection by the European Court of Human Rights and the Member States. As noted by Advocate General Sharpston, such an extension in the protection of fundamental rights by the Court of Justice to situations beyond the traditional remit of EU law, under the banner of European Citizenship, would be akin to stating that certain fundamental rights are so significant that they are among the fundamental rights that must be protected by the EU from impairment by the States:

A change of that kind would alter, in legal and political terms, the very nature of fundamental rights under EU law. It therefore requires both an evolution in the case law and an unequivocal political statement from the constituent powers of the EU (its Member States), pointing at a new role for fundamental rights in the EU.[129]

Thus, it can be argued that, even though there may be normative reasons for extending the scope of European Citizenship, depending on the evolution of European integration, the scope of European Citizenship should be distinguished from the scope of the market freedoms: the latter refer to economic rights and should be restricted to situations of inter-State movement with an economic purpose, while the former refers to a fundamental right of a more political nature.

Naturally, European Citizenship does have an impact on how to construe the market freedoms. For example, systemic considerations point to economically active citizens being granted social benefits at least equivalent to non-economically active citizens. As such, should the Court of Justice or the legislature increase the level of benefits available for inactive citizens, *ceteris paribus* the level of protection of (previously) active citizens should be at least similar? But this does not imply any alteration of the normative foundations of the market freedoms themselves, or any privileged status for the economic free movement of persons over other economic freedoms—without

[129] Opinion in *Zambrano*, para. 173. This would also raise serious issues of judicial architecture that would need to be addressed. For an example of previous discussions on Treaty amendments concerning the EU's judicial architecture, see Angus Johnston, 'Judicial Reform and the Treaty of Nice' (2001) 38 CML Rev 499.

detriment to any such privileged status which may accrue to individuals under their newly exalted status as European citizens.

V. Conclusion

While describing the main normative theories on the EU economic freedoms, two trends were identified, one for and the other against a common approach to the market freedoms.

In support of a common normative foundation of all market freedoms, one finds both formal and substantive arguments. Formally, all market freedoms are judicially enforceable rights against acts or omissions by the State that are subject to the same analytical framework based on the identification of a *prima facie* restriction followed by the application of a proportionality assessment. Substantively, the market freedoms are all instrumental to the realization of the same goal: a market without internal frontiers. That this overarching goal can support a uniform reading of the market freedoms can be derived from the Treaties, particularly Article 3(1) (c) EC and Article 26 TFEU; from theories of economic integration, according to which all market freedoms are required to remove obstacles to the creation of a common market; and from the imperatives of systemic coherence and legal certainty, particularly as the same situation can be subject to different freedoms depending on how it is framed before the courts.

The arguments against a common approach, on the other hand, are freedom-specific. While it was found that there is some support for the free movement of capital being subject to specific treatment, the main arguments for a differentiated treatment of the market freedoms focus on the free movement of people. These arguments, which have been gaining support in the literature, have focused on the free movement of people as a fundamental (human) right and on European Citizenship. Underlying this trend lurks a challenge to the centrality of the internal market in the European project that seeks to replace the instrumental nature of the economic freedoms in the creation of the common market with a wider rationale centred on the idea of European Citizenship and of a political Union that goes well beyond market integration.

SECTION II

The Freedoms

Section I set the stage for the analysis of how extra-legal constraints interact with more traditional legal approaches regarding the fundamental freedoms. This section will test the hypothesis that adding these extra-legal elements to traditional 'normative' discussions allows for the development of more comprehensive descriptive models of the law and its evolution, and for better contextualized normative debates.

In Chapter 1 it was shown that, in a world of divided powers, imperfect decision-makers and value pluralism, one should look beyond whether a decision is right or wrong in accordance with a certain 'evaluative' framework. Instead, one should look also into which entity is better placed to decide in the light of the relevant institutional context. It was also demonstrated that the Court of Justice can appoint itself as the best available decision-maker through its judgments on the scope of the market freedoms, which act as gatekeepers to the Court of Justice's balancing exercises.

In Chapter 2, we saw how the market freedoms are traditionally considered to have an identity of aim: to contribute to the completion and functioning of the internal market through the elimination of obstacles to economic free movement, and to the creation of an area without internal frontiers in which the free movement of goods, persons, services, and capital is ensured.[1] It is arguable, however, that the normative goals underpinning the internal market have evolved since the Union's inception in 1957—in particular under the influence of European Citizenship—and that some market freedoms are now subject to specific normative foundations.

The following chapters will try to understand how competing legal normative underpinnings led to developments in the case law, and the

[1] See Art. 26 TFEU. See also Case 355/85 *Driancourt v Cognet* [1986] E.C.R. 3231, and Case 98/86 *Mathot* [1987] E.C.R. 809.

impact that the institutional context has had in mediating and constraining the impact of the relevant legal normative inputs. The analysis in this section will focus on the scope of the market freedoms. In areas where the freedoms are treated identically, one can reasonably presume that the normative inputs anchoring legal practice and extra-legal constraints are similar for all freedoms.[2] On the other hand, in areas where it is arguable that the market freedoms are subject to differentiated treatment, it is a reasonable hypothesis that specific normative concerns and/or institutional constraints are at play. This means that the areas of the law where the freedoms are treated differently provide ideal grounds for trying to map out the interaction between legal normative concerns and extra-legal institutional constraints in the development of free movement law.

The method adopted in this section will consist of reviewing the case law on each of the areas where the market freedoms are subject to differentiated treatment, alongside the academic literature concerning those areas. Following this, an attempt will be made to demonstrate how institutional context matters to the development of the law by courts, and how taking this external dimension into account can add to traditional internal legal approaches. The analysis undertaken at this stage will be merely descriptive, and concerned with whether a contextual approach that adds institutional elements to traditional legal approaches can lead to a theory that is a better descriptive fit with the law than traditional legal approaches allow for. This descriptive analysis will be followed by an attempt to describe how normative approaches that adopt such a contextual approach might look like. It will also be argued that such contextual normative approaches are likely to be more attractive than decontextualized ones.

[2] But see fn. 9 of the Introduction.

3

The Concept of Restriction on Free Movement—An Introduction

I. Introduction

If the groundwork for the Court of Justice's leading role in creating the EU legal order was laid during the 1960s by the doctrines of direct effect and supremacy, this role was taken over in the 1970s by the market freedoms—in particular the free movement of goods, and, since the 1990s, the free movement of persons. The judicial removal of national measures posing unjustified obstacles to intra-Union trade was one of the main tools used to build the internal market, and the concept of restriction on free movement adopted by the Court of Justice set the threshold for identifying measures that posed such obstacles. In other words, the broader the concept of 'restriction' used, the greater the number of national rules that fell within the scope of the free movement provisions. This chapter will review the traditional tests developed by the Court of Justice concerning the concept of restriction on the market freedoms, which tend to fit with the tests proposed in the academic literature. These tests will be divided into four main groups that will be analysed in turn: discrimination tests; economic due-process tests; typological tests; and access-to-market tests.

II. A Bit of Legal History

Originally, all market freedoms to which direct effect had been granted were supposed to apply a test prohibiting discrimination on grounds of nationality. According to orthodox history, this first changed as regards the free movement of goods, which prohibits both quantitative restrictions—a well-known concept in International Economic Law referring to measures amounting, according to the circumstances, to a total or partial restraint of imports, exports, or goods in transit[1]—and measures having equivalent effect to quantitative restrictions. The traditional tale is that, in the 1970s, the concept of a measure having equivalent effect to a quantitative restriction was extended from referring merely to discriminatory measures into encompassing national measures whose mere existence was liable *per se* to have a restrictive effect on intra-State trade.[2] During the 1980s, this concept was further extended until the free movement of goods was held to prohibit any measure that might diminish the total volume of cross-border trade, in effect turning the free movement of goods into an economic due-process clause.[3] Following academic criticism,[4] in 1993 the Court of Justice expressly corrected its case law in *Keck and Mithouard* by adopting a typological approach.[5] As the story goes, while the free movement of goods expanded, the other freedoms lingered in relative neglect—with the provisions on capital not being granted direct effect, and those on persons still applying discriminatory tests—until the 1990s, when the Court of Justice expressly adopted more expansive tests for persons and capital, almost contemporaneously with its attempt to limit the scope of the free movement of goods.[6] The various tests adopted by the Court of Justice eventually coalesced around the concept of access-to-market, which the Court has recently applied to all freedoms, including goods.[7]

In this short historical prelude, we find four main tests regarding whether a national measure restricts free movement: discrimination; economic

[1] Case 2/73 *Geddo v Ente* [1973] E.C.R. 865.

[2] Case 8/74 *Dassonville* [1974] E.C.R. 837; Case 120/78 *Rewe-Zentral AG* [1979] E.C.R. 649 (*Cassis de Dijon*).

[3] In the so-called *Sunday Trading* cases: see *Torfaen*, Case C-312/89 *Conforama* [1991] E.C.R. I-00997, Case C-332/89 *Marchandise* [1991] E.C.R. I-1027, and *Stoke and Norwich v B&Q*.

[4] Particularly important was Eric L. White, 'In Search of the Limits to Article 30 of the EEC Treaty' (1989) 26 CML Rev 235, who as a member of the Commission legal service pressed this view on the Court of Justice in more than one hearing.

[5] *Keck and Mithouard*.

[6] See for establishment, Case C-340/89 *Vlassopoulou* [1991] E.C.R. I-2357; for services, Case C-76/90 *Säger* [1993] E.C.R. I-4221; for workers, *Kraus*.

[7] For services, Case C-384/93 *Alpine Investments* [1995] E.C.R. I-1141; for workers, Case C-415/03 *Bosman* [1995] E.C.R. I-4921; for capital, *Commission v UK*; for establishment, Case C-442/02 *CaixaBank* [2004] E.C.R. I-8961; and for goods, Case C-110/05 *Commission v Italy* [2009] E.C.R. I-00519.

due-process; typological; and access-to-market. They will now be addressed in turn.

III. Discriminatory Approaches

Prohibitions of discrimination on grounds of nationality were first adopted by anti-protectionist theories on the basis that measures that discriminate against foreigners are normally intended to protect nationals at their expense. Discrimination tests always include formal discrimination, but they can also look into related criteria, such as the intent of regulation—since a purportedly legitimate regulatory purpose can disguise protectionist intent—or the existence of material discrimination. In this latter case, the subject of examination is the effect of State measures, in particular whether they place a heavier burden on foreign goods than on national ones.[8]

The Treaties set out in Article 18 TFEU a general prohibition of discrimination on grounds of nationality, but it is the market freedoms, as *lex specialis*, that apply this principle in the context of the internal market.[9] That discrimination is prohibited under the market freedoms is unanimously accepted, but it should be noted that goods, services, and capital do not have nationality as such; it is discrimination on the grounds of their origins that is contrary to free movement law, even if sometimes nationality is used as shorthand.[10] Similarly, discrimination on the grounds of the company's seat—its registered office, administration, or principal place of business—serves as the equivalent to discrimination on grounds of nationality for legal entities.

Discrimination on grounds of nationality was the main test applied to the market freedoms until the early 1990s. The exception to this was goods, and it was in reaction to judicial developments regarding this freedom that structured defences of discrimination tests in EU economic free movement law

[8] Sykes, 'Regulatory Protectionism and the Law of International Trade', 16–23; Gráinne de Búrca, 'Unpacking the Concept of Discrimination in EC and International Trade Law' in Catherine Barnard and Joanne Scott (eds), *The Law of the Single European Market* (Hart Publishing 2001), 187–188.

[9] On workers, see Case C-40/05 *Lyyski* [2007] E.C.R. I-99, para. 34; on services, see Case C-341/05 *Laval* [2007] E.C.R. I-11767, para. 55; on establishment and capital, see Case C-311/08 *SGI* [2010] E.C.R. I-487, para. 32.

[10] Gareth Davies, *Nationality Discrimination in the European Internal Market* (Kluwer Academic Publishers 2003), 60.

were first elaborated. As will be seen below, in the early 1970s the Court of Justice decided that not only discriminatory measures but also indistinctly applicable product requirements[11] restricted the free movement of goods. Attempts were nonetheless made to rationalize this case law as still applying a discrimination test. In particular, it was argued that, since discriminatory measures could only be justified by reference to the grounds listed in the Treaty, mandatory requirements—i.e. grounds for the justification of national measures that restrict free movement without being provided for in the Treaties but that are nonetheless deemed legitimate by the Court of Justice—were not akin to Treaty derogations but were limits to the concept of restriction itself.[12] Furthermore, it was also argued that mandatory requirements and product requirements were used by the Court of Justice solely to identify situations that indirectly discriminated against foreign goods by imposing an *unjustified* 'double-regulatory burden' on imports. When these two arguments were coupled, it resulted that mandatory requirements were only available to justify product requirements, which meant that the Court of Justice only found a measure to be restrictive if it was discriminatory for the purposes of traditional discrimination tests or it was indirectly discriminatory by imposing an unjustified double-regulatory burden on imports.[13]

Following the *Sunday Trading* cases, which extended the concept of restriction to such an extent that virtually any rule susceptible of having an impact on the volume of trade was liable to infringe upon the free movement of goods, this position became descriptively untenable.[14] However, *Keck's* overruling of this case law, and its identification of product requirements and discriminatory selling arrangements as the only measures that were able

[11] Meaning legal requirements concerning the physical characteristics of products. See the more elaborate discussion on typological approaches belowin section V.

[12] Kingreen, 'Fundamental Freedoms', 573; Karen Banks and Giuliano Marenco, 'Intellectual Property and the Community Rules on Free Movement: Discrimination Unearthed' 15 ELRev 224, 238–241. See for a criticism of this position, Joseph Weiler, 'The Constitution of the Common Market Place: Text and Context in the Evolution of the Free Movement of Goods' in Paul Craig and Grainne de Búrca (eds), *The Evolution of EU law* (OUP 1999), 349. On the origins of the doctrine of mandatory requirements, see Section IV of this chapter.

[13] Gustavo Marenco, 'Pour une interprétation traditionelle de la notion de mesure d'effet equivalent à une restriction quantitative' (1984) 20 CDE 291, in particular 304–313 and 349; Louis Defalque, 'Le concept de discrimination en matiére de libre circulation des marchandises' (1987) 23 CDE 471. On the applicability of justifications not found in the Treaty to directly discriminatory measures, see fn. 145 of Chapter 6 below.

[14] See fn. 3 above.

to restrict the free movement of goods, resuscitated the plausibility of discrimination as the relevant judicial test.[15]

What are we to make of this approach? One should recall that prohibitions of discrimination are prescriptive impositions of equality standards consisting of a tripartite relation between two (or several) objects or persons who share one (or several) qualities alongside an inadmissible distinction criterion. Since discrimination refers to the unjustified differentiated treatment of similar situations, the first step in any analysis must be to determine whether the relevant situations are similar; and this, in turn, requires the prior identification of a *tertium comparationis*, i.e. the quality that the things being compared have in common that makes them similar. Secondly, one must then select the criteria used to distinguish/discriminate between two subjects sharing this *tertium comparationis* that are prohibited. This selection requires the pre-existence of normative reasons making the adoption of such criteria unacceptable. A discrimination test not following these steps can easily lead to the kind of arbitrary decisions that it purports to prevent.

In the light of this, the discrimination approaches adopted in the case law and in the literature are problematic. First, they seem to assume that domestic and foreign goods are similarly situated; but:

> *The problem is that one cannot presuppose any such thing. One must have criteria for determining which goods (or services or workers) are equivalent and hence worthy of equal treatment. No credible discrimination model can exist without definitions of what we mean by equivalent or similar situations. A failure to treat equivalent situations the same is a hall-mark of arbitrary behaviour.*[16]

Under WTO law, discrimination tests are preceded by a market equivalence analysis of the relevant products. Such analysis requires an economic and empirical assessment of the market in order to determine whether the relevant products are comparable, prior to determining whether those same products are subject to differentiated treatment. This is understood to be a difficult exercise and, as such, a variety of different criteria such as objective (physical characteristics, tariff classification, end-uses, or even the act of exportation) and economic (market definition) standards have been used.[17]

[15] *Keck and Mithouard*. See N. Bernard, 'Discrimination and Free Movement in EC Law' (1996) 45 ICLQ 95; Snell, *Goods and Services in EC Law*, 27–28, 45–46.

[16] Daniel Wilsher, 'Does *Keck* Discrimination Make Any Sense? An Assessment of the Non-Discrimination Principle Within the European Single Market' (2008) 33 ELRev 3, 5.

[17] Nicolas F. Diebold, *Non-Discrimination and the Pillars of International Economic Law—Comparative Analysis and Building Coherency* (Society of International Economic Law 2010), 4–7.

In EU law, however, the Court of Justice usually deems products to be comparable without going into the business of determining whether they effectively are so. This means that any commentator who seeks to advocate the application of a discriminatory approach by the Court of Justice has to identify a variety of *tertia comparationis* in order to explain the comparison of different things in the case law. For example, product requirements are unlawful because they discriminate on the basis of regulatory equivalence, with the host-State imposing an additional burden on products which have already been subject to rules pursuing the same regulatory goal in the home-State. On the other hand, selling arrangements will only be unlawful when they discriminate between products for which comparability was established on the basis of market equivalence.[18] The existence of multiple *tertia comparationis*, however, leads to completely different comparisons: even if measures that discriminate on the basis of regulatory equivalence may also indirectly discriminate on the basis of market equivalence, concerns about indirect discrimination against foreign products as they are placed in the market are incidental at best, and unproven at worst, because there is no effort to determine whether those products are market equivalent to begin with.[19]

The Treaties set forth that 'nationality' and 'the State of origin of a given product' are the relevant prohibited discrimination criteria. This is straightforward for cases of direct discrimination, but findings of indirect discrimination require an economic assessment of the practical effects of a measure. However, the Court of Justice has never seemed inclined to pursue the extensive empirical analysis its own test requires, relying instead on a series of intuitive rules that point towards discrimination but bear little relation to empirical evidence.[20] A good example of this can be found in a specific branch of case law that focuses on measures preventing both national and foreign economic agents from entering and competing in

[18] Wilsher, 'Does *Keck* Discrimination Make Any Sense?', 5–9.

[19] Findings of market equivalence are actually impossible in the case of product bans—ibid, 13—which is why they have to be accommodated as situations of regulatory equivalence. See Snell, *Goods and Services in EC Law*, 87. This does not only apply to bans on selling goods—Case 34/79 *Henn and Darby* [1979] E.C.R. 3795—but also to bans on the provision of services, for example in situations where, by requiring prior establishment, their provision is prevented—Case 39/75 *Coenen* [1975] E.C.R. 1547; Joined Cases C-110/78 and C-111/78 *Van Wesemael* [1979] E.C.R. 35.

[20] Wilsher, 'Does *Keck* Discrimination Make Any Sense?', 18–20.

consolidated national markets. Even though discriminatory effects are found on the grounds that measures protecting the existent players in a market—such as general bans on advertising[21] or requirements of physical presence in local markets[22]—affect foreign importers more adversely than domestic suppliers, such measures do not seem to distinguish on grounds of nationality.[23] Instead, the distinction is between established and incoming economic agents, or between local and non-local operators, regardless of their nationality.[24] In one of these cases, the Court of Justice went so far as to state that:

For a national measure to be characterised as discriminatory or protective within the meaning of the rules on the free movement of goods, it is not necessary for it to have the effect of favouring national products as a whole or of placing only imported products at a disadvantage and not national products.[25]

This is *prima facie* correct, since a measure that is detrimental to imports may also affect some national products. The problem with this approach is that it fails to provide any criteria to distinguish between those measures that may potentially affect a single imported product and those that amount to indirect discrimination for the purposes of the Treaty. The question is whether these two sets should actually overlap. After all, there are other options: is a measure to be prohibited if it applies to domestic and foreign products alike, as long as at least a single foreign product more is affected? Or should it be prohibited only if it applies mainly to foreign products? Or should a measure instead be deemed discriminatory only when it does not apply to foreign products the best treatment available for national products?

The approaches proposed in the literature and adopted by the Court of Justice completely evade the question of exactly what normative values are protected by the prohibition against discriminatory treatment. Since questions about how to distinguish between those measures that may potentially affect a single imported product and those that amount to indirect discrimination cannot be answered without a thorough understanding of

[21] Case C-412/93 *Leclerc-Siplec* [1995] E.C.R. I-0179 and Joined Cases C-34/95 to 36/95 *De Agostini* [1997] E.C.R. I-3843.

[22] See Case C-254/98 *TK-Heimdienst* [2000] E.C.R. I-151; Case C-322/01 *DocMorris* [2003] E.C.R. I-14887; Case C-141/07 *Commission v Germany* [2008] E.C.R. I-06935.

[23] As is made clear by Advocate General La Pergola's Opinion that there was no discrimination in *TK-Heimdienst*.

[24] Against this, see Tamara Perisin, *Free Movement of Goods and Limits of Regulatory Autonomy in the EU and WTO* (TMC Asser Press 2008), 36.

[25] *Commission v Germany*, para. 39.

what these values are, the Court of Justice's failure to answer this question has allowed for the finding of materially discriminatory effects in almost any situation. This derives from the fact that, since imports have to comply with different sets of rules, this may benefit domestic products or prevent imported products from enjoying a competitive advantage, simply because regulatory regimes are likely to push consumer behaviour in a way which will put the marketing of certain products—including imports—at a disadvantage, or because specific costs may arise from both the legal splintering of a company's activity into intra-State and inter-State activities and from that company's need to gain familiarity with foreign regulations.[26] As a result of the absence of parameters for the pursuit of comparison exercises, any factual difference in the impact of national rules on imported and domestic products can be considered discriminatory or protectionist, with the result that virtually any rule can be said to be discriminatory.

The use of discrimination tests in the free movement of persons suffers from similar problems. It is generally accepted that the Court of Justice has interpreted indirect discrimination broadly, using proxy criteria that allow for the identification of measures with the same effect as those that distinguish on the basis of nationality.[27] Moreover, the Court of Justice found that measures applying regardless of nationality, but which were empirically shown to apply mainly to nationals of other Member States, or that defined the conditions for the acquisition or retention of the right to benefits in such a way that they could only, or more easily, be satisfied by home-State nationals,[28] were also indirectly discriminatory.[29] In *O'Flynn*, a case on the free movement of workers, the Court of Justice tried to consolidate its case law on indirect discrimination by developing a formula:

[26] Damian Chalmers, 'Repackaging the Internal Market—The Ramifications of the *Keck* Judgement' (1994) 19 ELRev 385, 399; Maduro, 'Reforming the Market or the State?', 68; Snell, *Goods and Services in EC Law*, 85; Holger Spamann, 'Choice of Law in a Federal System and an Internal Market' [2001] Jean Monnet Working Paper 8/01, 33–34.

[27] Some go as far as asserting that any rule which had a territorial element was likely to be indirectly discriminatory—Spaventa, *Free Movement of Persons in the European Union*, 24–25.

[28] Case C-349/87 *Paraschi* [1991] E.C.R. I-4501, para. 23.

[29] Case 33/88 *Allué and Coonan* [1989] E.C.R. 1591; Joined cases C-259/91, C-331/91 and C-332/91 *Allué and Coonen and others* [1993] E.C.R. I-4309; Case C-272/92 *Spotti* [1993] E.C.R. I-5185.

> *...conditions imposed by national law must be regarded as indirectly discriminatory where, although applicable irrespective of nationality, they affect essentially migrant workers...or the great majority of those affected are migrant workers...where they are indistinctly applicable but can more easily be satisfied by national workers than by migrant workers...or where there is a risk that they may operate to the particular detriment of migrant workers.*[30]

However, the Court of Justice also stated that: '*It is not necessary in this respect to find that the provision in question does in practice affect a substantially higher proportion of migrant workers. It is sufficient that it is liable to have such an effect.*'[31] This formulation leads into the same kind of problems identified as regards material discrimination on the free movement of goods, since situations where there is a mere risk of foreigners being put in a worse situation than nationals can be deemed restrictive without the Court of Justice pursuing any empirical assessment as to whether this occurs in practice.[32] This includes, as with goods, situations where the restriction is local and thereby risks discriminating against non-local nationals as much as it does against foreigners.[33]

Virtually all cases concerning restrictions having a purely local dimension are good examples of how material discrimination can be incidental to virtually any national rule. The free movement of people leads to people having the right to choose the community where they live throughout the Union; but the mere existence of a community implies disadvantages to outsiders, which are not allowed to enjoy public goods or other local services in the same way as members of that community. Local obstacles will always exist, but if they are applied at an exclusively local level they are surely not being applied on grounds of nationality.[34] Findings of material discrimination seem, again, to result not from empirically grounded assessments, but from lack of thought concerning the identification of the values the law protects and lack of consideration of the necessary parameters required for the successful pursuit of discrimination analyses.

[30] Case C-237/94 *John O'Flynn* [1996] E.C.R. I-2617, para. 18.

[31] Ibid, para. 21. See also Case C-278/94 *Commission v Belgium* [1996] E.C.R. I-4307, para. 20; and Case C-332/05 *Cellozi* [2007] E.C.R. I-563, paras 26–27.

[32] See Gareth Davies, '"Any Place I Hang my Hat?" or: Residence is the New Nationality' (2005) 11 ELJ 43, 46–47.

[33] Case C-281/98 *Angonese* [2000] E.C.R. I-4139, concerning the demand for language certificates issued by the province of Bolzano in Italy as a requirement for bi-lingual speakers to gain access to employment; and *Commission v Italy*, concerning a requirement that, in order to be registered, dentists must have their residence or practise their profession in the district of the professional body or association where they are registered—thereby precluding the opening of secondary establishments—provide good examples.

[34] Davies, '"Any Place I Hang my Hat?" or: Residence is the New Nationality', 55–56.

Furthermore, it can be said that the Court of Justice has expressly abandoned nationality as the only criterion for discrimination regarding the free movement of persons. The very first case where a national measure was struck down as an unjustified restriction on the free provision of services concerned the situation of a Dutch lawyer who had moved to Belgium and was prevented from practising in the Netherlands by a residency requirement for lawyers practising there.[35] It was also held from an early stage that prohibiting establishment on the grounds that the relevant person already had a different place of establishment was restrictive, with the result that discrimination was prohibited not only against foreigners or companies trying to establish themselves in a host-State, but also against a State's own nationals when they were trying to establish themselves in a State other than the one where they resided.[36] For workers, the Court of Justice eventually also held that, alongside measures distinguishing on grounds of nationality, national legislation, which might place nationals at a disadvantage when they wished to extend their activities beyond the territory of a single Member State by placing those nationals who migrate in a worse position than those who have not, was prohibited unless justified.[37]

National measures are thereby unlawful not only when they distinguish on grounds of nationality, but also when they are found to discriminate against cross-border movement.[38] This can be said to have found expression in the case law on the free movement of persons, which contains provisions that

> ...*are intended to facilitate the pursuit by Community nationals of occupational activities of all kinds throughout the European Community, and preclude measures which might place them at a disadvantage when they wish to pursue an economic activity in the territory of another Member State.*[39]

[35] Case 33/74 *van Binsbergen* [1974] E.C.R. 1299.

[36] Case 107/83 *Klopp* [1984] E.C.R. 2971. This applies also to a person who is employed in one Member State and wishes, in addition, to work in another Member State in a self-employed capacity, or vice-versa: see *Stanton; Wolf and Dorchain*, Case C-351/90 *Commission v Luxembourg* [1992] E.C.R. I-3945.

[37] *Stanton*. This includes not only rules by a home-State which apply to nationals moving abroad, but also to those returning home: Case C-392/05 *Alevizos* [2007] E.C.R. I-3505. See also D. Martin, 'Discriminations, Entraves et Raison Impérieuses' [1998] CDE 561.

[38] It might very well be that the only reason this approach was never adopted for goods is that this is the only freedom which has different provisions for entry (imports) and exit (exports) situations. See Marek Szydlo, 'Export Restrictions within the Structure of Free Movement of Goods. Reconsideration of an Old Paradigm' (2010) 47 CML Rev 753, 753–754.

[39] Case C-527/06 *Renneberg* [2004] E.C.R. I-7735, para. 43; Case C-314/08 *Filipiak* [2009] E.C.R. I-11049, para. 58.

This development, however, gives rise to problems as to how to conceptualize the case law in light of the Treaties. Some have tried to interpret the case law as applying traditional discrimination tests,[40] while others have favoured a discrimination test while admitting that nationality was no longer the sole relevant criterion.[41] Yet another alternative was to conceptualize the case law as prohibiting discrimination against cross-border situations, according to which a restriction on free movement is found if the treatment a national rule grants to a situation containing cross-border elements is worse than that granted to exclusively domestic situations.[42]

The Court of Justice itself never seemed sure how to justify this approach in light of the Treaties. It considered in some cases that rules that discriminate against free movement indirectly discriminate on grounds of nationality, while in others it held that mobility is a prohibited criterion of differentiation under the Treaty. On yet other occasions, it held that discrimination against free movement constitutes an obstacle to free movement outside the scope of traditional discrimination analyses.[43]

Part of the reason for this confusion is that cases of indirect discrimination on grounds of nationality—which are identified by criteria like residence or employment in a foreign country—will collapse into discrimination against free movement when the complainant is a national residing abroad but working in her home-State, or is someone who has resided or worked abroad and decided to return to her home-State. In these cases, the only relevant difference between applying these different discrimination tests is the nationality of the complainant.[44] But another reason for this confusion is that, since material discrimination as used by the Court of Justice can be extended to encompass virtually any rule, measures discriminating against free movement can

[40] Denis Martin, 'Réflexions sur le champ d'application de l'Article 48 du Traité CE' [1993] CDE 555, 596.

[41] Esther Johnson and David O'Keefe, 'From Discrimination to Obstacles to Free Movement: Recent Developments Concerning the Free Movement of Workers' (1994) 31 CML Rev 1313, 1332; Spaventa, *Free Movement of Persons in the European Union*, 23.

[42] Cordewener, 'The Prohibitions of Discrimination and Restriction within the Framework of the Fully Integrated Internal Market', .

[43] Anastasia Iliopoulou and Helen Toner, 'A New Approach to Discrimination Against Free Movement? *D'Hoop v Office National de lÉmploi*' (2003) 28 ELRev 392. See, for services, Case C-198/89 *Tourist Guides Greece* [1991] E.C.R. I-00727, para. 16; Case C-154/89 *Tourist Guides France* [1991] E.C.R. I-00659, para. 12.

[44] See Case C-436/00 *X and Y* [2002] E.C.R. I-10829; Case C-269/07 *Commission v Germany* [2009] E.C.R. I-07811.

be reconceptualized as discrimination on grounds of nationality by looking at the facts differently.[45]

The problems with discriminatory approaches are the same throughout the freedoms: they fail to determine the relevant *tertium comparationis*; they have recourse to different prohibited discrimination criteria without any consideration of their normative foundations; and they use an indirect/material discrimination test which can be extended to encompass virtually any rule when, as is the Court of Justice's practice, no empirical assessment is pursued. These issues are pervasive both in academic approaches and in the Court of Justice's case law, demonstrating a deficient understanding of the necessary normative underpinnings of anti-discrimination tests.

The relevant question for any discrimination test is not merely how to distinguish between selective and non-selective rules, since economic rules will always 'select' some situations to regulate. The question is whether that specific 'selection' and the level of differentiation it entails are acceptable. The existing approaches reflect a lack of normative anchoring that makes the discrimination test too malleable and unclear to have any explanatory value.[46] The discrimination test is the most traditional and widely used tool in international economic law and constitutional law to identify protectionism; a structured theory of anti-protectionism was never articulated regarding the market freedoms. Furthermore, the market freedoms have been used to remove national measures posing obstacles to trade other than traditional protectionist ones.[47] A more sophisticated approach is required to determine why certain measures are acceptable and others not. Otherwise, discrimination-based approaches will risk prohibiting all national measures and will eventually overlap with economic due-process tests, to which we now turn our attention.[48]

[45] Say, from the perspective of an employer instead of the employee. See Case C-232/01 *van Lent* [2003] E.C.R. I-11525, particularly paras 19–21.

[46] Maduro, *We, the Court*, 43; Martin, 'Discriminations, Entraves et Raison Impérieuses', 632; Gareth Davies, 'Understanding Market Access: Exploring the Economic Rationality of Different Conceptions of Free Movement Law' (2010) 11 GLJ 671, 680.

[47] Perisin, *Free Movement of Goods and Limits of Regulatory Autonomy in the EU and WTO*, 39; Imelda Higgins, 'The Free and not so Free Movement of Goods Since *Keck*' (1997) 6 IrJEurL 166, 176; Maduro, *We, the Court*, 68–70.

[48] Maduro, *We, the Court*, 84 and 162; Piet Eeckhout, 'After *Keck and Mithouard*: Free Movement of Goods in the EC, Market Access and Non-Discrimination' in Thomas Cottier and Petros C. Mavroidis (eds), *Regulatory Barriers and the Principle of Non-Discrimination in World Trade Law* (The University of Michigan Press 2000), 203. This is also recognized by proponents of discriminatory approaches. See Snell, *Goods and Services in EC Law*, 85; Davies, 'Understanding Market Access', 676, apparently proposing *de minimis* limits to the amount of material discrimination necessary. Defending this approach, see the seminal

IV. Economic Due Process

The original departure from a discriminatory approach by the law on free movement is usually presented as the result of two cases on the free movement of goods. The most important is arguably the latter one, *Cassis de Dijon*, which adopted a notably elliptical formula:

Obstacles to movement within the Community resulting from disparities between national laws relating to the marketing of the products in question must be accepted in so far as those provisions may be recognised as being necessary in order to satisfy mandatory requirements…[49]

In the absence of such mandatory requirements, there was '*no valid reason why, provided that they have been lawfully produced and marketed in one of the Member States, alcoholic beverages should not be introduced in any other Member State*'.[50]

One possible interpretation of this case was that a product could be subject to non-discriminatory marketing rules in its country-of-origin but not in another country where it was also sold, unless the rules of the country-of-origin did not provide for an equivalent level of regulatory protection as the rules of the country of sale. In other words, *Cassis de Dijon* could be read as establishing a mutual recognition system that adopted a country-of-origin principle as long as regulatory equivalence existed between the relevant States.[51]

On the other hand, *Cassis de Dijon* also opened the door for a widening of the concept of restriction on the free movement of goods. The concept of obstacles had been previously developed in *Dassonville*, which had held that:

All trading rules enacted by Member States which are capable of hindering, directly or indirectly, actually or potentially, intra-Community trade are to be considered measures having an equivalent effect to quantitative restrictions.[52]

Donald H. Regan, 'Judicial Review of Member-State Regulation of Trade within a Federal or Quasi-Federal System: Protectionism and Balancing, "Da Capo"' 99 MichLRev 1853.

[49] *Cassis de Dijon*, para. 8.

[50] Ibid, para. 14.

[51] On this, or advocating this view of mutual recognition, Joseph Weiler, 'Mutual Recognition, Functional Equivalence and Harmonization in the Evolution of the European Common Market and the WTO' in Fiorella Kostoris Padoa Schioppa (ed.), *The Principle of Mutual Recognition in the European Integration Process* (Palmgrave Macmillan 2005), 25; Kalypso Nicolaïdis, 'Globalization with Human Faces: Managed Mutual Recognition and the Free Movement of Professionals' in Fiorella Kostoris Padoa Schioppa (ed.), *The Principle of Mutual Recognition in the European Integration Process* (Palmgrave Macmillan 2005), 142; Markus Möstl, 'Preconditions and Limits of Mutual Recognition' (2010) 47 CML Rev 405; Vassilis Hatzopoulos, 'Le principe de reconnaissance mutuelle dans la prestation des services' [2010] CDE 47.

[52] *Dassonville*, para. 5.

When articulated with *Dassonville*, *Cassis de Dijon* could be read in at least two ways in addition to a mutual recognition approach: as applying a pure country-of-origin principle, labelling as restrictive any double-regulation regardless of the level of regulation in the home and host-States; or, by focusing exclusively on the *Dassonville* formula, as prohibiting all individual national rules which could have an effect on intra-Union trade, even if non-discriminatory or protectionist, unless they were justified by mandatory requirements.

While *Cassis de Dijon* extended the concept of restriction to encompass perfectly reasonable disparities in national laws concerning the marketing of products, together with *Dassonville* it also opened the door to a market economy with no political regulation beyond that necessary to guarantee equal opportunity in the market and protect free competition. This latter possibility was bound eventually to emerge in the case law, and arguably it raised its head in *Cinétèque*, a case concerning whether a legal regime establishing a non-commercialization period between the end of the period of a film in movie theatres and the date of the start of commercialization of that same film through videocassettes could create barriers to intra-Union trade in videocassettes when these were already marketed in other Member States.[53] Advocate General Slynn argued that the purpose of the free movement of goods was merely to remove national measures protecting domestic products. Instead, a measure should only be found to be restrictive if it was directed at, discriminated against, or gave protection to domestic producers against imports—none of which could be said to be the case of the measure *sub judice*. The Court of Justice, however, ignored the Advocate General, and held that a legal regime establishing a non-commercialization period between the date when a film was no longer in movie theatres and the date when it was commercialized via video cassettes could create barriers to intra-Union trade in videocassettes when these were already marketed in other Member States. This case was soon followed by *Commission v France*, where the Court of Justice held that a total prohibition on the marketing of both national and foreign products intended to replace milk powder or concentrated milk and composed of products other than milk was contrary to the free movement of goods on the sole basis that it applied to imported products—even though the ban on sales applied equally to foreign and national products.[54] Both these cases took the *Cassis de Dijon* formula and ran with

[53] Case 60/84 and 61/84 *Cinéthèque* [1985] E.C.R. 2605.

[54] Case 216/84 *Commission v France* [1988] E.C.R. 793.

it, replacing the mutual recognition approach with a pure version of the country-of-origin principle: as long as a product was lawfully marketed in a Member State, preventing it from circulating in another Member State was a restriction on free movement that needed to be justified.

The decisions in these cases were soon followed by the so-called '*Sunday Trading*' cases, concerning national measures prohibiting the opening of commercial premises on Sundays.[55] The first of these cases read *Cinétèque* as having stated that a marketing prohibition

> *... applicable to domestic and imported products alike [was] not compatible with the principle of the free movement of goods provided for in the Treaty unless any obstacle to Community trade thereby created did not exceed what was necessary in order to ensure the attainment of the objective in view and unless that objective was justified with regard to Community law.*[56]

The Court of Justice went on to hold that a prohibition on marketing goods on Sundays was restrictive merely because it might restrict the total volume of sales.[57] The main justification for finding that non-discriminatory measures were restrictive ceased to be based on a country-of-origin principle, but focused instead on the impact, however slight, that a measure could have on imports, regardless of whether it had the same effect on national products. Since virtually any rule can have an impact on the total volume of trade,[58] this equated the free movement of goods with an economic due-process clause, i.e. a test according to which any rule that can impact on trade, and thus on economic freedom, is subject to judicial review as to whether it is justified.[59]

This test was not only identified from a descriptive standpoint in the academic literature:[60] some also actively defended it from a normative standpoint. It was argued that a clear application of the *Dassonville* formula, coupled

[55] See fn. 3 above. [56] *Torfaen*, para. 12.

[57] *Conforama*, para. 8; *Marchandise*, para. 9.

[58] White, 'In Search of the Limits to Article 30 of the EEC Treaty', 246.

[59] Since the Court of Justice can also apply this test to persons in situations where no economic interest exists—namely as regards European Citizenship—the concept of economic due-process is limited to the market freedoms. In a theory encompassing all free movement provisions—economic and non-economic—this would probably be more appropriately called a rule of reason, since it would require a general balancing of costs and benefits between differing public values. See Borgmann-Prebil, 'The Rule of Reason in European Citizenship'.

[60] Even though a number of cases militated against it, inasmuch as they held that national rules fell outside the scope of the free movement of goods in a manner inconsistent with the *Sunday Trading* cases: see Case C-260/89 *ERT* [1991] E.C.R. I-2925; Case 155/80 *Oebel* [1981] E.C.R. 1993; Case 75/81 *Blesgen* [1982] E.C.R. 1211; Case 148/85 *Forest* [1986] E.C.R. 3449; Case 286/81 *Oosthoek's* [1982] E.C.R. 4575; Case C-23/89 *Quietlynn* [1990] E.C.R. I-3059; Case C-69/88 *Krantz* [1990] E.C.R. I-00583.

with proper argumentation and the judicious use of balancing exercises, was an appropriate approach that could provide clear guidance on the precise practical application of the free movement of goods to Member States and national courts alike.[61]

On the other hand, normative arguments against this approach could also be found in the academic literature. The first such argument was that, whereas an economic due-process clause inherently espoused an ordo-liberal perspective, promoting the removal of any unjustified restriction on unfettered competition and free movement, this was not the underlying normative underpinning of the market freedoms.[62] The question was, as Advocate General Tesauro put it:

> *Is Article [34] of the Treaty a provision intended to liberalize intra-Community trade or is it intended more generally to encourage the unhindered pursuit of commerce in individual Member States?... [The latter option] means that any measure which might potentially reduce the volume of trade, however minimally, would be prima facie, a restriction on the free movement of goods... [In the former option, on the other hand] the purpose of Article [34] [would be] to ensure the free movement of goods in order to establish a single integrated market, eliminating therefore those national measures which in any way create an obstacle to or even mere difficulties for the movement of goods; its purpose is not to strike down the most widely differing measures in order, essentially, to ensure the greatest possible expansion of trade.*[63]

Secondly, findings of restriction require the Court of Justice to pursue balancing exercises; and the more situations in which the Court of Justice (and national courts) are required to pursue such a balancing, the more they become responsible for defining the appropriate regulatory policy. Should there be regulation? If so, who should regulate? Are there any substantive limits to what regulators may impose? If so, what are they? Answers to these questions require value judgements on broad policy questions, with the implication that economic due-process clauses raise serious issues of judicial

[61] See Laurence Gormley, '"Actually or Potentially, Directly or Indirectly?" Obstacles to the Free Movement of Goods' (1989) 9 YEL 197, and Laurence Gormley, 'Recent Case Law on the Free Movement of Goods: Some Hot Potatoes' (1990) 27 CML Rev 825, 857; Anthony Arnull, 'What Shall We Do on a Sunday?' (1991) 16 ELRev 112. See also, slightly differently, Wouter P. J. Wils, 'The Search for a Rule in Article 30 EEC: Much Ado About Nothing?' (1993) 18 ELRev 475.

[62] On the influence ordo-liberals had during the early stages of the European project, see Maduro, 'Reforming the Market or the State?', 55–56; Gerber, 'Constitutionalizing the Economy'.

[63] Advocate General Tesauro's Opinion in Case C-292/92 *Hünermund* [1993] E.C.R. I-6787, paras 1, 10 and 28. See also Advocate General van Gerven's Opinion in *Torfaen*.

legitimacy.[64] This is compounded by the fact that the proportionality test, as applied by the Court of Justice, is unable to produce a single coherent result for each situation, which became clear as different national courts reached contradictory decisions on whether rules prohibiting the opening of stores on Sundays were justified or not, thereby contradicting the arguments that economic due-process clauses could provide clear guidance and legal certainty.[65]

V. Typological Approaches

Criticisms of the economic due-process test were usually coupled with the suggested adoption of a different test.[66] One of these tests—developed by one of the Commission's agents at the Court of Justice, and advanced by some Advocates General[67]—was eventually adopted by the Court of Justice in *Keck and Mithouard*. This test built on a distinction, implicit in some interpretations of *Cassis de Dijon*, between rules requiring changes to be made to products before they could be marketed in a host-State and discriminatory rules.[68] Following this, the Court of Justice distinguished in *Keck* between rules concerning product requirements—meaning '*rules that lay down requirements to be met by [goods coming from other Member States where they are lawfully manufactured and marketed] (such as those relating to designation, form, size, weight, composition, presentation, labelling, packaging)*', which were deemed restrictive regardless of whether they were indistinctly applicable to national and foreign products alike—and rules concerning certain

[64] Maduro, 'Reforming the Market or the State?', 55–7; and Maduro, *We, the Court*, 35.

[65] J. Steiner, 'Drawing the Line: Uses and Abuses of Article 30 EEC' (1992) 29 CML Rev 749, 755–762.

[66] Kamiel Mortelmans, 'Article 30 of the EEC Treaty and Legislation Relating to Market Circumstances: Time to Consider a New Definition?' (1991) 28 CML Rev 115; Steiner, 'Drawing the Line', 769–772; Norbert Reich, 'The "November Revolution" of the European Court of Justice: *Keck*, *Meng* and *Audi* revisited' (1994) 31 CML Rev 459, 467.

[67] White, 'In Search of the Limits to Article 30 of the EEC Treaty'; Advocate General van Gerven's Opinion in *Torfaen*; Advocate General Tesauro's Opinion in *Hünermund*.

[68] This reading is typical of discriminatory approaches—see fn. 15 above. The similarity of tests may have to do with the fact that both Marenco and White were Commission Agents with the Court of Justice, which might also have something to do with the Court having adopted this particular typological test.

selling arrangements, which did not infringe the rules on free movement of goods unless they discriminated, in law or in fact, between the marketing of domestic and foreign products. In the Court of Justice's view, measures that respect these principles '*do not prevent access to the market, nor impede access any more than it impedes the access of domestic products*'.[69]

Keck was more reform than revolution: the *Dassonville* and *Cassis* tests were perfected in order to increase legal certainty and reduce the Court of Justice's caseload.[70] Following Advocate General Tesauro's lead, the typology adopted was seen as a means to distinguish between measures that merely reduce the economic attractiveness of pursuing a given activity and those measures that effectively restrict free movement rights within the framework of the Treaty.

Rather than solving the academic debate, however, *Keck* merely changed its focus. If, on the one hand, *Keck* was said to increase legal certainty, and to have clarified the case law by expressly repudiating ordo-liberal readings of the free movement of goods,[71] on the other hand it was argued that the *Keck* typology still did not accurately reflect the normative underpinning of the free movement of goods.[72] This latter argument was that a typological test will only be normatively apt if it is able perfectly to marry the nature of national measures to their effect. Since the effect of a measure may depend on the particular situation and structure of a specific market, while the nature of a measure has to be determined in the abstract, the nature of a measure and its effects may not always correspond. In the case of obstacles to the free movement of goods, an almost infinite range of domestic policies

[69] *Keck and Mithouard*, paras 15–17.

[70] Maduro, 'Reforming the Market or the State?', 58. The Court of Justice justified its decision thus, in para. 14:

In view of the increasing tendency of traders to invoke Article 30 of the Treaty as a means of challenging any rules whose effect is to limit their commercial freedom even where such rules are not aimed at products from other Member States, the Court considers it necessary to re-examine and clarify its case-law on this matter.

[71] Reich, 'The "November Revolution" of the European Court of Justice', 480; Stephen Weatherill, 'After *Keck*: Some Thoughts on How to Clarify the Clarification' (1996) 33 CML Rev 885, 886; Barnard, 'Fitting the Remaining Pieces into the Goods and Persons Jigsaw?', 42; Maduro, *We, the Court*, 83; Snell, *Goods and Services in EC Law*, 78, 98; Bernard, 'Discrimination and Free Movement in EC Law', 101.

[72] Advocate General Jacobs' Opinion in *Leclerc-Siplec*; Weatherill, 'After *Keck*'; Barnard, 'Fitting the Remaining Pieces into the Goods and Persons Jigsaw?'; Niamh Nic Shuibhne, 'The Free Movement of Goods and Article 28 EC: An Evolving Framework' (2002) 27 ELRev 408; Eeckhout, 'Constitutional Concepts for Free Trade in Services', 216, 225; Schillig, 'The Interpretation of European Private Law in the Light of Market Freedoms and EU Fundamental Rights', 290; Snell, *Goods and Services in EC Law*, 98–99 and 117.

can have an effect on both trade flows and market access: non-tariff barriers have such variety and complexity that they present serious definitional problems.[73] The nature of a measure, even if it may provide a good indication as to its effect, does not determine what this effect will be in every conceivable situation. This lack of correspondence between a measure's nature and effect was apparent in certain descriptive failings of the *Keck* typology, which was unable to encompass measures that undoubtedly have an effect equivalent to a quantitative restriction but are not easily categorized as either product requirement or selling arrangements—such as frontier inspections on imported goods[74] or rules on the exercise of intellectual property rights.[75]

It seemed that any attempt to maintain *Keck*'s formalistic approach and ensure that such an approach would fit a normative framework requiring that no genuine obstacle to free movement be left in placewould lead to either: an extension of the concept of product requirements to measures which restrict free movement even though they are not product requirements *per se*; or to a number of 'selling arrangements' being held discriminatory even though that was not really the case; or even to the Court of Justice ignoring the typology it had developed when that typology became inconvenient. Such an attempt may even lead to all of these outcomes combined. Arguably, this is exactly what happened.

The concept of product requirements has been extended beyond its original boundaries, to the point where it includes certain measures that regulate the marketing of a product but have an impact on its actual content or packaging.[76] A number of rules on selling arrangements were found to be discriminatory in cases where it was extremely controversial that this was actually the case, such as general restrictions on advertising[77] or requirements of physical presence in local markets.[78,79] Further, the *Keck* typology was ignored in a variety of cases

[73] Stanley D. Metzger, *Lowering Non-tariff Barriers*, 7–8; Robert Howse and Donal Regan, 'The Product/Process Distinction: An Illusory Basis for Disciplining "Unilateralism" in Trading' 11 EJIL 249, 253.

[74] Case 35/76 *Simmenthal* [1976] E.C.R. 1871; Case 190/87 *Moormann* [1988] E.C.R. 4689.

[75] Case 78/70 *Deutsche Grammophon* [1971] E.C.R. 487; Case 15/74 *Centrafarm v Sterling* [1974] E.C.R. 1147; Case 187/80 *Merck v Stephar* [1981] E.C.R. 2063; Joined Cases 55/80 and 57/80 *Musik-Vertrieb* [1981] E.C.R. 147.

[76] Case C-315/92 *Estée Lauder* [1994] E.C.R. I-00317; Case C-470/93 *Mars* [1996] E.C.R. I-1923; Case C-368/95 *Familiapress* [1997] E.C.R. I-3689, and, arguably, *Alfa Vita Vassilopoulos*.

[77] *De Agostini;* Case C-405/98 *Gourmet International* [2001] E.C.R. I-1795; Case C-239/02 *Douwe Egberts* [2004] E.C.R. I-7007.

[78] See *TK-Heimdienst; DocMorris; Commission v Germany*.

[79] See Wilsher, 'Does *Keck* Discrimination Make Any Sense?', 3. This relates to the possibilities for manipulation that normatively unanchored discrimination tests allow that were reviewed above—see in particular the text between fn. 26 and 46 above.

where it arguably did not fit the measures under review,[80] such as rules on inspections of imported products,[81] restrictions on transport,[82] obligations to collect data for statistical purposes,[83] and failures to act by a Member State.[84] Finally, in a number of cases, the focus was on the effects of a measure instead of on trying to apply the *Keck* typology.[85]

VI. Access to Market

In their attempts to criticize *Keck* while sympathizing with its goal of avoiding an economic due-process clause, Advocate General Jacobs and some commentators tried to advance the argument that, instead of adopting a typological approach for its own sake, *Keck* merely used such an approach as a means to identify those measures that restricted free movement by affecting a product's access to the market.[86]

To understand this new test for goods, it is important to describe the evolution of the field where the access to the market test was first applied autonomously—the free movement of persons. The Court of Justice had originally framed its approach to the free movement of persons under the banner of discrimination. Nonetheless, such an approach was descriptively inept. For example, from very early on, the Court of Justice had held that any rule which imposed upon a service provider an obligation to fulfil all requirements applicable to established persons in a host-State infringed upon the freedom to provide cross-border services. Any such requirement was only justified if the home-State did not have a similar level of control or supervision over the service provider as the host-State required for service providers based therein.[87] This approach was similar to that adopted in *Cassis de Dijon*.

[80] Or where it did fit but nevertheless the Court of Justice ignored the typology: Case C-337/95 *Evora* [1997] E.C.R. I-6013; Case C-358/95 *Morellato* [1997] E.C.R. I-1431.

[81] Case C-105/94 *Ditta A. Celestini* [1997] E.C.R. I-2971.

[82] Case C-350/97 *Wilfried Monsees* [1999] E.C.R. I-2921.

[83] Case C-114/96 *Kieffer and Thill* [1997] E.C.R. I-3629.

[84] *Commission v France*.

[85] Case C-189/95 *Franzén* [1997] E.C.R. I-5909 and Case C-323/93 *Crespelle* [1994] E.C.R. I-5077.

[86] Advocate General Jacobs' Opinion *Leclerc-Siplec*. See, in particular, Weatherill, 'After *Keck*'.

[87] *van Binsbergen*; *Van Wesemael*; Case 279/80 *Webb* [1981] E.C.R. 3305, *Commission v Germany*; Case C-355/98 *Commission v Belgium* [2000] E.C.R. I-1221.

There, a country-of-origin principle was coupled with mutual recognition requirements, which were recognized, as regards the free movement of goods, not to amount to discrimination but to an obstacle-based approach.[88] The Court of Justice eventually acknowledged that the free provision of services:

> *...require(s) not only the abolition of any discrimination against a person providing services on account of his nationality but also the abolition of any restriction on the freedom to provide services imposed on the ground that the person providing a service is established in a Member State other than the one in which the service is provided. In particular, the Member State cannot make the performance of the services in its territory subject to observance of all the conditions required for establishment; were it to do so the provisions securing freedom to provide services would be deprived of all practical effect.*[89]

In *Säger*, this formula was extended into a pure obstacle-based approach similar to that arising out of *Dassonville*, with the Court of Justice stating that the free provision of services:

> *...requires not only the elimination of all discrimination against a person providing services on the ground of his nationality but also the abolition of any restriction, even if it applies without distinction to national providers of services and to those of other Member States, when it is liable to prohibit or otherwise impede the activities of a provider of services established in another Member State where he lawfully provides similar services.*[90]

This replacement of discrimination by an obstacle-based approach for the free provision of services was mimicked in the fields of workers and establishment. The starting point for this was, again, mutual recognition, this time the mutual recognition of professional qualifications. This area was originally regulated by secondary legislation, particularly a number of Directives focusing on: (i) transitional measures, whereby, pending mutual recognition of diplomas, recognition was granted in certain areas to professionals who had pursued a professional activity for a certain period; (ii) co-ordinating training requirements and professional qualifications, in particular concerning health-related activities; (iii) co-ordinating national requirements applicable to architects; and (iv) the possibility of pursuing legal activities under a national title in another Member State.[91] Finally, in

[88] Hatzopoulos, 'Le principe de reconnaissance mutuelle dans la prestation des services', 73–74.

[89] *Tourist Guides Greece*, para. 16. See also *Tourist Guides France*; Case C-180/89 *Tourist Guides Italy* [1991] E.C.R. I-00709; Case C-375/92 *Commission v Spain* [1994] E.C.R. I-0923.

[90] *Säger*, para. 12.

[91] See Rolf Wägenbauer, 'Free Movement in the Professions: The New EEC Proposal on Professional Qualifications' (1986) 23 CML Rev 91, 94–97.

1985, the Commission submitted a new draft Directive 'on a *general* system of recognition of higher education diplomas' which added to, but did not replace, the existing sectoral directives on mutual recognition.[92]

Initially, the Court of Justice merely applied this secondary legislation without finding that any right to mutual recognition of diplomas arose directly from Treaty provisions, meaning that to refuse mutual recognition in the absence of secondary legislation was the States' prerogative.[93] But eventually the Court of Justice reversed its case law and started holding that national requirements concerning professional qualifications might have the effect of restricting the right of establishment or the free movement of workers, even if applied without any discrimination on grounds of nationality.[94] This was taken to its logical conclusion in *Kraus*, where the Court of Justice held that any national measure governing the conditions under which an academic title obtained in another Member State may be used was restrictive:

> ...*where that measure, even though it is applicable without discrimination on grounds of nationality, is liable to hamper or to render less attractive the exercise by Community nationals, including those of the Member State which enacted the measure, of fundamental freedoms guaranteed by the Treaty.*[95]

At this stage, a number of different obstacle-based approaches co-existed in the case law: *Dassonville* focused on trade rules capable of hindering inter-State trade; *Säger* looked into whether a measure was capable of prohibiting or otherwise impeding the cross-border provision of services; *Kraus* and *Gebhard* were concerned with whether a measure could hamper or render less attractive the exercise of the market freedoms. Nonetheless, all these formulae were interchangeable in the way they focused on situations or measures that might be liable to hinder or impede the cross-border exercise of market freedoms. Furthermore, these formulae faced the same problems as material discrimination and economic due-process clauses. Like material discrimination, any

[92] Council Directive 89/48/EEC [1988] OJ L 19, 16–23 on a general system for the recognition of higher-education diplomas awarded on completion of professional education and training of at least three years' duration, replaced by Council Directive 92/51/EEC [1992] OJ L 209, 25–45 on a second general system for the recognition of professional education and training to supplement Directive 89/48/EEC. See also Directive 2005/36/EC [2005] OJ L255/22 on the recognition of professional qualifications.

[93] Case 136/78 *Auer* [1979] E.C.R. 437; Case 271/82 *Auer II* [1983] E.C.R. 2727; Case C-61/89 *Bouchoucha* [1990] E.C.R. I-3551.

[94] Case 222/86 *Unectef v Heylens* [1987] E.C.R. 4097; *Vlassopoulou.*

[95] *Kraus*, para. 32.

disparity between national rules can be seen as an impediment to free movement inasmuch as persons or products might face stricter requirements in the host-State than in the home-State, or merely by requiring the product or person moving to adapt to a new set of legal rules. Like economic due-process clauses, these formulae may also be used to support the finding that reductions in the volume of economic activities, or limitations in the manner whereby such activities can be pursued, somehow impede or make less attractive the exercise of the market freedoms, particularly when those economic activities are subject to a lighter regulatory regime in their home-State.

The question that these formulae raised was, once again, how to distinguish between obstacles to cross-border economic activity that were prohibited for the purposes of the Treaty and those obstacles that are merely incidental to the legitimate regulation of economic activity. This question had been already addressed regarding goods by *Keck*'s typological approach. Hidden in this case's reasoning, however, was a justification for why only discriminatory selling arrangements could restrict the free movement of goods: namely, because a non-discriminatory selling arrangement would not '*prevent access to the market or impede access any more than it impedes the access of domestic product*'.[96]

Since *Keck* was adopted precisely as the tests on the free movement of persons were catching up with the original obstacle-based approach for goods, it is not surprising that it was thought by some that the reasoning in *Keck* was also applicable to market freedoms other than goods. In *Alpine*, a case concerning the free provision of services decided shortly after *Keck*, it was pleaded that a rule by the State of establishment prohibiting the practice of 'cold calling' by financial service providers to potential clients in other States, even when such States allowed 'cold calling' in their territory, concerned selling arrangements and should, as in *Keck*, only be found restrictive if the rule was discriminatory. The Court of Justice addressed this argument by holding that:

> *A prohibition such as that at issue is imposed by the Member State in which the provider of services is established and affects not only offers made by him to addressees who are established in that State or move there in order to receive services but also offers made to potential recipients in another Member State. It therefore directly affects access to the market in services in the other Member States and is thus capable of hindering intra-Community trade in services.*[97]

[96] *Keck and Mithouard*, para. 17.

[97] *Alpine*, paras 37–38. This reasoning has also been used to explain why *Keck*'s typological distinction is not applicable to certain analogous measure under the free movement of capital: see Case C-543/08 *Commission v Portugal* [2010] E.C.R. I-11241, paras 67–68.

Keck and *Alpine* were the first cases where the expression 'access to the market' is used.[98] While it is debatable whether *Alpine* embraced *Keck* or whether instead it expressly refused to do so, what is undeniable is that, while the Court of Justice stuck with the *Keck* typology in goods, it started having recourse to a test based on market access for the other freedoms. Having first expressly used the test in *Alpine* for the free provision of services, the Court of Justice soon after applied it to the free movement of workers in *Bosman*.[99] The relevant question concerned transfer indemnities rules, according to which professional footballers could not transfer to a new club unless they had paid their former club a transfer fee agreed upon between the two clubs or determined in accordance with the regulations of the relevant sporting associations. Advocate General Lenz admitted that pure obstacle-based approaches could entail a very broad concept of restriction on free movement, and observed that the Court of Justice had in *Keck* reined in the obstacle test for goods.[100] He further noted that:

> *[In* Alpine*, the Court of Justice] considered that the ground for the decision reached in* Keck and Mithouard *lay in the fact that the provision at issue in that case was not such as to 'prevent' access of foreign products to the market or 'impede such access more than it impedes access by domestic products'. The prohibition at issue in Alpine Investments, by contrast, 'directly affects access to the market in services in the other Member States and is thus capable of hindering intra-Community trade in services'. That reasoning can be applied to the field of [workers]. It must be noted in particular that the transfer rules at issue in the present case directly affect access to the employment market in other Member States.*[101]

The Court of Justice, even though following a different line of reasoning, went on to hold that the relevant rules directly affected players' access to the employment market in other Member States, and prohibited them.[102] In 2003, the Court of Justice extended the market access test to the free movement of capital,[103] and in the following year to establishment.[104] Finally, recent decisions in the field of goods point to the adoption of an access to market test, bringing the case law full circle and establishing

[98] Advocate General Tesauro's Opinion in *Hünermund*, particularly para. 25; *Keck and Mithouard*, para. 17.

[99] *Bosman*.

[100] See paras 204–205 of the AG's Opinion.

[101] AG's Opinion, para. 206. See also Advocate General Tizzano's Opinion in *CaixaBank*, paras 73-74.

[102] Ibid, para. 103.

[103] *Commission v UK*, paras 45–47.

[104] *CaixaBank*.

market access as the key criterion forthe Court of Justice's free movement jurisprudence.[105]

What is the meaning of 'market access', however? Even though a new arrival to the internal market scene, this concept is an old acquaintance in competition law and in industrial economic studies on barriers to entry.[106] The concept corresponds broadly to two different economic views: the first one, associated with Harvard's structure-performance-conduct paradigm, sees as a barrier to market access any kind of advantage enjoyed by established sellers allowing them to sell above a competitive price without new competitors entering the market. Barriers to entry exist each time the entrant cannot achieve the profit-levels post-entry that the incumbent enjoyed prior to its arrival.[107] This is a very broad approach, in that, unless the market is perfectly competitive, virtually any cost or obstacle in accessing a market—such as economies of scale, advertising, or capital requirements—will be deemed a barrier to entry.[108] If this conception were adopted for the market freedoms, any State regulation that can have a negative effect on a credible opportunity for trade would be susceptible to being deemed a restriction on free movement. The second approach, developed by members of the Chicago School, considers that barriers to entry are only those obstacles of regulatory or other origin that make it costlier for some firms to enter a market than for others. A barrier to market access is merely a cost of producing that must be borne by firms seeking to enter an industry but was not borne by firms already in that industry. If the incumbent faces a number of market constraints in entering the market, the existence of similar constraints for newcomers is not deemed a barrier; only if the constraints are higher for the newcomer will a barrier be detected.[109] Apart from these two main approaches, there are a variety of other proposals concerning what should constitute a barrier to entry.[110] In particular, new institutionalist approaches

[105] *Commission v Italy*; Case C-142/05 *Mickelsson and Roos* [2009] E.C.R. I-04273. See also Shuibhne, 'The Free Movement of Goods and Article 28 EC: An Evolving Framework', 411; Jukka Snell, 'The Notion of Market Access: A Concept or a Slogan?' (2010) 47 CML Rev 437, 460.

[106] Ioannis Lianos, 'Shifting Narratives in the European Internal Market' (2010) 21 EBLRev 705, 728; Davies, 'Understanding Market Access: Exploring the Economic Rationality of Different Conceptions of Free Movement Law', 681–682.

[107] Joe S. Bain, *Industrial Organization* (2nd edn, Wiley 1968), 252; James Milton Ferguson, *Advertising and Competition; Theory, Measurement, Fact* (Ballinger Pub. Co. 1974), 10.

[108] Harold Demsetz, 'Barriers to Entry' (1982) 72 AmEconRev 47, 47–48.

[109] George J. Stigler, *The Organization of Industry* (R.D. Irwin 1968), 67–70.

[110] R. Preston McAfee, Hugo M. Mialon and Michael A. Williams, 'What is a Barrier to Entry?' (2004) 94 AmEconRev 461, 461–463.

distinguish between economic barriers and anti-trust barriers. The difference lies in the relevant time dimension: some barriers that are relevant for antitrust purposes—because they reduce the welfare of consumers relative to a situation where entry would otherwise be possible in the shorter term—are not so from an economic, long-term perspective, where the dominant position will eventually be replaced by a more competitive market. Relevant barriers from an antitrust perspective are not exclusively economic barriers, but also those deemed socially undesirable in the shorter term; as such, the relevance of economic perspectives is of limited use here.[111]

The relevance of competition law conceptions is, however, bound to be limited in identifying obstacles to the market freedoms.[112] More importantly, there is no indication that the Court of Justice had any such approach in mind when it adopted market access as a test. The goal of adopting market access seemed, as with *Keck*, to be to limit the scope of the concept of restriction by distinguishing between measures that merely reduce the economic attractiveness of pursuing a given activity and measures that effectively restrict free movement rights within the framework of the Treaty.[113] Even if this implies a rejection of a test based on the Harvard school conception of barrier to entry, it does not in any way imply that other conceptions borrowed from competition law are relevant for determining what 'access to market' means in the context of economic free movement.

In the light of the lack of normative anchoring of a judicial test based on market access other than the fact that it constitutes an attempt to develop a non-discriminatory alternative to economic due-process clauses, market access has been criticized as requiring an intuitive approach or as being a mere slogan.[114] These criticisms are not without merit. As with material discrimination, a more sophisticated approach seems to be necessary. The risks inherent in its lack of normative anchoring are apparent in market access's drift towards an economic due-process clause, going against its own original normative foundations. This can be seen in a number of cases where it was

[111] Ibid, 463–465.

[112] A different option would be to use market access as it is usually applied by the WTO, but market access here applies only to measures concerning actions on imports which take place at the border, while the test at EU level is an effects-based one. See Snell, 'The Notion of Market Access?', 439–443.

[113] Eeckhout, 'After *Keck and Mithouard*', 204.

[114] Spaventa, *Free Movement of Persons in the European Union*, 95–99; Snell, 'The Notion of Market Access?'.

found that the mere fact that general regulatory restrictions on the pursuit of economic activities existed, that one of various possible ways of competing in the market was prohibited, that local partioning of markets occurred, or even that less onerous regulatory requirements existed elsewhere, all constituted restrictions on market access.[115] This risk is also particularly evident in the case law on free movement of capital concerning the prohibition of golden shares, where restrictions were found on access to the market for corporate control even though the market was defined extremely narrowly—the relevant company—and where the Court of Justice's reasoning was that national provisions creating golden shares are restrictive:

> ... *to the extent to which they create instruments liable to limit the ability of investors to participate in the share capital [in a company] with a view to establishing or maintaining lasting and direct economic links with it which would make possible effective participation in the management or control of that company, reduce the interest in acquiring a stake in that capital [and are thereby restrictions inasmuch as]direct investors from other Member States, whether actual or potential, may have been deterred from acquiring a stake in the capital of that company.*[116]

The underlying *rationale* for this is, for all purposes, undistinguishable from an economic due-process clause.[117]

The main problem with differentiating between a purely deregulatory tool and a test focused on the removal of obstacles to the internal market is that measures reducing the economic attractiveness of pursuing a given activity will also have a detrimental effect on the pursuit of cross-border activities

[115] See, for workers, Case C-176/96 *Lethonen* [2000] E.C.R. I-2681 and Case C-325/08 *Olympique Lyonnais* [2010] E.C.R. I-02177; for establishment, *CaixaBank*, particularly paras 12–15 and Case C-134/05 *Commission v Italy* [2007] E.C.R. I-6251, Case C-389/05 *Commission v France* [2008] E.C.R. I-5337, Joined Cases C-171/07 and C-172/07 *Apothekerkammer des Saarlandes* [2009] E.C.R. I-04171, Case C-384/08 *Attanasio* [2010] E.C.R. I-02055; for services, Joined Cases C-94/04 and C-202/04 *Cipolla* [2006] E.C.R. I-2107; for goods, see Case C-108/09 *Ker-Optika* [2010] E.C.R. I-12213. See, for a cogent analysis, Eleanor Spaventa, 'Caixa-Bank Case Note' (2005) 42 CML Rev 1151, 1156–1161.

[116] Case C-212/09 *Commission v Portugal* [2011] E.C.R. I-10889, para. 67 (the emphasis is mine).

[117] Similarly, Snell, 'The Notion of Market Access?', 463. See also *Commission v Portugal*, para. 71. On cases concerning general rules on shareholding limits in certain sectors, see Case C-81/09 *Idrima Tipou* [2010] E.C.R. I-10161, particularly para. 59, according to which a restriction exists concerning an indistinctly applicable measure setting shareholding limits for companies holding licences to found, establish, and operate a television station because foreign companies '*know less about the realities of media life in Greece and are not necessarily acquainted with the various groups or alliances represented amongst the shareholders of [such] a company*'.

in that field. As a result, a more sophisticated approach than the one currently adopted by the Court of Justice is required. Advocate General Jacobs, when first proposing a judicial test based on market access, suggested that a *de minimis* approach should be adopted for all cases, except when there is direct discrimination, with any measure that substantially restricts market access being deemed an obstacle to free movement for the purposes of the Treaties. However, the concept of substantial restriction on market access has not been adopted by the Court of Justice, which has always refused to apply a *de minimis* test. Instead, the Court of Justice resorted to the concept of 'directly' affecting access to the market,[118] perhaps as a counterpoint to the 'too uncertain and indirect' doctrine.[119] In the absence of a properly structured normative underpinning for market access, however, the consequences of this approach to market access are similar to material discrimination: it leads to all those measures constraining market behaviour and limiting free competition, regardless of whether they pose obstacles to the cross-border exercise of the market freedoms, being deemed *prima facie* restrictive. It leads, in other words, back into an economic due-process clause.

VII. Conclusion

The judicial test used by the Court of Justice to identify measures posing unjustified obstacles to intra-Union trade is critical to the Court of Justice's role in the creation and maintenance of the internal market.

The Court of Justice originally adopted a test based on discrimination on grounds of nationality—the traditional test in international economic law for the identification of protectionist barriers. However, as a result of its failure to determinate the relevant *tertium comparationis*, its recourse to different prohibited discrimination criteria without any consideration of their normative foundations, and its improper and un-empirical use of indirect/material discrimination tests, the concept of discrimination was extended to the point where virtually any rule could be found to be restrictive. In the case of the free movement of goods, this led to the adoption of an economic

[118] Opinion in *Leclerc-Siplec*, paras 39–40. See *Alpine*, para. 38; *Bosman*, para. 103; and Advocate General Tizzano's Opinion in *CaixaBank*, paras 62–66.

[119] This was first applied as a limit to market access in Case C-190/98 *Graf* [2000] E.C.R. I-493.

due-process test, which constituted a clear normative over-expansion of the scope of this market freedom, and, as such, led to an eventual retrenchment by the Court of Justice around a typological test. However, since the nature of a national measure does not necessarily correspond to its effect on intra-State trade, typological tests do not match the normative foundations of the free movement of goods or the other market freedoms, with the result that the Court of Justice ended up developing a new, obstacle-based test based on market access that seems now to apply to all market freedoms.

Each test adopted by the Court of Justice failed to distinguish between-measures that merely reduce the economic attractiveness of pursuing a given activity, and those measures that effectively restrict economic free movement rights within the framework of the Treaty. The main reason for this seems to be a lack of clarity regarding the normative foundations of the market freedoms. A study of these foundations is thus required, and will be pursued in the next chapter.

4

Restricting Free Movement Rights—Unpacking the Normative Foundations

I. Introduction

The previous chapter identified a variety of different tests regarding the concept of restriction on economic free movement that have been both adopted by the Court of Justice and advanced in the academic literature. There is seemingly a consensus that the concept of restriction reflects concerns with the creation of the internal market, and is to be contained within two boundaries: first, it is not disputed that the market freedoms are supposed to prevent protectionist measures (*minimum content*); and, secondly, it is accepted that the market freedoms do not reflect a deregulatory agenda according to which any national measure can be subject to review regarding its rationality (*maximum content*). What the normative underpinnings of the concept of restriction are in between these two extremes is not clear; and this vagueness ultimately seems to correspond to a lack of specification of the normative underpinnings of the market freedoms. While they are instrumental to the creation of a European internal market, the market freedoms nonetheless fail to specify how market integration is to proceed, or what kind of integrated European market is envisioned.

This chapter will begin by reviewing the implications of adopting certain judicial tests regarding the concept of restriction on economic free movement, before moving into the analysis of the normative ideas which can be said to underlie each of those tests. This analysis will reveal that each judicial test regarding the concept of restriction on economic free movement can be underpinned by a variety of autonomous normative concerns. It will be further demonstrated that most discussions about the concept of restriction on economic free movement not only ignore this normative polysemy of judicial tests, but also tend to overlook the existence of related normative debates, and to focus on negative integration to the detriment of more integrated models of European integration.[1]

II. What Do the Market Freedoms Do?

What is the impact of adopting a specific judicial test to determine whether a national measure infringes a market freedom? As we have already seen, such tests identify the national measures that will be subject to a proportionality assessment by courts in order to establish whether they are justified. But, behind this apparently simple consequence, one can discern a variety of other implications for State autonomy, for the EU's competence to legislate, and for the level and kind of regulation that may be adopted. It is to these implications, and to how they are usually perceived in the academic literature, that this section is devoted.

A. Static perspectives

Through the market freedoms, a large number of State actions become subject to review by the Court of Justice. When the Court decides that a national rule falls within the scope of the market freedoms, it makes an institutional choice: it takes ultimate control away from the ordinary national legislative process and subjects these rules to the jurisdiction of the courts.[2] Even if a *prima facie* restrictive national measure is deemed justified, the Court of Justice will have the ultimate say about its validity, thereby centralizing the ultimate decision-making power at the EU level regardless of whether the relevant national measures fall within the scope of the EU's legislative competences.[3]

[1] The question of which relative roles should be played by negative and positive integration is a question which any trade system must face, and one that must be answered when establishing the normative foundations of the judicial tests regarding European negative integration—see Weiler, 'Mutual Recognition, Functional Equivalence and Harmonization in the Evolution of the European Common Market and the WTO', 25; Perisin, *Free Movement of Goods and Limits of Regulatory Autonomy in the EU and WTO*, 9.

[2] Gregory Shaffer, 'A Structural Theory of WTO Dispute Settlement: Why Institutional Choice Lies at the Centre of the GMO Case' (2008) 41 JILP 1, 4.

[3] See, just as an example, Case C-438/05 *Viking* [2007] E.C.R. I-10779, para. 40 and the case law referred to therein.

This has consequences at what will be called the horizontal level, concerning the level of regulatory options left to Member States in non-harmonized areas and to the Union in harmonized ones, and at the vertical level, concerning the division of regulatory competences between the Union and its Member States.

Horizontally, the market freedoms set substantive limits to the exercise of legislative powers at both the national and EU levels.[4] At the national level, when a measure is caught within the scope of the market freedoms, the ultimate decision as to its legitimacy falls to the Court of Justice, which may, by means of a proportionality test, determine whether the manner in which a State protects its public interests is acceptable. Further to this, in certain cases—namely those concerning mandatory requirements and other justifications not provided for by the Treaties—the Court of Justice may even determine what public interests a State can legitimately pursue. The result is that a Member State loses part of its autonomy to legislate and Member States, other than the State subject to the Court of Justice's decision but with similar measures in place, will find themselves under the 'shadow of the law', and under pressure to amend out-of-step rules in accordance with the Court of Justice's case law.[5] Similarly, EU legislation can be assessed as to its conformity with the substantive orientation of the market freedoms, even if this has only seldom occurred.[6]

At the vertical level, the market freedoms not only centralize ultimate decision-making powers in the Court of Justice, but are also instrumental in the attribution of competences to the Union: the broader the concept of restriction used, the larger the number of rules susceptible to being deemed contrary to EU law, and of being harmonized under Articles 114 to 118 TFEU.[7] Nonetheless, it should be noted that deciding that a national

[4] Schillig, 'The Interpretation of European Private Law in the Light of Market Freedoms and EU Fundamental Rights', 296–297.

[5] Sweet and Caporaso, 'From Free Trade to Supranational Polity', 128

[6] And even more seldom resulted in the invalidation of EU secondary law: see Joined Cases 80 and 81/77 *Commissionnaires Réunis v Receveur des douanes* [1978] E.C.R. 927, para. 35; Case 41/84 *Pinna* [1986] E.C.R. 1; Case 20/85 *Roviello* [1988] E.C.R. 2805; Piet Eeckhout, 'The European Court of Law and the Legislature' (1998) 18 YEL 1, 12–14. However, EU legislation can be indirectly reviewed by the Court of Justice when it assesses whether a national measure that is compliant with Union legislation nonetheless infringes upon the fundamental Treaty provisions: see Case C-208/07 *Chamier-Glisczinski* [2009] E.C.R. I-06095, para. 66 and other cases quoted there.

[7] Matej Avbelj, 'European Court of Justice and the Question of Value Choices' [2004] Jean Monnet Working Paper 06/04, 19. Evidence that litigation and negative integration led to an increase in EU legislation—presumably to replace regulatory holes left in the Member States by the negative integration that preceded it—has been empirically observed. See Sweet and Fligstein, 'Institutionalizing the Treaty of Rome', 45–46, 51–53.

rule falls within the scope of the market freedoms does not *per se* lead to the replacement of national measures for EU measures, nor does the adoption of Union measures depend only on the finding that national measures constitute prohibited obstacles to economic free movement.[8] Article 114 TFEU is obviously not the only positive competence rule in the Treaty, as the EU has a variety of legislative competences that are not related to the market freedoms, or even to the internal market. However, the impact of Article 114 TFEU is hard to overstate, since it not only allows the EU to re-regulate at the European level what the market freedoms deregulate at the national level, but it can also be used to remove obstacles to trade beyond those falling within the scope of the market freedoms, such as those arising from non-restrictive discrepancies between national laws.[9] In any event, even if there were a perfect correspondence between the provisions on negative and positive integration, this would not automatically lead to legislative harmonization. Instead, the Commission would still be required to muster the political will to submit the necessary legislative proposals, which must then assemble the necessary level of political support among the Member States and in the European Parliament. Moreover, compliance with the constitutional constraints set by Article 5 TEU further requires that harmonizing measures respect the principles of proportionality and subsidiarity.

In short, the impact of the scope of the market freedoms and of Article 114 TFEU on EU competences must be distinguished, even if the Union's legislative competence is triggered each time a measure is deemed restrictive.[10] While the scope of the market freedoms is instrumental to the vertical allocation of competences in the EU, a finding that a national measure restricts free movement is a sufficient, but not necessary, trigger for harmonization. The scope of the market freedoms (i.e. centralization) will only correspond to an extension of Union competences under Article 114 TFEU (i.e. harmonization) if there is a complete absence of *ex ante* restraint from Member States and EU institutions in adopting harmonized rules, and if

[8] Loïc Azoulai, 'The Court of Justice and the Social Market Economy: The Emergence of an Ideal and the Conditions for its Realization' (2008) 45 CML Rev 1335, 1341.

[9] Gareth Davies, 'Can Selling Arrangements be Harmonised?' (2005) 30 ELRev 370, 375–378. This is also apparent from Case C-380/03 *Tobacco Advertising II* [2006] E.C.R. I-11573, para. 80.

[10] Which is a further reason for there being no equivalence between a test where a market freedom would have a vast scope and be subject to light review at the justification stage, and a test imposing a stricter scope for the market freedoms but applying a stricter review at justification stage, even when the final outcome of the cases would be the same.

the Court of Justice fails to review EU legislation under the principles of proportionality and subsidiarity *ex post*.[11]

To summarize, when determining the scope of the market freedoms and what the legitimate justifications for their restriction are, the Court of Justice's decisions have implications of two types. From a vertical perspective, the market freedoms act as positive competence rules, with the Court of Justice being instrumental to the allocation of competences between the EU and the Member States. From a horizontal perspective, the market freedoms operate as negative competence rules: what matters is not the allocation of competences within the EU and the States but the scope of EU law itself, and here the Court of Justice's role looms even larger as it becomes the ultimate decider of what regulatory options are available within the Union. From this interplay of vertical and horizontal effects arises the functional consequence that the market freedoms are inherently deregulatory, since the Court of Justice can only strike down legislative measures but cannot legislate itself—in other words, the greater the degree of centralization in the Court of Justice (via the free movement rules), the greater the prospect of deregulation of national markets. On the other hand, the market freedoms trigger the possibility of the EU political process stepping in, so that the broader the concept of restriction used, the greater the prospect of re-regulation at EU level (subject to the assembly of the required support among the EU's law-making institutions). This re-regulation, however, will be different from national regulation, inasmuch as the EU regulatory process has more numerous and diverse participants than national processes, benefits from inputs provided by previous market outsiders, and may adopt different regulatory goals and methods.[12]

B. *A dynamic perspective*

Our understanding of the impact of the market freedoms can be improved by taking into account insights from studies on US federalism. One particularly important insight is that the impact of the market freedoms is dynamic,

[11] Stephen Weatherill, 'Better Competence Monitoring' (2005) 30 ELRev 23, 25–28; Perisin, *Free Movement of Goods and Limits of Regulatory Autonomy in the EU and WTO*, 91–108. See Case C-376/98 *Tobacco Advertising I* [2000] ECR I-8419, *British American Tobacco*; Case C-210/03 *Swedish Match* [2004] E.C.R. I-11893, *Tobacco Advertising II*.

[12] National deregulation might paradoxically lead to greater levels of formal regulation as the social distance and distrust between regulators and regulated actors in liberalized markets increases. This results in laws and regulatory processes becoming more formal, transparent, and legalistic, replacing more informal mechanisms. See on this Kelemen, *Eurolegalism: The Transformation of Law and Regulation in the European Union*, 23.

as a consequence of the free movement of economic factors between jurisdictions that these freedoms allow and resulting regulatory competition.[13]

Regulatory competition depends on federal or quasi-federal entities creating and enforcing rights of entry into and exit from States for products and production factors, while simultaneously not encroaching on those States' regulatory autonomy. This allows local regulators to compete in a market for legal rules. In the EU, the market freedoms create the conditions for the existence of regulatory competition by making available comparative information, and by granting economic agents the ability to move and choose between different jurisdictions. In particular, consumers are able to show their preferences in products and services (*voting with their purses*), businesses may choose to relocate to more favourable environments (*voting with their feet*), and private agents may vote or lobby their public authorities for different rules (*voice*). In turn, different rule-making entities are forced to compete in the market for legal rules, which may theoretically lead to a convergence of standards.[14] Some argue that this convergence results in a race-to-the-bottom in regulation—effectively, deregulation—while others contend that it leads to optimal levels of regulation instead.[15]

The dynamic perspective adds to the static perspective in a variety of ways. It points to the fact that the market freedoms change the incentives of market and political agents within Member States, and thus affect State autonomy in ways that are not considered from a static perspective. It demonstrates that a dynamic process of regulatory competition may lead to the creation of common rules throughout the internal market which do not come top-down from European institutions, but arise instead bottom-up as a result of competitive pressures in the market for legal rules. Additionally, it focuses on the fact that, even if the adopted tests seek to protect existing levels of regulation put in place by States, deregulation may still emerge as a consequence of economic agents searching for the least onerous regulatory regime.

[13] Which was first identified in C. Tiebout, 'A Pure Theory of Local Expenditures' (1956) 64 Journal of Political Economy 416.

[14] Jeanne-Mey Sun and Jacques Pelkmans, 'Regulatory Competition in the Single Market' (1995) 33 JCMS 67, 69–77; Catherine Barnard and Simon Deakin, 'Market Access and Regulatory Competition' [2001] Jean Monnet Working Paper 9/01, 2–4. On the origin of these concepts, see Albert O. Hirschman, *Exit, Voice, and Loyalty: Responses to Decline in Firms, Organizations, and States* (Harvard University Press 1970).

[15] This is an empirically debatable question, particularly in the EU context. See, for example, Scharpf, *Governing in Europe: Effective and Democratic?* 86–101; Catherine Barnard, 'Social Dumping and the Race to the Bottom: Some Lessons for the European Union from Delaware?' (2000) 25 ELRev 57.

III. What Ought the Market Freedoms To Be Doing?

The above review of the practical implications of the market freedoms allows us to map out three different ways to approach them from a normative perspective, concerning, respectively, the desirability of centralization, deregulation, and harmonization.

First, one can focus on the impact of the market freedoms on the centralization of powers at EU level. From this perspective, normative positions vary in a continuum between defending extreme centralization of powers in EU bodies, and particularly the Court of Justice—proponents of which will usually favour a broad test—and arguing for decentralization and the maximization of State autonomy—which will usually lean towards a narrow test.[16] Secondly, one can look into the deregulatory effects of the market freedoms, with the normative positions varying from defending the market freedoms as neo-liberal tools protecting the unencumbered pursuit of economic activity by removing unjustified national rules—which would point towards a very broad test—or seeing them merely as an otherwise economically agnostic means to remove obstacles to inter-State trade and protectionist measures—a position traditionally associated with a narrower test.[17] In the light of *Keck*, the deregulation v. economic agnosticism debate appears to have been replaced in the academic literature by discussions concerning the balancing of the virtues of regulatory competition when compared to legislative harmonization. One side of the argument is that regulatory pluralism is desirable because centralized rules are more distant from the regulated entities, tend to limit the opportunities for meaningful political participation, are more subject to capture by interest groups, imply severe procedural costs inherent in the implementation of common rules in large, heterogeneous areas, and pre-empt regulatory competition in the areas in which they are adopted.[18] Regulatory pluralism is said not only to allow the

[16] It should be noted that this perspective also overlaps with debates on the value of judicial review as opposed to legislative autonomy. I thank Damian Chalmers for his comments on this point.

[17] On broad tests leading to deregulation, see critically Spaventa, *Free Movement of Persons in the European Union*. On the debate, see Wolf Sauter and Harm Schepel, *State and Market in European Union Law: The Public and Private Spheres of the Internal Market before the EU Courts* (Cambridge University Press 2009), 4–15.

[18] Majone and Baake, *Dilemmas of European Integration*, 145;Snell, *Goods and Services in EC Law*, 38–40.

content of rules to take into account local specificities and more effectively to match the preferences of citizens, but also to promote diversity and innovation in legal solutions, the flow of information on effective law-making, and competition between legal orders.[19] Against this, and in favour of harmonization, it is argued that regulatory competition can be sub-optimal, not only because of the risks of a race-to-the-bottom and deregulation, but also because it can lead to market failures being left unattended.[20] Furthermore, since governments regulate a number of economic activities not handled satisfactorily by competitive markets in the first place, it has been argued that regulatory competition may lead to the re-emergence of market failures which were previously addressed by corrective national regulation.[21] It is also argued that harmonization is useful as a means of reducing transaction costs, and better placed to deal with natural monopolies, systemic risks, and regulatory drift.[22]

One can therefore, for heuristic purposes, develop a taxonomy of the mainstream debates on the scope of the market freedoms as concerning themselves with the balancing of centralization v. decentralization, deregulation v. economic agnosticism, and harmonization v. regulatory pluralism.

IV. Towards a Contextualized Perspective

This section will begin with a critical review of the static and dynamic models presented above, following which it will attempt to deconstruct how the

[19] Although some authors have pointed to discrepancies between economic models and empirical results: see Sun and Pelkmans, 'Regulatory Competition in the Single Market', 83–85.

[20] These traditionally include market externalities, market power, and asymmetric information. See John Kay and John Vickers, 'Regulatory Reform: An Appraisal' in Giandomenico Majone (ed.), *Deregulation or Re-regulation* (Pinter 1990), 225–230; Cass R. Sunstein, *After the Rights Revolution: Reconceiving the Regulatory State* (Harvard University Press 1990), 47–73; A. I. Ogus, *Regulation: Legal Form and Economic Theory* (Hart 2004), 30–46; Andrew Johnston and Phil Syrpis, 'Regulatory Competition in European Company Law after *Cartesio*' (2009) 34 ELRev 378, 392; Kalypso Nicolaïdis, 'Mutual Recognition of Regulatory Regimes' [1997] Jean Monnet Working Papers, 11–12.

[21] Hans-Werner Sinn, 'The Selection Principle and Market Failure in Systems Competition' (1997) 66 JPE 247.

[22] Simon Deakin, 'Legal Diversity and Regulatory Competition: Which Model for Europe?' (2006) 12 ELJ 440, 441–443; Neil Fligstein and Alec Stone Sweet, 'Constructing Polities and Markets: An Institutionalist Account of European Integration' (2002) 107 AmJSoc 1206, 1312.

different normative models of European integration interact with the judicial formulae used to identify national measures that restrict economic free movement.

A. Refining our understanding of the impact of the market freedoms

The above analysis of the impact of the market freedoms offers important insights. In particular, the static perspective allows us to understand that the concept of restriction on economic free movement is relevant to determine the deregulatory impact of the market freedoms on national markets and the level of centralization of powers at EU level. The dynamic perspective, in turn, points to the impact of the market freedoms in the development of common European standards, and illustrates the choice parameters between harmonization and regulatory competition.

Nonetheless, these perspectives seem to be somewhat lacking. From a static perspective, we have seen above that the market freedoms may be seen as deregulatory because the Court of Justice can strike down national measures but not regulate *ex novo*. On the other hand, the market freedoms may also be perceived as re-regulatory tools stimulating the adoption of harmonized regulation. While there are good reasons behind arguments that the market freedoms are both deregulatory and re-regulatory devices, the prevailing view at any given moment will be the result of specific institutional realities external to the legal content of the market freedoms. When the Court of Justice replaces the parameters of acceptability of a certain regulatory scheme, this will have a deregulatory effect if the possibility of re-regulation is blocked, as commonly occurred prior to the adoption of the Single European Act. If this is not the case, and the political mechanisms necessary for re-regulation to occur are operating smoothly, a *prima facie* deregulatory decision may well have preponderantly re-regulatory effects.

What is more, a closer look at the ways in which the market freedoms operate demonstrates that the market freedoms need not be deregulatory at all, even if the political channels for re-regulation are closed. It was in a context where the political mechanisms of re-regulation were foreclosed that the Court of Justice first developed a tool that enabled it to disapply national rules without deregulating national markets—mutual recognition.

Mutual recognition, as seen in chapter 3, was first adopted in *Cassis de Dijon*, a case concerning a prohibition on importing liqueur from France into Germany, on the grounds that it had an alcoholic content inferior to the minimum allowed for the marketing of alcoholic beverages in

Germany.[23] The Court of Justice held that disparities between national laws concerning the marketing of products were contrary to the free movement of goods because they could hinder trade between Member States, and that the host-State should recognize the marketing rules set by the home-State unless its own (different) rules were justified. This was understood as expanding the concept of restriction on the free movement of goods to encompass disparities in national laws on product requirements, a vast expansion on the scope of the concept as understood until then. In particular, the Court of Justice in *Cassis* picked up a lead from the EU legislature, which had previously adopted a Directive imposing on Member States an obligation to take all necessary steps to abolish not only distinctly applicable measures hindering imports, but also: '*measures governing the marketing of products which deal, in particular, with shape, size, weight, composition, presentation, identification or putting up and which are equally applicable to domestic and imported products*'.[24] *Cassis de Dijon*'s reference to disparities between national laws on the marketing of products can be related to the types of rules listed in Directive 70/50/EEC. Even if the Court of Justice did not refer to it expressly in its decision, the Commission's interpretation of this case was that:

> *...a Member State may not in principle prohibit the sale in its territory of a product lawfully produced and marketed in another Member State even if the product is produced according to technical or quality requirements which differ from those imposed on its domestic products... [This refers in particular to] rules covering the composition, designation, presentation and packaging of products as well as rules requiring compliance with certain technical standards.*[25]

It was in the light of this that *Cassis* was interpreted as having adopted mutual recognition, which meant that, even when acting in a host-State, an economic agent was only subject to the rules on technical standards of its home-State and was thereby freed from the onus of complying with two or more sets of rules.

[23] *Cassis de Dijon.*

[24] Commission Directive 70/50/EEC [1969] OJ L 13 on the abolition of measures which have an effect equivalent to quantitative restrictions on imports and are not covered by other provisions adopted in pursuance of the EEC Treaty, Art. 3.

[25] Communication from the Commission concerning the consequences of the judgment given by the Court of Justice on 20 February 1979 in *Cassis de Dijon*. It has been remarked that the Commission fished around for a case of this sort and worked closely with the plaintiffs to bring it forward: see Kalipso Nicolaïdis, 'Kir Forever? The Journey of a Political Scientist in the Landscape of Mutual Recognition' in Miguel Poiares Maduro and Loïc Azoulai (eds), *The Past and Future of EU Law: The Classics of EU Law Revisited on the 50th Anniversary of the Rome Treaty* (Hart Publishing), 449.

As we have also seen, this case law eventually led to the adoption of an economic due-process clause by the Court of Justice, with attendant deregulatory consequences. Mutual recognition, however, does not lead so much to deregulation as to the transfer of regulatory authority from one jurisdiction to another. Mutual recognition can be thought of as a contract between governments mandating the transfer of regulatory authority from one jurisdiction to another. As stated by Nicolaïdis:

If a professional can operate, a product be sold or a service provided lawfully in one jurisdiction, they can operate, be sold or provided in any other participating jurisdiction, without having to comply with the regulations of those other jurisdictions. The 'recognition' involved here is the 'equivalence', 'compatibility' or at least 'acceptability' of the counterpart's regulatory system; the 'mutual' part indicates that the reallocation of authority is reciprocal and simultaneous.[26]

Underlying mutual recognition is the idea that, if the standards of different Member States are functionally equivalent, there is no good reason for a State to exclude products coming from another State from its markets. By mandating that the regulatory standards of the home-State must be accepted as functionally equivalent to those of a host-State, the Court of Justice replaced the deregulatory effects of the freedoms with the imposition of a different regulatory standard.[27] Since different Member States can adopt different approaches for the protection of public interests, the determination of the level at which equivalence is found is a pre-requisite for mutual recognition to occur, with this determination requiring the Court of Justice to balance how much the regulatory autonomy of the Member State must be sacrificed for the sake of the functioning of the internal market.[28] Through mutual recognition, the Court of Justice substitutes a European value assessment for the national one, and imposes its own evaluation as to the necessary level of regulatory protection. In some situations, the Court of Justice will follow secondary legislation in establishing the equivalence level, as was the case in *Cassis* and in the case law on alternative labelling policy.[29] In other situations, however, there may

[26] Nicolaïdis, 'Globalization with Human Faces', 133.

[27] Nicolaïdis, 'Mutual Recognition of Regulatory Regimes', 2–14. This may, occasionally, lead to harmonization through regulatory competition: see Miguel Poiares Maduro, 'So Close and Yet So Far: The Paradoxes of Mutual Recognition' (2007) 14 JEPP 814.

[28] Nicolaïdis, 'Globalization with Human Faces', 144–146; Möstl, 'Preconditions and Limits of Mutual Recognition', 411.

[29] Where the Court of Justice had recourse to secondary legislation when striking down national law imposing certain product requirements by considering that labelling information on product characteristics would provide an equivalent level of protection: see Council

be no European standards which the Court of Justice can have recourse to. However, since mutual recognition does not allow Member States to maintain different levels of protection, the Court of Justice must nonetheless establish the minimum level at which equivalence is to be found, which will usually become the maximum allowed European standard. It is in the light of this preliminary assessment that the Court of Justice then goes on to determine whether the regulatory objectives in the origin and destination countries are 'equivalent': as a rule, when a State's requirements go beyond the 'European' maximum standard, no derogation can be successfully invoked.[30] From this perspective, the whole mandatory and imperative requirements' doctrines should be understood as maintaining the equivalence assessments regarding different regulatory regimes within reasonable limits in order to ensure that mutual recognition is politically and sociably acceptable.[31] Mutual recognition still implies a loss of regulatory autonomy for the Member State, by delinking the exercise of sovereign power from its territorial anchor through a reciprocal allocation of jurisdictional authority to prescribe and enforce laws;[32] but it is a middle way, less intrusive than outright deregulation or harmonization, which gives the lie to models arguing that the market freedoms lead to either judicially enforced deregulation of national markets or to increased legislative harmonization.

The dynamic model is more sophisticated than the static one in that it takes into account the existence of a federal or quasi-federal system as a relevant consideration when identifying the effects unleashed by the market freedoms. Still, in its pure form, even the dynamic model is insufficiently contextualized, taking as a given the existence of an ideal federal system without looking into the specific characteristics of the EU.[33] After all, any complex

Directive 79/112/EEC [1978] OJ L33/01 relating to the labelling, presentation, and advertisement of foodstuffs for sale to the ultimate consumer, and Case 130/80 *Kelderman* [1981] E.C.R. 527, *Commission v France*, and Case 76/86 *Commission v Germany* [1989] E.C.R. 121. See other examples in Maduro, *We, the Court*, 72–74.

[30] Jacques Pelkmans, 'Mutual Recognition in Goods. On Promises and Disillusions' (2007) 14 JEPP, 702.

[31] Nicolas Bernard, 'La libre circulation sous l'angle de la compétence' [1998] CDE 11.

[32] Kenneth Armstrong, 'Mutual Recognition' in Catherine Barnard and Joanne Scott (eds), *The Law of the Single European Market* (Hart Publishing 2001), 332; Möstl, 'Preconditions and Limits of Mutual Recognition', 407; Kalypso Nicolaïdis, 'Trusting the Poles? Constructing Europe through Mutual Recognition' (2007) 14 JEPP 682, 691.

[33] Arguing that this theory in its purest version is too abstract even for the US reality, see Simon Deakin, 'Reflexive Governance and European Company Law' (2009) 15 ELJ 224, 231.

market system—including markets for laws—requires the establishment of a system of rules that ensures a minimum degree of order and security, and allows for the enforcement of market arrangements.[34] As Deakin has stated:

> *All markets rest on institutional foundations. These 'rules of the game' are not solely concerned with protecting existing markets, by enforcing contracts and penalising collusion. At a more basic level, they constitute markets by defining the elements of exchange, and in so doing inevitably frame the process of competition. The market for laws is no different.*[35]

In particular, 'pure' regulatory competition requires that all relevant products and production factors be equally mobile—or at least equally able to threaten to move—to a State which better meets their preferences, and that market failures be dealt with aptly.[36] This ideal framework does not actually occur in practice: since these ideal parameters are almost never met, they cannot be assumed but must be assessed in each particular case instead.[37] An abstract model of regulatory competition is a heuristically useful device, but it will necessarily fail to identify some relevant characteristics of the applicable institutional framework. For example, it is generally accepted that labour is far less mobile than capital in the EU, which would seem to indicate that centralized action might be required in this field.[38] Also, traditional regulatory competition debates focus on whether decentralization, which ensures regulatory heterogeneity and protects local peculiarities, is preferable to centralization through judicial or legislative balancing. But in the EU, should a market failure (re-)emerge as a result of regulatory competition, it could be dealt with not only through harmonization but also by ensuring

[34] North, *Institutions, Institutional Change and Economic Performance*, 47. In effect, most systems require much more than this: see Ogus, *Regulation*, 3, 16–28. On the other hand, in an ideal neoclassical world without information costs, rules would be largely irrelevant, as *per* the Coase Theorem.

[35] Deakin, 'Legal Diversity and Regulatory Competition', 440. See also Fligstein, 'Markets as Politics', 658. A more expressive illustration was provided by Bertrand Russell, *History of Western Philosophy* (Routledge 2004), 704, who stated: '"Free competition", in orthodox economics, is a very artificial conception, hedged in by legal restraints. You may undersell a competitor, but not kill him.'

[36] Deakin, 'Legal Diversity and Regulatory Competition', 442, points out that Tiebout's work was an application of theories of general equilibrium typical at the time, where ideal conditions were assumed and institutional considerations ignored.

[37] Joel Trachtman, 'Regulatory Competition and Regulatory Jurisdiction' (2000) 3 JIEL 331–332. On particular rules defining and limiting regulatory competition in the EU, see, for example, Maduro, *We, the Court*, 133–135.

[38] Johnston and Syrpis, 'Regulatory Competition in European Company Law after *Cartesio*', 392.

that national standards of protection are equivalent through mutual recognition, which not only creates the conditions for wider regulatory competition within the EU,[39] but also establishes mechanisms to prevent the re-emergence of most of the market failures that the national measures were dealing with in the first place.[40]

B. Contextualizing normative debates

In addition to the limitations identified above, it is also worth noting that debates about the ideal form of negative integration are part of wider debates about the general goals and ideal models of European integration which contain elements of both negative and positive integration. Thus, to understand debates on negative integration, one must also understand those general models of European integration to which they are related.

For simplification and exposition purposes, we can adopt a taxonomy of different models of integration found in the academic literature: a centralized constitutional model; a competitive constitutional model; and a decentralized constitutional model.[41] These overarching heuristic models conceptualize both positive and negative integration. When dealing with the latter, they tend to be connected to specific understandings of what the concept of restriction on economic free movement should be and what it is meant to achieve.

The centralized constitutional model advocates the creation of mechanisms for the peaceful resolution of disputes and the adoption of harmonized rules as a way to defuse horizontal friction between Member States and promote political and economic stability. Proponents of this model will tend to side with broad tests—which lead to the ultimate decision regarding the legitimacy of a large number of national laws resting with the EU, and particularly with the Court of Justice, and to an expansion of the areas where harmonization is possible at EU level.

[39] Deakin, 'Legal Diversity and Regulatory Competition', 452.

[40] Jacques Pelkmans, 'Mutual Recognition in Goods and Services: An Economic Perspective' in Fiorella Kostoris Padoa Schioppa (ed.), *The Principle of Mutual Recognition in the European Integration Process* (Palgrave Macmillan 2005), 92, 115.

[41] Maduro, *We, the Court*, 108–149. Similar models have been developed for international economic law. Alan O. Sykes, 'The (Limited) Role of Regulatory Harmonization in International Goods and Services' (1999) 2 JIEL 49, distinguishes between models supporting regulatory harmonization, mutual recognition, and policed de-centralization. Armin von Bogdandy, 'Legitimacy of International Economic Governance' in Stefan Griller (ed.), *International Economic Governance and Non-Economic Concerns* (Springer-Verlag 2003), 103, identifies a federal model, a coordinated interdependence model, and a liberal model.

The decentralized constitutional model favours the maintenance of Member States' autonomy (arguing that this is the best approach to co-ordinating national regulatory systems by allowing for regulatory pluralism), for the Court of Justice to be economically agnostic, and for a focus on ensuring that people and products from other Member States are able to compete on truly equal terms with the host-State's nationals and domestic products. This model points towards a decentralized system where Member State competence is preserved and the quest for regulatory uniformity through the European courts and institutions is abandoned, thus siding with a narrow test on the grounds that such a test would prevent the Court of Justice from overriding decisions best left for national legislatures, while reducing the attribution of legislative competences to the Union.

The competitive constitutional model is subject to a sub-distinction as to whether it favours competition at the national or at the European level.[42] The former model advocates the deregulation of national markets, and is associated with broad tests through which courts can enforce the basic tenets of ordo-liberalism, i.e. increasing individual autonomy, controlling governmental abuses and maximizing economic welfare. The latter model merely favours regulatory competition, and will tend to favour a narrow test—thereby protecting regulatory pluralism—as long as free movement and the conditions for the creation of regulatory competition are possible and harmonization at EU level is limited.[43]

While the models enumerated in this taxonomy identify different 'ideal' normative visions regarding the EU's 'ever closer Union', each of them fails to take into account some of the realities of EU integration which are addressed by the other models.[44] The centralized constitutional model overlooks how the Treaties merely provide the EU with a limited set of competences. The competitive constitutional model in its ordo-liberal version ignores the fact that the EU does not have a strictly deregulatory bent, as is made clear by the existence of derogations to the Treaty freedoms and of a variety of

[42] This version of the model was not developed by Maduro, but I add it here because it helps fill what I perceive to be a gap in his taxonomy, which appears to result from the assumption that regulatory competition will lead to a race-to-the-bottom and should be equated with deregulation.

[43] Bernard, 'Discrimination and Free Movement in EC Law', 102–8; Spaventa, *Free Movement of Persons in the European Union*, 85–86. Against, arguing that it tends towards a broad test, see Maduro, *We, the Court*, 109.

[44] Maduro, ibid, 109.

harmonization competences attributed to the EU.[45] In its regulatory competition guise, on the other hand, the competitive constitutional model fails to recognize both the relevance of the political goals of the Union going beyond efficiency or market integration, and the role of centralized rules in both making regulatory competition possible and remedying its defects. Finally, the de-centralized constitutional model sees the Treaties and the EU as little more than free-trade agreements, to which the lie is given not only by the extent of the EU's competences but also by a number of political developments, particularly those that have taken place since the Single European Act and the Maastricht Treaty.

Naturally, the descriptive limitations of these 'ideal' models are at least partially the result of their purity, and each normative 'ideal' may still be valid and attractive on its own. But what we must question is how helpful these models are in assisting us in finding the normative underpinnings of the market freedoms as developed and applied in practice.

To begin with, while these models partially overlap (in as much as they agree on the desirability of some sort of European integration), they answer different questions concerning the nature of European positive and negative integration. This can be exemplified by bringing together these models with the different normative debates identified above concerning the scope of the market freedoms. The centralized constitutional model takes a position on the harmonization v. regulatory pluralism debate in favour of harmonization, and on the centralization v. decentralization debate in favour of centralization, but has nothing to say on the deregulation v. economic agnosticism debate. The competitive constitutional model in its ordo-liberal mode takes a position on the deregulation v. economic agnosticism debate in favour of deregulation, and on the centralization v. decentralization debate in favour of centralization, but is unconcerned with the question of harmonization v. regulatory pluralism. In its 'regulatory competition' variant, this model takes a position on the harmonization v. regulatory pluralism debate with a presumption in favour of pluralism, and on the centralization v. decentralization debate with a presumption in favour of decentralization, but it does not address the deregulation v. economic agnosticism debate. Lastly, the de-centralized constitutional model takes a position on the deregulation v. economic agnosticism debate in

[45] Wolf Sauter, 'The Economic Constitution of the European Union' (1998) 4 ColumJEurL 27, 57–63; I.E. Schwartz, 'Rechtsangleichung und Rechtswettbewerb im Binnenmarkt—Zum europäischen Modell' 42 (2007) EuR, 198–202.

favour of economic agnosticism, and on the centralization v. decentralization debate in favour of decentralization, but on harmonization v. regulatory pluralism (while it is arguable that it would favour regulatory pluralism[46]) it ignores the question of how regulatory competition may impact State regulation.

This partially overlapping pattern reflects the fact that, like the 'ideal' models of European integration, the normative debates about the scope of the market freedoms—centralization v. decentralization, deregulation v. economic agnosticism, and harmonization v. regulatory pluralism—themselves overlap partially, but are effectively autonomous. They are heuristic simplifications of a much more complex reality, developed to try to make sense of specific questions raised during particular moments of the process of European Integration, and reflect the different cognitive frameworks available to those looking into those questions at the time.[47] This illustrates that the main problem of trying to find a single normative underpinning for the various tests proposed by the Court is that a judicial test is no more than a crude shorthand allowing courts and lawyers to pursue their activity, while simultaneously carrying with them a multiplicity of (possibly conflicting) meanings and normative concerns.[48]

To illustrate this, remember that broad tests are usually related to centralization, harmonization, and deregulation while narrow tests, on the other hand, are associated with State autonomy, regulatory pluralism, and economic agnosticism. Concerning the ideal models of European integration, we have also pointed out that the centralized constitutional model is usually connected with broad tests and the de-centralized constitutional model tends to be associated with narrow tests. The competitive constitutional model does not necessarily favour either, even if its ordo-liberal version was traditionally associated with broad tests, and its regulatory pluralistic version with narrow, economically agnostic tests. In short, this means that judicial tests are advanced as reflecting specific positions in each of the centralization v. decentralization, harmonization v. regulatory pluralism, and deregulation v.

[46] This seems to result from this model's defence of the maintenance of State autonomy, while the normative debates regarding the concept of restriction on free movement focus precisely on the impact of negative integration on State autonomy.

[47] On the concept of cognitive frameworks, see fn. 27 of Chapter 1.

[48] This is related to the indeterminacy of any concept. As remarked by Joseph Raz, 'The Problem of Authority: Revisiting the Service Conception' (2006) 90 MinnLRev 1003, 1011: explanations such as normative theories may strive to replicate the indeterminacies of the concepts they explain, but it is almost impossible for a concept to replicate that explanation perfectly.

economic agnosticism debates; and they are usually also used as projections of a certain 'ideal' model of European integration. However, as we have seen, these debates are autonomous, and they only partially match the 'ideal' models of European integration. The result is that all tests carry with them different, sometimes conflicting, normative concerns. For example, broad limits to national regulation can be argued for on the basis that they favour either a deregulated or a European re-regulated market.[49] This means that some supporters of deregulation support broad tests because they see it as leading to the advancement of market liberalization, while that same test can be defended by someone who favours broad tests as a means to centralization (say, a proponent of a unified European State) but does not particularly care about the level of regulation in the internal market.

This mix of normative foundations is further complicated by the fact that the institutional context matters for the normative connotations of each test, and that justifications to *prima facie* restrictions on free movement act as safety-valves that mediate and soften the implications of this normative mix in practice. Should the context change, someone's position concerning the relevant test would change as well, even if the underlying normative position being defended did not. For example, ordo-liberals and proponents of a centralized European State could find common ground when most or all regulations were produced at State level and the EU's political process was blocked. But when Treaty amendments resuscitated the EU's political process and allowed for the development of a European social model, leading to an increase in EU legislation, ordo-liberals may have found that deregulatory approaches could be more successfully pursued at the national level, and started to support a restrictive reading of the market freedoms. On the other hand, centralizers would then find themselves in the company of supporters of a well-regulated market—who had previously supported a narrow test, as they opposed deregulation—in supporting a broad test.

Further, institutional changes can have an impact of the nature of normative debates themselves. This can be seen in the change in focus from the deregulatory effect of the market freedoms to a focus on the impact of regulatory competition. With the Single European Act and the Maastricht Treaty, the channels for re-regulation at EU level were opened, and a multiplicity of EU legislation started being produced. Accordingly, it no longer made sense to debate the effects of the market freedoms in terms of regulation v.

[49] Maduro, *We, the Court*, 103.

deregulation. Instead, the question became whether it was better to preserve national rules through a narrow test and let regulatory competition run its course, or to adopt a broad test that could lead to the deregulation of national markets but allowed for EU harmonization.

What sustains a specific approach regarding the preferable concept of restriction on economic free movement appears to be a coalition of persons and agents with different normative agendas coalescing around a judicial test in a specific context. Underlying each normative concern is a theory—on protecting international trade, on the constitutional division of competences in the EU, on the appropriate level of regulation in the market—which is a heuristic simplification of reality that needs to be transformed into legal criteria through the judicial interpretation and application of rules. Different normative goals will tend to be compatible in certain settings, and give rise to coalitions of proponents of a common approach even though those proponents have disparate normative concerns. But the world may change, and it may be found that apparently compatible goals are contradictory after all. In other words, the same judicial test can be used to defend completely different, usually unrelated, and sometimes contradictory normative concerns. Defending a specific normative position in terms of the judicial test to be adopted by the Court of Justice ignores the limitations of a specific formula in encapsulating a whole normative theory. More importantly, adopting such a posture also prevents a reflection on how multiple normative concerns interact in practice, leading to the case law being misunderstood, inasmuch as other relevant historical and institutional element are ignored.

V. Conclusion

The concept of restriction on free movement influences both the allocation of competences between the EU and the Member States and the regulatory options left open to Member States. In particular, the market freedoms have inherently deregulatory effects, while also allowing for increased re-regulation at EU level. Furthermore, the market freedoms lead to regulatory competition between Member States by creating a market for legal rules in which these States must compete.

In the light of this, normative debates on the scope of the market freedoms (and hence, on the nature of negative integration) have concerned themselves with the balancing of their effects regarding centralization v.

decentralization, deregulation v. economic agnosticism, and harmonization v. regulatory pluralism. However, these debates suffer from insufficient contextualization, in particular as regards their role within wider debates on the nature of European integration. When we compare these two different, but related levels of debate—on the nature of European integration, and on the specific nature of negative integration and the market freedoms—we find that they look at different questions concerning the nature of European positive and negative integration.

The reason for this is that all these models are heuristic simplifications of a complex reality that, as a result, overlap partially in their concerns but address autonomous questions. The same goes for judicial tests, which are no more than pragmatic tools carrying a multiplicity of (possibly conflicting) meanings and normative concerns which may vary depending on the institutional context in which they are applied.

As a consequence, in order to understand the judicial tests on the concept of restriction on free movement, one must not only look into the fundamental freedoms' normative content but also into the relevant institutional context in which they are applied, as will be done in the next chapter.

5

Re-framing the Concept of Restriction

I. Introduction

The previous chapter found that the traditional normative underpinnings of the various conceptions of restriction on economic free movement are under-determined and insular in relation to each other and to the wider context of European integration. This chapter will review how adding certain extra-legal considerations to the normative approaches reviewed above can improve our understanding of the law. It will do so by explaining how such extra-legal considerations help to make sense not only of the case law on general concepts of restriction on economic free movement, but also of the traditional debates surrounding such concepts. In this chapter, it will also be demonstrated how such considerations allow for the incorporation of sector-specific concepts of restriction on economic free movement that are usually not dealt with, or even acknowledged by traditional approaches to the concept of restriction on economic free movement. Finally, suggestions will be made on how extra-legal considerations can be of use in developing more attractive normative approaches to the market freedoms and the concept of restriction on economic free movement.

II. Institutional Context and Free Movement Law

We have seen that the judicial tests adopted by the Court of Justice and described in the academic literature for identifying restrictions on the market freedoms tend to be both descriptively inept and normatively vague. To understand the case law, one must look beyond decontextualized normative considerations, and take the relevant extra-legal considerations into account as well. As noted in Chapter 1, one relevant consideration in this respect is that the Court of Justice must abide by the prevailing canons for legal reasoning, judicial methodology, and logics of presentation in order to ensure its own legitimacy and the obedience of national courts. In effect, what the Court of Justice decides will not matter unless its decisions are given effect.[1] As Weiler once stated:

Constitutional actors in the Member States accept the European constitutional discipline not because, as a matter of legal doctrine, as is the case in the federal state, they are subordinate to a higher sovereignty and authority attaching to norms validated by the federal people, the constitutional demos. They accept it as an autonomous voluntary act, endlessly renewed on each occasion... The French or the Italians or the Germans are told: in the name of the peoples of Europe, you are invited to obey... This process also operates at the Community level. Think of the European judge... who must understand that, in the peculiar constitutional compact of Europe, his decision will take effect only if obeyed by national courts... This... will instil a measure of caution and tolerance.[2]

If adopting certain normative positions regarding the market freedoms implies taking sides in controversial debates of constitutional importance, one should not be surprised to find the Court of Justice eschewing fully theorized decisions while trying to make sure its actions appear as legitimate judicial activity—by abiding by recognized forms of legal reasoning and following precedent—in order to ensure that its decisions are found to be persuasive and, more importantly, obeyed. Mutual recognition provides perhaps the best example of this strategy.

Surprisingly, mutual recognition is usually ignored as such in debates about the concept of restriction on economic free movement. In the academic literature, mutual recognition is simultaneously associated with obstacle-based tests, particularly economic due-process clauses,[3] and with discrimination approaches.[4] This reflects the normative indeterminacy that underpins both these approaches and allows for the incorporation of mutual

[1] Karen Alter, *The European Court's Political Power*(OUP 2009), 92–109.

[2] Weiler, 'In Defence of the Status Quo', 21–22.

[3] This is understandable, since the adoption of both mutual recognition and economic due-process clauses by the Court of Justice originated in the same two cases, *Dassonville* and *Cassis de Dijon*. See Laurence Gormley, 'Reasoning Renounced? The Remarkable Judgement in *Keck and Mithouard*' (1994) [5] EBLRev 63.

[4] Marenco, 'Pour une interprétation traditionelle de la notion de mesure d'effet equivalent à une restriction quantitative'; Snell, *Goods and Services in EC Law*.

recognition into either of them. For mutual recognition to be identified as a form of discrimination requires an extension of discrimination tests' traditional underpinnings. The 'dual-burden' thesis is wholly alien to classic trade law: it requires the assumption—unnecessary under traditional discrimination law—that a set of regulations in a State provides adequate protection for consumers in a second State, meaning, innovatively, that obstacles arising from the mere existence of disparate rules restrict free movement and can be challenged in court. Mutual recognition thus removes more obstacles to trade, in particular, those obstacles created by the mere existence of different legal regimes applicable to the same product or person, than is traditionally required to set up a liberal trade regime. On the other hand, the fact that mutual recognition goes beyond traditional discrimination tests does not in any way imply the adoption of an ordo-liberal perspective or of an economic due-process clause.

It is a fact, however, that one can observe a development from the adoption of mutual recognition in *Cassis de Dijon* to the implementation of an economic due-process clause in the *Sunday Trading* cases. How then are we to explain this?

The answer starts from the observation that mutual recognition is an under-theorized judicial tool that attempts to produce a pragmatic solution acceptable to all parties. The price that the Court of Justice paid for such pragmatism was to eschew normative foundations strong enough to prevent the case law from departing from them. The story of these departures, already described in Chapter 3, is the story of the path-dependent evolution of judicial tests on the concept of restriction on economic free movement. It is a tale that begins with the notably elusive language of *Cassis*, which stated that:

Obstacles to movement within the Community resulting from disparities between national laws relating to the marketing of the products in question must be accepted in so far as those provisions may be recognised as being necessary in order to satisfy mandatory requirements . . .[5]

As previously described, this not only opened the door to mutual recognition, but also seemed to allow for a pure country-of-origin principle, i.e. a rule requiring the disapplication of the country-of-sale's rules (unless they are justified), and their replacement by the rules of the country-of-origin. Then, in *Cinéthèque*, the Court of Justice held that, as long as a

[5] *Cassis de Dijon*, para. 8.

product was lawfully marketed in a Member State, preventing it from circulating in another Member State was a restriction on the free movement of goods that needed to be justified regardless of there being regulatory equivalence or not. Since the absence of a requirement of regulatory equivalence turns mutual recognition into a pure country-of-origin principle, the result was that *Cinéthèque* formally extended the case law beyond mutual recognition.

On the other hand, the Court of Justice in *Cinéthèque* left unaddressed whether the case law was applying merely a pure country-of-origin principle, or if other types of obstacles could also be caught under the free movement of goods, as was arguably possible under the *Dassonville* formula that:

> *All trading rules enacted by Member States which are capable of hindering, directly or indirectly, actually of potentially, intra-Community trade are to be considered measures having an equivalent effect to quantitative restrictions.*[6]

When the first *Sunday Trading* case read *Cinéthèque* as focusing on the concept of obstacle to trade instead of on the country-of-origin principle (which clearly did not apply to measures prohibiting stores from opening on Sundays), the move towards an economic due-process clause, and to a concept of restriction on the free movement of goods able to prohibit any measure that reduces the volume of imports, was complete.[7]

Strikingly, a similar development can be observed in the free movement of persons, if at a later date than for goods.[8] The Court of Justice developed its concept of restriction on the free provision of services by focusing on discrimination against free movement, considering that any obligation on a service provider to fulfil all requirements applicable to established persons in the host-State was a denial of its freedom to provide cross-border services.[9] The Court of Justice explained this line of reasoning on the basis that specific requirements imposed on a person who does not reside in the State where the services were to be provided would not be contrary to the Treaty if justified; those requirements, however, were not justified when the service provider was already subject to similar requirements in its State of establishment.[10] The similarity between this approach and that adopted in *Cassis de Dijon* is apparent.

[6] *Dassonville*, para. 5. [7] See fn. 53 to 57 in Chapter 3 above.

[8] This precedence of goods may relate to the existence of higher levels of litigation concerning it than existed for the other market freedoms. See Schmidt, 'Who Cares About Nationality?', 11.

[9] See fn. 87 to 88 in Chapter 3 above. [10] *Van Wesemael*, paras 27–28.

For the free movement of workers and the right of establishment, the adoption of the obstacle-based approach followed a longer path, which, nonetheless, ran through mutual recognition as well. Mutual recognition regarding the establishment of persons in another Member State was for a long time restricted to the enforcement of a number of Directives—the earliest of which concerned very specific and carefully delineated professions. This reflected both the sensitivity of the topic and the related difficulty in coming up with acceptable regulatory equivalence criteria in this area.[11] These concerns can be seen in the Court of Justice's case law: in *Auer*, the Court of Justice held that an Austrian veterinarian who could practise in Italy could not practise in France, where he was established, until the relevant Directive on the mutual recognition of diplomas was brought into force.[12] On the same day that this case was decided, the Court of Justice acknowledged that a Member State had to recognize a foreign qualification obtained by one of its nationals because a Directive was in place which set forth parameters for the protection of the States' legitimate interests.[13] To reinforce the point, when the *Auer* case came before the Court of Justice again after the relevant Directive's implementation date, with the French State still not having implemented it, mutual recognition was acknowledged to result from the Directive's direct effect.[14] This case law was restated in subsequent decisions, with the Court of Justice repeatedly upholding the Member States' right to refuse mutual recognition in the absence of EU legislation, on the grounds that the regulation of the exercise of professional activities in their territory, as long as it was pursued in a non-discriminatory fashion, was the States' prerogative.[15] Eventually, proposals to create a general system of mutual recognition of professional qualifications introduced the concept of a 'regulated profession'—those professions where the conditions for taking up or pursuing a professional activity are directly or indirectly governed by laws, regulations, or administrative provisions requiring possession of evidence of education and training, or an attestation of competence—and the idea that, when controlling access to such a profession, host-States had to take into account qualifications obtained in another Member State.[16] In a case decided after the adoption of the first general recognition Directive, but

[11] See fn. 91 to 92 in Chapter 3 above.
[12] *Auer*.
[13] Case 115/78 *Knoors* [1979] E.C.R. 399.
[14] *Auer II*. See similarly Case 5/83 *Rienks* [1983] E.C.R. 4233.
[15] Case 246/80 *Broekmeulen* [1981] E.C.R. 2311; Case 292/86 *Gullung* [1988] E.C.R. 111.
[16] See fn. 91 to 94 in Chapter 3 above.

applying to a situation which had occurred before such adoption, the Court of Justice finally decided that, even in the absence of secondary legislation, national requirements concerning qualifications could restrict the right of establishment, particularly when they took no account of knowledge and qualifications acquired in another Member State.[17]

The Court of Justice's reasoning in this case distilled the general recognition system developed in the Directives by imposing an obligation upon each Member State to examine whether, and to what extent, diplomas and professional qualifications awarded by other Member States were equivalent to the diplomas and qualifications required by them for the exercise of a regulated profession in their territory. A similar obligation applied to considerations of professional experience.[18] Since judicial mutual recognition was only required for situations falling outside the scope of secondary legislation, this case law applied to situations not covered by the mutual recognition Directives.[19] However, the case law was also used to extend or plug gaps in the mutual recognition system, particularly as the system erected by the general mutual recognition Directives did not apply to professions that were subject to specific Directives.[20]

Under pressure from this application of mutual recognition principles by the Court of Justice, the test for finding restrictions to the free movement of persons eventually changed from a discrimination- to an obstacle-based approach. It was first acknowledged that the free provision of services:

> *...require(s) not only the abolition of any discrimination against a person providing services on account of his nationality but also the abolition of any restriction on the freedom to provide services imposed on the ground that the person providing a service is established in a Member State other than the one in which the service is provided. In particular, the Member State cannot make the performance of the services in its territory subject to*

[17] *Unectef v Heylens.*

[18] See Case C-313/01 *Morgenbesser* [2003] E.C.R. I-13467; Case C-238/98 *Hocsman* [2000] E.C.R. I-6623; Case C-345/08 *Peśla* [2009] E.C.R. I-11677. Arguing that this corresponds to the Directive's system, Barnard, *The Substantive Law of the EU*, 317–319.

[19] Essentially, these cases were those that either fell outside the scope of the relevant Directives—see *Commission v Spain*—or that addressed situations occurring before such Directives had been implemented. See *Vlassopoulou*. See also, Advocate General Jacobs' Opinion in Case C-104/91 *Borrell* [1992] E.C.R. I-3003, paras 11 and 16.

[20] See Article 2 of both of the above mentioned Directives. See also Case C-319/92 *Haim* [1994] E.C.R. I-00425, for dental practitioners, and Case C-55/94 *Gebhard* [1995] E.C.R. I-4165 and *Morgenbesser* for lawyers.

observance of all the conditions required for establishment; were it to do so the provisions securing freedom to provide services would be deprived of all practical effect.[21]

Similarly, and almost simultaneously, the Court of Justice started holding that rules on professional qualifications were able to hinder nationals of other Member States in the exercise of their right of establishment or the cross-border movement of workers, even if applied without any discrimination on grounds of nationality.[22] Finally, in *Säger*—a case concerning a rule subjecting the provision of patent renewal services in Germany by an undertaking established in the UK to the prior issue of an administrative licence in Germany for which the possession of certain professional qualifications was required—the Court of Justice adopted a pure obstacle-based approach similar to that arising out of *Dassonville*, by stating that the free provision of services:

...requires not only the elimination of all discrimination against a person providing services on the ground of his nationality but also the abolition of any restriction, even if it applies without distinction to national providers of services and to those of other Member States, when it is liable to prohibit or otherwise impede the activities of a provider of services established in another Member State where he lawfully provides similar services.[23]

In *Kraus*, the Court of Justice adopted a similar approach for the free movement of workers and the right of establishment, holding that any national measure governing the conditions under which an academic title obtained in another Member State may be used is restrictive:

where that measure, even though it is applicable without discrimination on grounds of nationality, is liable to hamper or to render less attractive the exercise by Community nationals, including those of the Member State which enacted the measure, of fundamental freedoms guaranteed by the Treaty.[24]

More than an outcome required by specific normative underpinnings, these developments are better understood as the result of litigants arguing within the bounds of existing law, with the potential beneficiaries of new precedent providing positive feedback to prior developments by following through on incentives to test the limits of the law in a context of normative under-determination. A similar observation can be made for the development of the market access test in *Alpine* and its subsequent drift into something akin to an economic due-process clause, and for the case law on goods post-*Keck*.[25]

[21] *Tourist Guides Greece*, para. 16. See also *Tourist Guides France; Commission v Italy; Commission v Spain*.

[22] *Unectef v Heylens; Vlassopoulou*, paras 15–17.

[23] *Säger*, para. 12.

[24] *Kraus*, para. 32.

[25] See fn. 97 to 105 in Chapter 3 above.

The reason for the case law's tendency to gravitate from judicial tests grounded on relatively narrow normative underpinnings to broader tests seems to be that the entities more likely to plead on the basis of the market freedoms are those who stand to benefit from increased inter-State movement rights and economic freedom and also have the means to go to court to pursue their preferences. Not all possible judicial paths are, after all, as likely to be followed: litigants will only push for those paths that are likely to be of benefit to them. Those who enjoy direct benefits from free movement are more likely to plead and try to extend their scope. Simultaneously, it is arguable that the costs of increased free movement are likely to be diffuse, with those incurring such costs not having sufficient incentives or means to start judicial actions.

This system of judicial incentives—which is consistent with findings that corporations, public interest groups, and enforcement agencies tend to be repeat players in starting legal procedures under the market freedoms—can create a stream of cases arguing for the market freedoms' extension without any equivalent counter-balancing pressure at the judicial level, other than those arising from the institutional environment in which the Court of Justice operates.[26] From this perspective, a retrenchment, such as the one in *Keck*, is an outlier, which may be explained by the Court of Justice's concern with docket control, as a reaction to expressions of displeasure about the increased scope of the Court of Justice's jurisdiction from various entities, as a response to academic criticism and expressions of concern about the normative coherence of the case law, or even by a mix of all these elements.[27]

On the other hand, a case such as *Keck* is not likely to create positive feedback: the typical claimant seeking the protection of the market freedoms will usually not plead for the narrowing of their scope. The result is that the judicial test on the concept of restriction on economic free movement will remain static or, as arguably happened in practice, renewed pressure for its

[26] Such as the role of Member States as interveners in the judicial process. This, however, only amounts to a defensive role, and even Member States must argue in accordance with existing precedent, which seems to indicate that the role of the Member States as interveners can, like a dike, slow the rising free movement tide, but is unable to stop it altogether.

[27] Arguably, the best (anecdotal) evidence that all of these elements played a role is that the Court of Justice reacted to increased academic and judicial criticism about its case law, as it was being flooded with similar cases during the *Sunday Trading* saga, by endorsing an approach that was advanced by one of the Commission's agents. Its adoption was justified as being needed to check: '*the increasing tendency of traders to invoke Article 30 of the Treaty as a means of challenging any rules whose effect is to limit their commercial freedom even where such rules are not aimed at products from other Member States*'. See para. 14 of *Keck and Mithouard*.

extension will again surface under a new guise as litigants continue to try to extend their free movement rights.[28]

A focus on path-dependence need not blind us to the role that the shared cognitive frameworks, values, and concerns of a legal community can play in the development of the law. As is apparent from *Keck*, normative considerations can buck institutionally based trends. Furthermore, the normative theories developed to rationalize the evolution of the case law influenced its development by providing greater levels of theorization, in the form of normative and explanatory theories on the concept of restriction on free movement. This could then be adopted by courts and litigants when deciding and pleading cases, alongside theories about the normative unity or disunity of the freedoms and related requirements of systemic interpretation.[29]

The outcome of *Cassis* was an incompletely theorized mix of traditional normative ideas about anti-protectionism with novel ideas about European integration. In effect, the *Cassis* reasoning attracted virtually no attention until the Commission issued an interpretative Communication rationalizing it, *ex post*, in accordance with certain classificatory frameworks, which were then picked up by a community of EU legal academics and practitioners.[30] On the other hand, and as we have seen, purely normative approaches were of limited use in unearthing the meaning of judicial tests. The result was that—locked-in, constrained by path-dependency, and pressured by claimants who perceived and reacted to the existent choice-set by attempting to alter the existing institutional framework at the margin and by the reactions of other institutional players[31]—the Court of Justice gave precedence to the formulae it created over their potential normative foundations, thereby detaching the judicial tests from their original normative *rationale*, and even from most of their *ex post* rationalizations.

A consequence of all this is that institutionally driven developments can affect the content of the law's normative *substrata*. In other words, normative

[28] See fn. 151 in Chapter 1 above, including Connant, *Justice Contained*, 19, 21–38. See also Schmidt, 'Who Cares About Nationality?', 11.

[29] Examples of these theories can be found for discrimination (Marenco, 'Pour une interpréta-tion traditionelle de la notion de mesure d'effet equivalent àune restriction quantitative'), economic due-process (Gormley, '"Actually or Potentially, Directly or Indirectly?"'), typological approaches (White, 'In Search of the Limits to Article 30 of the EEC Treaty'), and market access (Weatherill, 'After *Keck*'), to name only the most relevant.

[30] See, famously, Communication from the Commission concerning the consequences of the judgment given by the Court of Justice on 20 February 1979 in Case 120/78 (*Cassis de Dijon*), already referred in fn. 25 of Chapter 4. Another example of this can be found in the Commission's White Paper on 'Completing the Internal Market' [1985]. See also Connant, *Justice Contained*, 12.

[31] Connant, *Justice Contained*, 12–13.

considerations do not reflect concepts or conceptions that exist *a priori*, but instead come into existence as a result of a constitutive process inherent to legal practice. For example, since negative integration, of necessity, leads to some overlap between the removal of obstacles to intra-State trade and deregulation, in the absence of a careful application of normative criteria the pressures exerted by economic agents eventually led, through incremental change, to the finding that any rule which might potentially restrict economic freedom also restricted the free movement of goods. It was the normative under-theorization of the various judicial tests on the restriction on the free movement of goods that allowed litigants to argue, and the Court of Justice to conclude, that a judgment prohibiting measures by a Member State (the country-of-sale) preventing the sale of products coming from another Member State because such products did not comply with the country-of-sale's rules on product requirements—as in *Cassis de Dijon*—implied that all national measures prohibiting the marketing of products with certain characteristics needed to be justified, regardless of whether those products were imported or not, as in *Cinéthèque*. It was this same under-theorization that subsequently allowed the Court to further conclude that any measure that can potentially restrict the volume of sales of imported and domestic products alike is restrictive unless justified, thereby transforming the free movement of goods into an economic due-process clause, as in the *Sunday Trading* cases. Similar developments can be said to have occurred as regards the free movement of persons, and eventually to have led to the apparent adoption of market access as a judicial test applicable across all freedoms.[32]

These developments do not reflect an improved divination of the original meaning of the market freedoms, but are instead the result of a discursive process which brought about an evolution in the accepted meaning of those provisions through: (i) sophisticated reflection on their possible normative underpinnings by a professional legal class operating in particular institutional contexts; and (ii) pressure by litigants who took advantage of this reflection to argue for increased rights to free movement on the basis of normative and systemic coherence.

III. A More Comprehensive Description

Apart from the academic literature focusing on economic free movement generally, there are different branches of scholarship that focus instead

[32] Schmidt, 'Who Cares About Nationality?', 11.

on specific areas of free movement law. The existence of these specialized branches constitutes a blind-spot in more general discussions on the concept of restriction on economic free movement and points to the existence of multiple concepts of restriction on economic free movement—an issue that needs to be addressed by anyone attempting to develop an analytical framework fully able to explain the law on economic free movement. This section will now review these areas of the law, and identify the specificities in the concept of restriction on economic free movement they adopt.[33]

A. Direct taxation

Direct taxation raises a number of particular issues for free movement law. Tax rules are inherently territorial, applying criteria such as residence and place of work.[34] For example, international tax law tends to distinguish between taxation at source (meaning at the place where the taxable income or activity occurred) and taxation of the worldwide income of residents. This gives rise to the possibility of double taxation, which is usually dealt with in double taxation agreements ('DTA's) by giving precedence to taxation at source and granting a corresponding credit at the place of residence.

With the exception of the free movement of capital, which expressly allows Member States to discriminate for tax purposes on the basis of residence,[35] there is a general presumption that national rules that apply territory-based criteria are *prima facie* prohibited under the market freedoms because they indirectly discriminate on grounds of nationality[36] or against free movement.[37] Therefore, it would seem that national rules on direct taxation would fall within the scope of the market freedoms.

[33] The following areas of the law are those which the author has identified as being subject to specific judicial tests regarding whether they restrict economic free movement or not. There may well be other areas not subject to the general concept of restriction on free movement, but the author is unaware of them.

[34] As acknowledged in Case 270/83 *Commission v France* [1986] E.C.R. 273 (*Avoir Fiscal*). See also Case C-175/88 *Biehl* [1990] E.C.R. I-1779; Jan Wouters, 'Fiscal Barriers to Companies' Cross Border Establishment' (1994) 14 YEL 73, 103. This is also the case for non-physical entities: Laenerts and Bernardeau, 'L'encadrement communautaire de la fiscalité directe', 42.

[35] But, following Case C-319/02 *Manninen* [2004] E.C.R. I-07477, this, when articulated with the prohibition of Art. 58 (3) on arbitrary restriction, is to be read in accordance with the case law on tax discrimination applicable to the other market freedoms. See Usher, 'Monetary Movements and the Internal Market', 200–207.

[36] See Case C-42/02 *Lindman* [2003] E.C.R. I-13519.

[37] Case C-234/01 *Gerritse* [2003] E.C.R. I-5933; Case C-39/04 *Fournier* [2005] E.C.R. I-2057; Case C-17/00*De Coster* [2001] E.C.R. I-9445; Case C-136/00 *Danner* [2002] E.C.R. I-8147;

The Court of Justice has, however, decided otherwise. In *Schumacker*, it held that, where direct taxes are concerned, the situations of residents and non-residents are not comparable because income received in the territory of a State by a non-resident is in most cases only part of her total income. A non-resident's personal ability to pay tax, determined by reference to her aggregate income and her personal and family circumstances, was held to be easier to assess at the place where her personal and financial interests are centred, which tends to be the place where she has her usual abode. This means that the use of residency-based criteria for the purposes of direct taxation is not indirectly discriminatory, except when a non-resident receives no significant income in the State of residence and obtains a significant part of her taxable income in another State.[38] This case law has since become entrenched for the free movement of workers,[39] and has been extended to the right of establishment,[40] the free provision of services,[41] European Citizenship,[42] and arguably the free movement of capital as well.[43] It has also been further established that the situation of residents and non-residents includes '*all the tax advantages connected with the non-resident's ability to pay tax which are not taken into account either in the State of residence or in the State of employment*'[44] and is comparable when the amount earned by a non-resident in a Member State is 90 per cent or more of her total income.[45]

The peculiarity of this case law lies in the way the discrimination test is applied, in particular in the attention the Court of Justice pays to the *tertium comparationis*—an attention which is effectively absent in the traditional use of discrimination tests by the Court. What the Court of Justice has held, correctly, is that if the situation of residents and non-residents is

Case C-330/07 *Vermögensverwaltungs-Gesellschaft* [2008] E.C.R. I-9099; *Filipiak*. As seen above, indirect discrimination on grounds of nationality sometimes overlaps with discrimination against free movement: see Case C-294/97 *Eurowings* [1999] E.C.R. I-7447, para. 37.

[38] Case C-279/93 *Schumaker* [1995] E.C.R. I-0225.

[39] Case C-336/96 *Gilly* [1998] E.C.R. I-2793; *Renneberg*.

[40] Case C-80/94 *Wielockx* [1995] E.C.R. I-2493; *Asscher*; Case C-329/05 *Meindl* [2007] E.C.R. I-1107.

[41] *Gerritse*. [42] Case C-520/04 *Turpeinen* [2006] E.C.R. I-10685.

[43] Case C-376/03 *D.* [2005] E.C.R. I-2421; Case C-510/08 *Mattner* [2010] E.C.R. I-3553. See also Laenerts and Bernardeau, 'L'encadrement communautaire del al fiscalité directe', 76.

[44] Case C-182/06 *Lakebrink* [2007] E.C.R. I-6705, para. 34.

[45] Case C-391/97 *Gschwind* [1999] E.C.R. I-5451. A. Castro Oliveira, 'Workers and Other Persons: Step-by-Step from Movement to Citizenship—Case-Law 1995–2001' (2002) 39 CML Rev 77, 121, criticizes this decision by arguing that residents and non-residents were, in this case, in a comparable situation.

not objectively comparable as regards direct taxation, no discrimination can be said to exist even if a criterion that is *prima facie* prohibited is being used by national legislation. Residence requirements are thereby *prima facie* lawful in direct taxation unless the situation of residents and non-residents is comparable,[46] which means that the relevant question for the Court of Justice when deciding these cases is how to identify the situations where residents and non-residents are in an objectively comparable position. The Court of Justice held that a resident is in a comparable position to a non-resident when she earns the majority of her income in a State other than the one where she resides, making it impossible for the State of residency to take into account her situation. The underlying idea seems to be that such a person becomes a 'virtual' resident of the State where the majority of income is earned, which justifies requiring the host-State to take into account the non-resident's personal and family circumstances in the same way it does for its residents.[47] This approach requires a State other than the one of residence to take into account facts which are usually known only to the latter—an exercise which is made possible by the existence of EU secondary legislation providing for ways through which States can obtain information from tax authorities from other countries. In effect, by creating the pre-conditions for the comparability of the situation of residents and non-residents, this secondary legislation appears to have been essential to the development of this case law in the first place.[48]

Apart from this particular take on the *tertium comparationis*, direct taxation is also conspicuous for the concept of restriction it uses.[49] The Court of Justice started using the language of obstacle-based tests for cases of direct taxation soon after such a test was adopted for the free movement of persons, even if in virtually every case it then went on to pursue a discrimination-based analysis that focused on whether national rules led to differentiated treatment and whether the situations of the claimant and

[46] Paul Farmer, 'Article 48 EC and the Taxation of Frontier Workers' (1995) 20 ELRev 310, 316.

[47] Peter Wattel, 'The EC Court's Attempts to Reconcile the Treaty Freedoms with International Tax Law' (1996) 33 CML Rev 233, 227; Melchior Wathelet, 'The Influence of Free Movement of Persons, Services and Capital on National Direct Taxation: Trends in the Case Law of the Court of Justice' (2000) 20 YEL 1, 10.

[48] *Schumaker*, para. 45; *Wielockx*, para. 26. See Council Directive 77/799/EEC of 19 December 1977 concerning mutual assistance by the competent authorities of the Member States in the field of direct taxation [1977] OJ 1977 L 336

[49] This is arguably also the case for indirect taxation: see Jukka Snell 'Non-Discriminatory Tax Obstacles' (2008) 56 ICLQ 339, 340–350.

of the persons receiving such differentiated treatment were comparable.[50] Even though, theoretically, the free movement provisions apply in the same way to tax and non-tax rules, an obstacle-based approach sits uneasily with the concept of national sovereignty in tax law. Direct taxation is an area in which mere discrepancies between the laws of Member States can pose clear obstacles to free movement. The combination of source-based and residence-based taxation criteria can lead to double taxation, the very definition of an obstacle created by different national rules. Moreover, a number of differences in national tax law, for example the tax rate, could be construed as obstacles under the mutual recognition or 'additional cost' criterion.[51]

As such, an obstacle-based approach could easily lead to an economic due-process clause, an implication not lost on private tax litigants. In what has been identified as a reaction by the Court of Justice to a barrage of cases testing the limits of this case law, the Court subsequently seemed to revert explicitly to a discrimination-based analysis.[52] In *Marks and Spencer*, a case on UK rules limiting the amounts parent-companies could deduct on losses incurred by non-resident subsidiaries, Advocate General Maduro explicitly argued for an extension of the test applicable to direct taxation beyond non-discrimination, in an attempt to bring it in line with the rest of the case law on the market freedoms.[53] The Court of Justice, without explicitly disagreeing with the Advocate General, instead argued that the UK measure discriminated both on grounds of nationality and against free movement. A restriction was found because the rules applied '*different treatment for tax purposes to losses incurred by a resident subsidiary and losses incurred by a non-resident subsidiary*'.[54] An explicit defence of this purely discriminatory approach was subsequently pursued by Advocate General Geelhoed, who argued that cumulative burdens resulting from the parallel exercise of

[50] Advocate General Maduro's Opinion in Case C-446/03 *Marks & Spencer* [2005] E.C.R. I-10837, paras 27–28. See, for example: for workers, Case C-385/00 *de Groot* [2002] E.C.R. I-11819; for services, *De Coster*, *Lindman*; for establishment, Case C-307/97 *Saint-Gobain* [1999] E.C.R. I-6161, Case C-250/95 *Futura* [1997] E.C.R. I-2417 *X and Y*, Case C-324/00 *Lankhorst-Hohorst* [2002] E.C.R. I-11779, Case C-168/01 *Bosal* [2003] E.C.R. I-9409, and, more recently, Case C-48/13 *Nordea Bank Danmark*, decided on 17 July 2014, and Case C-326/12 *van Caster*, decided on 9 October 2014. See also S. Kingston, 'A Light in the Darkness: Recent Developments in the ECJ's Recent Tax Jurisprudence' (2007) 44 CML Rev, 1334; Snell, 'Non-Discriminatory Tax Obstacles', 350–354.

[51] Kingston, 'A Light in the Darkness', 1330–1331.

[52] See *D.*; Case C-403/03 *Schempp* [2005] E.C.R. I-6421; Kingston, 'A Light in the Darkness', 1335.

[53] Advocate General Maduro's Opinion in *Marks & Spencer*, paras 31–40.

[54] Ibid, paras 31–34.

Member State's fiscal sovereignty 'restrict' cross-border activity, but that on closer analysis two types of 'restriction' can arise in such circumstances. The first (which were termed 'quasi-restrictions') are restrictions resulting inevitably from the co-existence of national tax systems, which give rise to '*distortions of economic activity resulting from the fact that different legal systems must exist side-by-side*'. The second (which he termed 'true restrictions') are '*restrictions that go beyond those flowing inevitably from the co-existence of national tax systems*'. The Advocate General then went on to suggest that '*all "truly" restrictive national direct tax measures will also, in practice, [be] directly or indirectly discriminatory measures*', distinguishing between obstacles '*resulting from disparities or differences between the tax systems of two or more Member States*', which did not restrict the market freedoms, and '*obstacles resulting from discrimination, which occurs as a result of the rules of just one tax jurisdiction*', which did.[55] This reasoning appears to have been adopted by the Court of Justice, which has for all purposes abandoned even the trappings of an obstacle-based approach in this field in favour of a discrimination-oriented test.[56]

This is not to say that the Court of Justice has not developed other strategies to remove non-discriminatory obstacles in this field, particularly those arising from the possibility of double-taxation.[57] The Court of Justice has considered that the Treaty does not prohibit national instruments that minimize such obstacles, such as the application of a tax credit mechanism with a view to precluding double-taxation.[58] It has also extended the scope of the free movement provisions so that they are able to assess whether DTAs entered into by Member States—which are international treaties *prima facie* excluded from the market freedoms' scope—are in accordance with the Treaty.[59] But in all these cases, the Court of Justice went to extremes to stress that what it was assessing was whether the national rules of Member States were discriminatory, that mere differences between national direct taxation laws do not fall within the scope of the market freedoms, and that, whenever

[55] See Advocate General Geelhoed's Opinion in Case C-374/04 *Test Claimants* [2006] E.C.R. I-11673, paras 32-41. See, similarly, Advocate General Sharpston's Opinion in Case C-96/08 *CIBA* [2010] E.C.R. I-2911, paras 26–29.

[56] Kingston, 'A Light in the Darkness', 1336–1341; Michael J. Graetz and Alvin C. Warren, 'Dividend Taxation in Europe: When the ECJ Makes Tax Policy' (2007) 44 CML Rev 1577. But path-dependency still plays its role; the Court of Justice sometimes refers to the relevant obstacle test before applying a discrimination test—see, for example, *CIBA*, para. 19; Case C-284/09 *Commission v Germany* [2011] E.C.R. I-09879, para. 72.

[57] International double taxation is not a restriction on the market freedoms: see Case C-513/04 *Kerckhaert and Morris* [2006] ECR I-10967.

[58] *Gilly*, Laenerts and Bernardeau, 'L'encadrement communautaire de la fiscalité directe', 70–71.

[59] *Saint-Gobain*, paras 57–60; *de Groot; Gerritse; Turpeinen*.

a DTA is deemed discriminatory, it is because the laws in question are coordinated, and hence there can be said to be no restrictions arising from pure differences between national laws.[60]

B. Social security

The integrity of the various national social security schemes, each requiring a minimum contribution on an annual basis and a minimum number of years of such contributions before benefits are granted, meant that a worker, whose contribution record would entitle her to benefits in case of unemployment, could have to sacrifice such coverage if she decided to migrate to another Member State. Further, refusal by national authorities to pay benefits to claimants residing outside their jurisdiction could compound this obstacle.[61] To address this issue, the Treaties provided for the co-ordination of the various national social security systems, by requiring the amendment of national laws.[62] The secondary legislation adopted for this purpose was based on a number of principles.[63] Persons covered by EU legislation were assimilated to nationals, requiring the removal of national laws which put migrants at a disadvantage. A person should, if she decided to move, see the social protection to which she was entitled replaced by an equivalent protection in the host-State through the aggregation of the social benefits that the person had accrued in different Member States, and by the guarantee that such aggregated benefits would be paid in whatever Member State the person lawfully resided.[64] Furthermore, in the case of payment of cash benefits, Member States were precluded from withdrawing or reducing benefits on

[60] *Alevizos.*

[61] Derrick Wyatt, 'The Social Security Rights of Migrant Workers and their Families' (1977) 14 CML Rev 411, 411–412; A. C. Page, 'The Scope of Community and National Rules against the Overlapping of Social Security Benefits' (1989) 17 CML Rev 211, 211.

[62] Art. 51 EEC. See J. Seché, 'The Revision of Regulations nos. 3 and 4 (Social Security and Migrant Workers) in Light of their Interpretation by the Court of Justice' (1968) 6 CML Rev 170, 171.

[63] Particularly Regulation no. 1408/71 [1971] OJ L 149 OF; replaced by Regulation no. 883/2004 [2004] OJ L 166 on the coordination of social security systems. See A. Pieter van der Mei, *Free Movement of Persons Within the European Community* (Hart Publishing 2003), 63–64; Vicki Paskalia, 'Co-ordination of Social Security in the European Union: An Overview of Recent Case Law' (2009) 46 CML Rev 1177, 1180.

[64] Walter Munch and Jean-Claude Séché, 'Les Droits de l'Étranger dans les Communautés Européenes' [1975] CDE 251, 261–262.

the ground that the recipient was a resident in a Member State other than the one whose institution was responsible for payment.[65]

The case law of the Court of Justice on social security restricted itself to the enforcement of this secondary legislation, with the market freedoms being applied only to the few situations falling outside its scope. This may explain why the concept of restriction on economic free movement as used in this area seemed to follow the principles resulting from that legislation, and to focus on precluding national legislation that might place European citizens at a disadvantage when they wished to extend their activities beyond the territory of a single Member State.[66] Situations that could lead a worker to lose, as a consequence of the exercise of her right to free movement, the advantages in the field of social security guaranteed to her by the laws of a single Member State, especially when those advantages represented the counterpart of contributions already paid, were found to be contrary to the free movement of persons because they placed her in a worse situation than that of a worker who had never migrated.[67] Similarly, legislation by a Member State requiring contributions to be made to a social security scheme by persons already affiliated to a social security scheme in another Member State without providing any additional benefits was prohibited, since such legislation disadvantages the pursuit of occupational activities in a second Member State by imposing costs without any corresponding benefit.[68]

Other than these situations of discrimination against free movement, the Court has consistently held that the Treaty offers no guarantee to a person that extending her activities into more than one Member State, or transferring them to another Member State, will be neutral as regards social security. Given the disparities in the social security legislation of the various Member States, such an extension or transfer may be to the person's advantage in terms of social security or not, depending on the circumstances. It follows that any variations in treatment that arise from differences between national social security laws are in accordance with EU law, so long as these variations affect in the same way those to whom the laws apply, according to objective criteria, and without regard to their

[65] Wyatt, 'The Social Security Rights of Migrant Workers and ther Families', 413.

[66] See *Stanton*.

[67] Case C-228/07 *Petersen* [2008] E.C.R. I-6989, para. 43 and case law cited therein.

[68] Case C-53/95 *Kemmler* [1996] E.C.R. I-0703; Joined cases C-393/99 and C-394/99 *INASTI* [2002] E.C.R. I-2829.

nationality.[69] The idea seems to be that, since the Treaty provides not for the harmonization, but for the coordination of social security rules, the competences of the Member States are to be protected. This prevents the Court of Justice from finding obstacles in the mere disparity of regulations and from giving full effect to obstacle tests.

There is one exception to this, however, which concerns the receipt of health services abroad. Article 22 of Regulation 1407/71 required prior authorization from the home-State for the receipt of certain health-benefits by its nationals in another Member State. This requirement was challenged in two ground-breaking cases: *Decker*,[70] concerning a refusal by the Luxembourg social security authorities to reimburse a pair of spectacles bought in Belgium on the basis of a Luxembourg prescription; and *Kohll*,[71] concerning a refusal by those same Luxembourg authorities to allow dental treatment in Germany for one of its citizens. Both of these refusals were valid under the Regulation, but the Court of Justice held that the situations fell outside its scope. The Regulation, it was held, was

> ...*not intended to regulate, and hence did not in any way prevent the reimbursement by Member States at the tariffs in force in the competent State, of costs incurred in connection with treatment provided in another Member State, even without prior authorisation.*[72]

In both these cases, the traditional obstacle-based test was adopted and the authorization requirements were deemed restrictive,[73] with the result that an alternative procedure, under which reimbursement of the cost of cross-border care is not a privilege but a judicially enforceable right which can only be limited in exceptional circumstances, was created.[74] The striking thing about these cases and the case law arising from it, however, is that they are the only decisions in the field of social security that follow the more

[69] Case C-92/02 *Kristiansen* [2003] E.C.R. I-14597; Case C-493/04 *Piatkowski* [2006] E.C.R. I-2369, para. 34.

[70] Case C-120/95 *Nicolas Decker* [1998] E.C.R. I-1831.

[71] Case C-158/96 *Kohll* [1998] E.C.R. I-1931.

[72] Ibid, para. 27.

[73] *Decker*, paras 31–36; *Kohll*, paras 31–36. See also Matthew Moore, 'Freedom of Movement and Migrant Workers' Social Security: An Overview of the Case Law' (2002) 39 CML Rev 808, 816.

[74] Barnard, *The Substantive Law of the EU*, 395–403; Mei, *Free Movement of Persons Within the European Community*, 288; V. Hatzopoulos, '*Killing* National Health and Insurance Systems but *Healing* Patients? The European Market for Healthcare Services after the Judgements of the ECJ in *Vanbraekel* and *Peerbooms*', [2002] 39 CML Rev 696.

general concept of restriction that is used in the case law on the economic free movement of persons.[75]

C. The free movement of companies and their primary seat

Yet another area where the Court of Justice seems to apply a specific test that differs from its general approach to the concept of restriction on economic free movement concerns the transfer of the primary seat of corporations. Two main theories can be said to exist in this regard. The 'Sitztheorie', or real seat theory, postulates that a company's legal capacity is determined by reference to the law applicable in the place where its actual centre of management and control is located. In accordance with this theory, the removal of the centre of management and control from a real seat jurisdiction may presuppose the winding-up of the relevant company, with all the consequences this entails in company and tax law, while the establishment by a foreign company of its centre of management and control in a real seat jurisdiction might require a company to be newly incorporated. Some jurisdictions that adopt the real seat doctrine do not impose such strict requirements and allow a company to move to another Member State without being dissolved. However, in its pure form, real seat jurisdictions refuse to recognize companies originating from other legal orders, even if this movement is in accordance with the laws of the companies' State of origin. They either disqualify them or submit them to their own (real-seat) legal order when those companies' centres of management and control move into their territory.[76] The second theory, known as 'Gründungstheorie', or incorporation theory, holds instead that legal capacity is determined in accordance with the law of the State in which the company was incorporated regardless of where its centre of management and control is located.

[75] Case C-368/98 *Vanbraekel* [2001] E.C.R. I-5363, para. 44; Case C-157/99 *Geraets-Smits & Peerbooms* [2001] E.C.R. I-5473, paras 61–69; *Commission v France*, para. 91; *Müller-Fauré*, para. 44; Case C-8/02 *Leichtle* [2004] E.C.R. I-2641, para. 30; Case C-444/05 *Stamatelaki* [2007] E.C.R. I-3185, paras 25–29; Case C-211/08 *Commission v Spain* [2010] E.C.R. I-5267, paras 56–72; Case C-512/08 *Commission v France* [2010] E.C.R. I-08833, para. 32; Case C-173/09 *Elchinov* [2010] E.C.R. I-08889, paras 41–45; Case C-255/09 *Commission v Portugal* [2011] E.C.R. I-10547, paras 74–75. The present case law can be summarily described as holding that prior authorization for reimbursement of costs constitutes, for both patients and service providers, an obstacle to free movement. This is likely to be justified for systems of intra-mural (hospital) care or extra-mural care requiring the use of major and costly equipment exhaustively listed in the national legislation, but not for general extra-mural (out-of-hospital) care or for systems based on reimbursement. See Barnard, *The Substantive Law of the EU*, 401.

[76] Eddy Wymeersch, 'The Transfer of the Company's Seat in European Community Law' (2003) 40 CML Rev 661, 662, 668–671.

Articulating these models in a single economic space where economic free movement is protected is a difficult exercise, with the types of movement in Table 5.1 being possible:

Table 5.1: Real seat and incorporation theories

From \ To	Incorporation	Real-seat
Incorporation	I	II
Real-seat	III	IV

Movement I (the rules of the original State of incorporation apply) and Movement IV (the rules of the host-State apply) do not pose issues concerning which jurisdiction a company is subject to, but Movement II can lead to two legal orders claiming jurisdiction over a company, and Movement III may result in a company being left unregulated. Furthermore, even in situations where company movement is possible and it is clear which jurisdiction will apply after that movement takes place, there may be national rules setting forth conditions for that movement being allowed in the first place.

The complexity of this issue was reflected in its treatment in the Treaties. Article 54 TFEU provides for a number of different connection factors—registered office, central management, or principal place of business—as being relevant to determine the nationality of a company. Article 220 of the EC Treaty (now revoked) provided for Member States entering into agreements to address the transfer of their primary seat but no convention has ever been agreed in this area.

The first question to reach the Court of Justice in this area concerned a Movement I situation. The case, *Daily Mail*, concerned the validity of a requirement of prior authorization from the UK Treasury for the outbound movement from the UK of a company wanting to establish its central management in the Netherlands without losing legal personality or ceasing to be a United Kingdom company.[77] The Court of Justice, held that the right of establishment prohibits the home-State from hindering the establishment in another Member State of a company incorporated under its legislation by means of both secondary establishment and/or taking part in the

[77] Case 81/87 *Daily Mail* [1988] E.C.R. 5483. The reason for this condition was that the company would cease to be resident in the UK for corporate tax purposes.

incorporation of a company in another Member State, but decided that the transfer of the primary seat fell outside the scope of this freedom. Holding that companies are creatures of national law, and that their existence, functioning, and extinction is to be regulated by that law alone, the Court decided that the conditions under which a company may transfer its central management and control from one Member State to another were governed by the national laws of the State in which it was incorporated and of the State to which it wished to move. In the absence of harmonization, the Court of Justice held that differences in national legislation concerning the relevant connection factor, and on the possibility of transferring a company's seat, must be dealt with by future legislation or international conventions.

Daily Mail merely looked into the rules of the State-of-incorporation, and its reasoning left open the question of what to do if the rules of the State-of-incorporation were not compatible with those of the host-State. In *Überseering*, a question regarding a Movement II situation, i.e. where two legal orders claim jurisdiction over a company, reached the Court of Justice.[78] The case focused on a real-seat jurisdiction, Germany, which refused to recognize a company incorporated under the law of the Netherlands that had moved its centre of management and control to Germany. The result was that the company was denied all legal capacity until it was reincorporated in Germany, even though the company's actions were lawful under Dutch law.[79] The Court of Justice found that the situation fell within the scope of the market freedoms, holding that the reasoning in *Daily Mail* applied only to relations between a company and the Member State under whose laws it had been incorporated when that company wished to transfer its actual centre of management and control to another Member State whilst retaining its legal personality in the State of incorporation. In this sense, *Daily Mail* was distinguished as an 'emigration' case. *Überseering*, was, instead, an immigration case, and the refusal to recognize a company validly incorporated in another Member State which had no problem with the company moving its centre of management and control elsewhere was held to be a restriction on the right of establishment. Thus, and in contrast to what one might have expected to be derived from *Daily Mail*, it was decided that not

[78] Case C-208/00 *Überseering* [2002] E.C.R. I-9919.

[79] Wymeersch, 'The Transfer of the Company's Seat in European Law Community', 671, 682—these are so-called 'bipatride' companies. The opposite situation would be a Movement III situation, which can leave a company unregulated. This is usually prevented by the home-State requiring the winding-up of the company in order to allow it move to another Member State. See the discussion on Case C-210/06 *Cartesio* [2008] E.C.R. I-9641 below.

all differences between legal systems on the subject of change of primary seat fell outside the scope of the right of establishment.[80] In *Inspire Art*,[81] a case concerning a Dutch law imposing a number of obligations upon the exercise of a UK company's business activities in the Netherlands, this line of reasoning was further elaborated and extended to inbound Movement I situations.

At this point in time, the law seemed to be that while inbound situations fell within the scope of the right of establishment, outbound situations did not. This was at odds with the main corpus of free movement law according to which inbound and outbound situations were subject to the same standards.[82] However, while the Court of Justice was refusing to eradicate obstacles to the outbound movement of a company's primary seat, it was also creating, together with the EU's political process, the conditions for the circumvention of these same obstacles.

The most conspicuous means by which the Court of Justice did this was by allowing companies to set a primary establishment in one Member State, even if they then went on to pursue all their activities through secondary establishments in other Member States. In *Centros*, the Court of Justice expressly accepted that a company could be formed in a Member State solely for the purpose of establishing itself in another State where its main, or indeed entire, business was to be conducted through a secondary branch.[83] From a practical standpoint, this made the distinction between primary and secondary establishment virtually meaningless.[84]

Obstacles to the transfer of the primary seat were also addressed through the transformation of companies. *Daily Mail* meant that the market freedoms did not create a right for companies to transfer their primary seat to another Member State '*while retaining their status as companies incorporated under the legislation of the first Member State*'.[85] In *Sevic*, a case concerning a decision by the German authorities to refuse the registration of a merger of a German company with a Luxembourg company on the grounds that German law only provided for mergers between companies established in Germany, the Court of Justice held that restrictions on mergers fell within the scope of the free movement provisions, further restricting the scope of

[80] *Überseering*, para. 82. See also António Frada de Sousa, 'Company's Cross-Border Transfer of Seat in the EU after *Cartesio*' [2009] Jean Monnet Working Paper 07/09, 18.

[81] Case C-167/01 *Inspire Art* [2003] E.C.R. I-10155.

[82] Wymeersch, 'The Transfer of the Company's Seat in European Law Community', 675–676.

[83] Case C-212/97 *Centros* [1999] E.C.R. I-1459.

[84] Wymeersch, 'The Transfer of the Company's Seat in European Law Community', 680–681.

[85] *Daily Mail*, para. 24.

Daily Mail to those outbound situations where legal personality is retained in the State of incorporation.[86]

The EU legislator also started devising ways to facilitate the transfer of a company's main seat. The first instrument for this was the *Societas Europaea* ('SE') Regulation, allowing public limited liability companies to transfer their registered office from one Member State to another. The public limited company intending to transfer its seat abroad would, however, first have to convert itself into an SE in its home-State. The SE would subsequently transfer its registered office to the host-State and, finally, convert itself back into a public limited company subject to the *lex societatis* of that host-State.[87] Secondly, the cross-border merger Directive allowed limited liability companies to transfer their registered office to another Member State with a change of *lex societatis* through a cross-border merger—in particular, by setting up a subsidiary in the Member State where it wanted to move its registered office and then merging with that subsidiary.[88]

In short, while the market freedoms seemed only able to remove obstacles to the inbound movement of a company's seat, a number of alternatives were devised to circumvent obstacles to outbound movement through case law and legislation on secondary establishment, cross-border mergers, and *ad hoc* company structures.[89]

This state of affairs gave rise to a particular tension, since the decision in *Centros* seemed to imply that the validity of the incorporation of a company in one Member State could not be called into question in a second Member State on the grounds that its centre of management and control was not located in the State of incorporation. In other words, *Centros* seemed to establish that the real seat theory itself was an obstacle to free movement prohibited by the Treaty.[90] This ignited an academic debate

[86] Case C-411/03 *SEVIC* [2005] E.C.R. I-10805. See Gert-Jan Vossestein, 'Companies' Freedom of Establishment after *Sevic*' (2006) 4 EBLRev 177, 179.

[87] Council Regulation No. 2157/2001 [2001] OJ L 294 on the Statute for a European Company.

[88] Directive 2005/56/EC [2005] OJ L 310 on cross-border mergers of limited liability companies. This is similar to the system prevailing in the US, which espouses the incorporation doctrine. See Jan Wouters, 'European Company Law: *Quo Vadis*?' (2000) 37 CML Rev 257; Mathias M. Siems, 'The Impact of the European Company (SE) on Legal Culture' (2005) 28 ELRev 431, Deakin, 'Legal Diversity and Regulatory Competition: Which Model for Europe?'

[89] de Sousa, 'Company's Cross-Border Transfer of Seat in the EU after *Cartesio*', 55, 60–61; Johnston and Syrpis, 'Regulatory Competition in European Company Law after *Cartesio*', 385–386.

[90] de Sousa, 'Company's Cross-Border Transfer of Seat in the EU after *Cartesio*', 7; Wulf-Henning Roth, 'From *Centros* to *Uberseering*: Free Movement of Companies, Private International, Law and Community Law' (2003) 52 ICLQ 177, 187.

about whether the real-seat doctrine ran contrary to the free movement provisions or not.[91]

This question was put before the Court of Justice in *Cartesio*, a case concerning a company wishing to transfer its operational headquarters from a real-seat jurisdiction—Hungary—to another country—Italy—while remaining registered and regulated by its State of incorporation.[92] The Hungarian authorities required the company to liquidate itself and reconstitute in Italy. Advocate General Maduro argued quite forcefully that the requirement to liquidate a company when it moved its centre of management and control to another Member State, as required by the real-seat theory, was contrary to the right of establishment because it treated cross-border situations less favourably than purely national situations. He argued for the reversal of *Daily Mail* on the grounds that the Court of Justice had consistently held that rules on the transfer of seat fell within the scope of the right of establishment, that the distinction between 'exit' and 'access' situations ran against the general analytical framework of the right of establishment, and that even though the right of establishment did not preclude the adoption of either the real-seat or incorporation theories, it prevented them from being applied to their fullest logical extent.[93] However, the Court of Justice did not follow the Advocate General and upheld *Daily Mail*, deciding that differences in national legislation should be dealt with by the European legislature, and that a Member State was allowed to prevent a company governed by its laws from retaining that status if that company intended to reorganize itself in another Member State by moving its seat to its territory, thereby breaking the connecting factor required under the national law of the State of incorporation.[94] On the other hand, the Court of Justice further narrowed the scope of application of *Daily Mail*, holding that its reasoning in that case did not extend to situations where a company moves to another Member State with an attendant change as regards the national law applicable, in particular

[91] Adopting this position, see Peter Dyrberg, 'Full Free Movement of Companies in the European Community at Last?' (2003) 18 ELRev 528, 531; similarly, but with qualifications, Wymeersch, 'The Transfer of the Company's Seat in European Law Community', 680–687; Erik Werlauff, 'Cross-Border Transfers of SE Companies' (2004) 1 EurCoL 121. Defending the real seat theory, see Roth, 'From *Centros* to *Uberseering*', 190–193.

[92] Case C-210/06 *Cartesio* [2008] E.C.R. I-9641.

[93] Opinion, paras 25–31.

[94] How much the Court of Justice's position was influenced by the years-long failure to adopt the 14th Company Law Directive on the cross-border transfer of the registered office of limited companies is impossible to say. See, on this, <http://ec.europa.eu/internal_market/company/seat-transfer/2004-consult_en.htm>.

when a company converts into a company type governed by the law of the host-State. The Court of Justice also held that a liquidation or winding-up requirement was a restriction on the right of establishment inasmuch as it prevented a company from converting itself into a company governed by the law of the other Member State, to the extent permitted under that law.[95]

In conclusion, it is clear that the possibility of disparate treatment between outbound and inbound situations subsists in so far as the transfer of a company's primary establishment is concerned, which goes against the general rule that inbound and outbound situations are to be treated equally.[96] This is reminiscent of another area where this distinction was first elaborated: the export of goods, to which the next section is devoted.

D. *Export of goods*

The free movement of goods is the only freedom that has different provisions for entry (imports) and exit (exports) situations, and is also the only freedom where the Court of Justice explicitly adopted different approaches for inbound and outbound situations.[97] In *Groenveld*, a case decided shortly after the Court of Justice expanded its test for imports in *Cassis de Dijon*, the Court held that the concept of measures having equivalent effects to quantitative restrictions on exports was different from that applicable to imports. As a result, and as regards exports, the free movement of goods was found merely to preclude national measures the aim or effect of which was (i) to restrict the flow of exports; and (ii) to thus establish a difference in treatment between the domestic trade of a Member State and its export trade; (iii) in such a way as to confer a particular advantage on domestic production or on the domestic market of the Member State in question.[98] The dominant reading of this decision was that

[95] It should be noted that, at the time of the decision, no Member State had such rules in place: Johnston and Syrpis, 'Regulatory Competition in European Company Law after *Cartesio*', 387. A case which was the mirror image of *Cartesio* was put before the Court in Case C-378/10 *Vale* [2012], decided on 12 July, which concerned a refusal by the Hungarian authorities to recognize the conversion of a company established under Italian law and with its centre of management and control in Italy into a company governed by Hungarian law and with its centre of management and control in Hungary. However, in this case a restriction was easily found because Hungarian law allowed for the conversion of domestic companies, which meant the actions of the Hungarian authorities discriminated between domestic and cross-border company conversions.

[96] de Sousa, 'Company's Cross-Border Transfer of Seat in the EU after *Cartesio*', 38–39.

[97] Szydlo, 'Export Restrictions within the Structure of Free Movement of Goods', 753–754.

[98] Case 15/79 *Groenveld* [1979] E.C.R. 3409, para. 7. See also *Oebel*, para. 17; *Oosthoek's*, para. 13; Case 172/82 *Inter-Huiles* [1983] E.C.R. 555, para. 12; Case 237/82 *Kaas* [1984] E.C.R. 4025, paras 22–23; Case C-339/89 *Alsthom Atlantique* [1991] E.C.R. I-00107, paras 13–14; Case C-412/97 *ED v Fenocchio* [1999] E.C.R. I-3845, para. 10; *Case C-205/07 Gysbrechts and Santurel Inter [2008] E.C.R. I-09947*, para. 40.

the free movement of goods only prohibited discriminatory measures in so far as exports were concerned.[99] However, since the 'too uncertain and indirect effect' doctrine was found to also apply to exports,[100] and, in some cases, the Court of Justice appeared to indicate that measures such as bans on exports and other non-discriminatory obstacles could also restrict the free movement of goods,[101] it was arguable that national rules on exports were subject an effects-based test with a broader scope than a mere prohibition of discriminatory measures.[102] Regardless of which reading was to prevail, and even though the normative grounds for the distinction between them were not clear,[103] it was consensual that the test on exports was different, and less broad, than the test for imports and for outbound movement as applied to the other market freedoms.[104]

More recently, however, a convergence between the rules on exports and imports has been observed. In *Gysbrechts*, the Court of Justice decided that a Belgian rule prohibiting a supplier from requiring an advance or payment before expiry of the period for withdrawal for distance-sales amounted to a restriction on exports. The measure itself was indistinctly applicable, but the Court of Justice held that it affected cross-border sales more than intra-State trade because the actual effect of the measure was greater for goods being exported than for goods marketed in the domestic market. The reason for this was that suppliers face greater obstacles to bringing legal proceedings against consumers who default on their payment if they reside in another Member State, especially when the sales involve relatively small sums.[105] However, it is clear that, even if it reduced the flow of exports, the Belgian law did not differentiate between domestic and export trade, and did not confer

[99] Weatherill, 'After *Keck*: Some Thoughts on How to Clarify the Clarification', 902.

[100] *ED v Fenocchio*, para. 11.

[101] Case 118/86 *Nertsvoederfabriek Nederland* [1987] E.C.R. 3883, para. 11; *Monsees*, para. 22; Case C-47/90*Delhaize frères* [1992] E.C.R. I-3669, paras 13–14.

[102] Holding that an effects-based test, when applied to rules that apply irrespective of nationality, has to have some protective effect to constitute an impediment to trade, see Advocate General Fenelly's Opinion in *Corsica Ferries France*, para. 29.

[103] See, in an attempt to provide such grounds, Alexandre Defossez, 'L'Histoire d'une Divergence et d'une Possible Réconciliation: l'article 29 CE' (2009) XLV CDE 409, 420–421. Critical of this distinction, see Advocate General Trstenjak's Opinion in *Gysbrechts and Santurel Inter*, paras 42–48.

[104] For example, it is not clear why the marketing of goods and services should be treated differently, but that's what *Groenveld* and *Alpine* do: see Oliver and Roth, 'The Internal Market and the Four Freedoms', 420.

[105] *Gysbrechts and Santurel Inter.*

any particular advantage upon domestic trade at the expense of foreign production or trade. On the contrary, if anything the measure placed Belgian exporters in a potentially worse situation than traders active in the State where the customers resided.[106] It is therefore not surprising that, unlike the Court, Belgium, the Commission, and the Advocate General all considered that the measure did not restrict the free movement of exported goods.

This case is, perhaps, part of a trend whereby the Court of Justice has started to extend to exports the test applicable to imports with the aim of developing an overarching formula for the free movement of goods.[107] However, the Court of Justice has not overruled *Groenveld*, nor has it come up with a new test for exports in its stead. As such, exports are *prima facie* still subject to a different test as to the concept of restriction from the one applying generally to the market freedoms at large.[108]

E. *Discrepancies and context*

Each of the sectors reviewed above is subject to a judicial test which differs from the more general approach applicable to the market freedoms *in totum*. What is more, these specific tests are not found in respect of different market freedoms, where different concepts of restriction are usually identified and for which the justifications identified in Chapter 2 were developed; instead, the same judicial test applies to all the market freedoms in a certain area of the law. Lastly, if in some cases—namely exports and the transfer of seat—legal commentators and Advocates General have generally criticized the case law for departing from the general approach, in others—such as social security, but particularly direct taxation—such a departure is not so much criticized as acknowledged, described, and rationalized.

How are we to explain this? It has been noted by political scientists that, while the EU generated an increasing volume of rules and expanded its authority into new areas, developments in those areas were not coordinated. Separate policy domains emerged through positive integration as

[106] As observed by Advocate General Trstenjak in para. 34–40 of her Opinion, before defending the adoption of an 'exit from the market' test, and proposing a substantially similar solution to that adopted by the Court of Justice in this case.

[107] See Case C-293/02 *Jersey Produce* [2005] E.C.R. I-9543; Case C-161/09 *Kakavetsos-Fragkopoulos* [2011] E.C.R. I-00915, particularly Advocate General Mengozzi's Opinion, paras 46–48. See also Anthony Dawes, 'A Freedom Reborn? The New Yet Unclear Scope of Article 29 EC' (2009) 34 ELRev 639, 642.

[108] Stéphanie Rodrigues, 'Cronique de Jurisprudence Communautaire—Marché intérieur' [2009] CDE 217, 230; Tryfonidou, 'Further Steps on the Road to Convergence Among the Market Freedoms', 53.

responses to separate sets of societal demands, with self-interested actors exploiting EU rules and arenas—for example, by taking their concerns to the Commission, the Court of Justice, or the Parliament, and urging them to act.[109] These separate policy domains seem to have been relevant to the development of free movement law. It has been observed repeatedly throughout this book how the existence of secondary legislation was relevant to the development of the Court of Justice's primary law. The reasons for this can be said to relate both to canonical understandings of systemic interpretation, and to attempts by the Court of Justice to advance the law in a consensual way that respects, or appears to respect, the preferences of other relevant institutional actors.

On the other hand, if the political mechanisms for positive integration are blocked, not only will the actions of economic and political agents be channelled towards negative integration, but the risks of the Court of Justice's decisions being overruled by the political process become very small. As is well known, the Court of Justice's role in bringing about the internal market by granting directly enforceable rights to individuals with a stake in EU integration and in adopting a broad interpretation of the market freedoms initially co-existed with limited positive integration and unanimity requirements for the adoption of EU legislation. The unblocking of EU political channels[110] and increase in secondary legislation from the 1980s onwards reduced the Court of Justice's institutional autonomy even as the relevant economic free movement provisions and their underlying normative goals remained the same (and as the goals of European integration expanded). Simultaneously, however, the law's path-dependency generated a pull in the opposite direction which kept the Court of Justice locked-in and subject to pressures from self-interest maximizing litigants.

The co-existence of both general and specific concepts of restriction reflects this tension between the specific institutional context in certain sectors—for example, the political sensitivity and absence of harmonization in direct taxation or the system of co-ordination and secondary legislation for social security—with the more general values and context governing general judicial tests on the concept of restriction on economic free movement, leading to different institutional calculi concerning the acceptable

[109] Stone Sweet, Sandholtz, and Fligstein, *The Institutionalization of Europec*.

[110] This unblocking is relative, obviously: the move from unanimity to qualified majority voting facilitates the adoption of secondary legislation, but the hurdles for its adoption are still quite high.

scope of the market freedoms in specific sectors. The evolution of the case law on the various freedoms reflects a similar tension between different path-dependent lines of case law, on the one hand, and the pressures, on the other hand, for the convergence of the tests applicable to the various market freedoms derived from concerns with the law's coherence and the use of systemic arguments by litigants and Advocates General.[111] Traditional debates about the concept of restriction on economic free movement do not deal with the existence of a multiplicity of tests that were dealt with above. However, these tests are relevant to understand those debates because it is only by looking at the discursive process between all of the relevant institutional agents, and at the normative theories that they might defend from time to time, that we can try to make sense of all of these phenomena within a single analytical framework.

Identifying the specific role that institutional and normative constraints play in each of the areas of the law reviewed above will not be attempted here. Even if identifying institutional constraints helped us to understand the case law better than if we merely looked at normative considerations, the impact of those constraints is still controversial within political science itself.[112] Each situation is deeply contextual and going beyond a somewhat superficial identification of the relevant normative and institutional inputs requires a detailed analysis that falls beyond the scope of this book.[113] Nonetheless, even this cursory review suffices to demonstrate that institutional constraints are relevant to the evolution of free movement law, and that taking them into account helps to make sense of the law and allows for the development of more comprehensive descriptive models.

[111] This is made particularly clear in the review of the law on exports and on the transfer of a company's primary seat discussed above.

[112] See, on the impact of the possibility of State override and non-compliance on the Court of Justice's decision-making, the debate found in: Clifford Carruba, Mathew Gabel, and Charles Hankla, 'Judicial Behavior under Political Constraints: Evidence from the European Court of Justice' (2008) 102 AmPolitSciRev 435; Alec Stone Sweet and Thomas L. Brunell, 'The European Court of Justice, State Noncompliance, and the Politics of Override' (2012) 106 AmPolitSciRev 204; and Clifford Carruba, Mathew Gabel and Charles Hankla, 'Understanding the Role of the European Court of Justice in European Integration' (2012) 106 AmPolitSciRev 214.

[113] Such studies are effectively pursued in the literature mentioned at the beginning of Section III, which is specifically devoted to each of these fields. Nonetheless, the role that specific normative and institutional inputs play in each of these areas clearly merits further research.

IV. Normative Implications

A. The broader picture

The concept of restriction on economic free movement—alongside other elements concerning the scope of the market freedoms which will be reviewed in Chapter 6—is a tool that the Court of Justice uses to decide when to balance a variety of interests and values concerning European economic integration, instead of leaving such balancing to other decision-making entities such as the EU and national political processes. The sensitivity of some issues, the pre-existence of different modes of regulation, and the institutional consequences of finding a restriction on economic free movement for the allocation of legislative competences within the EU can all change the incentives for negative integration and the Court of Justice's institutional calculus, even if all substantive normative considerations remain the same. It is within a discursive framework that includes both legal normative and extra-legal, institutional considerations that the Court of Justice determines its scope of action; and it is by taking into account this framework that we can understand why the Court of Justice is the entity better placed to decide *in some situations but not in others*.

What is at stake in the Court of Justice's decisions on the scope of the market freedoms is a choice between various models of European integration and the numerous normative concerns these models carry with them. The Treaties' statement that one of the EU's goals is to create an internal market does not really help in determining what such a market should look like. There is nothing fixed about an internal market—while most sovereign States have one, almost all look different as a result of their specific institutional and regulatory characteristics. Article 3 (3) TEU sets about the creation of an internal market that is supposed to contribute simultaneously to, *inter alia*, balanced economic growth and price stability, a highly competitive social market economy, and a high level of protection and improvement of the quality of the environment and social justice. It should be clear that, apart from the different meanings that can be attributed to expressions such as 'competitive social market economy', the exclusive pursuit of one goal, such as economic growth, might undermine the achievement of other goals, such as those related to social justice and the protection of the environment.[114] The

[114] K. Mortelmans, 'The Common Market, the Internal Market and the Single Market, What's in a Market?' (1998) 35 CML Rev 101, 118.

balancing of these different goals, a task of the utmost political significance, is thereby required, but neither this provision nor the Treaties provide a complete picture as to what the division of competences between the Member States and the EU, or between the Court of Justice and the EU legislature should be.[115]

In other words, the Court of Justice is left with the duty of choosing between multiple and contentious normative views on what the EU and its internal market should be. A preliminary question in this situation must be why the Court of Justice should decide these matters in the first place. A number of answers are possible. First, even if courts lack the institutional capacity to take into account the same number of considerations and interests as representative political bodies, they may nonetheless provide a forum for voices otherwise unable to be adequately represented in national and European political processes, and thereby serve an important corrective role.[116] Secondly, the Court of Justice has formal legitimacy granted by the Treaties, but it cannot effectively impose its views on the rest of the European Union. These institutional limitations may point towards the Court of Justice being the organization better placed to allocate competences between relevant decision-makers—including itself—since those same limitations make it less likely that the Court will be able to exercise excessive power or abuse this role when compared to other institutional alternatives. In other words, the Court of Justice will likely be the least dangerous branch, which is why the ultimate power regarding the allocation of competences should be granted to it. Furthermore, the Court of Justice's concern with the enforcement of its decisions and with its legitimacy creates pressure for the adoption of incompletely theorized agreements, which have the advantage of requiring prior reasoned argument and of consisting of compromise solutions acceptable to most, if not all, parties. This means that the Court of Justice is not the last word in the development of European integration, but merely a voice, and a moderating one at that, in a more complex discursive process.

These insights do not point to any specific concept of restriction *per se*, but they can guide normative approaches that seek to find such a concept and think contextually about how better to match their proposals as to what the law should be with specific normative agendas. The observations above provide insights into two different facts. The first is that the role of the market freedoms in reconciling divergent social traditions in a competitive 'single'

[115] I thank Stephen Weatherill for having pointed this out to me.
[116] This is the thesis in Maduro, *We, the Court*, as I understand it.

marketplace means that the Court of Justice's role in effecting such reconciliation needs to be determined.[117] The second insight is that such determination is highly contextual.

The main consequence of a measure being found restrictive is that the Court of Justice determines that it—or a national court—is the best-placed institution to pursue a balancing exercise between the need for European integration and the Member State's regulatory autonomy. Accordingly, the question underlying any assessment of whether a measure restricts free movement is one of comparative institutional choice, in particular whether in the relevant institutional context, the Court of Justice is better placed than other institutional alternatives to determine the balance between European integration and the State's regulatory autonomy, between centralization and decentralization, and between different regulatory options. This is not a question that can be answered in the abstract: the specific context in which the Court of Justice operates is relevant. What is more, that context not only changes, it does so by the Court of Justice's own actions, by reactions to such actions, and by autonomous initiatives of other relevant institutional actors. The Court of Justice operates in an institutional environment which might dispute its judgments and react to them: it is the historical interaction between the Member States, the Court of Justice, and other EU institutions that determines both the on-going and ever-(slightly)-changing balance of powers within the EU and the content of the Union's economic constitution.[118] That constitution is open, in the sense that its contents concerning the level of regulation and the attribution of competences will be the result of a discursive process between all the relevant institutional agents and the normative theories they might defend from time to time.

This leads us to the second insight, that the Court of Justice has good reasons to avoid definitively answering normative questions concerning the nature of the internal market. The choice of the Court of Justice as the relevant decision-maker is an imperfect one: being the best institutional alternative does not mean that the Court of Justice is a perfect institutional alternative, able to identify normatively ideal outcomes. There is no good reason why the Court of Justice should determine on its own what kind of single market is to be created—that is a contentious issue requiring the

[117] Niahm Nic Shuibhne, 'Settling Dust? Reflection on the Judgments in *Viking* and *Laval*' (2010) 21 EBLRev 681, 701–703.

[118] More broadly, on the inherent role of conflicting tensions and their constant management by pluralist market societies, see Albert O. Hirschman, 'Social Conflicts as Pillars of Democratic Market Society' (1994) 22 PolTheo 203.

continuous balancing of different normative considerations. The existence of discrepancies in the concept of restriction on economic free movement can thus even be applauded as demonstrating sensitivity to context. Since positive integration is more developed in some sectors than in others, the incentives for negative integration may vary, and specific normative and institutional considerations may provide reasons why the Court of Justice's institutional calculi should be different in different areas.[119]

B. *A proposal concerning judicial tests*

Courts are constrained by both formal and informal rules as to how they pursue their role, but they are also constrained by their own limitations as to what they can effectively do. This relates both to their resources, and to their ability to investigate, understand, and make the substantive social decisions that may be required of them. These constraints interact with the determinants of litigation to determine the institutional ability of the adjudicative process.[120]

It is common to find in the literature concerning the way courts deal with such limitations references to rules and standards. As was described in Chapter 1, this is also a traditional classificatory device used by legal agents attempting to rationalize case law.[121] To summarize what was said there, standards implicitly grant competence to courts, ensuring greater flexibility in dealing with cases that cannot be easily foreseen or made to fit with the normative underpinnings of the law. Rules reduce uncertainty, facilitate settlement, and allow courts to allocate decision-making elsewhere, but tend to be both over- and under-inclusive in relation to their normative underpinnings.

The finding of a restriction on economic free movement carries with it different, possibly conflicting, normative considerations concerning both the identification of obstacles to free movement, the nature of the internal market, and the ideal allocation of competences in the EU, covering an immense variety of situations. This means that a standard-based approach

[119] It should be noted that these calculi include a consideration of the Court of Justice's own legitimacy—after all, what the Court may preserve of its legitimacy in avoiding certain controversies and adopting incompletely theorized approaches, it may lose in criticisms from the legal community for vagueness, for creating difficulties for national courts, for confusing market participants, etc.

[120] Komesar, *Law's Limits*, 38.

[121] See fn. 104 to 108 in Chapter 1 above.

would seem to be the best option when developing the ideal judicial test to identify restrictions on economic free movement. In effect, economic due-process clauses, the market access test, and the discrimination tests as applied by the Court of Justice would seem closer to standards than rules.

The problem with this, as with the adoption of any standard-based judicial test, is that, as the amount and complexity of litigation increases, the lack of clear normative underpinnings can lead to that judicial test's overextension. Simultaneously, concerns about the Court of Justice's physical capacity, scale, and even legitimacy might drive the Court to adopt rules. This is what appears to have occurred with the free movement of goods in *Keck*, and to a certain extent with the developments concerning tax and social security. However, the main problem with the adoption of rules is their natural normative under- and over-inclusiveness, which may lead courts progressively to extend their scope until those rules resemble standards.[122]

In truly complex issues, where the heterogeneity of the cases submitted before the Court of Justice might mean that a rule does not encompass a situation that should be subject to judicial scrutiny, the Court will have to decide whether to give prevalence to the relevant normative considerations or to institutional concerns regarding the consistency, coherence and path-dependency of the law. As complexity and numbers increase, all alternative solutions become imperfect. The tension between the flexibility courts might obtain through the adoption of standards, and the reduction in litigation and the sharing of competence with other institutions that simple rules allow, may lead to cycling between rules and standards as a least-bad situation is attained.[123]

This insight can be formulated in a slightly different fashion: due to the way in which they operate, the market freedoms function as a tool for policing the borderline between legitimate and illegitimate national regulation. As European integration evolves, an increase in the heterogeneity of cases submitted will follow, leading to the adoption of complex, standard-based tests.[124] These standard tests, in turn, can become more manageable and predictable by the development of specific rules applicable to similar situations

[122] The best example of which is arguably the slide from a typological test to market access in goods.

[123] Komesar, *Law's Limits*, 159–160.

[124] Empirical demonstration that increases in inter-State trade correspond to increases in the amount of litigation reaching the Court of Justice is found in Stone Sweet, Sandholtz, and Fligstein, *The Institutionalization of Europe*, 49–51. It is also demonstrated that increases in inter-State trade correspond to increases in the levels of positive integration—see, ibid, 52.

that can be subject to the same rule.[125] This can be said to be the case of the judicial tests developed for the areas of economic free movement law reviewed above. Since they were subject to specific normative and institutional considerations, and, as such, to different comparative institutional choice assessments, the Court of Justice adopted rule-like approaches to the identification of restrictions on economic free movement which were exceptions to the standard applied more generally to the market freedoms. It is true that pressure by litigants and the pull of legitimate normative concerns can limit the usefulness of such rules and lead to the renewed adoption of standards. Nonetheless, since the incentives for litigation mean that there is a constant pressure for an increase in the scope of the market freedoms, rules can serve an important role in anchoring the case law and preventing normative drifts.

The starting point for developing a concept of restriction on economic free movement should be to acknowledge that first, even if the market freedoms share a normative unity concerning the goal of creating an internal market, such normative unity is under-determined and hides debates between diverse visions of the European common market; and, secondly, that, as was seen above, there is no good reason for the Court of Justice to decide such debates on its own. The Court of Justice is rather better suited, institutionally, to participate in the discursive process whereby such debates take place by being a forum for pragmatic compromises reflecting possible, not ideal equilibriums. While gains in legal certainty and freeing resources achieved by adopting rules may correspond to losses in normative coherence, and vice-versa, this is not necessarily a bad thing.[126] Quite the opposite, it is a reflection of the institutional role that courts are better suited to pursue, and may reflect both the institutional realities of enforcement and the political/sociological facts of greater or lesser degrees of agreement concerning the market freedoms' normative underpinnings.

Nonetheless, more care about the normative underpinnings of the case law, and an acknowledgement that the stream of cases reaching the Court of Justice will pressure it towards a continuous expansion of the scope of the market freedoms, seem to be in order. If due care is taken, a standard like market access—which reflects the fact that, while the market freedoms' goal is to promote market integration, they do not support the adoption of economic

[125] Similarly, see Wils, 'The Search for a Rule in Article 30 EEC'.

[126] Miguel Poiares Maduro, 'Harmony and Dissonance in Free Movement' in Mads Andenas and Wulf-Henning Roth (eds), *Services and Free Movement in EU Law* (OUP 2002), 65.

due-process clauses—could become an appropriate tool for dealing with cases which, at heart, are about such a complex, normatively under-determined topic as the ideal scope of the market freedoms. On the other hand, it may be possible or desirable to adopt rules for certain areas of the law. These rules can complement, simplify, or, in some rare cases, even go against the chosen standard. In these situations, and if properly drafted, a rule may be able to address most situations arising before a court, while the general free movement standard will only play a residual role and deal with issues of over- or under-inclusiveness vis-à-vis the relevant normative concerns.

From this perspective, the proposal of rule-like tests by Advocates General, the existence of exceptions to the main 'market access' standard in certain areas of the law, the co-existence of the *Keck* typology and a market access test concerning the free movement of goods, and the existence of settled derogations from even *prima facie* restrictions, are all expressions of institutional memory and of the tentative equilibriums that have been achieved between normative coherence and legal certainty.[127] Each test, however, is an attempt to answer the same question: when is the Court of Justice the best institutional option to decide a certain issue in light of the relevant normative goals? Within the scheme of the Treaties, the scope of the market freedoms is the legal tool to address this issue.

It is only by taking into account all of the relevant normative and institutional concerns that such a question can be dealt with fruitfully. Existing standards and rules are judicial tools reflecting the variety of situations reaching the Court of Justice, while also providing a modicum of legal certainty and coherence. They reflect prior comparative institutional choices, provide classificatory frameworks, and allow for argumentative frameworks within which legal and judicial debates can take place.

V. Conclusion

Developments in free movement law result from the interaction of legal, normative and extra-legal, institutional inputs. One important institutional

[127] On the first point, see Advocate General Lenz' Opinion in *Bosman*; Advocate General Fennely's Opinion in *Graf*; and Advocate General Kokott in *Mickelsson and Roos*. On the second point, see Section III above, and on the last point, see my contribution: Pedro Caro de Sousa, 'Through Contact Lenses, Darkly: is Identifying Restrictions to Free Movement Harder than Meets the Eye? Comment on *Ker-Optika*' (2012) 37 ELRev 79.

input is that, while litigants must argue within the bounds of existing law, potential beneficiaries of free movement law are in a privileged position to provide positive feedback to prior extensions of free movement rights. As a result, there seems to be an ingrained tendency for the expansion of the scope of the market freedoms. This tendency may, however, be counter-balanced by the shared cognitive framework, values, and concerns of the European legal community.

In the past, normative considerations have bucked institutionally based expansionary trends. Simultaneously, attempts to rationalize institutionally driven developments in the law have led to changes in its normative underpinnings, i.e. the normative foundations of the law were shown to be constituted as a result of legal practice. As was demonstrated, the various judicial tests on the concept of restriction, and the numerous legal theories developed to justify them, do not reflect an improved divination of the original meaning of the market freedoms, but are instead the result of a discursive process which brought about an evolution in the accepted meaning of the relevant legal provisions.

There are also specific tests in respect of certain areas of the law that differ from—and are ignored by—the more general approaches said to apply to the market freedoms *in totum*. The co-existence of both general and specific concepts of restriction reflects a tension between the specific concerns regarding certain areas of the law, and the wider normative values and institutional context governing free movement law.

In short, a descriptive model that takes into account both normative and institutional dimensions will provide a better fit to the law than models that merely look at one of these dimensions. This insight is also relevant for the development of normative analyses on the market freedoms.

The concept of 'restriction on economic free movement' is key to identifying which national measures fall within the scope of the market freedoms. Due to the way in which they operate, these freedoms function as a tool for policing the borderlines between legitimate and illegitimate national regulation. In particular, the main consequence of a measure being found restrictive is that the Court of Justice thereby assumes the responsibility for determining whether that measure is legitimate—which is the result of a balancing of the conflicting demands of European integration and the State's regulatory autonomy.

However, even if the market freedoms share a normative unity concerning the goal of creating an internal market, such normative unity is under-determined and hides different visions of the European common market. Accordingly, an important question underlying any assessment of whether a measure restricts free movement is one of comparative institutional choice—in an environment of normative indeterminacy, why should the Court of Justice be entitled to pursue this balancing exercise instead of other institutional options? This means that normative theories about the market freedoms must go beyond decontextualized normative considerations and take into account the relevant institutional context in which these freedoms are applied.

The Court of Justice operates in an institutional environment that may dispute its assessment and react to it: it is the historical interaction between the Member States, the Court of Justice, and other EU institutions that determines the on-going and ever-(slightly)-changing balance of powers in the EU, and the content of the Union's economic constitution. That constitution is open, in the sense that its contents concerning the level of regulation and the attribution of competences will be the result of a discursive process between all the relevant institutional agents and the normative theories they might defend from time to time. The Court of Justice is rather well suited, institutionally, to be a forum for debate and for the adoption of pragmatic compromises that balance all these concerns.

Reflecting this, it has been argued that a normatively under-determined standard should be adopted as the judicial test for identifying restrictions on free movement. Such a standard would reflect both the institutional realities of enforcement, and the political/sociological facts of greater or lesser agreement concerning the market freedoms' normative underpinnings. Further, this standard could, where the institutional context so requires, or normative consensus so allows, be complemented by specific rules applicable to certain areas of the law.

Adopting this perspective is to embrace open-ended judicial formulae that reflect the absence of a consensual and definitive vision of the internal market, and acknowledge the limitations of the Court of Justice in coming up with and imposing such a vision on its own. The question of when the Court of Justice should intervene is both normative and institutional, and an open one at that—but, arguably, such is the nature of standards and European integration alike.

6

The Fundamental Freedoms' Scope—Beyond Restriction

I. Introduction

It used to be that when a party to judicial proceedings had national law against her, she would lose the case. Now, she may find relief by pleading that the applicable national measure infringes upon her free movement rights. Nonetheless, a finding by the court that a national measure restricts economic free movement rights does not suffice for a case pleaded on that basis to succeed. In practice, a set of additional requirements must be met in order for a situation to fall within the scope of free movement law, and ensure the party's success:

i. the facts must disclose a cross-border element;
ii. the party must pursue an activity which is economic in nature; and
iii. there must be a connection between the cross-border element and the exercise of the economic free movement right.

Further, in some situations a specific question arises regarding whether someone's economic free movement rights can be infringed by private legal entities or by individuals.

While these requirements for the enforcement of economic free movement rights are separate from the concept of restriction on economic free movement, they pursue a similar purpose: to determine when a specific fact-situation falls within the scope of the market freedoms. In practice, these requirements tend to limit the effects of a finding that a national measure restricts economic free movement—a national measure that is found to restrict economic free movement may nonetheless still be lawfully applied by national courts and administrative bodies as long as the facts lead to the situation *sub judice* falling outside the scope of free movement law.[1]

This chapter will further demonstrate the value of the analytical approach developed in the previous chapters by applying it to these requirements regarding the scope of the market freedoms that go beyond the concept of restriction on economic free movement. Each requirement will be reviewed in turn, first by identifying the normative concerns underpinning it, secondly by unearthing the relevant institutional inputs, and, lastly, through an analysis of the law and its development that incorporates both legal, normative considerations, and extra-legal, institutional elements. The chapter will close with a section concerning the normative implications of adopting this approach for these areas of the law.

II. Cross-Border Movement

A. The normative dimension

The free movement provisions have as their goal the creation of an internal market. However, as noted above, an internal market can have various configurations. It is easy to argue that obstacles to economic movement within Member States are obstacles to the creation of an internal market and that, as such, both cross-border and purely internal situations should fall within the scope of the market freedoms. On the other hand, the Treaty rules on economic free movement, with the exception of the provisions on free movement of workers, seem to indicate that cross-border situations alone will be subject to EU law.[2] In this reading, purely internal situations should fall outside the scope of the market freedoms, which could be said to be in line with the inter-governmental and subsidiary nature of the European legal order

[1] As a result, the Court of Justice may well simultaneously deem a measure to be unlawful in the context of an infringement proceeding (Art. 258 TFEU) and consider that its application in practice is lawful when issuing a preliminary ruling regarding a specific factual scenario (Art. 267 TFEU).

[2] See, for goods, Art. 28, 30, 34, and 35 TFEU, which all include prohibitions *between Member States* on custom duties on imports and exports and all charges having equivalent effect. For establishment and services, see Art. 49 and 56 TFEU, which prohibit restrictions on such freedoms on nationals *of a Member State in the territory of another Member State*. Finally, Art. 63 TFEU prohibits all restrictions on the free movement of capital *between Member States* (and also third countries).

by limiting the scope and purposes of EU law and protecting the regulatory autonomy of the Member States.[3]

These different options were explicitly reflected in the different solutions proposed by the Advocate General and the Court of Justice in *Saunders*.[4] This case dealt with whether a criminal sanction imposed on a British citizen requiring her to remain in Northern Ireland and not go to Wales or England for a period of three years infringed upon the free movement of workers. Advocate General Warner held that: '*The true question is not whether the case has any connection with another Member State, but whether and, if so, to what extent Community law confers rights on a person.*' From this perspective, what mattered was not whether the relevant factual situation was circumscribed to a single Member State, but whether the national measure infringed upon the substance of rights conferred by the free movement provisions—meaning these provisions could apply even to purely internal situations. However, the Court of Justice reasoned instead that the free movement of workers did not restrict the power of Member States to lay down rules in purely internal situations, and, as such, the national measure *sub judice* did not infringe upon the free movement of workers.

The different approaches of the Advocate General and the Court of Justice in this case are reminiscent of, and seem to have been influenced by, two criteria used in private international law to distinguish between international and internal situations: the Advocate General's approach is reminiscent of the 'juridical' criterion, which looks into whether more than one legal system is connected to a case, while the Court of Justice's is similar to a 'geographical' test, focusing on where the facts of the case take place.[5] Advocate General Geelhoed neatly encapsulated the procedural implications of this:

The main question is this: is it the facts in the main proceedings that determine whether the Court must answer the questions referred to it for a preliminary ruling, or is it the nature and substance of the national measure? If it is the facts in the main proceedings that are decisive, the Court clearly will not answer the question where the main proceedings have no cross-border elements... If it is the substance of the national measure that is decisive, the Court should consider how far the national legislation may have an external effect. Only if there is no—potential—external effect should the Court refrain from answering the question referred to it.[6]

[3] Tryfonidou, *Reverse Discrimination in EC Law*, 9.

[4] Case 175/78 *Saunders* [1979] E.C.R. 1129.

[5] Hans Ulrich Jessurun d'Oliveira, 'Is Reverse Discrimination Still Permissible under the Single European Act?' in *Forty Years on: The Evolution of Postwar Private International Law in Europe* (Kluwer 1990), 73–74.

[6] Opinion in Joined Cases C-515/99, C-519/99 to C-524/99, and C-526/99 to C-540/99 *Reisch* [2002] E.C.R. I-2157, paras 79-82.

Following *Saunders*, the Court of Justice adopted the geographical approach for all market freedoms, using the canonical formulae that the free movement provisions did not apply to activities which have no factor linking them with any of the situations governed by EU law and/or that were confined in all aspects within a single Member State—the so-called 'purely internal situations' doctrine.[7]

Recently, however, this doctrine has been eroded.[8] In *Lancry*,[9] the Court of Justice held that the prohibition of custom duties set forth in Article 28 TFEU extended to custom duties imposed on goods crossing the internal frontiers of a Member State, at least inasmuch as such duties could also be applied to imported goods. The distinction from national goods, in the light of the prohibition of border controls and the conclusion of the internal market, was seen to be practically impossible.[10] This was further developed in *Jersey Produce*, where the Court of Justice held that, even though an internal customs duty applied only to the export of potatoes from Jersey to the United Kingdom:

> *that does not rule out the possibility that such potatoes, once within the United Kingdom, might then be re-exported to other Member States, with the result that the contribution in question may be levied on goods which, after having passed through the United Kingdom in transit, are in fact exported to other Member States.*[11]

Hence, whenever it is impossible to identify whether potential imports or exports will be affected by a custom duty, such a duty will infringe EU law even where it applies to products that are in a purely internal situation.[12] This

[7] d'Oliveira, 'Is Reverse Discrimination Still Permissible under the Single European Act?', 73–74; Tryfonidou, *Reverse Discrimination in EC Law*, 30–31. See for goods, *Mathot*, Case C-60/91 *Morais* [1992] E.C.R. I-2085; for establishment, *Tourist Guides Greece*, Joined Cases C-64/96 and C-65/96 *Uecker and Jacquet* [1997] E.C.R. I-3171; for services, Case 20/87 *Gauchard* [1987] E.C.R. 4879, Joined Cases C-54/88, C-91/88, and C-14/89 *Nino* [1990] E.C.R. I-3537, and Case C-152/94 *Buynder* [1995] E.C.R. I-3981; for capital, Case C-513/03 *van Hilten-van der Heijden* [2006] E.C.R. I-10653.

[8] As observed in Chapter 2, this erosion was quite spectacular regarding European Citizenship. In particular, it has been decided that the purely internal situations doctrine will not apply when a national measure results in a denial of the genuine enjoyment of the substance of European Citizenship rights—particularly when the European citizen is forced to leave the Union. See the decisions in *Zambrano*, *McCarthy*, and *Dereci*.

[9] Joined Cases C-363/93, C-407/93, C-408/93, C-409/93, C-410/93, and C-411/93 *Lancry* [1994] E.C.R. I-3957; Case C-72/03 *Carbonati Apuani* [2004] E.C.R. I-8027; and Case C-254/13 *Orgacom* (decided on 2 October 2014).

[10] Oliver and Roth, 'The Internal Market and the Four Freedoms', 431; Cyril Ritter, 'Purely Internal Situations, Reverse Discrimination, *Guimont*, *Dzodzi* and Article 234' (2006) 31 ELRev 690, 706.

[11] *Jersey Produce*, para. 65.

[12] Tryfonidou, *Reverse Discrimination in EC Law*, 75.

approach was transposed into Article 34 TFEU in *Pistre*, a case concerning an appeal brought by French nationals accused of selling goods produced in France under the description 'montagne'. This was allowed only in relation to products prepared in the French territory after the producer had obtained an authorization from the French authorities. In the case at hand, all the relevant legislation had been complied with but no authorization had been obtained. Choosing not to look into the specific facts of the case, the Court of Justice held that:

Article [34 TFEU] cannot be considered inapplicable simply because all the facts of the specific case before the national court are confined to a single Member State. In such a situation, the application of the national measure may also have effects on the free movement of goods between Member States, in particular when the measure in question facilitates the marketing of goods of domestic origin to the detriment of imported goods. In such circumstances, the application of the measure, even if restricted to domestic producers, in itself creates and maintains a difference of treatment between those two categories of goods, hindering, at least potentially, intra-Community trade.[13]

This statement could be read as implying that the Court of Justice has to look into the substance of the national measure and its potential external effects, instead of into where the facts of the case occur, in order to determine whether the application of national measures infringed on the free movement of goods—in effect overturning *Saunders*.[14] On the other hand, the Court of Justice went on to decide that since it was '*accepted that the domestic legislation in question could be applied to products imported from other Member States, it follows... that it constitutes an obstacle to intra-Community trade*'—thereby reiterating that the free movement of goods protected imported goods, and that the situation was not purely internal.

This apparent contradiction between *obiter dicta* and *ratio decidendi* was clarified in *Guimont*, where the Court of Justice distinguished *Pistre* as extending the scope of the free movement of goods to purely domestic situations only if the relevant national measure directly discriminates against imports. Concerning indistinctly applicable rules, it held: '*it is clear from the Court's case law that such a rule falls under Article [34] of the Treaty only in so far as it applies to situations that are linked to the importation of goods in intra-Community trade*'.[15] However, the Court of Justice then went on to state that a preliminary reference request from a national court would only

[13] Joined Cases C-321/94 to C-324/94 *Pistre* [1997] E.C.R I-2343, paras 44-45.

[14] See, in this sense, Tryfonidou, *Reverse Discrimination in EC Law*, 71.

[15] Case C-448/98 *Guimont* [2000] E.C.R. I-10663, para. 20–21.

be refused if it was quite obvious that the interpretation of EU law sought bore no relation to the actual nature of the case or to the subject matter of the main action. Because it was possible that a reply could be useful to the national court if national law were to require that the rights which a foreign producer derives from EU law must also be enjoyed by national producers, the Court of Justice decided to take the case.[16]

Following *Guimont*, in *PreussenElektra* the Court of Justice dismissed out of hand arguments to the effect that the case was not admissible because the situation *sub judice* had no cross-border element. Instead, it held that it was for the referring court to determine whether the question was relevant and stated that: '*it is not obvious that the interpretation sought bears no relation to the actual facts of the main action or its purpose*'.[17] This line of case law was progressively adopted for the free movement of capital,[18] services,[19] establishment,[20] and might currently also be applicable for workers.[21] Thus, the Court of Justice appears to be moving away from its traditional geographical approach, and to be willing to review measures applying to purely internal situations as long as the referring national courts consider the question to be relevant, even if it is not clear on what basis EU law would apply to the situation at hand.

Alongside this procedural development, the 'purely internal situations' doctrine has also been eroded by a reduction in the number of situations susceptible of being deemed purely internal. It is settled law that a situation will have a link with economic free movement law if it involves a potential, but not merely hypothetical exercise of a market freedom.[22] The distinction between hypothetical and potential exercises of a market freedom is not exactly clear, however, and the Court of Justice has steadily increased the number of situations deemed to have potential links with EU law.[23] This

[16] Ibid, paras 20–23. [17] Case C-379/98 *PreussenElektra* [2001] E.C.R. I-2099, para. 52.

[18] *Reisch*.

[19] Case C-6/01 *Anomar* [2003] E.C.R. I-8261. See Stefan Enchelmaier, 'Always at Your Service (Within Limits)' (2011) 36 ELRev 615, 617.

[20] Case C-250/03 *Mauri* [2005] E.C.R. I-1267.

[21] See Advocate General Léger's Opinion in Case C-152/03 *Ritter-Coulais* [2006] E.C.R. I-1711, fn. 47.

[22] See for the free movement of workers Case 180/83 *Moser* [1984] E.C.R. 2539, para. 18; Case C-41/90 *Höfner and Elser* [1991] E.C.R. I-1979, para. 39. On the application of this principle to all provisions on the free movement of persons, see Case C-299/95 *Kremzow* [1997] E.C.R. I-2629.

[23] Niamh Nic Shuibhne, 'Free Movement of Persons and the Wholly Internal Rule' (2002) 39 CML Rev 731, 736.

is apparent as regards the free movement of goods, as we saw, as a result of *Lancry*, *Pistre*, and *Guimont*. Further, concerning the free provision of services, while the Court of Justice reiterated that it does not apply to purely hypothetical situations, it also held that to trigger this freedom there is no need to prove the existence of a previously determined service recipient as long as she is determinable:[24] the existence of either virtual or merely possible future recipients suffices.[25] The result is that the case law no longer insists on a specific exercise of inter-State movement, as long as a potential effect on the intra-State provision of services can be found.[26] As in *Pistre*, a situation might fall within the scope of the market freedom even when all the facts of the case are located within a single Member State.[27]

In short, while the 'purely internal situations' doctrine still stands, its effects have been significantly limited, both substantively and procedurally. Substantively, it has been limited by the Court of Justice's decision to focus on the effects of a measure in certain situations, such as internal custom duties, instead of focusing on the specific facts of the case—i.e. by the partial replacement of the 'geographic' with the 'juridical' criterion—and by the blurring and expansion of the 'geographic' criterion resulting from the consideration of 'potential' situations.

Behind these developments lies the fact that the Court of Justice never provided a coherent normative theory for the 'purely internal situations' doctrine to begin with. In effect, the geographical/juridical distinction is, like the 'purely internal situations' doctrine, an analytical tool for the identification of situations falling outside the scope of the market freedoms, which relates to concerns with the protection of areas of State regulatory autonomy outside the reach of EU law. The 'purely internal situations' doctrine reflects a vision of the internal market that is concerned solely with the abolition of obstacles to free movement across State borders while ignoring intra-State obstacles, but the reasons underpinning the adoption of this particular

[24] Hatzopoulos, 'Recent Developments of the Case Law of the ECJ in the Field of Services', 58. See *Alpine Investments*; Joined Cases C-51/96 and C-191/97 *Deliège* [2000] E.C.R. I-2549; *Gourmet International*; Case C-355/00 *Freskot* [2003] E.C.R. I-5263.

[25] *Alpine; Omega*; Case C-215/03 *Oulane* [2005] E.C.R. I-01215. See Vassilis Hatzopoulos and Thien Uyen Do, 'The Case Law of the ECJ concerning the Free Provision of Services: 2000-2005' (2006) 43 CML Rev 923, 926.

[26] Tryfonidou, *Reverse Discrimination in EC Law*, 85; Enchelmaier, 'Always at Your Service (Within Limits), 618.

[27] Compare Case C-108/98 *RI.SAN.* [1999] E.C.R. I-5219 with Case C-410/04 *ANAV* [2006] E.C.R. I-3303.

vision were never disclosed. Furthermore, this vision of the internal market has been attacked in the light of recent normative concerns, particularly those regarding reverse discrimination, which arises when those people not encompassed by the free movement provisions, and particularly those people involved in purely internal situations, are left worse off than those involved in cross-border situations. Arguments against reverse discrimination hold that, on the basis of the adoption and development of European Citizenship, of the protection of fundamental rights, and of the principle of equality enshrined in the Treaties' prohibition of discrimination on grounds of nationality, EU law should protect nationals against their own State in the same way as it protects foreigners.[28]

The relevance of concerns with reverse discrimination is particularly evident in the *Guimont* case law, which limited the effect of the 'purely internal situations' doctrine from a procedural standpoint. According to this case law, cases without cross-border elements may nonetheless be admissible because the Court of Justice's decision may be useful if:

national law were to require, in proceedings such as those in this case, that a national producer must be allowed to enjoy the same rights as those which a producer of another Member State would derive from Community law in the same situation.[29]

However, in the development of this case law, the Court of Justice avoided engaging in an assessment of how to balance the protection of State autonomy and the prevention of reverse discrimination.[30] On the academic side, some commentators have inferred justifications for a more extensive protection of fundamental rights, European Citizenship, and the free movement of persons from the dilution of the 'purely internal situations' doctrine.[31] However, this academic literature passes over the fact that similar developments have occurred regarding the free movement of goods, and, as a result,

[28] Shuibhne, 'Free Movement of Persons and the Wholly Internal Rule'; Alina Tryfonidou, 'Reverse Discrimination in Purely Internal Situations: An Incongruity in a Citizen's Europe' (2008) 35 LIEI 43.

[29] *Guimont*, para. 23.

[30] With the exception of the Opinion of Advocate General Sharspton in *Zambrano*, which is a case on European Citizenship.

[31] Spaventa, 'Seeing the Wood Despite the Trees?', 36–39; Tryfonidou, 'Reverse Discrimination in Purely Internal Situations', 58; Herwig Verschueren, 'Reverse Discrimination: An Unsolvable Problem?' in Paul Minderhoud and Nicos Trimikliniotis (eds), *Rethinking the Free Movement of Workers: The European Challenges Ahead* (Wolf Legal Publishers 2009), 118.

fails to explain the parallel erosion of the 'purely internal situations' doctrine across the full spectrum of the market freedoms, and to reflect on what the normative justifications for these developments might be outside the free movement of persons.[32]

Ultimately, the erosion of the 'purely internal situations' doctrine appears to stem from its normative indeterminacy and under-theorization. Without proper normative underpinnings, questions about the type and amount of (geographical) cross-border elements required for a situation to fall within the scope of the market freedoms are susceptible, through the manipulation of whether a situation may potentially or hypothetically have a cross-border element, to become questions about whether a situation has a sufficient (juridical) connection with the economic free movement provision. Similarly, questions about whether a situation falls within the scope of a freedom can easily be framed in geographical terms. In this way, the Court of Justice is able to manipulate the 'purely internal situations' doctrine in order to reach the solutions it prefers, but to the detriment of the normative coherence of the law.

B. The institutional dimension

In the light of this normative uncertainty, taking institutional elements into account helps to make sense of the logic behind the purely internal situations doctrine, the development of the law in this area, and the implications of such developments.

To begin with, the absence of fully fledged justifications for the law on purely internal situations and its development—other than diffuse concerns with setting limits to the reach of EU law, the protection of national regulatory autonomy, and reverse discrimination—should not cause surprise by now. As has been repeatedly remarked, courts will usually decide cases on the particulars facts of the case without needing to engage with large-scale normative questions: courts may enlist silence as a device for producing consensus despite disagreement and uncertainty by adopting incompletely theorized outcomes. The existence of potential disagreements that judges must paper over or negotiate in order to achieve a single collegial decision may

[32] The main exception to this is Tryfonidou, *Reverse Discrimination in EC Law*. See also Alina Tryfonidou, 'Resolving the Reverse Discrimination Paradox in the Area of Custom Duties' (2011) 22 EBLRev 311, arguing that the focus with preventing reverse discrimination regarding the free movement of goods is to maintain a properly functioning market where competition is undistorted.

also be relevant to explain why the developments in the case law seem not to have been properly justified and give an impression of a lack of theorization.

The development of the 'purely internal situations' doctrine, from this perspective, may be the result of the case law's initial position, i.e. a somewhat random choice by a specific set of judges regarding the scope of economic free movement law. This choice then became entrenched as a result of the particular institutional dynamics of the EU's adjudicative process. However, the case law's under-theorization left it open to the erosion of its (implicit) normative foundations through the adoption of decisions that seemed to go against them, which, in turn, led, through the use of the rationale of those decisions, to the development of strands of case law with their own normative foundations.

The prevalence of institutional elements is evident in the way the development of justifications centred on the free movement of persons—fundamental rights, European Citizenship, etc.—failed to prevent the extension of the *Guimont* case law, and its apparent concerns with reverse discrimination, to the free movement of goods and capital. This is, according to the analytical framework developed in this book, anything but surprising. On the one hand, the acknowledgement by the Court of Justice that such normative concerns with reverse discrimination were the basis for these extensions would be tantamount to a change of the normative substrata of the market freedoms, and of the very 'internal market' concept adopted by the Court of Justice when addressing these freedoms. This would hardly be justifiable in the light of the cases that point in this direction.[33] On the other hand, the observed developments result naturally from the imperatives of systemic coherence and the prevalent modes of legal reasoning, even in the absence of concurring normative reasons. Similarly, the absence of a properly theorized normative basis for the tweaking of the geographical criterion, which is a consequence of the Court of Justice's manipulation of 'hypothetical' and 'potential' scenarios in order to determine whether a measure is contrary to the free provision of services, meant that there was no reason not to extend this case law to the other freedoms—a development made likely by the institutional dynamics of legal reasoning and the existence of litigants with an

[33] It can be argued, I think successfully, that such a change has not occurred because the *Guimont* case law merely provides guidance to States should they wish to prevent reverse discrimination, and does not extend the scope of the market freedoms to intra-State situations. This is not to say, however, that such an extension will not occur, particularly in light of the under-theorization of this case law.

interest in expanding the scope of the market freedoms.[34] Likewise, once the 'juridical' criterion was adapted for certain situations affecting the free movement of goods, there appeared to be no good reason not to extend this criterion to the free movement of persons.

In other words, institutional elements are likely to be driving the evolution of the law in this area, to the detriment of normative considerations. This is a consequence of the thinness of the normative grounds underpinning the law, which makes it likelier that the specific institutional dynamics of path-dependency and legal reasoning will determine the development of the law, and that the Court of Justice will be able to adopt *ad hoc* decisions that can take on a life of their own. It is the combination of these elements that seems to be leading to the erosion of the 'purely internal situations' doctrine across all the market freedoms.

Taking into account institutional considerations, however, has a power that goes beyond improving our ability to make sense of the law. After all, even if developments in this area of the law had a purely normative basis, they would still have institutional implications. For example, the 'purely internal situations' doctrine has both procedural and substantive implications. Substantively, the impact of the 'purely internal situations' doctrine is that the free movement rules have no effect on situations whose facts and effects are confined within a single Member State, even if such a measure falls within the scope of the market freedoms regarding situations with a cross-border element.[35] This means that the application of the same national measure can be simultaneously lawful and unlawful, depending on the factual situation in which that measure is applied. As a result, a Member State is merely required to disapply the relevant measure in cross-border situations, but is allowed to apply it in purely internal situations.[36] From this perspective, the erosion of the 'purely internal situations' doctrine can result in an extension of the substantive scope of the market freedoms.[37]

[34] For example, companies might potentially want to expand to another country, workers may be interested in potentially seeking jobs abroad, and suppliers of goods may be preparing for the eventuality of competing in another market.

[35] See on goods, Joined Cases 314/81 to 316/81 and 83/82 *Waterkeyn* [1982] E.C.R. 4337, *Oosthoek's*; on services, see Case 52/79 *Debauve* [1980] E.C.R. 833, Höfner and Elser; on workers, see Case C-332/90 Steen [1992] E.C.R. I-341, Case C-379/92 *Peralta* [1994] E.C.R. I-3453, Case C-212/06 Government of Communauté française and Gouvernement wallon [2008] E.C.R. I-1683; on establishment, see Nino. There is no case law on capital of which I am aware.

[36] This is particularly clear in Case 407/85 *Drei Glocken* [1988] E.C.R. 4233. See also Ritter, 'Purely Internal Situations, Reverse Discrimination, *Guimont*, *Dzodzi* and Article 234', 691. It should be noted that it is this substantive effect that leads to reverse discrimination.

[37] On all of the above, see P. P. Craig and G. De Búrca, *EU Law: Text, Cases, and Materials* (5th. edn, OUP 2011), 462–474.

However, the 'purely internal situations' doctrine, also has a number of procedural implications. In particular, the doctrine operates as a gatekeeper to the preliminary reference mechanism: if a case referred by a national court dealt with a purely internal situation, the Court of Justice would traditionally refuse to pursue any assessment of the relevant measures. This refusal, however, has no implication regarding the substantive status of a measure under EU law: that measure could still be subject to review by the Court of Justice either under an infringement procedure brought by the Commission against a Member State or by a litigant whose situation has a cross-border element.

The *Guimont* case law reversed the Court of Justice's traditional case law regarding the admissibility of preliminary references by allowing cases on the basis of hypothetical prohibitions of reverse discrimination at the national level, which means that the risk of the Court of Justice delivering purely theoretical rulings has become real.[38] From this perspective, while the extension of the material scope of the market freedoms leads to the Court of Justice dealing with reverse discrimination itself, the *Guimont* case law leaves this question for Member States' courts and governments.[39]

In a way, the *Guimont* case law is a return to the Court of Justice's approach in the earlier stages of European integration. The Court of Justice was initially very liberal in this area, holding that facts were a matter for national courts, and that the Court of Justice was not empowered to investigate them or question the grounds or purpose of the request for interpretation.[40] Eventually, the Court of Justice asserted control over its docket in the *Foglia* decisions, through which the Court assumed authority for determining the scope of its jurisdiction.[41] In particular, the Court of Justice held that a genuine dispute was required for a preliminary reference to be admissible, and it had no jurisdiction to deliver 'advisory opinions on general or hypothetical

[38] See Advocate General Tizzano's Opinion in *Anomar*, para. 23. Ritter, 'Purely Internal Situations, Reverse Discrimination, *Guimont*, *Dzodzi* and Article 234', 700, is critical of this.

[39] The Court of Justice is here using the 'purely internal situation' doctrine strategically as a tool for institutional choice, deciding which cases it wants to deal with directly and those that are better dealt with by national courts or legislatures. Both approaches are theoretically apt to deal with normative concerns about reverse discrimination, but the existence of different institutional options reveals how the Court of Justice is able to adopt different strategies on how to balance concerns about reverse discrimination and the protection of State autonomy.

[40] See, for example, Case 6/64 *Costa v ENEL* [1964] E.C.R. 585; *Simmenthal*.

[41] Case 104/79 *Foglia I* [1980] E.C.R. 745; Case 244/80 *Foglia II* [1981] E.C.R. 3045.

questions'.[42] Since then, and until the decision in *Guimont*, the Court of Justice had refused to answer hypothetical questions.

The *Guimont* approach to the 'purely internal situations' doctrine represents a limited return to the original, pre-*Foglia*, case law on the Court of Justice's jurisdiction in preliminary reference cases: it effectively opens the door to test cases in situations without any direct link with EU law. While this does not directly lead to a substantive extension of the scope of the market freedoms, it nonetheless has very serious consequences in this respect. A decision by the Court of Justice that a national measure is contrary to the market freedoms, adopted in a case without any cross-border element, may not make any difference to the outcome of that specific case, but it places the Member State in the 'shadow of the law' and under pressure to amend its rules—which become inapplicable to cross-border situations. As a result, the *Guimont* approach increases the pool of litigants, the Court of Justice's workload, and the level of control the Court of Justice is able to exert on national regulatory autonomy. On the other hand, the blurring between 'hypothetical' and 'potential' situations leads to an increase in the substantial scope of the market freedoms, because, in an internal market, the possibility of a measure having a 'potential' impact on cross-border situations is inherent.[43]

Taken together, these substantive and procedural developments lead to a relaxation of the requirements for submitting national measures to review by the Court of Justice. In these developments, one can find an implicit institutional choice: after all, claims that the 'purely internal situations' doctrine should be limited, or even eliminated, are calls for an expansion of EU powers and, incidentally, those of the Court of Justice. On the other hand, the differentiated treatment of 'purely internal situations' that are brought within the scope of the market freedoms, and those that are left outside this scope to be dealt with under the *Guimont* case law, may well lead to the development of different normative foundations through the adoption of

[42] This is not the only reason for the Court of Justice to refuse to pass judgement: it may also do so when the questions have no relation to the facts or subject matter of the main action (Case C-18/93 *Corsica Ferries Italia* [1994] E.C.R. I-1783), when the questions are not articulated clearly enough for the Court of Justice to give any meaningful response (Case C-318/00 *Bacardi-Martini* [2003] E.C.R. I-905), and when the facts are insufficiently clear for the Court of Justice to be able to apply the relevant legal rules (Case C-157/92 *Banchero* [1993] E.C.R. I-1085).

[43] Spaventa, *Free Movement of Persons in the European Union*, 153.

ex post attempts to rationalize this difference. Normative and institutional considerations are, here as elsewhere, closely intertwined.

III. Economic Aim

A. The normative dimension

The market freedoms are instrumental to the completion and functioning of the internal market through the elimination of obstacles to economic free movement. As such, their goal is to protect cross-border movement with an economic aim. While it is generally easy to identify movement with an economic aim, the existence of different conceptions of economic activity may lead to definitional issues in borderline situations.

There can be said to be three main conceptions of economic activity: a first conception focuses strictly on the production of goods and services; a second one considers that economic activity includes not only the production of goods and services, but also their distribution and consumption; and a third approach focuses on the production and distribution of goods and services which are provided against measurable amounts of money or other material requirements of well-being.[44]

The existence of various conceptions of economic activity is reflected in EU law,[45] and is particularly visible when one compares competition law with free movement law. EU competition law can only be applied to undertakings, i.e. entities engaged in economic activity, regardless of their legal status.[46] It is considered that an undertaking is engaged in economic activity when it has the potential to provide goods or services and make a profit under market conditions, with the exception of when that undertaking's activities

[44] Alfred Marshall, *Principles of Economics: An Introductory Volume* (8th edn, Macmillan 1949); A. C. Pigou, *The Economics of Welfare* (4th edn, Macmillan 1962).

[45] See Case C-519/04 P *Meca-Medina* [2006] E.C.R. I-6991, para. 33. See also Advocate General Maduro's Opinion in Case C-205/03 P *FENIN* [2006] E.C.R. I-6295, para. 51; and Advocate General Kokott's Opinion in Case C-284/04 *T-Mobile Austria* [2007] E.C.R. I-05189, para. 61. Similarly, see Communication from the Commission to the European Parliament, the Council, the European Economic and Social Committee and the Committee of the Regions Accompanying the Communication on 'A single market for 21st century Europe' Services of general interest, including social services of general interest: a new European commitment [2007] COM 2007 725 Final 5.

[46] *Höfner and Elser*, para. 21.

are in the public interest or are pursued in the exercise of official authority. In other words, an entity is engaged in economic activities for the purposes of EU competition law when it acts like a for-profit entity that is able to respond to market demand, regardless of whether it is remunerated for the goods or services it provides.[47] However, only the offering of products seems to be relevant to the conception of economic activity adopted by EU competition law: demand-side activities are not deemed to be economic, at least as regards the purchase of goods on the market for use in the provision of public services.[48]

The conception of economic activity adopted by free movement law is somewhat different: it focuses on both the provision *and* demand for goods or services against some kind of remuneration.[49] This means that activities that are not remunerated but have profit-making potential fall within the scope of competition law but not of free movement law, while activities which are remunerated but do not have any profit-making potential fall within the scope of free movement law but not of competition law. For example, activities that are deemed to be in the public interest—such as the maintenance of air navigation safety and the protection of the environment[50]—or which operate under the principle of solidarity—such as the payment of benefits out of social security schemes[51]—do not fall within the scope of competition law because it is considered that they are not pursued with a view to achieving profits, even though these activities might fall within the scope of the free movement provisions inasmuch as they are remunerated. On the other hand, for the purposes of competition law, an activity might be deemed economic independently of the way in which it is financed, meaning that activities that are financed by the State without any remuneration—such as employment

[47] See Joined Cases C-180/98 to C-184/98 *Pavlov* [2000] E.C.R. I-6451, para. 75; Case C-364/92 *Eurocontrol* [1994] E.C.R. I-0043; *Meca-Medina*, para. 41; and Advocate General Maduro Opinion in *FENIN*, paras 13–14. See also Niamh Dunne, 'Knowing When To See It: State Activities, Economic Activities, and the Concept of Undertaking' (2010) 16 ColumJEurL 427, 436. On remuneration not being a necessary element for the conception of economic activity adopted in EU competition law, see Case T-155/04 *Selex* [2006] E.C.R. II-4797, para. 77

[48] Mark Furse, *Competition Law* (OUP 2008), 22. See *FENIN*.

[49] Okeoghene Odudu, 'Economic Activity as a Limit to Community Law' in Catherine Barnard and Okeoghene Odudu (eds), *The Outer Limits of European Union Law* (Hart Publishing 2009), 230–231.

[50] Advocate General Maduro's Opinion in *FENIN*, para. 15.

[51] Case C-159/91 and C-160/91 *Poucet and Pistre* [1993] E.C.R. I-637.

procurement by State agencies—might fall within the scope of competition law but not of the free movement provisions.[52]

It is unclear what the normative reasons were for the Court of Justice to adopt these different conceptions of economic activity for competition and free movement law. While determining whether an activity is economic does not pose significant problems on most occasions, in those borderline situations when it is not clear whether an activity is economic or not, the lack of a proper normative underpinning of the case law comes to the fore. For example, the concept of remuneration for services was traditionally understood as meaning consideration for a service to be normally agreed upon between the providers and recipients of services.[53] While it was commonly accepted that remuneration need not be paid by the service recipients themselves,[54] the concept of remuneration has been recently extended well beyond its former limits to cover payments that are only indirectly related to the service provided, in the sense that the remuneration does not need to be agreed between the parties, it need not be provided by the service recipient, and it can even be subject to subsequent reimbursement by a third party.[55] In applying this new concept of remuneration, the Court of Justice sometimes acts incoherently. For example, the provision of services in the area of public education is held not to be economic for the purposes of the Treaty because the State is deemed not to be seeking to engage in gainful activity, and the system in question is, as a general rule, funded from the public purse and not by pupils or their parents.[56] However, this reasoning is not applicable to the public provision of hospital health services under an insurance scheme that provides benefits in-kind, even though similar arguments would seem to apply.[57] These inconsistencies do not seem susceptible to being explained by normative arguments regarding the nature of economic activity, even though they are evidence of an absence of due consideration of the relevant normative foundations of such a concept.

[52] *Höfner and Elser*, paras 21–22.

[53] Case 263/86 *Humbel* [1988] E.C.R. 5365, para. 17; *Freskot*, para. 55.

[54] Case 352/85 *Bond van Adverteerders* [1988] E.C.R. 2085.

[55] Pedro Cabral, 'The Internal Market and the Right to Cross Border Medical Care' (2004) 19 ELRev 673, 677; Hatzopoulos and Do, 'The Case Law of the ECJ Concerning the Free Provision of Services', 946–947; Lorna Woods, *Free Movement of Goods and Services within the European Community* (Ashgate 2004), 168–174.

[56] *Humbel* and Case C-109/92 *Wirth* [1993] E.C.R. I-6447.

[57] *Peerbooms* and *Vanbraekel*. In both cases, the Advocate General argued the situation did not fall within the market freedoms' scope.

Similar phenomena can be observed for the free movement of goods and capital. There is case law indicating that goods need not be part of an economic transaction at all, but only susceptible to being part of an economic transaction, in order to fall within the scope of the free movement of goods. In effect, it has been remarked that Article 34 TFEU: '*which does not itself use the word "trade", cannot be interpreted as limited to transactions by or between traders*'.[58] Similarly, Advocate General Jacobs has held that:

objects can benefit from the Treaty provisions concerning the free movement of goods, whether or not they are being transported across national frontiers for the purposes of sale or resale... [The free movement of goods can be extended], for instance, to the importation of goods by a private individual for the purposes of personal consumption.[59]

Regarding the free movement of capital, Annex I to Directive 88/361 includes a Section XI on 'Personal Capital Movement', allowing for the free movement of capital of, *inter alia*, gifts and endowments, dowries, inheritances and legacies, the transfer of assets by residents in the event of emigration, at the time of their installation, or during their period of stay abroad, and the transfer of immigrants' savings to their previous country of residence during their period of stay.[60] None of these movements of capital seem to be of an economic nature, but are instead examples of situations where individuals would like to transfer money without wanting to engage in any economic transactions.[61]

Again, this clearly cannot be justified on the basis of different considerations of what might qualify as economic activity. Instead, these cases seem to reflect a complete absence of consideration of the economic aim of the market freedoms, and what its normative foundations might be.[62]

[58] Advocate General Warner's Opinion in *Henn and Darby*.

[59] Case C-2/90 *Walloon Waste* [1992] E.C.R. I-4431; Advocate General's second Opinion, para. 15

[60] Council Directive 88/361/EEC

[61] See, as a good example, Case C-25/10 *Missionswerk* [2011] E.C.R. I-00497, where a restriction on the free movement of capital was found for rules that made a legacy to a not-for-profit organization abroad less valuable than if the legacy had been made to a not-for-profit in the State where the deceased had previously resided or worked. The main rule concerning inheritances seems to be that rules that have the effect of reducing the value of the inheritance of a resident of a State other than the Member State in which the assets concerned are situated, and which taxes the inheritance of those assets, are restrictive—see *van Hilten-van der Heijden*, para. 44 and the case law cited therein. Similarly, for rules that infringe upon the free movement of capital by restricting gifts to charities, see Case C-318/07 *Hein Persche* [2009] E.C.R. I-00359.

[62] For the argument that this indicates that Art. 34 TFEU covers the non-economic free movement of goods, see Odudu, 'Economic Activity as a Limit to Community Law', 238–239.

B. *The institutional dimension*

Again, a fuller picture of the case law emerges if one takes into account the role that institutional dynamics play in environments of normative indeterminacy. The requirement that free movement must have an 'economic aim' for it to fall within the scope of the market freedoms limits the reach of EU law and preserves an area of autonomy over non-economic areas for Member States.[63] But the categorization of certain activities as economic does not work merely as a device for the allocation of competences between the EU and the Member States: it also operates as a device to determine whether the Court of Justice and/or the European political process should be able to overrule Member State choices.

In the absence of a careful consideration of the relevant normative and institutional underpinnings of the law, decisions by the Court of Justice on whether an activity is economic or not—or whether a certain type of movement needs to be economic to fall within the scope of the market freedoms at all—seem to constitute unprincipled, or at least unjustified, comparative institutional choices. From an institutional perspective, this may reflect the Court of Justice's pragmatic streak, which enables it to use the conception of 'economic activity' or even 'remuneration' malleably to get rid of cases it does not want to deal with, or to adjudicate on cases it would not have competence to decide on beforehand.[64]

Furthermore, and as seen above, the greater the level of normative indeterminacy, the more important is the role played by institutional constraints. This helps to explain the inconsistencies in the law: the developments reviewed above seem to be outgrowths of *sui generis* or pragmatic decisions, which are allowed to metastasize in the absence of normative constraints. On the one hand, and in the light of the specific incentives for litigation that permeate free movement law, this is likely to allow for a constant increase in the scope of the market freedoms and the reach of EU law—an assumption that is broadly in line with the case law reviewed above. But, on the other hand, such an unruly development is also likely to provoke a reaction, because the law craves

[63] With the obvious exception of when EU competences over non-economic areas exist. See Odudu, 'Economic Activity as a Limit to Community Law' 226

[64] Spaventa, *Free Movement of Persons in the European Union*, 54–58; Hatzopoulos, '*Killing* National Health and Insurance Systems but *Healing* Patients?' (2002) 39 CML Rev 683, 693–694. For a famous example of an ingenious, if normatively incoherent, use of the concept of economic activity by the Court of Justice, one need only see how the Court avoided having to decide on the prohibition of abortion in Ireland in Case C-159/90 *Grogan* [1991] E.C.R. I-4685.

coherence and the legal community will seek to impose order, with the result that this body of law and its developments are likely to be rationalized, which will probably lead to changes to its very normative foundations in the future.

IV. From Fundamental Freedoms to Rights of Free Movement—the Connecting Factor

A. The normative dimension

> *The simple exercise of the right of free movement within the Community is not in itself sufficient to bring a particular set of circumstances within the scope of Community Law; there must be some connecting factor between the exercise of the right of free movement and the right relied on by the individual.*[65]

It is technically still the law that the economic free movement rights granted by the Treaties must be exercised in a cross-border situation for an economic purpose. Nonetheless, there are various strands in the case law under which the free movement rights of individuals will be engaged merely because a situation has a cross-border element and the right-bearer pursues an economic activity, even though any connection between these two elements is absent.

The Court of Justice first departed from the traditional requirement of a connecting factor between the cross-border element and the right to economic free movement in *Cowan*. This was a case concerning the award of State compensation for harm caused in France to the victim of an assault resulting in physical injury. A national measure subjected the award to the condition that the victim either held a residence permit or was a national of a country which had entered into a reciprocal agreement on the matter with France.[66] As the French State argued, this requirement posed no obstacle to economic free movement, but the Court of Justice nonetheless considered this rule to be contrary to the free provision of services because the situation concerned tourists, i.e. service recipients who had travelled across State borders. This decision clearly departed from the existing case law on economic free movement, and it was arguable that it was concerned instead

[65] Para. 5 of Advocate General Tesauro's Opinion in *Singh*.

[66] *Cowan*.

with granting an autonomous status to the Treaties' prohibition of discrimination on grounds of nationality.

This line of analysis would seem to find support in *Bickel and Franz*, a case concerning a refusal to grant German-speaking foreigners in Italy a right to use their own language in interactions with the judicial and administrative authorities based in the Bolzano province, when such a right was granted to German-speaking Italians.[67] In this case, the Court of Justice decided that such a refusal was prohibited by the general prohibition of discrimination on grounds of nationality arising from Article 18 TFEU. The issue with this approach is that the general prohibition of discrimination on grounds of nationality in the Treaty is only applicable where a previous link to EU law exists—or, as the Treaty puts it, when a situation falls 'within the scope of application of the Treaties'. While the Court of Justice ignored the issue in *Bickel and Franz*, Advocate General Jacobs in his Opinion in this case tried to establish such a link by reference to European Citizenship—a possibility that was not open to the Court of Justice in *Cowan*, since this is a case that was decided prior to the adoption of European Citizenship.[68]

A second strand of cases where there is no obvious connection between cross-border movement and the right to economic free movement relates to European Citizens' right to a family life in their home-State.[69] The paradigmatic example of this is *Carpenter*.[70] Mr Carpenter was a British national who married, in the UK, a Philippines' national who had overstayed her allowed leave. The British authorities ordered her deportation but the Court of Justice found a sufficient link to EU law on the grounds that Mr Carpenter conducted a business whereby he provided services to advertisers established in other Member States, and occasionally travelled there for business purposes. Accordingly, the Court of Justice went on to hold that the deportation of Ms Carpenter from the United Kingdom, where the couple resided, would be detrimental to the couple's family life and,

[67] *Bickel and Franz*.

[68] Under European Citizenship, the right to move need not have been exercised for an economic purpose, so the mere existence of cross-border movement by a EU national will bring Art. 18 TFEU into play. Also seeing *Cowan* as related to European Citizenship, Damian Chalmers, G. T. Davies, and Giorgio Monti, European Union law (3nd edn, Cambridge University Press 2014), 482.

[69] See *Singh* and Case C-291/05 *Eind* [2007] E.C.R. I-10719. See also Miguel Poiares Maduro, 'The Scope of European Remedies: The Case of Purely Internal Situations and Reverse Discrimination' in Claire Kilpatrick, Tonia Novitz and Paiul Skidmore (eds), *The Future of Remedies in Europe* (Hart Publishing 2000), 124.

[70] Case C-60/00 *Carpenter* [2002] E.C.R. I-6279.

therefore, to the conditions under which Mr Carpenter exercised a market freedom. However, there was no link between Mr Carpenter exercising his freedom to provide services and his wife's right to reside in the UK. After all, it is not as if this right to family life was being interfered with as a result of Mr Carpenter pursuing cross-border economic activities. Even accepting, for argument's sake, that the situation *sub judice* possessed a cross-border element—which is doubtful—the contested measure did not interfere with Mr Carpenter's ability to engage in cross-border movement for the purpose of providing services in another Member State.[71]

This absence of connection between the exercise of cross-border movement and economic free movement rights is also present in the Court of Justice's case law on whether third-country nationals who are relatives of European citizens who moved into another State should be allowed to join them there directly from outside the EU without previously being allowed to reside in the European citizen's State of origin.[72] The argument against EU law allowing relatives who are third-country nationals to join EU nationals in their State of residence is that EU law grants family reunification rights in order for people to move freely between Member States. An impediment to that movement would only arise if the relatives of a European citizen, who previously resided lawfully with them in the territory of a Member State, would, as a result of that European citizen's movement to another Member State, lose the right to reside with her. This would only occur if the family members were already lawfully residing with the EU national before she moved to another Member State.[73] Accordingly:

[71] In her Opinion in Joined Cases C-456 and 457/12 *O and S*, decided on 12 March 2014, para. 117, Advocate General Sharpston valiantly tries to read *Carpenter* in accordance with traditional case law by inferring a necessary premise that there was a '*causal connection between Mr Carpenter's exercise of economic free movement and his Filipino wife's residence in Mr Carpenter's Member State of nationality and residence*' inasmuch as '*Mr Carpenter was dependent on her so far as she looked after his children, did the homemaking and thereby indirectly contributed to his success*'. The Court of Justice, in its 12 March 2014 decision in Case 457/12, seems to have adopted such a reading of *Carpenter* at para. 13. The problem with this is that the causal connection is indirect—as the Advocate General herself recognizes, the premise is necessary for the conclusion that deporting Mr Carpenter's wife would prevent Mr Carpenter from pursuing his activities abroad, but whether her deportation would have caused such an outcome '*is unclear and does not form part of the Court's reasoning*'.

[72] This situation was not addressed by Council Directive 73/148/EEC [1973] OJ 1973 L 172 on the abolition of restrictions on movement and residence within the Community for nationals of Member States with regard to establishment and the provision of services, or by Directive 2004/38/EC.

[73] Tryfonidou, 'Family Reunification Rights of (Migrant) Union Citizens', 637–638.

*it is the family situation as it exists at the time the Community national decides to go to another Member State which should be taken into account. [*National immigration rules do not restrict the right of*] a national who has already exercised his rights to free movement and apparently has not been dissuaded from using that right for reasons related to the non-admission of third-country-national family members.*[74]

This was the *rationale* behind old cases such as *Morson*[75] and more recent ones such as *Akrich*.[76] However, in *Jia*[77] and particularly in *Metock*,[78] the Court of Justice chose to hold instead that the relevant question is whether the third-country national is a family member of a European citizen. Whether the refusal of the extension of the claimed family reunification rights impeded the exercise of the free movement right or not was deemed to be irrelevant.[79]

A last line of cases where it appears that no connection is required between cross-border movement and the purpose for which economic free movement rights were established concerns changes in the State of residence by persons who continue to pursue their economic activities in their States of origin. This line of cases deals with the rights of workers and self-employed people who have moved their residence to another Member State but continue to pursue their economic activities in their home-State,[80] and with situations where an individual controlling a number of undertakings in her home-State moves into another State without any economic intent.[81] The Court of Justice held that all these cases fell within the scope of the market freedoms, even though the cross-border movement that took place could not be said to have occurred in order to gain access to the markets of other Member States.[82]

In short, even though economic free movement rights were created in order to protect cross-border movement with an economic aim, in all these

[74] Advocate General Geelhoed's Opinion in Case C-1/05 *Jia* [2007] E.C.R. I-001, para. 70.

[75] *Morson and Jhanjan.* [76] Case C-109/01 *Akrich* [2003] E.C.R. I-9607.

[77] *Jia.* [78] Case C-127/08 *Metock* [2008] ECR I-6241.

[79] Alina Tryfonidou, 'Jia or "Carpenter II": The Edge of Reason' (2007) 32 ELRev 908, 913–915

[80] *Ritter-Coulais; Government of Communauté française and Gouvernement wallon*; Case C-152/05 *Commission v Germany* [2008] E.C.R. I-00039 *Renneberg*. Examples of traditional case law can be found in Case C-112/91 *Werner* [1993] E.C.R. I-00429; Case C-293/03 *Gregorio My* [2004] E.C.R. I-12013.

[81] *N*, Case C-464/05 *Geurts* [2007] E.C.R. I-9325.

[82] Tryfonidou, 'In Search of the Aim of the EC Free Movement of Persons Provisions', 1596–1604.

cases the unrelated presence of cross-border movement and an economically active EU national sufficed to bring a situation within the scope of EU law.[83]

One thing that all these cases have in common is that they are concerned with the free movement of individuals. It is therefore plausible that normative considerations on the special status of individuals in the EU underlie this case law. The *rationale* behind this can perhaps be traced to the influence that European Citizenship has had on the market freedoms—particularly because European Citizenship protects cross-border movement even if such movement occurs without any economic aim. This influence is apparent in a growing body of academic literature already reviewed in Chapter 2, which, starting from the observation that a unitary approach to the free movement of persons appears to have been adopted in the Court of Justice's language,[84] holds that the different Treaty provisions on the economic free movement of people are complementary to a general freedom for the movement of individuals and juridical persons.[85] This academic literature submits that European Citizenship has had an impact on the case law on the market freedoms and has led the Court of Justice to read the free movement provisions as protecting the human rights of any European citizen moving across State borders.[86]

These normative arguments point towards the economic free movement of persons having a more exalted normative status than the other freedoms.[87] This would mean that the normative underpinnings of the market freedoms have changed from merely protecting the right to move for the purpose of taking up an economic activity, to protecting the rights of all economically active persons whose situation has a cross-border dimension. If this is the

[83] Schiltz, 'Akrich', 252.

[84] Hatzopoulos, 'Recent Developments of the Case Law of the ECJ in the Field of Services', 70.

[85] Scheuing, 'Freizügigkeit als Unionsbürgerrecht', 753; Weatherill, 'Discrimination on Grounds of Nationality in Sport', 59; Snell, *Goods and Services in EC Law*, 9; Dollat, *Libre circulation des personnes et citoyenneté: enjeux et perspectives*, 26; Snell, 'And Then There Were Two', 69–70; Hilson, 'Discrimination in Community Free Movement Law', 453; Oliver and Enchelmaier, 'Free Movement of Goods', 666.

[86] Spaventa, 'Seeing the Wood Despite the Trees?', 39–44. This can reflect the idea that the basic common values of European States lie in respect for human rights, which, hence, should be protected by the Court of Justice: see Advocate General Jacob's Opinion in Case C-168/91 *Konstantinidis* [1993] E.C.R. I-1191; Neussl, 'European Citizenship and Human Rights'.

[87] See Chapter 2 and this chapter's Section II.

case, the scope of the market freedoms will now cover the situations of all economically active European citizens, provided that the situation involves a cross-border element and regardless of whether the exercise of free movement is related to the pursuit of an economic activity.[88]

B. *The institutional dimension*

If the normative *substrata* of the free movement of persons have indeed changed, a relevant question is: When did this happen, and by whose authority? After all, there is no indication in the drafting of the Treaties (or in secondary legislation) that European Citizenship altered the goals of the market freedoms to be something other than to enable cross-border movement between Member States for economic purposes, instrumentally to the creation of a common market. Furthermore, in most cases a connection is still required between cross-border movement and the pursuit of an economic aim—the strands in the case law reviewed above are exceptions to this rule.

Looking into the institutional dynamics operating in the background allows us to answer these questions and understand the logic behind these developments in the law. To begin with, it should be made clear how the existence of case law that deviates from the norm can lead to changes in the normative foundations of the law: (a) through *ex-post* rationalization and categorization; (b) *via* the effects of lock-in and path-dependency; and (c) under influence of a legal culture that prizes systemic coherence and regularity. Arguably, this is what happened.

The adoption of decisions under the market freedoms which are detached from the internal market rationale may be the result of judicial mistakes, pragmatism, or even concerns with the just outcome of a given case (as perceived by the judges). In themselves, these decisions are too limited to change the normative *substrata* of the law—and allowance should also be made for the fact that, given enough cases, the Court of Justice will eventually come up with decisions that do not fit too neatly with any given normative framework, particularly as it is operating in an environment of normative uncertainty. However, some of these cases may be given greater prominence by legal commentators, or even develop into their own strand of case law. When this happens, it is likely that the legal community will try to rationalize these developments by reference to a specific normative framework, which is arguably what happened in this case, particularly as regards

[88] Tryfonidou, 'Family Reunification Rights of (Migrant) Union Citizens'.

the family reunification cases. In other words, the normative foundations of the market freedoms did not change—if they changed at all—from one moment to another. It was through *ex-post* rationalization—that took into account the logic of legal reasoning and which was in line with a certain normative bent prevalent in the scholarship—that this potential change in the normative foundations of the case law came to light in the first place. From there, it was but a small step to argue that, in the light of the principles of systemic coherence and non-arbitrariness, this change did not apply only to the specific strands of case law where the connection between cross-border movement and the pursuit of economic aims was severed, but to all law on the economic free movement of individuals—a change that may well come to pass as a result of this argument being advanced.

Taking into account institutional considerations also helps us to identify the implications that these developments may have. As seen above, the requirements that a situation falling under the scope of the market freedoms must have a cross-border element and be concerned with the pursuit of an economic activity were susceptible to being stretched, which resulted in an expansion in the scope of the market freedoms. This expansion, however, pales in comparison to the impact that eliminating the required connection between the exercise of cross-border movement and the subjective right to pursue economic activities across borders may have.

This can be seen in *Carpenter*, which exemplifies how decoupling cross-border movement from the right to economic free movement leads to a stretching of the market freedoms to breaking point. After all, under a simple reading of this case, the fact that one may engage in cross-border movement and in economic activities in more than one Member State is able to bring one within the scope EU law, even in situations not directly related to such cross-border movement or the pursuit of economic activities. This line of reasoning significantly expands the possibilities litigants have to use the market freedoms to challenge Member States' national measures resulting from *prima facie* legitimate democratic processes. It means that the Court of Justice will be called upon to second-guess Member States' decisions in areas outside the traditional scope of EU law, without any prior consideration as to why the Court of Justice is better suited to pursue such an assessment than national institutions.

Normative arguments defending this case law on the basis of the expansion of European Citizenship and the protection of fundamental rights are, implicitly, calls for a greater role for the courts and, eventually, the EU political process to the detriment of the Member States' political processes. What is more, they also require the Court of Justice to take on a load for which an international court—the European Court of Human Rights—is already responsible. That the Court must decide on issues of fundamental rights protection in areas falling within the scope of EU law results clearly enough from the case law, and appears to be justified by the fact that EU law is ultimately responsible for outcomes in these fields.[89] Whether it should do so in areas not traditionally falling within the scope of EU law is a question with which these normative claims usually fail to engage.

As previously in this book, we find that institutional questions can be dressed in normative clothes, while the normative claims themselves—that European Citizenship allows for the expansion of the market freedoms, and that the protection of fundamental rights at EU level should prevail over the mechanisms of protection at national level—are interlinked with, and make no sense except by reference to, specific institutional contexts.

V. Private Action and Free Movement—The Question of Horizontal Effect

There is no doubt that the market freedoms are able to affect private relationships—as demonstrated by the fact that EU law can apply to private disputes, which are the main source of preliminary references. Nonetheless, the question remains whether, in addition to State action, actions by private parties are susceptible to falling within the scope of the market freedoms—a question identified as being about the horizontal effect of the market freedoms.[90] However, 'horizontal effect' does not exclusively refer to relationships between private parties, in the same way that vertical effect does not refer exclusively to relationships between the EU and its Member States. The effect of EU law between Member States can also be said to be horizontal, while the relationship between Union law and individuals is clearly vertical. Regardless, the expression 'horizontal effect' is commonly, and imprecisely, used in the academic literature when dealing with the question of whether

[89] This includes the application of the general principles of EU law relating to fundamental rights and, more recently, of the rights contained in the Charter of Fundamental Rights: see Case C-617/10 *Åkerberg Fransson*, decided on 26 February 2013, paras 19–22; and Case C-390/12 *Pfleger*, decided on 30 April 2014, paras 30–35.

[90] Cruz, 'Free Movement and Private Autonomy', 605; Chalmers, Davies, and Monti, *European Union Law*, 296.

private behaviour can infringe on free movement rights—a usage that will be adopted in this chapter, even if the Court of Justice has never used it.[91]

A. The normative dimension

The original academic debate on the horizontal effect of the market freedoms arose from disputes between two opposing camps regarding the relative roles of competition law and free movement law in the context of the Treaties.

One camp argued that private action could restrict, at the very least, the free movement of people—a position which was supported by a number of Court of Justice decisions concerning rules emanating from private entities that aimed to regulate in a collective manner gainful employment and the provision of services.[92] The reasons presented by the Court of Justice for considering that such private rules fall within the scope of the free movement of persons were threefold: (i) the market freedoms create rights which courts must protect, and the removal as between Member States of obstacles to the economic free movement of persons would be compromised if the State barriers removed by that freedom could be replaced by new obstacles raised by associations or organizations not governed by public law (the *effect utile* argument); (ii) since working conditions in different Member States are governed sometimes by provisions laid down by law or regulation, and sometimes by agreements or other acts concluded or adopted by private persons, to limit the scope of the free movement of persons to public acts would prevent them from being uniformly applied throughout the EU (the uniform application argument); (iii) there is nothing in the relevant provisions restricting the direct effect of the provisions on economic free movement of persons to public action (the general wording proposition).[93]

This camp also observed that the Court of Justice applied competition law and market freedoms to the same situations, and that this made sense from a systemic perspective because it reflected the existence of situations

[91] Joanna Krzeminska-Vamkava, 'Horizontal Effect of Fundamental Rights and Freedoms—Much Ado About Nothing? German, Polish and EU Theories Compared after *Viking Line*' [2009] Jean Monnet Working Paper 11/09, 7.

[92] Case 13/76 *Donà v Mantero* [1976] E.C.R. 1333; *Bosman*; *Deliège*; Case C-309/99 *Wouters* [2002] E.C.R. I-1577.

[93] Detlef Schaefer, *Die unmittelbare Wirkung des Verbot der nichttarifären Handelshemmnisse (Art. 30 EWGV) in den Rechtsbezienhungen zwischen Privaten* (Lang 1987), 147–154; Torsten Körber, 'Innerstaatliche Anwendung und Drittwirkung der Grundfreiheiten' (2000) 35 EuR 932, 941; Stefaan van den Bogaert, 'Horizontality: the Court Attacks?' in Catherine Barnard and Joanne Scott (eds), *The Law of the Single European Market* (Hart Publishing 2001), 125.

with both public and private elements.[94] While competition law only applies to undertakings, this concept encompasses any entity engaged in an economic activity regardless of its legal status.[95] This means that public bodies such as public authorities, State-owned corporations, bodies entrusted by the State with particular tasks, and quasi-governmental bodies, can be subject to competition law whenever they pursue economic activities, with the result that their actions are thereby susceptible to falling simultaneously within the scope of both free movement provisions and competition rules.[96] At the same time, private entities do not fall within the scope of competition law when they are not undertakings, which would mean that, unless their actions were to fall within the scope of the market freedoms, they would fall outside the scope of EU law altogether—which would be inappropriate should they have regulatory powers and/or be able to raise private obstacles to free movement.[97] Ultimately, it was argued, free movement law and competition law share the same goal—the creation of a common market—and are complementary; as such, there is no impediment to applying both sets of rules concurrently.[98]

Another camp, however, argued that, while the market freedoms cover State action, private action should be covered by the provisions on competition law alone. If either competition law or the market freedoms did not regulate a situation, this was not the result of a legal gap, but because some

[94] Case 311/85 *Vlaamse Reisbureaus* [1987] E.C.R. 3801. See K. Mortelmans, 'Towards Convergence in the Application of the Rules on Free Movement and on Competition?' (2001) 38 CML Rev 613, 625.

[95] *Höfner and Elser*, paras 21-22 and 74-75 and cases mentioned therein. See, for a detailed analysis, Okeoghene Odudu, *The Boundaries of EC Competition Law* (OUP 2006), 23–45.

[96] Richard Whish, *Competition Law* (6th edn, OUP 2009), 85–86; Mortelmans, 'Towards Convergence in the Application of the Rules on Free Movement and on Competition?', 634–635.

[97] Examples of private parties not being deemed undertakings can be seen in Case C-96/94 *Spedizioni Marittima del Golfo* [1995] E.C.R. I-2883, paras 23–25; Case C-343/95 *Cali & Figli* [1997] E.C.R. I-1547, para. 23; Case C-35/96 *Commission v Italy* [1998] E.C.R. I-3851, paras 41–44; *Eurocontrol*, para. 30; *Wouters*, para. 57; Case C-67/96 *Albany* [1999] E.C.R. I-5751, para. 60; Joined Cases C-115/97 to C-117/97 *Brentjens'* [1999] E.C.R. I-6025, para 57.

[98] M. Waelbroeck, 'Les rapports entre les règles de concurrence applicables aux enterprises dans la CEE' in F. Capotorti and others (eds) *Liber Amicorum Pierre Pescatore* (Nomos 1987). 782, 793; Pierre Pescatore, 'Public and Private Aspects of European Community Competition Law', 10 Fordham Int'l LJ, 383–386; Cruz, *Between Competition and Free Movement*, 87; C. Krenn, 'A Missing Piece in the Horizontal Effect "Jigsaw": Horizontal Direct Effect and the Free Movement of Goods' (2012) 49 CML Rev, 205–206.

situations were explicitly excluded from the scope of the Treaty in order to protect a sphere of regulatory autonomy for the Member States.[99]

On the other hand, until recently the law was that the free movement of persons had horizontal effect, while the free movement of goods did not.[100] Unsurprisingly, this led to the recent development of additional arguments based on the special status of people under EU law. These arguments took two different forms, which we should by now be familiar with: a first, earlier version held that the free movement of workers, due to its specific social significance and the fact that it does not fall within the scope of competition rules, is subject to special treatment; the second approach went beyond the realm of market integration and anchored the doctrine of horizontal direct effect in a general prohibition of non-discrimination based on human rights and/or European Citizenship.[101]

A very important consequence of these debates, which went broadly unnoticed, was a focus on the horizontal 'direct' effect of the market freedoms to the detriment of the other types of horizontal effect those freedoms might have. It is however undisputed that the market freedoms can affect the outcome of private disputes—and hence the lawfulness of private behaviour—even when they do not apply directly to that behaviour. In reality, the issue of horizontal direct effect only came up in a small number of cases, while the overwhelming majority of disputes about whether private behaviour infringed upon free movement rights were instead decided by reference to the State measure regulating that behaviour.

[99] Gustavo Marenco, 'Competition between National Economies and Competition between Businesses—A Response to Judge Pescatore', (1986-1987) 10 Fordham Int'l LJ, 424–432; MacGowan and Quinn, 'Could Article 30 Impose bligations on Individuals?', 167–168; White, 'In Search of the Limits to Article 30 of the EEC Treaty', 264; G. Orlandini, Right to Strike, Transnational Collective Action and European Law: Time to Move On?' (2007) Jean Monnet Working Paper 01/05, 8; Jukka Snell, 'Private Parties and the Free Movement of Goods and Services' in Mads Andenas and Wulf-Henning Roth (eds), *Services and Free Movement in EU Law* (OUP 2002), 211–212.

[100] See, on goods, Joined Cases 177 and 178/82 *van de Haar* [1984] E.C.R. 1797; Case 19/84 *Pharmon v Hoechst* [1985] E.C.R. 2281, para. 22; Case 434/85 *Allen and Hanburys* [1988] E.C.R. 1245, paras 8–10; *Vlaamse Reisbureaus*; Case C-316/95 *Generics* [1997] E.C.R. I-3929, para. 17; Case C-159/00 *Sapod Audic* [2002] E.C.R. I-5031. For a possible exception to this, see Case 58/80 *Dansk Supermarked* [1981] E.C.R. 181. For the controversy around it, see Cruz, 'Free Movement and Private Autonomy', 608–609.

[101] Cruz, *Between Competition and Free Movement*, 92; Chalmers, Davies, and Monti, *European Union Law*, 820; H. Schepel, 'Constitutionalising the Market, Marketising the Constitution, and to Tell the Difference: On the Horizontal Application of the Free Movement Provisions in EU Law' (2012) 18 ELJ 177, 180; Krenn, 'A Missing Piece in the Horizontal Effect "Jigsaw"', 184–185.

This impact of the market freedoms on private behaviour is a result of their status as constitutional rights hierarchically superior to national law.[102] In effect, debates about horizontal effect are not exclusive to the market freedoms: they are inherent in the creation of a system of judicial adjudication of constitutional rights.[103] A cursory review of the scholarship on comparative constitutional law provides examples of how constitutional rights regulate private behaviour in a number of different ways, and makes clear that the question of whether fundamental rights have, or should have horizontal effect is a classical topic of constitutional law across the world.[104] From a comparative perspective, constitutional rights may:

- have no horizontal effect, which is the case only where constitutional rights are not judicially enforceable at all, or are only enforceable against the State;[105]
- have direct effect, i.e. constitutional rights are directly effective in regulating private behaviour and do not require to be implemented via legislative or administrative acts;[106]

[102] See fn. 2 and 3 in Chapter 2 above.

[103] Marc Tushnet, 'The Issue of State Action/Horizontal Effect in Comparative Constitutional Law' I (2003) I•CON 79.

[104] Marc Tushnet, 'The Relationship between Judicial Review of Legislation and the Interpretation of Non-Constitutional Law, with Reference to Third Party Effect', in A. Sajó and R. Uitz (eds) *The Constitution in Private Relationships* (Eleven International Publishing 2005), 170 in A. Sajó and R. Uitz (eds) *The Constitution in Private Relationships* (Eleven International Publishing 2005), 170 169.

[105] This is arguably the case in the USA, where the law is that: (i) apart from the Thirteenth Amendment, both the text of the Constitution and authoritative precedent make clear that the Constitution binds only governmental actors and not private individuals; (ii) courts are not under an obligation to interpret private law in accordance with the Constitution. See S. Gardbaum, 'The Effect of Constitutional Rights' (2003) 102 Mich L. Rev 387, 388, who nonetheless argues that this extreme position is tempered by the supremacy clause and the fact that private law is subject to constitutional law (i.e. private law may be deemed inconstitutional), with the result that constitutional rights indirectly govern private law and private actions. Ibid, 390–391; S. Gardbaum, 'The Myth and the Reality of American Constitutional Exceptionalism' [2008] Jean Monnet Working Paper 07/08, 50–51; Marc Tushnet, 'The Issue of State Action/Horizontal Effect in Comparative Constitutional Law', 81. For a plausible explanation of the historical-institutional background for the apparently restrictive 'State-action' doctrine in the USA, see M. Kumm and V. Comella, 'What Is So Special about Constitutional Rights in Private Litigation?' in A. Sajó and R. Uitz (eds), *The Constitution in Private Relationships* (Eleven 2005), 267, 272–283.

[106] This type of effect for constitutional rights is adopted in Ireland, whose legal order contains a 'constitutional tort' for those situations where fundamental rights are infringed upon: see S. Banda, 'Taking Indirect Horizontality Seriously in Ireland: A Time to Magnify the Nuance' (2009) DULJ 263, 264–268.

- have indirect effect, meaning that it is incumbent upon the legislative and executive branches to regulate private relationships in such a way as to ensure respect for constitutional rights, and upon the courts to interpret private law in accordance with those rights;[107]
- give rise to positive duties of action by the State, which are usually complementary to direct and indirect effect, in order to protect private parties from acts by third parties that may infringe on their rights. Inasmuch as any such infringement takes place, the State is responsible for it, and courts may be responsible for striking down laws that make such the infringement possible.[108]

While it is clear from comparative constitutional law that different legal orders adopt different approaches to how constitutional rights regulate private behaviour, it is also clear that, as long as some type of horizontal effect is adopted, no substantive difference arises from the adoption of any particular approach; i.e. these approaches are interchangeable and outcome-neutral, with the only practical differences between them concerning the way in which procedural questions are framed. For example, under horizontal direct effect, private parties would be the addressees of the decision instead of public authorities, and the actions of those parties would be reviewed as regards their compatibility with constitutional rights instead of the relevant law or absence thereof. The substantive outcome, however, would be the same in both scenarios: since courts are under an obligation to uphold constitutional law, the fact that private parties may not invoke a direct constitutional infringement by the other party merely

[107] Alexy, *A Theory of Constitutional Rights*, 355; Claus-Wihelm Canaris, 'Drittwirkung der gemeinschaftsrechtlichen Grundfreiheiten' in Hartmut Bauer and others (eds), *Umwelt, Wirtschaft und Recht* (Mohr Siebeck 2002), 34; Krzeminska-Vamkava, 'Horizontal Effect of Fundamental Rights and Freedoms', 11; Canotilho, *Direito Constitucional e Teoria da Constituição*, 422. This approach to the horizontal effect of constitutional rights has been prevalent in Germany since the German Federal Constitutional Court's decision in *Lüth* BVerfGE 7 198 (205), according to which: '*Basic rights are primarily to protect the citizen against the State, but as enacted in the Constitution they also incorporate an objective scale of values which applies, as a matter of constitutional law, throughout the entire legal system*', with the result that constitutional rights 'radiate' into all areas of the legal system, requiring constitutional rights to be taken into account when interpreting private law.

[108] Also known as *Schtutzpflicht* in Germany. See Alexy, *A Theory of Constitutional Rights*, 302 ff; Mattias Kumm, 'Who is Afraid of the Total Constitution? Constitutional Rights as Principles and the Constitutionalization of Private Law' (2006) 7 GLJ 341, 350–351; Canotilho, *Direito Constitucional e Teoria da Constituição*, 374, 384–385. This doctrine can also be found in the case law of the European Court of Human Rights since the *Belgian Linguistic case (No 2)* [1968] 1 EHRR 252.

means that the court is instead required to interpret existing private law in accordance with the constitution, to declare such law unconstitutional if such interpretation is not possible, or to condemn the State for failing to regulate such behaviour, with exactly the same balancing exercise being imposed on courts from a substantive standpoint.[109]

A consequence of this is that, in systems where constitutional rights are protected through indirect effect and the imposition of positive protection duties upon States—such as the EU, which demands that national law be interpreted in accordance with EU law; if such *interprétation conforme* is not possible, that national courts disapply national laws that infringe upon the market freedoms; and under which Member States have a duty of sincere cooperation with the EU under Art. 4(3) TEU [110]—the question of horizontal direct effect will only arise in those rare situations that are left untouched by the relatively thick regime of regulation that States nowadays have in place to regulate private interactions—in other words, when situations fall outside the control of the State's judicial apparatus (such as social arrangements, or when private entities acquire regulatory powers akin to those of the State).[111] This explains the limited number of cases dealing with whether private behaviour falls within the scope of the market freedoms.

The imposition of positive duties incumbent upon the State is close to horizontal indirect effect, inasmuch as both impose on courts, as State bodies, a duty to hand down decisions that respect the constitutional rights of the parties by either interpreting private law in accordance with constitutional rights or, when such law is explicitly contrary to constitutional rights, by considering it unlawful. Arguing that this duty should merely be considered an element of a wider *Schtutzpflicht* incumbent on both courts and the legislature, see Hermes, 'Grundrechtsschutz durch Privatrecht auf neuer Grundlage?' [1990] NJW 1764. For the argument that *mittelbare Drittwirkung* and *Schutzpflicht* are very similar, if dogmatically distinct, see Ingo von Münch, Josep Ferrer i Riba, and Pablo Salvador Coderch, *Zur Drittwirkund der Grundrechte* (Lang 1998), 24–28.

[109] Stephen Gardbaum, 'Where the (State) Action is' (2006) 4 I•CON 760; Krzeminska-Vamkava, 'Horizontal Effect of Fundamental Rights and Freedoms', 13–18; Kumm, 'Who is Afraid of the Total Constitution?', 352–359.

[110] On the principle of *interprétation conforme*, see Case 14/83 *von Colson* [1984] E.C.R. 1891; Case C-106/89 *Marleasing* [1990] E.C.R. I-04135; Case C-91/92 *Faccini Dori* [1994] E.C.R. I-03325. On the disapplication of national law contrary to EU law, see *Simmenthal.*

[111] Mark Tushnet, 'The Relationship between Judicial Review of Legislation and the Interpretation of Non-Constitutional Law, with Reference to Third Party Effect', 170; Gardbaum, 'Where the (State) Action is', 767. A good example of this type of situation can be found in Canada, where certain rules—such as common law—are largely exempt from judicial constitutional review. See Cheryl Saunders, 'Constitutional Rights and the Common Law' in András Sajó and Renáta Uitz (eds), *The Constitution in Private Relationships* (Eleven International Publishing 2005), 195–199.

As with constitutional rights in other legal orders, choosing between different approaches to the horizontal effect of the market freedoms does not affect their substance, but merely what legal actions are available to enforce the rights arising from them. This is particularly obvious in the development of the law on the horizontal effect of the free movement of goods. Debates about the horizontal effect of this freedom first arose in a number of cases on IP rights in which the Court of Justice identified the IP right's 'specific object': for example, for patents the 'specific object' would be the right for the holder to be the first to place a patented product in a given market and enjoy the economic benefit arising from it. The exercise of the right to this 'specific object' would 'exhaust' the IP right, with the result that, whenever the exercise of a right by a private party exceeded its 'specific object'—e.g., if the patentee tried to prevent the importation of the product into her own Member State when such a product had already been lawfully marketed in another Member State—such exercise would infringe upon Article 34 TFEU.[112] This doctrine seemed to imply that it was the private parties' actions that restricted the free movement of goods, leading to a lively academic debate on whether this was (and should) be the case.[113] The issue was apparently solved when the Court of Justice held that it was the laws granting IP rights to private parties, and not the exercise of those rights by individuals, which were subject to Article 34 TFEU.[114] It thus became settled law that the actions of private persons did not *per se* restrict the free movement of goods.[115] In reality, whether the free movement of goods was infringed upon by private parties exercising IP rights or by the national laws granting such rights in the first place did not alter the substantive outcome of the case: in the end,

[112] *Merck v Stephar*, paras 9–10; Joined Cases C-267/95 and C-268/95 *Beecham Group v Europharm* [1996] E.C.R. I-6285, para. 33.

[113] For the argument in favour of the horizontal effect of the free movement of goods, see Walter Van Gerven, 'The Recent Case Law of the Court of Justice Concerning Articles 30 and 36 of the EEC Treaty' (1977) 14 CML Rev 5; Pescatore, 'Public and Private Aspects of European Community Competition Law', 373; Waelbroeck, 'Les rapports entre les règles sur la libre circulation des merchandises et les règles de concurrence applicables aux enterprises dans la CEE', 782–786. For the argument against it, see Marenco, 'Competition between National Economies and Competition between Businesses, 420; MacGowan Quinn, 'Could Article 30 Impose Obligations on Individuals?', 163; EL White, Karen Banks and Giuliano Marenco, 'Intellectual Property and the Community Rules on Free Movement: Discrimination Unearthed' (1990) 15 ELRev 224.

[114] See *Pharmon v Hoechst*, para. 22; *Allen and Hanburys*, paras. 8–10; *Generics* [1997], para. 17.

[115] *van de Haar*; *Vlaamse Reisbureaus*; Case C-159/00 *Sapod Audic* [2002] E.C.R. I-5031. For a possible exception to this, see *Dansk Supermarked*. For the controversy around it, see Cruz, 'Free Movement and Private Autonomy', 608–609.

the situation would have been considered contrary to the free movement of goods regardless of whether the Court of Justice decided that it was private action or public conduct that infringed upon this market freedom. Hence, upholding the effect of market freedoms on private relationships can be done by either granting the market freedoms direct or indirect horizontal effect, or by imposing on the State a duty to protect them, without any difference in the substantive outcome of a case.[116]

This goes some way towards explaining the nature of the debate on the horizontal effect of the market freedoms reviewed at the beginning of this section, and its focus on systemic and formal arguments. In reality, each camp in that debate seemed to be engaged in the rationalization of previous decisions, and the only truly substantive arguments used related to the different treatment of the free movement of persons and the free movement of goods.

In particular, and as we have seen above, it was argued that the free movement of workers, due to its specific social significance and the fact that it does not fall within the scope of competition rules, is subject to special treatment and/or that the free movement of persons benefits from horizontal direct effect as a result of normative concerns about the protection of human rights and/or European Citizenship. The main issue with these arguments is that they are unable to explain the evolution of the case law, i.e. they have limited value even as rationalizations of legal developments. First, attribution of horizontal direct effect to the free movement of persons first took place in the 1970s,[117] a period when the case law was expanding the scope of the free movement of goods while seemingly attributing a secondary status to the other fundamental freedoms. This makes it unlikely that these normative justifications were at play. Secondly, the three arguments presented by the Court of Justice for the attribution of horizontal direct effect to the free movement of persons—which were reviewed above—in no way indicate that the normative underpinnings for this attribution relate to the privileged status of that freedom. Lastly, not only are these arguments unable to explain the Court of Justice's zigzags concerning the horizontal effect of the free movement of goods, but the adoption and development of European Citizenship by the Court of Justice—which occurred in the late 1990s and early 2000s[118]—is

[116] Advocate General Maduro's Opinion in *Viking*, paras 38–40.

[117] In *Walrave* (a case decided in 1974) and *Donà v Mantero* (a case decided in 1976).

[118] In particular, as a result of decisions adopted between 1998 (*Martínez Sala*) and 2002 (*Baumbast*), even though the Court of Justice has kept expanding the scope and impact of European Citizenship to this day, as is made clear by the *Zambrano* and *Dereci* decisions.

actually contemporaneous with its eventual attribution of horizontal direct effect to the free movement of goods.

In effect, at the turn of the millennium, when it had been settled law for decades that the free movement of goods did not have horizontal direct effect, the Court of Justice expanded the horizontal effect of the free movement of goods in two decisions. The first decision, *Commission v France*, from 1997, concerned a failure by the French State to prevent actions by private parties obstructing the free movement of fruit and vegetables originating from Spain.[119] The second one, *Schmidberger*, from 2003, dealt with the failure by the Austrian State to prevent a demonstration that resulted in the complete closure of a major transit route between northern Europe and northern Italy.[120] In both cases, the Court of Justice was asked to consider whether omissions by a Member State to suppress individuals' activities, which impeded cross-border trade, restricted the free movement of goods, and considered that it did do so. This approach was new, in that, even though in both cases an assessment of the lawfulness of collective actions undertaken by private individuals was implied, the decisions did not identify obstacles erected through the conduct of private persons *per se*, but focused instead on the failure by the State to prevent such conduct.[121] On this basis, one could arguably distinguish between a principle of direct horizontal effect for persons—meaning that it was possible for private action to fall within the scope of the free movement of persons—and indirect State liability for goods—meaning that, even though private action would not be able to restrict this free movement right *per se*, States could still be held liable for their failure to regulate such private activity.

This distinction, however, was ignored by the Court of Justice in *dicta* in *Viking*, a case on the right of establishment, which read these cases as making it '*apparent that restrictions [on the free movement of goods] may be the result of actions by individuals or groups of such individuals rather than caused by the State*',[122] thereby opening the scope of Article 34 TFEU to private actions that restrict the free movement of goods.[123]

[119] *Commission v France*, para. 31. [120] *Schmidberger*, para. 64.

[121] Orlandini, 'Right to Strike, Transnational Collective Action and European Law', 23.

[122] *Viking*, paras 62–63.

[123] Derrick Wyatt, 'Horizontal Effect of Fundamental Freedoms and the Right to Equality after *Viking* and *Mangold*, and the Implications for Community Competence' (4) [2008] CYELP 1, 8.

B. The institutional dimension

In the absence of normative reasons for adopting one type of horizontal effect over another, one would expect institutional considerations to have an even greater power than usual in explaining the observed developments in the law, and in identifying the implications of adopting one type of horizontal effect instead of another.

One can only speculate as to the motivations of the judges involved, but one justification the Court of Justice provided for the adoption of horizontal direct effect for the free movement of persons was that there was nothing in the relevant provisions requiring that they only apply to public action. Since the Treaties do not explicitly address the question of horizontal direct effect, and in the absence of substantive normative reasons to decide otherwise, there was no impediment to the attribution of direct horizontal effect to the free movement of persons, particularly in areas where Member States left sectoral regulation to private entities. A second type of consideration relates to systemic issues which were reflected in the traditional debates concerning horizontal direct effect reviewed above. Since collective labour agreements and workers do not fall within the scope of competition law, unlike other types of private economic activity, this meant that EU law was unable to control regulations—and, potentially, remove obstacles to free movement—in these fields. From this standpoint, principles of interpretation of EU law such as the principle of effectiveness and of uniform application—which were invoked by the Court of Justice—may indeed point towards these types of private actions falling within the scope of the free movement provisions in order to ensure that all relevant public and private activity falls within the scope of the Treaty.

The different treatment to which individual market freedoms were subject is also demonstrative of courts' tendency to find solutions that are acceptable on results and on low-level principles without taking sides in large-scale controversies—and of the judicial drift that can result therefrom. In its decisions, the Court of Justice never directly engaged with the academic discussions, or expressly reneged on its previous case law, but merely focused on the facts at issue. Its decisions reflected 'incompletely theorized agreements on particular outcomes':[124] they were not fully theorized, nor did they attempt to be. Instead, the Court of Justice's decisions duly followed the prevailing canon for legal reasoning, judicial methodology, and logics of presentation

[124] Sunstein, *Legal Reasoning and Political Conflict*, 4–5.

to reach solutions that, even though duly justified, were limited to the questions that had been addressed to it.

A good example of this is yet again the IP saga, where the Court of Justice's assertion that the exercise of an intellectual property right could restrict the free movement of goods was in no way a sweeping proposition that the free movement of goods had horizontal direct effect. Instead, it was merely a logical step in a piece of legal reasoning that concluded that certain IP rights provided in national law were able to restrict the free movement of goods if exercised.[125] Nor did the subsequent focus of the Court of Justice on national rules granting rights to individuals include an outright rejection of horizontal direct effect: both sets of decisions merely included statements to the effect that the exercise of the IP right or, subsequently, the application of national provisions allowing the exercise of such rights restricted free movement, but this fell short of endorsing one type of horizontal effect over another.

A similar lack of theorization can be found in the development of direct horizontal effect for the free movement of persons. By invoking *effet utile*, uniform application, and general wording to justify its adoption of horizontal direct effect, the Court of Justice made reference to underlying principles of EU law that could support its conclusion that certain types of 'collective regulation' may fall within the scope of the free movement provisions. On the other hand, the concept of 'collective regulation' pops up, as unannounced as Venus from the waves of Cyprus, and has never been subject to any detailed analysis as to its meaning and content. This has allowed the Court of Justice to elude abstract theoretical debates on whether the free movement provisions should have horizontal direct effect, and if so to what extent, and to focus instead on the problem at hand—in the relevant cases, the problems arising from the regulation of certain types of professional activities by international bodies outside the control of the State.[126]

In other words, it cannot be excluded that the first cases on horizontal direct effect did not consider the issue in depth, and adopted lines of reasoning that were in line with the wording of the Treaties, apt to deal with the

[125] A step borrowed from competition law (see Joined Cases 56 and 58/64 *Consten and Grundig* [1966] E.C.R. 299) and which may relate to how IP rights straddle both competition and free movement law (see for example *Deutsche Grammophon*, para. 11). For a detailed analysis, see D. G. Goyder, Joanna Goyder and Albertina Albors-Llorens, *Goyder's EC Competition Law* (5th edn, OUP 2009).

[126] See, particularly, *Walrave*, paras 17–22; also see how the arguments remain exactly the same, and similarly focused, in *Bosman*, paras 82–86.

cases at hand, and broadly satisfactory to both its addressees and the legal community at large. From these humble and under-theorized beginnings, however, small differences escalated and metastasized into bigger ones. This is again a reflection of the fact that legal change will usually be incremental and constrained by the embeddedness of customs, legal traditions, codes, and conducts that lead both to lock-in and path-dependency. It also reflects that fact that the feedback process characteristic of precedent based-systems can lead to small early events having a large, and surprising, impact on the eventual outcome of the case law, particularly in under-theorized areas.

However, this institutional dynamic has serious implications. First, institutionally led developments may cause the law to clash with its basic normative foundations. By treating the free movement of persons as having direct horizontal effect, and the free movement of goods as not having such an effect, a (legal) cognitive pattern was created that pushed would-be litigants to accept previous case law and plead in accordance with it—particularly in the absence of any particular incentive or normative reasons to argue differently, since the substantial outcome for plaintiffs was the same regardless of the type of horizontal effect adopted. This approach, however, failed to deal with potential situations such as one where the activity of a vast number of individuals prevented the free movement of agricultural products from Spain to France. In this case, there was a clear obstacle to the free movement of goods that was not created by private economic activity or by national law. Since, within the cognitive framework created by the Court of Justice's case law, no action was possible against private persons under the free movement of goods, the Commission had to bring an action not against those individuals who disrupted the cross-border trade in agricultural products, but instead against the French State for failing to control them.[127] In the light of this new datum, when a later protest blocked a road linking Austria to Italy, the question could now be framed by the referring court as being focused on the failure of the relevant public powers to ban the demonstration instead of on the acts of the demonstrators.[128]

A second implication of this type of institutional dynamic is that it may lead, as a consequence of judicial drift and the constitutive nature of the normative foundations of the law, to a change in those very normative foundations. For example, so far as the free movement of persons is concerned, it was accepted that the Treaties' non-discrimination imperative applied not only to the action of public authorities but also to rules of any other

[127] *Commission v France.* [128] *Schmidberger.*

nature aimed at regulating in a collective manner gainful employment and the provision of services.[129] However, the thin theorization in place to justify horizontal direct effect for the free movement of persons was never explicitly confined to 'collective regulations'. The case law could entail that only private acts with effects akin to State action were prohibited, including discrimination on grounds of nationality by private entities when the effect of this would be similar to State-sponsored discrimination; or it could mean instead that private parties were not allowed to discriminate on grounds of nationality *tout court*. The question of whether private parties were allowed to discriminate on grounds of nationality reached the Court of Justice in *Angonese*. This was a case about a competition for a post with a private banking undertaking in Bolzano that required, as one of the conditions for entry into the competition, the possession of a certain certificate of bilingualism (in Italian and German) which could only be obtained in that Italian province. The Court held that this condition discriminated on grounds of nationality and, implicitly, that private discriminatory behaviour infringes upon the free movement of workers regardless of whether such behaviour consists of attempts to regulate paid labour collectively or contracts between individuals.[130] This development seemed finally to have taken the free movement of persons—or at least workers—beyond the other freedoms by extending the kind of restrictions that it encompassed, requiring a somewhat different normative foundation for it. This different normative foundation, however, was never articulated.[131]

Even in the face of these institutionally led developments, however, normativity does have its pull, and as such the question remained: apart from the institutional context and the constraints it imposes, why should the various market freedoms be treated differently as regards their horizontal effect? The recognition that there is no such reason—as powerfully articulated by Advocate General Maduro—may be the reason behind the startling *obiter dicta* in *Viking* implying that the free movement of goods also has horizontal direct effect.[132]

[129] *Walrave; Donà v Mantero; Bosman; Deliège; Wouters.*

[130] *Angonese*. See also Case C-94/07 *Raccanelli* [2008] E.C.R. I-5939. This leaves open the question of whether the prohibition of measures which do not regulate employment in a collective manner but are non-discriminatory can also apply to private persons, a question still unaddressed by the Court of Justice.

[131] Except by Cruz, *Between Competition and Free Movement*. This line of case law has had a very limited impact. The exception is *Raccanelli*, which effectively applied this principle to a private entity operating in the public interest.

[132] *Viking*, para. 62. See also Advocate General Maduro's Opinion in this case, paras 36–40.

Taking into account the institutional dimension is also fruitful as regards the identification of the implications of choosing between different types of horizontal effect in practice. In particular, while different types of horizontal effect are, from a normative perspective, outcome-neutral, they may lead to different solutions regarding civil liability and the payment of damages to those whose free movement rights were infringed upon. The question of what type of horizontal effect should be adopted is, ultimately, a question about who should be responsible for unregulated private behaviour. If horizontal direct effect is adopted, *prima facie* it will be the private party who will be liable for infringing upon the market freedoms. If, instead, horizontal effect is indirect, and in particular if it is found that the Member State has a positive duty to act to prevent private behaviour susceptible of infringing upon the market freedoms, then that Member State will be liable for private conduct that infringes upon free movement rights. These implications, together with substantive and systemic considerations, should be taken into account when engaging in normative debates regarding what the law on the horizontal effect of the market freedoms should be, as will be demonstrated in the next section.

VI. Some Normative Suggestions

The insights that arise from taking into account the institutional dimension are relevant to the development of better contextualizzed normative approaches. Such approaches are better contextualized not only because they take into account the institutional implications of adopting a certain line of case law, but because they are also able to account for the effects of the co-existence of various normative approaches, the lack of normative coherence in the case law, and, ultimately, the constitutive nature of legal practice on the law's normative foundations.

This section will use these insights to sketch normative suggestions regarding the areas of the law reviewed above. A first suggestion will focus on the scope of the market freedoms, i.e., on the cross-border element, economic aim, and connecting factor required for the application of the market freedoms—issues that, like the concept of restriction on economic free movement reviewed in the previous chapters, are relevant to the identification of situations in which national measures are subject to proportionality assessments pursued by the Court of Justice. Since, unlike what could have been assumed, the issue of horizontal direct effect of the market freedoms was shown not to relate to their scope, a different type of normative approach—unrelated to the scope of the market freedoms—will have to be sketched.

A. The scope of the market freedoms

A number of trends in the case law were identified above that have serious institutional implications as a result of the expansion of the scope of the market freedoms. Regarding the cross-border element, it was pointed out that the substantive scope of the market freedoms has expanded, while the *Guimont* case law has led to an indirect expansion of the impact of the market freedoms on national regulatory autonomy by opening the door to test cases whose outcomes are able to force regulatory changes by placing Member States under the shadow of the law. Concerning economic aim, it was observed how, in the few cases in which this issue arose, the case law lacked normative coherence. And, when reviewing the case law on the connecting factor between the exercise of free movement rights and the purpose for which such rights are granted, it was clear that this connecting factor was ignored in a number of cases, with serious implications regarding the number of situations susceptible to falling within the scope of the market freedoms.

This analysis revealed some constants. First, in all these areas, it was found that the law's normative underpinnings are under-theorized, which has the consequence of letting institutional dynamics determine the evolution of the law. As a result of these dynamics—and particularly due to pressure from self-interested litigants—the trend in all these areas of the law has been to extend the number of cases susceptible of falling within the scope of the market freedoms—with the implication that the Court of Justice became empowered as the ultimate arbiter of the validity of national law in direct proportion to the extension of the scope of EU law.

As a consequence of, and reaction to, this normative indeterminacy, a number of new normative grounds have been developed. These grounds focus on concerns about reverse discrimination, the adoption and development of European Citizenship, and the increasing importance of fundamental rights' protection. Since the light theorization of the market freedoms also enables new normative pressures to produce major effects without any previous consideration of how old and new normative concerns should interact, and since all new normative grounds point towards a further expansion of the scope of the market freedoms—particularly as regards the free movement of persons—it is to be expected that these grounds will lead to an increasing number of situations being caught by the market freedoms.

There is a consequence to a measure falling within the scope of the market freedoms that is particularly relevant when considering these developments: that measure will become subject to review under EU law standards, including regarding its adequacy *vis-à-vis* the EU's fundamental rights' standards. As Advocate General Sharpston put it:

> *According to the Court's settled case law, EU fundamental rights may be invoked when (but only when) the contested measure comes within the scope of application of EU law. All measures enacted by the institutions are therefore subject to scrutiny as to their compliance with EU fundamental rights. The same applies to acts of the Member States taken in the implementation of obligations under EU law or, more generally, that fall within the field of application of EU law. This aspect is obviously delicate, as it takes EU fundamental rights protection into the sphere of each Member State, where it coexists with the standards of fundamental rights protection enshrined in domestic law or in the ECHR.*[133]

While this may delight proponents of extending the scope of the market freedoms as a way to better protect fundamental rights, the institutional consequences of such an extension in scope are that the Court of Justice would be able to replace decisions by national judicial and democratically elected bodies in areas where the normative grounds justifying European intervention are either slim or—when the extension of the scope of the market freedoms results merely from institutional dynamics—non-existent. This follows from the fact that decisions about the scope of the free movement provisions inherently imply comparative institutional choices, since free movement rules, when triggered, re-allocate Member State competences to the EU and/or subject areas that were under the exclusive remit of the EU's political process to judicial control.

In order to make sure that the scope of the fundamental freedoms does not go beyond what its normative foundations and the Court of Justice's institutional ability to enforce them allow, it is crucial not only that greater attention be paid to the decontextualized normative goals underlying the case law but also to its institutional implications. Better reasoning and theorization of the relevant substantive normative underpinnings of the law is undoubtedly in order, but institutional considerations should be recognized as normative concerns of equal importance for the Court of Justice's decision-making process. In the end, the absence of consideration of institutional realities and

[133] Advocate General Sharpston's Opinion in *Zambrano*, para. 156.

implications does not eliminate them; it merely prevents a properly reasoned consideration of all the relevant normative and institutional choices which the Court of Justice has to make in its case law.

As such, a contextualized normative approach should begin by trying to clarify the normative underpinnings of the case law. Regardless of the value of the normative arguments that have been advanced regarding European Citizenship and the protection of fundamental rights, the goals of the market freedoms were not altered by European Citizenship or any of the Treaty amendments, and thus their purpose is still *prima facie* to enable Member State nationals to move between Member States for an economic purpose, thereby assisting in the creation of a common market.[134] This brings to the forefront the need to separate the normative concerns underpinning the market freedoms and the protection of other individual rights in the EU, a point that is supported by systemic considerations. In particular, these new normative grounds apply to situations where the free movement of individuals is at stake. However, as we saw in Chapter 2, all market freedoms entail, to a greater or lesser degree, the possibility of people crossing borders, with the result that an approach common to the market freedoms based on the protection of rights intrinsic to individuals or European Citizenship would not be common at all, but would instead require different approaches to be adopted within each market freedom depending on whether individual free movement occurred or not.

A better option would be to rationalize the case law on the protection of individuals under the market freedoms as relating to European Citizenship alone. In other words, the scope of European Citizenship should be distinguished from the scope of the market freedoms: the latter refer to economic rights and should be restricted to situations of inter-State movement with an economic purpose, while the former refers to a fundamental right of a more political nature which covers situations that may overlap with, but are more extensive than, those falling under the market freedoms. Debates about the nature of European Citizenship are effectively debates about the nature and direction of European integration beyond the economic sphere. As such, it would increase normative clarity if the Court of Justice and the relevant legal and political communities were to address the nature and impact of European Citizenship on its own.[135] Distinguishing between situations covered by European Citizenship and

[134] Kadelbach, 'Union Citizenship', 465; Tryfonidou, 'In Search of the Aim of the EC Free Movement of Persons Provisions', 1612.

[135] Or, at the very least, try explicitly to deal with the impact of European Citizenship in construing a more complex normative framework for the market freedoms.

those covered by the market freedoms should lead to greater clarity in the reasoning of the Court of Justice, increased doctrinal consistency in its decisions, and a clear distinction between those rights which are merely economic and those which are something more—and, hopefully, to a renewed and more rigorous analysis of the characteristics of each, and to a clearer and more exalted status for European Citizenship as a cornerstone of the European project.

While one may disagree with the above suggestion, it would be hard to deny that the enhanced normative precision that would result from it is desirable, particularly because it allows greater clarity regarding the importance of institutional considerations. This can be seen from the fact that the institutional issues arising from the expansion in scope of the market freedoms would also arise if a too-broad approach to European Citizenship were adopted. As with the market freedoms, the scope of European Citizenship affects the Court of Justice's jurisdiction and determines when the Court must engage in proportionality assessments that second-guess national political preferences. As a consequence, expansive approaches to the scope of the fundamental freedoms increase the potential for conflicts regarding the institutional allocation of competences between the European courts and national courts and legislatures.[136] Such approaches also increase the risks of the Court of Justice being swamped with litigation unrelated to the goals of the market freedoms or European Citizenship, thereby raising serious issues concerning the Court of Justice's institutional scale and ability, even as it proposes to impose its decisions on institutions which might be better placed to deal with the issues at hand in the first place.[137] These consequences should be taken into account by anyone suggesting expansive readings of the fundamental freedoms.

In other words, there is a need for greater normative coherence in the development of the case law—if nothing else, as a means to anchor the case law and limit institutionally driven increases in the scope of the market freedoms. In order to achieve these goals in the light of the market freedoms'

[136] See, as an example of such conflict, the German Constitutional Court's *Lisbon* decision.

[137] It should be noted that a similar issue of institutional comparative analysis was crucial in the Court of Justice's decision not to apply a UN resolution in Joined Cases C-402/05 P and C-415/05 P *Kadi* [2008] E.C.R. I-06351—see in particular Advocate General Maduro's Opinion, particularly para. 54. It is perhaps a concern with the institutional legitimacy of the Court of Justice to pursue these assessments that explains the wide margin of appreciation that the Court leaves to Member States when balancing fundamental rights—see, for example, *Schmidberger* and *Omega*. For the argument that the Court of Justice merely seeks to determine whether Member States protect minimum standards, see Charles F. Sabel and Oliver Gerstenberg, 'Constitutionalising an Overlapping Consensus: The ECJ and the Emergence of a Coordinate Constitutional Order' (2010) 16 ELJ 511.

normative foundations, it is submitted that the 'purely internal situations' doctrine should be preserved in some form. In this respect, the juridical criterion should perhaps be adopted, particularly in the light of the practical limitations of the geographical criterion, as evidenced in *Lancry* and *Pistre*, and the fact that the juridical criterion allows the Court of Justice to focus expressly on the scope of the market freedoms. The juridical criterion seems, in particular, to be amenable to unified analytical treatment with the concept of restriction on free movement, without implying a complete reversal of precedent, in a way that the geographical criterion is not. Secondly, a more normatively consistent approach to the concept of economic activity should be pursued. And lastly, the need for a link between cross-border movement and the economic aim for which the right to such movement is granted should be re-affirmed, with those situations deviating from it—and thus from the *telos* of the market freedoms—being addressed, if at all, under European Citizenship.[138]

B. Horizontal effect

It was observed above, as respects the horizontal effect of the market freedoms, that there is an absence of normative reasons supporting the adoption of one type of horizontal effect over another. Simultaneously, while different types of horizontal effect are substantively outcome-neutral, this does not mean that there are no other reasons for choosing between them—particularly, since different types of horizontal effect can lead to different solutions regarding who should be ultimately liable for private behaviour contrary to free movement rights.[139]

It would in general be simpler, and more in accordance with the structure of the Treaty, for national courts to be under a duty to interpret national law in accordance with the fundamental freedoms, and for States to be subject to liability for breaches of their protection duties.[140] Indirect horizontal

[138] Meaning that the normative and institutional issues regarding the protection of cross-border movement without an economic aim should be dealt with exclusively under the *aegis* of European Citizenship. On this, see my 'Quest for the Holy Grail—Assessing the Normative Overlap between the Market Freedoms and EU Citizenship' (2014) 20 ELJ 499.

[139] This is not an academic question: see *Raccanelli*. See also a description of civil liability procedures following *Laval* in Mia Rönnmar, 'Laval returns to Sweden: The Final Judgment of the Swedish Labour Court and Swedish Legislative Reforms' (2010) 39 ILJ 280.

[140] Against this, arguing for horizontal direct effect, see Schaefer, *Die unmittelbare Wirkung des Verbot der nichttarifären Handelshemmnisse (Art. 30 EWGV) in den Rechtsbezienhungen zwischen Privaten*; arguing for both horizontal direct and indirect effect as complementary tools, see Krzeminska-Vamkava, 'Horizontal Effect of Fundamental Rights and Freedoms', 40.

liability by States—including a duty by national courts to interpret national law in accordance with the fundamental freedoms, and State liability in cases where omissions on the State's part lead to the infringement of subjective rights arising from the fundamental freedoms—has the advantage of providing a single uniform solution applicable to all potential factual scenarios, and of making the attribution of liability independent from how much each Member State impinges on private relationships. Another advantage to this approach is that, even though private parties might have recourse to the justifications provided in the Treaty, these are directed at States and not at individuals: it is hard to see how individuals might benefit from them in practice. Furthermore, this approach leaves to the relevant Member State the means to regulate private relationships in accordance with the principle of subsidiarity. Lastly, adopting a general indirect horizontal approach has the advantage of allowing for direct actions in European courts against Member States for infractions committed by private parties, arguably the reason why this approach was adopted for the free movement of goods in the first place.[141]

Concerning damages, this approach would lead to an acceptable allocation of liability between States and private parties. Whenever a private party is found to have infringed both the fundamental freedoms and a national rule, it would be liable for damages under national law. On the other hand, whenever the relevant structure to protect a fundamental freedom has not been put in place by a Member State—either through legislative omission or the adoption of a law infringing upon the fundamental freedoms—that Member State would then be liable for its failures in this regard. In other words, only Member States could be held liable for infringements of the fundamental freedoms *qua* fundamental freedoms.[142]

From a purely institutional standpoint, it would be preferable to allow Member States' legislative and administrative bodies discretion on how to deal with private action that might restrict free movement, without courts

[141] Stoppel, 'Grundfreiheitliche Schutzpflichten der Mitgliedstaaten im Europäischen Gemeinschaftsrecht', 247–250 and 260–261; Alison McDonnell, *A Review of Forty Years of Community Law: Legal Developments in the European Communities and European Union* (Kluwer 2005), 149; Kingreen, 'Fundamental Freedoms', 578–583; Schillig, 'The Interpretation of European Private Law in the Light of Market Freedoms and EU Fundamental Rights', 293.

[142] Nevertheless, this normative position is not the position currently adopted by the Court of Justice in cases other than those on the free movement of goods: see Peter Szczekalla, 'Grundfreiheitliche Schutzpflichten—eine "neue" Function der Grundfreiheiten des Gemeinschaftsrechts' (1998) 113 DVBl 219.

abandoning their powers to make sure that the exercise of this discretion duly protects the fundamental freedoms.[143] The direct submission of private behaviour to judicial review under the fundamental freedoms could very well result in excessive legal uncertainty, since it would require courts to balance competing individual rights in an immense (and immensely varied) number of situations, to the detriment of well-established private law concepts.[144] What is more, considerations of ability and scope clearly point towards courts not being entrusted with a duty to review all private behaviour that may infringe upon the market freedoms. Courts should, inasmuch as possible, leave to legislatures and private law the creation of rules arbitrating disputes between private parties, thereby avoiding the need to engage in delicate balancing exercises every time a dispute comes before them.

In other words, courts should rather ascertain, in the light of the market freedoms, whether the balancing outcomes which the legislative branch or private law arrived at are legitimate, or, in cases where there is a legal *lacuna*, whether State action is required. In order to achieve this, the focus should be placed not on the specific conduct of private agents but on the interpretation of rules allowing or constraining such conduct, and exceptionally on the need for such rules. In exceptional circumstances, where State regulation is absent, it cannot be excluded that the best option may occasionally be to apply the constitutional right directly to the situation at hand, while still deeming the State to be liable for its failure to act. But this would need to be assessed on a case by case basis, and reflect the exceptional nature of those situations.

It should be noted that some of these institutional considerations are also relevant to the assessment of the *Angonese* case law. From an institutional perspective, this case law may require courts to pursue balancing exercises whenever an individual discriminates on grounds of nationality, an exercise which may well exceed the courts' scope or ability.[145] If the law is that all

[143] Koen Muylle, 'Angry Farmers and Passive Policemen: Private Conduct and the Free Movement of Goods' 23 ELRev 467 473–474.

[144] Schillig, 'The Interpretation of European Private Law in the Light of Market Freedom and EU Fundamental Rights', .

[145] Further, it is unclear what type of justifications may be invoked to legitimize discriminatory behaviour. The law is that Member States may only have recourse to the derogations provided for in the Treaty in order to justify discriminatory measures, and these derogations do not seem to be applicable to individual behaviour. However, it is arguable that in a number of cases concerning discriminatory national rules, the Court of Justice nonetheless applied court-made derogations, even if without admitting it was doing so. See, for example, *Walloon Waste* and *PreussenElektra* and the more recent Case C-573/12 *Ålands vindkraft AB* (decided on 1 July 2014) and Joined

discrimination by individuals on grounds of nationality is prohibited, it will be incumbent on courts to review those situations and to see whether private action was proportional. However, this institutional allocation of competences seems to have been made without taking into account the ability of courts to pursue such an assessment in all the individual situations that may come before them, and without considering the advantages of the available institutional alternatives—such as national or EU measures (which are subject to review by national and European courts under the market freedoms), or even market outcomes. As argued by Advocate General Maduro:

> *The case of an individual shopkeeper who refuses to purchase goods from other Member States would not be liable to obstruct the functioning of the common market. The reason is that suppliers from other Member States would still have the opportunity to market their goods through alternative channels. Moreover, the shopkeeper would in all likelihood suffer from competition from retailers who had fewer qualms about buying foreign goods and who, as a result, might be able to offer lower prices and a larger choice to consumers. That prospect alone would probably be adequate to deter behaviour of this kind. Thus, the market will 'take care of it'. In those circumstances, there is no ground for Union law to intervene. The implication is that the rules on freedom of movement apply directly to any private action that is capable of effectively restricting others from exercising their right to freedom of movement.*[146]

This institutional point, in turn, relates to the normative dimension of the market freedoms. If the goal of the market freedoms was to prevent all private discriminatory behaviour on grounds of nationality, the institutional critique developed above would still be factually valid but its critical sting would be significantly blunted, since it would be clear that the market freedoms require just such a role for the courts. However, the *Angonese* case law also seems to be at odds with the normative *telos* of the economic free movement provisions—to remove obstacles to the functioning of the common market—since, while discriminatory measures by States can be presumed

Cases C-204 to C-208/12 *Essent Belgium* (decided on 11 September 2014), among others. See also Maduro, *We the Court*, 52; Snell, *Goods and Services in EC Law*, 185; Cruz, *Between Competition and Free Movement*, 95; P Gilliaux, 'Les entraves à la liberté de circulation des personnes' (2009) XLIV CDE 407, 426; and Advocate General Bot's Opinion in *Essent*, paras 86–97. More relevant for our point here, it may be argued that Articles 15 to 17 of the Charter of Fundamental Rights provide general justifications, to which individuals may have recourse to legitimize their discriminatory behaviour, inasmuch as they require a core of their private autonomy not to be affected by the fundamental freedoms. See Röthel, 'Grundfreiheiten und Private Normgebung', 916; Schepel, 'Constitutionalising the Market, Marketing the Constitution, and to Tell the Difference', 197–198; Krenn, 'A Missing Piece in the Horizontal Effect "Jigsaw"', 213–214.

[146] Opinion in *Viking*, para. 42–43.

to create obstacles to free movement, discriminatory conduct by specific individuals will usually not suffice for a restrictive effect on free movement to be found.

As a rule, private parties are unlikely to have enough influence to prevent others from enjoying their rights to free movement, and, as such, decisions applying horizontal direct effect should be exceptional. It is true that any discrimination on grounds of nationality by States is prohibited under the fundamental freedoms but this relates to concerns about State power in the normative, socio-economic, and cultural spheres. Any State measure that discriminates on grounds of nationality becomes immediately suspected of creating obstacles to trade, is deemed to be *prima facie* unlawful, and is subject to judicial review. There is no reason for this to be the case for all private action. Instead, only when private action discriminating on grounds of nationality is susceptible to having an effect akin to State action should it fall within the scope of the fundamental freedoms, thereby ensuring that the same concept of restriction on free movement is applicable to both State and private actions.[147] Such an option would seem to reflect an optimal alignment of institutional realities and normative requirements.

VII. Conclusion

This chapter demonstrated that institutional dynamics are driving the evolution of the law in a number of areas related to the scope of the market freedoms. This analysis disclosed some constants in these dynamics. First, it was found that the greater the level of normative indeterminacy, the more important is the role played by institutional constraints. Secondly, it was observed how developments in the law could be explained as the result of a specific institutional dynamic that results from a feedback process, characteristic of precedent-based systems, which arises from the interaction between legal decisions and reactions to them by self-interested legal and economic agents. This particular dynamic means that small events can have a large impact on the eventual development of the law, particularly in under-theorized areas. Thirdly, as a result of these dynamics—and of pressure from self-interested litigants—the trend in all the areas of the law reviewed is for an extension in

[147] Similarly, for goods, see Krenn, 'A Missing Piece in the Horizontal Effect "Jigsaw"', 211.

the number of cases susceptible of falling within the scope of the fundamental freedoms. And fourthly, law that is developed as a result of institutional dynamics will nonetheless be subject to a normative pull—particularly when the law has reached a point that risks going against even its under-theorized foundations—and/or to attempts to rationalize these developments as evidence of new normative foundations.

This chapter further exemplified how insights arising from taking into account the institutional dimension are relevant to the development of better normative approaches. Such approaches are more attractive, first, because they are better contextualized, and able to take into account the institutional implications of adopting a certain line of case law. They are also more attractive because they allow one to consider the consequences of the lack of normative coherence in the case law, and how normative approaches come into existence. Ultimately, taking into account the institutional dimension discloses the constitutive nature of legal practice on the law's normative foundations, and thereby allows one to understand the value and the role that one's own normative contribution may play in the development of the law.

Conclusion

De-contextualized ideas about law are not wrong as such: they can reflect the phenomenology of the law and refine our intuitions about it. They nonetheless have a number of disadvantages over contextualized approaches. First, de-contextualized approaches are descriptively inferior to contextualized ones because they ignore the role that the human element and the institutional context play in the development and application of the law. Secondly, they develop prescriptive suggestions that may well ignore the fact that legal decisions are adopted in an institutional environment that constrains what the law can be and do.[1]

By taking into account the interplay between legal reasoning and institutional setting, one can hope to identify better descriptive and prescriptive approaches to the Court of Justice's role and to Europe's particular brand of constitutionalism. A contextualized approach will be superior to de-contextualized ones because it acknowledges that debates about 'pure' normative concerns hide institutional questions. For example, debates about the nature of European integration or rights are also debates about the scope of State autonomy and about the discretionary power of courts over legislatures. On the other hand, since different bodies may be perceived as favouring different normative agendas—for example, the Court of Justice tends to be seen as pursuing a more supranational model of integration when compared to the Council of Ministers—it is not uncommon for specific normative orientations to be advanced under the guise of institutional arguments. This is a reflection of the fact that, as a political actor, the Court of Justice's decisions carry both substantive and institutional implications. Thus, debates

[1] This perspective can be framed as Realist, as opposed to Moralist, to use a distinction recently elaborated in American jurisprudence: see Brian Leiter, 'In Praise of Realism (and Against "Nonsense" Jurisprudence)' (2012) 100 GeoLJ 865.

on such substantive normative topics as the 'correct' concept of restriction on free movement, the 'nature' of European Citizenship, or even, and most flagrantly, the protection of human rights at EU level, do not make complete sense without taking into account the specific constitutional architecture of the EU and the logic of constitutional tolerance underpinning it.

The main claim of this book is that a contextualized theory, explaining the interplay between legal/normative and extra-legal/institutional elements and how such interplay should be addressed and incorporated into the scheme of European constitutionalism, allows for a more comprehensive descriptive and normative approach to the law than de-contextualized theories are able to produce. A contextualized approach does not require merely the incorporation of institutional elements into normative theories, or vice-versa. Instead, contextualized approaches call first for those de-contextualized normative theories to be properly fleshed out, since only then can their institutional consequences be appreciated properly. Facts and norms are mediated through the practice of legal reasoning; but such mediation can only be understood if the relevant facts and norms are previously known themselves. Acknowledging this feedback loop between theoretical idealism and institutional realities is a first step to understanding the role that legal reasoning plays in EU integration, and for developing better descriptive and prescriptive approaches to EU law.

This book has attempted to sketch a contextualized approach by incorporating insights from disciplines concerned with law, and EU law in particular, into the existing modes of legal discourse. In particular, this book has tried to demonstrate how a contextualized approach might work by reference to the fundamental freedoms, to their development, and to the analysis of normative debates concerning them. It has done so by explicitly starting from a value-pluralist perspective: when balancing the interests inherent in free movement with those pursued by the Member States, the Court of Justice has to arbitrate between incommensurate values and/or between values the measurement of which the Court is unable to verify empirically. In such a situation, reasons run out and the Court of Justice's decision-making becomes co-extensive with the exercise of discretion.

Since free movement rights do not remove charged political questions from political strife so much as lead to a greater role for courts in addressing those questions, the result is that the Court of Justice must address extremely sensitive questions under a veneer of seemingly politically neutral legal reasoning. What this makes clear is that the Court of Justice's recourse to proportionality when applying free movement law has the effect of assigning to the Court of Justice the power to determine what institution—including, among others, itself—is best suited to decide certain questions, and to control the extent to which other institutions may exercise their powers. In the light of this, the first question one must ask has to be why the Court of Justice should decide these issues to begin with. This is a question of comparative institutional choice; and the Court of Justice answers this question as regards the fundamental freedoms mainly by determining their scope. When a measure falls under the scope of the fundamental freedoms, the Court of Justice decides that it is the best institutional option to decide whether that measure is legitimate and, as such, the Court of Justice can decide to balance the relevant values at play itself, delegate such a task to other entities, particularly national legal processes and courts, or even create the conditions and incentives for the European political process to take over.

Starting from these premises, it was demonstrated how taking into account both normative and institutional elements helps to make better sense of the case law than de-contextualized approaches that take only one of these dimensions into account. In particular, it was demonstrated: that different normative theories tend to co-exist in judicial formulae and in the law in general; that de-contextualized normative perspectives are able to provide only partial descriptive models of the law; that acknowledging the plurality of normative interests at play and the normative indeterminacy of the law leads to better explanations of free movement law and its development; and that contextual approaches that add institutional elements to this normatively pluralistic perspective are able not only to produce better descriptive models of the law and its evolution, but also to explain how the normative interests and concerns identified by the legal community have come into existence and changed over time, particularly as a result of attempts to categorize and rationalize the law.

Under a contextualized approach, one can develop a general theory of free movement rights that centres on the scope of the fundamental freedoms, coupled with the idea of moral pluralism at the balancing stage. True, this is a high-level, abstract analytical framework, but combining an acknowledgement of normative pluralism and indeterminacy in the law with institutional insights allows for the common treatment of all free movement provisions. At the same time, a contextualised approach can also explain, and take into account, the various peculiarities found in specific fields of free movement law, such as distinctions based on individual fundamental freedoms, differences anchored in sectorial specificities, and even questions concerning the extension of the scope of the fundamental freedoms to private individuals.

Such an analytical framework is able to make descriptive sense, both formally and substantively, of free movement law, simultaneously at its most general level—where formal common structures seem to be undeniable, and a minimum common substantive content can be found—and at its most detailed levels—where substantive variations and greater normative specification exist.

This analytical framework can also be adopted for normative debates. After all, there are normative consequences to the descriptive model that was just sketched: assuming that normative assessments of legal questions pursued under practical reason should be kept within the realm of what is possible, descriptive assessments set limits and provide context to debates about what the law should be. If, as results from the descriptive analysis pursued in this book, the Court of Justice is merely one among a variety of other political institutions with decision-making powers that operate in a world of divided powers, imperfect decision-makers, and value pluralism, then the relevant normative questions are not merely whether decisions should be taken in accordance with certain 'evaluative' normative frameworks but, prior to this, whether these decisions should be adopted by a judicial entity or by another organization instead. This preliminary assessment must not focus exclusively on purely legal, de-contextualized normative considerations, but on the relative advantages and disadvantages of particular decision-making bodies, requiring a comparative institutional assessment that takes into account both normative and institutional considerations. Since, as we have seen, this choice is pursued by the Court of Justice through the determination of the scope of the market freedoms, normative debates concerning such a scope will be more fruitful if they take both normative and institutional concerns into account, and focus first on whether a measure should fall within the scope of the market freedoms—in other words, whether the Court of Justice should decide a certain question—and only subsequently on whether that decision was correctly reached on the merits.

Throughout this thesis, a number of normative positions were advanced, both concerning whether the Court of Justice is the best institutional option available to decide on a number matters, and concerning the merits of some lines of case law. These positions required not only the addition of institutional elements to de-contextualized normative positions, but also previous assessments of these normative positions on their own terms. This is a reflection of the fact that contextualized normative debates will have to embrace complexity and deal simultaneously with de-contextualized normative debates, purely institutional questions, and the interaction between them. The normative positions advanced in this book are examples of how one can embrace such complexity, and it is also naturally submitted that they are more attractive than de-contextualized normative approaches. Furthermore, as a result of the incorporation of insights related to the institutional dynamics driving the evolution of the law, the normative suggestions advanced in this book are simultaneously aware of the limited role that they may play in the evolution of the law's normative *substrata* and of where they stand in relation to other normative theories. In other words, contextualized normative approaches are self-aware, in that they acknowledge and take into account the role that legal scholarship plays in the development of the law.

An important point that should be emphasized is that one can legitimately disagree with the normative suggestions advanced in this book and still agree that normative debates should explicitly encompass both 'substantive' normative issues and institutional realities. Similarly, one may find purely theoretical or moral normative positions more attractive than contextualized ones, and still agree that the descriptive model provided here is a better fit than the de-contextualized models available.

Lastly, this book poses a challenge to political science, and in particular to schools of thought which do not take the law seriously, in particular the attitudinal and the structural approaches. By insisting that judges either follow their own personal policy preferences or those of the Member States, each of these schools can undoubtedly provide—and has provided—particular insights into the role that judges and Member States' policy preferences play in deciding cases and developing the law. But, by demonstrating the importance of the law and requiring that it be taken into account as a relevant ideational influence and a serious constraint on legal agents' behaviour, this book points to a serious limitation in those schools of thought. Without purporting to have been able to operationalize how the law constrains and frames the actions of the relevant legal agents, it has nonetheless been demonstrated that the law generates cognitive frameworks shared by the various players in the legal process and, thus, plays a role in both creating and restricting possible future paths for legal developments. This book hopefully opens possibilities of research into how the law affects the conduct of relevant legal agents, and into how they, in turn, influence the development of the law.[2]

[2] Similarly, and proposing exactly such a type of research concerning path-dependency, see Schmidt, 'Who Cares About Nationality?', 14 and 21.

In the end, the underlying intuition of this book is that, if the EU is a work in progress, that must of necessity be the nature of its constitutional law as well and that, if the direction and implications of the EU project are unclear, its basic provisions will share this under-determination and malleability, and reflect the institutional realities in which such provisions are applied. As stated in another context:

> *The erection of a new government, whatever care or wisdom may distinguish the work, cannot fail to originate questions of intricacy and nicety; and these may, in a particular manner, be expected to flow from the establishment of a constitution founded upon the total or partial incorporation of a number of distinct sovereignties.' Tis time only that can mature and perfect so compound a system, can liquidate the meaning of all the parts, and can adjust them to each other in a harmonious and consistent whole.*[3]

A new constitutional order needs a new constitutionalism; and a new constitutionalism requires a different vocabulary and a new set of tools refined over time in parallel with the development of this new polity. It is the role of EU legal theory to help to develop such vocabulary and tools. Hopefully, this book will contribute to this endeavour with its acknowledgment that the life of European law has not been merely logic, but also experience.[4] The Court of Justice is merely one of the participants in that experience, and the fact that the law it created is not perfectly logical should not detract from attempts to understand it, and, particularly, to try to improve it. Virtue is not necessarily rational, and, for all else that may transpire from this book, it should be clear that underlying it is a view of the European project as an endeavour to create a community out of disparate, and at times warring peoples that is a most noble experience at heart.

[3] Alexander Hamilton, John Jay, and James Madison, *The Federalist Papers* (IndyPublish.com 2002), No. 82 (A. Hamilton).

[4] Oliver Wendell Holmes, *The Common Law* (Dover edn, Dover 1991), 1; Weiler, *The Constitution of Europe*, 94.

BIBLIOGRAPHY

Alexander R, 'The Evolution of Social Behavior' (1974) 5 Annual Review of Ecology and Systematics 325

Alexy R, *A Theory of Legal Argumentation: The Theory of Rational Discourse as Theory of Legal Justification* (Adler R and MacCormick N tr) (Clarendon Press 1989)

Alexy R, *A Theory of Constitutional Rights* (Rivers J tr) (OUP 2001)

Alter K, *Establishing the Supremacy of European Law* (OUP 2003)

Alter K, *The European Court's Political Power* (OUP 2009)

Andenas M, 'The Interplay of the Commission and the Court of Justice in Giving Effect to the Right to Provide Financial Services' in Craig P and Harlow C (eds), *Lawmaking in the European Union* (Kluwer 1998), 333-335

Armstrong K, 'Mutual Recognition' in Barnard C and Scott J (eds), *The Law of the Single European Market* (Hart Publishing 2001)

Aquinas St T, *Summa Theologiae: A Concise Translation* (McDermott T tr) (Eyre and Spottiswoode 1989)

Aristotle, *Politics* (Dover 2000)

Arnull A, 'What Shall We Do on a Sunday?' (1991) 16 ELRev 112

Arnull A, *The European Union and its Court of Justice* (2nd edn, OUP 2006)

Arnull A, Wyatt D, and Dashwood A, *Wyatt and Dashwood's European Union Law* (6th edn, Sweet & Maxwell 2011)

Augustine, St, *The City of God* (Marcus Dods tr) (Hendrickson 2009)

Avbelj M, 'European Court of Justice and the Question of Value Choices' [2004] Jean Monnet Working Paper 06/04

Azoulai L, 'The Court of Justice and the Social Market Economy: The Emergence of an Ideal and the Conditions for its Realization' (2008) 45 CML Rev 1335

Bain JS, *Industrial Organization* (2nd edn, Wiley 1968)

Bamberger KA and Guzman AT, 'Keeping Imports Safe: A Proposal for Discriminatory Regulation of International Trade' (2008) 98 CLR 1405

Banda S, 'Taking Indirect Horizontality Seriously in Ireland: A Time to Magnify the Nuance' (2009) DULJ 263, 264-265

Banks K and Marenco G, 'Intellectual Property and the Community Rules on Free Movement: Discrimination Unearthed' (1990) 15 ELRev 224

Barnard C, 'Social Dumping and the Race to the Bottom: Some Lessons for the European Union from Delaware?' (2000) 25 ELRev 57

Barnard C, 'Fitting the Remaining Pieces into the Goods and Persons Jigsaw?' (2001) ELRev 35, 40

Barnard C, *The Substantive Law of the EU* (3rd edn, OUP 2010)

Barnard C and Deakin S, 'Market Access and Regulatory Competition' [2001] Jean Monnet Working Paper 9/01

Beck, G, *The Legal Reasoning of the Court of Justice of the EU* (Hart, 2013)

Beetham D, *The Legitimation of Power* (MacMillan, 1991)

Beetham D and Lord C, *Legitimacy and the EU* (Dyson K and Featherstone K eds) (Longman 1998)

Behrens P, 'Die Konvergenz der wirtschaftlichen Freiheiten im europäischen Gemeinschaftrecht' (1992) 27 EuR 145

Berlin I, *Four Essays on Liberty* (OUP 1969)

Bernard N, 'Discrimination and Free Movement in EC Law' (1996) 45 ICLQ 82

Bernard N, 'La libre circulation sous l'angle de la compétence' (1998) 34 CDE 11

Bickel AM, *The Least Dangerous Branch: The Supreme Court at the Bar of Politics* (1962)

Bix B, *Law, Language and Legal Determinacy* (Clarendon Press 1993)

Bleckman A, 'Die Freiheiten des Gemeinsamen als Grundrechte' in Bieber R and Nickel D (eds), *Das Europa der zweiten Generation—Gedächtnisshrift für Christoph Sasse*, vol II (N. P. Engel Verlag 1981), 665

Bodin J, *Six Books of the Commonwealth* (Blackwell 1955)

Bogaert Svd, 'Horizontality: The Court Attacks?' in Barnard C and Scott J (eds), *The Law of the Single European Market* (Hart Publishing 2001), 125

Bogdandy Av, 'Legitimacy of International Economic Governance' in Griller S (ed.), *International Economic Governance and Non-Economic Concerns* (Springer-Verlag 2003), 103

Borgmann-Prebil Y, 'The Rule of Reason in European Citizenship' (2008) 14 ELJ 328

Bossche PVd, 'Looking for Proportionality in WTO Law' (2008) 35 LIEI 283

Búrca Gd, 'The Principle of Proportionality and its Application in EC Law' (1993) 13 YEL 105

Búrca Gd, 'Unpacking the Concept of Discrimination in EC and International Trade Law' in Barnard C and Scott J (eds), *The Law of the Single European Market* (Hart Publishing 2001), 187-188

Cabral P, 'The Internal Market and the Right to Cross Border Medical Care' (2004) 19 ELRev 673

Cananea Gd, 'The Italian Constitutional Court and the European Court of Justice: From Separation to Interaction' (2008) 14 EPL 523

Canaris C-W, *Systemdenken und Systembegriff in der Jurisprudenz* (Cordeiro AM tr) (2nd edn, Duncker und Humblot 1983)

Canaris C-W, 'Drittwirkung der gemeinschaftsrechtlichen Grundfreiheiten' in Bauer H and others (eds), *Umwelt, Wirtschaft und Recht* (Mohr Siebeck 2002), 34

Canotilho JJG, *Direito Constitucional e Teoria da Constituição* (3rd edn, Almedina 1998)

Cappelletti M and others, *Methods, Tools and Institutions. Book 1. A Political, Legal and Economic Overview* (Walter de Gruyter 1986)
Carlier J-Y, 'Le devenir de la libre circulation des personnes dans l'Union Européenne: regard sur la directive 2004/38' 42 [2006] CDE 13
Carruba C, Gabel M, and Hankla C, 'Judicial Behavior under Political Constraints: Evidence from the European Court of Justice' (2008) 102 AmPolitSciRev 435
Carruba C, Gabel M, and Hankla C, 'Understanding the Role of the European Court of Justice in European Integration' (2012) 106 AmPolitSciRev 214
Chalmers D, 'Repackaging the Internal Market—The Ramifications of the Keck Judgement' (1994) 19 ELRev 385
Chalmers D, Davies GT, and Monti G, *European Union Law* (3rd edn, Cambridge University Press 2014)
Chander A, 'Globalization and Distrust' (2005) 114 Yale LJ 1197
Cheney DL and Seyfarth RM, *Baboon Metaphysics: The Evolution of a Social Mind* (University of Chicago Press 2007)
Christiano TD, 'Democracy: Normative Theory' in Smelser NJ and Bates PB (eds), *International Encyclopedia of the Social & Behavioral Sciences*, vol V (Elsevier 2001), 3413
Christie G, *Philosopher Kings?* (OUP 2011)
Clark I, *International Legitimacy and World Society* (OUP 2007)
Clark I, *Legitimacy in International Society* (OUP 2007)
Closa C, 'The Concept of Citizenship in the Treaty on the European Union' (1992) 29 CML Rev 1137
Closa C, 'Citizenship of the Union and Nationality of Member States' (1995) 32 CML Rev 487
Cohen-Eliya M and Porat I, 'American Balancing and German Proportionality: The Historical Origins' (2010) 8 I•CON 263
Connant L, *Justice Contained—Law and Politics in the European Union* (Cornell University 2002)
Constant B, *Principes de politique: Applicables à tous les gouvernements* (Hachette Littératures 2006)
Conway G, 'Levels of Generality in the Legal Reasoning of the European Court of Justice' (2008) 14 ELJ 787
Cordewener A, 'The Prohibitions of Discrimination and Restriction within the Framework of the Fully Integrated Internal Market' in Vanistendael F (ed.), *EU Freedoms and Taxation* (IBDF 2006), 4–10
Cover R, 'Foreword: Nomos and Narrative' (1982) 97 HarvLRev 1
Craig P, 'Constitutions, Constitutionalism, and the European Union' (2001) 7 ELJ 125
Craig P and De Búrca G, *EU Law: Text, Cases, and Materials* (5th edn, OUP 2011)
Cruz JB, 'The Legacy of the Maastricht-Urteil and the Pluralist Movement' (2008) 14 ELJ 389

Cruz JB, *Between Competition and Free Movement* (Hart Publishing 2002)

Cruz JB, 'Free Movement and Private Autonomy' (1999) 24 ELRev 603

d'Oliveira H, 'Is Reverse Discrimination Still Permissible under the Single European Act?' in *Forty Years On: The Evolution of Postwar Private International Law in Europe* (Kluwer 1990), 73–74

d'Oliveira H, 'European Citizenship: Its Meaning, Its Potential' in Dehousse R (ed.), *Europe After Maastricht: An Ever Closer Union?* (LBE, 1994)

Dahl R, *On Democracy* (Yale University Press 1998)

Dahl R, 'Democracy' in Smelser NJ and Baltes PB (eds), *International Encyclopedia of the Social & Behavioral Sciences*, vol V (Elsevier 2001), 3406-3408

Daniele L, 'Non-discriminatory Restrictions to the Free Movement of Persons' (1997) 22 ELRev 191

Dashwood A and Wyatt D, *Wyatt and Dashwood's European Union Law* (6th edn, Sweet & Maxwell 2011)

Davies G, *Nationality Discrimination in the European Internal Market* (Kluwer Academic Publishers 2003)

Davies G, '"Any Place I Hang my Hat?" or: Residence is the New Nationality' (2005) 11 ELJ 43

Davies G, 'Can Selling Arrangements be Harmonised?' (2005) 30 ELRev 370

Davies G, 'Understanding Market Access: Exploring the Economic Rationality of Different Conceptions of Free Movement Law' (2010) 11 GLJ 671

Dawes A, 'A Freedom Reborn? The New Yet Unclear Scope of Article 29 EC' (2009) 34 ELRev 639

Deakin S, 'Legal Diversity and Regulatory Competition: Which Model for Europe?' (2006) 12 ELJ 440

Deakin S, 'Reflexive Governance and European Company Law' (2009) 15 ELJ 224

Defalque L, 'Le Concept de Discrimination en Matière de Libre Circulation des Marchandises' (1987) 23 CDE 471

Defossez A, 'L'Histoire d'une Divergence et d'une Possible Réconciliation: l'Article 29 CE' (2009) XLV CDE 409

Dellavalle S, 'Constitutionalism beyond the Constitution: The Treaty of Lisbon in Light of Post-National Public Law' [2009] Jean Monnet Working Paper 03/09

Demsetz H, 'Barriers to Entry' (1982) 72 AmEconRev 47

Deniau J-F, *The Common Market* (4th revised edn, Barrie & Rockliff 1967)

Dickson J, *How Many Legal Systems? Some Puzzles Regarding the Identity Conditions of, and Relations between, Legal Systems in the European Union* (SSRN 2008)

Diebold NF, *Non-Discrimination and the Pillars of International Economic Law—Comparative Analysis and Building Coherency* (Society of International Economic Law 2010)

Dogan M, 'Conceptions of Legitimacy' in Hawkesworth M and Kogan M (eds), *Encyclopedia of Government and Politics vol I* (2nd edn, Routledge 2003), 110

Dollat P, *Libre circulation des personnes et citoyenneté: enjeux et perspectives* (Bruylant 1998)

Dougan M, 'The Constitutional Dimension to the Case Law On Union Citizenship' (2006) 31 ELRev 613
Dougan M and Spaventa E, 'Educating Rudy and the Non-English Patient: A Double-Bill on Residency Rights under Article 18 EC' (2003) 28 ELRev 699
Douglas-Scott S, 'In Search of European Citizenship' (1998) 18 YEL 29
Drexl J, 'Competition Law as Part of the European Constitutions' in Bogdandy Av and Bast J (eds), *Principles of European Constitutional Law* (Hart Publishing 2006), 659
Dunne N, 'Knowing When to See It: State Activities, Economic Activities, and the Concept of Undertaking' (2010) 16 ColumJEurL 427
Dworkin R, *Taking Rights Seriously* (Harvard University Press 1977)
Dyevre A, 'Making Sense of Judicial Lawmaking: A Theory of Theories of Adjudication' (EUI, 2008/09), <http://cadmus.eui.eu/dspace/bitstream/1814/8510/1/MWP_2008_09.pdf>
Dyrberg P, 'Full Free Movement of Companies in the European Community at Last?' (2003) 18 ELRev 528
Eeckhout P, 'The European Court of Law and the Legislature' (1998) 18 YEL 1
Eeckhout P, 'After *Keck and Mithouard*: Free Movement of Goods in the EC, Market Access and Non-Discrimination' in Cottier T and Mavroidis PC (eds), *Regulatory Barriers and the Principle of Non-Discrimination in World Trade Law* (The University of Michigan Press 2000), 203
Eeckhout P, 'Constitutional Concepts for Free Trade in Services' in Búrca Gd and Scott J (eds), *The EU and the WTO—Legal and Constitutional Issues* (Hart Publishing 2001), 215
Ehlermann CD, 'The Contribution of EC Competition Policy to the Single Market' (1992) 29 CML Rev 257
Ehlers D, 'General Principles' in Ehlers D (ed.), *European Fundamental Rights and Freedoms* (de Gruyter 2007), 193
Eleftheriadis P, 'Aspects of European Constitutionalism' (1996) 21 ELRev 32
Elsuwege PV, 'Shifting the Boundaries? European Citizenship and the Scope of Application of EU Law' (2011) 38 LIEI 263
Ely JH, *Democracy and Distrust: A Theory of Judicial Review* (Harvard University Press 1980)
Enchelmaier S, 'Always at Your Service (Within Limits)' (2011) 36 ELRev 615
Farmer P, 'Article 48 EC and the Taxation of Frontier Workers' (1995) 20 ELRev 310
Ferguson JM, *Advertising and Competition; Theory, Measurement, Fact* (Ballinger Pub. Co. 1974)
Ferguson N, *The Cash Nexus* (Penguin Books, London 2001)
Fiss O, 'Objectivity and Interpretation' (1982) 34 StanLRev 739
Fligstein N, 'Markets as Politics' [1996] 61 AmSociolRev 656
Fligstein N, *The Architecture of Markets: An Economic Sociology of Twenty-First-Century Capitalist Societies* (Princeton University Press 2001)

Fligstein N and Sweet AS, 'Constructing Polities and Markets: An Institutionalist Account of European Integration' (2002) AmJSoc 1206, 1312

Follesdal A and Hix S, 'Why There is a Democratic Deficit in the EU: A Response to Majone and Moravcsik' (2006) 44 JCMS 533

Frenz W, 'Grundfreiheiten und Grundrechte' (2002) 38 EuR 603

Friedman B, 'The Politics of Judicial Review' (2005) 84 TexLRev 257

Friedman B and Delaney EF, 'Becoming Supreme: The Federal Foundation of Judicial Supremacy' (2011) 111 ColumLRev 1137

Fritzsche A, 'Discretion, Scope of Judicial Review and Institutional Balance in European Law' (2010) 47 CML Rev 361

Fuller LL, 'The Forms and Limits of Adjudication' [1978] 92 HarvLRev 353

Fukuyama F, *The Origins of Political Order* (Profile 2011)

Furse M, *Competition Law* (OUP 2008)

Galston WA, *Liberal Pluralism: The Implications of Value Pluralism for Political Theory and Practice* (Cambridge University Press 2002)

Gardbaum S, 'The Effect of Constitutional Rights' (2003) 102 Mich L Rev 387, 388

Gardbaum S, 'Where the (State) Action is' (2006) 4 I•CON 760

Gardbaum S, 'The Myth and the Reality of American Constitutional Exceptionalism' [2008] Jean Monnet Working Paper 07/08

Gerber DJ, 'Constitutionalizing the Economy: German Neo-Liberalism, Competition Law and the "New" Europe' (1994) 42 AmJCompL 25

Gergen MP, 'The Selfish State and the Market' (1988) 66 TexLRev 1097

Gerven Wv, 'The Recent Case Law of the Court of Justice Concerning Articles 30 and 36 of the EEC Treaty' (1977) 14 CML Rev 5, 37–42

Gerven Wv, 'The Effect of Proportionality on the Actions of Member States of the European Community: National Viewpoints from Continental Europe' in Ellis E (ed.), *The Principle of Proportionality in the Laws of Europe* (Hart Publishing 1999), 37–42

Gibson JL, Caldeira GA, and Baird VA, 'On the Legitimacy of National High Courts' (1998) 92 AmPolitSciRev 343

Gillette CP, 'Lock-In Effects in Law and Norms' (1998) 78 BULRev 813

Gilliaux P, 'Les entraves à la liberté de circulation des personnes' (2009) XLIV CDE 407

Ginsburg T, 'The Global Spread of Judicial Review' in Caldeira GA, Kelemen RD and Whittington KE (eds), *The Oxford Handbook of Law and Politics* (OUP 2008)

Giorgi F and Triart N, 'National Judges, Community Judges: Invitation to a Journey through the Looking-glass—On the Need for Jurisdictions to Rethink the Inter-Systemic Relations Beyond the Hierarchical Principle' (2008) 14 ELJ 693

Giubboni S, 'Free Movement of Persons and European Solidarity' (2007) 13 ELJ 360

Gkoutzinis A, 'Free Provision of Services in the EC Treaty and the Law of Contractual Obligations relating to Banking and Financial Services' (2004) 41 CML Rev 119

Gormley L, '"Actually or Potentially, Directly or Indirectly?" Obstacles to the Free Movement of Goods' (1989) 9 YEL 197

Gormley L, 'Recent Case Law on the Free Movement of Goods: Some Hot Potatoes' (1990) 27 CML Rev 825

Gormley L, 'Reasoning Renounced? The Remarkable Judgement in *Keck and Mithouard*' [1994] EBLRev 63

Goyder DG, Goyder J and Albors-Llorens A, *Goyder's EC Competition Law* (5th edn, OUP 2009)

Graetz MJ and Warren AC, 'Dividend Taxation in Europe: When the ECJ Makes Tax Policy' (2007) 44 CML Rev 1577

Groussot, X, 'European Rights and Dialogues in the Context of Constitutional Pluralism' in Avbelj M and Komárek J (eds), Constitutional Pluralism in the EU and Beyond (Hart Publishing 2012)

Gormley L, 'Rock the KaZaA: Another Clash of Fundamental Rights' (2008) 45 CML Rev 1745

Gormley L, 'European Rights' and Dialogues in the Context of Constitutional Pluralism' in Avbelj M and Komárek J (eds), *Constitutional Pluralism in the EU and Beyond* (Hart Publishing 2012)

Gray J, *Enlightenment's Wake: Politics and Culture at the Close of the Modern Age* (Routledge 2007)

Groussot X, 'Rock the AaZaH: Another Clash of Fundamental Rights' (2008) 45 CML Rev 1745, 1762

Habermas J, 'Law and Morality' in McMurrin SM (ed.), *The Tanner Lectures on Human Values*, vol VIII (University of Utah 1988), <http://tannerlectures.utah.edu/_documents/a-to-z/h/habermas88.pdf>

Habermas J, 'Citizenship and National Identity: Some Reflections on the Future of Europe' in Beiner R (ed.), *Theorising Citizenship* (State University of New York 1995), 265–267

Habermas J, *Between Facts and Norms* (Polity Press 1996)

Hailbronner K and Thym D, 'Zambrano Case Opinion' (2011) 48 CML Rev 1253

Hamilton A, Jay J, and Madison J, *The Federalist Papers* (IndyPublish.com 2002)

Hart HLA, Bulloch PA and Raz J, *The Concept of Law* (2nd edn, Clarendon Press 1994)

Hathaway OA, 'Path Dependence in the Law: The Course and Pattern of Legal Change in a Common Law System' (2001) 86 IowaLRev 601

Hatzopoulos V, 'Recent Developments of the Case Law of the ECJ in the Field of Services' (2000) 37 CML Rev 43

Hatzopoulos V, 'Killing National Health and Insurance Systems but Healing Patients? The European Market for Healthcare Services after the Judgements of the ECJ in Vanbraekel and Peerbooms' (2002) 39 CML Rev 683

Hatzopoulos V and Do TU, 'The Case Law of the ECJ concerning the Free Provision of Services: 2000-2005' (2006) 43 CML Rev 923

Hatzopoulos V, 'Le principe de reconnaissance mutuelle dans la prestation des services' (2010) 46 CDE 47

Heater D, *What is Citizenship?* (Polity Press 1999)

Held D, 'Between State and Civil Society: Citizenship' in Andrews G (ed.), Citizenship (Lawrence & Wishart 1991), 19

Héritier A, 'Overt and Covert Institutionalization in Europe' in Sweet AS, Sandholtz W and Fligstein N (eds), *The Institutionalization of Europe* (OUP 2001), 159

Hermes, 'Grundrechtsschutz durch Privatrecht auf neuer Grundlage?' [1990] NJW 1764

Higgins I, 'The Free and Not So Free Movement of Goods Since Keck' (1997) 6 IrJEurL 166

Hilson C, 'Discrimination in Community Free Movement Law' (1999) 24 ELRev 445

Hilson C, 'What's in a Right? The Relationship between Community, Fundamental and Citizenship Rights in EU Law' (2004) 29 ELRev 636

Hinarejos A, 'Extending Citizenship and the Scope of EU Law' (2011) 70 CLJ 309

Hirschman AO, *Exit, Voice, And Loyalty: Responses to Decline in Firms, Organizations, and States* (Harvard University Press 1970)

Hirschman AO, 'Social Conflicts as Pillars of Democratic Market Society' (1994) 22 PolTheo 203

Hirschman AO, *The Passions and the Interests: Political Arguments for Capitalism Before its Triumph* (Princeton University Press 1997)

Hitiris T, *European Community Economics: A Modern Introduction* (Harvester Wheatsheaf 1988)

Hobbes T, *Leviathan* (Dalloz 2004)

Holmes OW, *The Common Law* (Dover edn, Dover 1991)

Hölscheidt S, 'Abschied vom subjecktif-öffentlichen Recht?' (2001) 37 EuR 376

Howard AED, 'A Traveler from an Antique Land: The Modern Renaissance of Comparative Constitutionalism' (2009) 50 VaJInt'l L 3

Howard JA and Renfrow DG, 'Social Cognition' in Delamater J (ed.), *Handbook of Social Psychology* (Springer 2006), 262-269

Howse R and Regan D, 'The Product/Process Distinction: An Illusory Basis for Disciplining "Unilateralism" in Trading' (2000) 11 EJIL 249

Iliopoulou A and Toner H, 'A New Approach to Discrimination Against Free Movement? D'Hoop v Office National de lÉmploi' (2003) 28 ELRev 392

Jacobs F, 'Recent Developments in the Principle of Proportionality in EC Law' in Ellis E (ed.), *The Principle of Proportionality in the Laws of Europe* (Hart Publishing 1999), 1, 3

Jacobs F, 'Citizenship of the European Union—A Legal Analysis' (2007) 13 ELJ 591

Jans J, 'Proportionality Revisited' (2000) 27 LIEI 239

Joerges C and Neyer J, 'From Intergovernmental Bargaining to Deliberative Political Processes: The Constitutionalisation of Comitology' (1997) 3 ELJ 273

Johnson E and O'Keefe D, 'From Discrimination to Obstacles to Free Movement: Recent Developments Concerning the Free Movement of Workers' (1994) 31 CML Rev 1313

Johnston A, 'Democracy in the European System: Towards a Critical Approach' (1998) 9 European Law Students Association Selected Papers in European Law 77

Johnston A, 'Judicial Reform and the Treaty of Nice' (2001) 38 CML Rev 499

Johnston A and Syrpis P, 'Regulatory Competition in European Company Law After Cartesio' [2009] 34 ELRev 378

Kadelbach S, 'Union Citizenship' in Bogdandy Av (ed.), *Principles of European Constitutional Law* (Hart Publishing 2006), 465

Kaplan HB, 'The Concept of Institution: A Review, Evaluation, and Suggested Research Procedure' (1960) 29 SocForces 176

Kaplow L, 'Rules versus Standards: An Economic Analysis' (1992) 42 Duke LJ 557

Kay J and Vickers J, 'Regulatory Reform: An Appraisal' in Majone G (ed.), *Deregulation or Re-regulation* (Pinter 1990), 225-230

Kelemen RD, *Eurolegalism: The Transformation of Law and Regulation in the European Union* (Harvard University Press 2011)

Kelemen RD 'The Political Foundations of Judicial Independence in the European Union' (2012) 19 JEPP 43

Kingreen T, 'Fundamental Freedoms' in Bogdandy Av and Bast J (eds), *Principles of European Constitutional Law* (Hart Publishing 2006), 550–583

Kingreen T and Störmer R, 'Die subjektiv-öffentlichen Rechte des primären Gemeinschaftsrechts' (1998) 34 EuR 263

Kingston S, 'A Light in the Darkness: Recent Developments in the ECJ's Recent Tax Jurisprudence' (2007) 44 CML Rev 1321

Komárek J, 'Judicial Law Making and Precedent in Supreme Courts' [2011] LSE Law, Society and Economy Working Papers 4/2011

Komesar N, *Imperfect Alternatives—Choosing Institutions in Law, Economics, and Public Policy* (The University of Chicago Press 1994)

Komesar N, *Law's Limits: The Rule of Law and the Supply and Demand of Rights* (Cambridge University Press 2001)

Koopmans T, 'The Birth of European Law at the Crossroads of Legal Traditions' (1991) 39 AmJCompL 493

Körber T, 'Innerstaatliche Anwendung und Drittwirkung der Grundfreiheiten' (2000) 35 EuR 932

Kostakopoulou D, 'Ideas, Norms and European Citizenship: Explaining Institutional Change' (2005) 68 MLJ 233

Kovar R and Simon D, 'La Citoyenneté Européenne' (1993) 29 CDE 285

Krenn C, 'A Missing Piece in the Horizontal Effect "Jigsaw": Horizontal Direct Effect and the Free Movement of Goods' (2012) 49 CML Rev 177

Krzeminska-Vamkava J, 'Horizontal Effect of Fundamental Rights and Freedoms—Much Ado About Nothing? German, Polish and EU Theories Compared after Viking Line' [2009] Jean Monnet Working Paper 11/09

Kumm M, 'Who is the Arbiter of Constitutionality in Europe?' (1999) 36 CML Rev 351

Kumm M, 'Who is Afraid of the Total Constitution? Constitutional Rights as Principles and the Constitutionalization of Private Law' (2006) 7 GLJ 341

Kumm M and Comella V, 'What is So Special about Constitutional Rights in Private Litigation?' in Sajó A and Uitz R (eds), *The Constitution in Private Relations* (Eleven 2005), 267

Laenerts K and Bernardeau L, 'L'encadrement communautaire de la fiscalité directe' (2007) 43 CDE 19

Laffan B, 'The Politics of Identity and Political Order in Europe' (1996) 34 JCMS 81

Lange Rd, 'Paradoxes of European Citizenship' in Fitzpatrick P (ed.), *Nationalism, Racism and the Rule of Law* (Dartmouth 1995), 103

Larenz K, *Methodenlehre der Rechtswissenchaft* (Lamego J tr, Springer-Verlag 1991)

Lasser M, 'Anticipating Three Models of Judicial Control, Debate and Legitimacy: The European Court of Justice, the Cour de Cassation and the United States Supreme Court' [2003] Jean Monnet Working Paper 1/03

Lasser M, *Judicial Deliberations: A Comparative Analysis of Judicial Transparency and Legitimacy* (OUP 2004)

Lavranos N, 'Regulating Competing Jurisdictions Among International Courts and Tribunals' (2008) 68 ZaöRV 575

Leiter B, 'Rethinking Legal Realism—Towards a Naturalised Jurisprudence' [1997] TexLRev, 267

Leiter B, 'In Praise of Realism (and Against "Nonsense" Jurisprudence)' (2012) 100 GeoLJ 865

Lenaerts K, 'Interlocking Legal Orders in the European Union and Comparative Law' (2003) 52 ICLQ 873

Lianos I, 'Shifting Narratives in the European Internal Market' (2010) 21 EBLRev 705

Lindseth PL, 'Democratic Legitimacy and the Administrative Character of Supranationalism: The Example of the European Community' (1999) 99 ColumLRev 628

Lipset SM, 'Some Social Requisites of Democracy: Economic Development and Political Legitimacy' (1959) 53 AmPolitSciRev 69

Loughlin M, *Foundations of Public Law* (OUP 2010)

Loughlin M, 'What is Constitutionalisation?' in Dobner P and Loughlin M (eds), *The Twilight of Constitutionalism?* (OUP 2010), 65–66

MacBean AI and Snowden PN, *International Institutions in Trade and Finance* (Allen & Unwin 1981)

MacCormick N, 'Beyond the Sovereign State' (1993) 56 MLR 1

MacCormick N, 'The Maastricht-Urteil: Sovereignty Now' (1995) 1 ELJ 259
MacCormick N, *Questioning Sovereignty: Law, State, and Nation in the European Commonwealth* (OUP 1999)
MacCormick N, *Practical Reason in Law and Morality* (OUP 2008)
MacGowan N and Quinn M, 'Could Article 30 Impose Obligations on Individuals?' (1987) 12 ELRev 163
Mackintosh M, Brown V and Costello N, *Economics and Changing Economies* (Open University Press 1996)
Maduro MP, 'Reforming the Market or the State? Article 30 and the European Constitution: Economic Freedom and Political Rights' (1997) 3 ELJ 55
Maduro MP, *We, the Court—The European Court of Justice and the European Economic Constitution—A Critical Reading of Article 30 of the EC Treaty* (Hart Publishing 1998)
Maduro MP, *A Crise Existencial da Constituição Europeia* (FDUNL 1999)
Maduro MP, 'The Scope of European Remedies: The Case of Purely Internal Situations and Reverse Discrimination' in Kilpatrick C, Novitz T and Skidmore P (eds), *The Future of Remedies in Europe* (Hart Publishing 2000), 124
Maduro MP, 'Harmony and Dissonance in Free Movement' in Andenas M and Roth W-H (eds), *Services and Free Movement in EU Law* (OUP 2002), 65
Maduro MP, 'Europe and the Constitution: What if This is as Good as it Gets?' in Weiler JHH and Wind M (eds), *European Constitutionalism Beyond the State* (Cambridge University Press 2003)
Maduro MP, 'Contrapunctual Law: Europe's Constitutional Pluralism in Action' in Walker N (ed.), *Sovereignty in Transition—Essays in European Law* (Hart 2006), 501.
Maduro MP, 'So Close and Yet So Far: The Paradoxes Of Mutual Recognition' (2007) 14 JEPP 814
Maduro MP, 'Courts and Pluralism: Essay on a Theory of Judicial Adjudication in the Context of Legal and Constitutional Pluralism' in Avbelj M and Komárek J (eds), *Constitutional Pluralism in the EU and Beyond* (Hart Publishing 2012), 20
Maher I, 'National Courts as European Community Courts' (1994) 14 LS 226
Majone G and Baake P, *Regulating Europe* (Routledge 1996)
Majone G and Baake P, 'Europe's "Democratic Deficit": The Question of Standards' (1998) 4 ELJ 5
Majone G and Baake P, *Dilemmas of European Integration: The Ambiguities and Pitfalls of Integration by Stealth* (OUP 2005)
Malecki M, 'Do ECJ Judges All Speak With The Same Voice? Evidence of Divergent Preferences from the Judgments of Chambers' (2012) 19 JEPP 59
Mancini GF, 'Crosscurrents and the Tide at the European Court of Justice' (1995) 4 IrJEurL 120
Marenco G, 'Pour une Interprétation Traditionnelle de la Notion de Mesure d'Effet Equivalent à une Restriction Quantitative' (1984) 20 CDE 291
Marenco G, 'Competition between National Economies and Competition between Businesses—A Response to Judge Pescatore' (1986-1987) 10 Fordham Int'l LJ 420

Marshall A, *Principles of Economics: An Introductory Volume* (8th edn, Macmillan 1949)

Martin D, 'Réflexions sur le champ d'application de l'Article 48 du Traité CE' (1993) 29 CDE 555

Martin D, 'Discriminations, Entraves et Raison Impérieuses' (1998) 34 CDE 561

Mather J, 'The Court of Justice and the Union Citizen' (2005) 11 ELJ 722

Mattli W and Slaughter A-M, 'Constructing the European Community Legal System from the Ground Up: The Role of Individual Litigants and National Courts' [1996] Jean Monnet Working Paper 6/96

McAfee RP, Mialon HM and Williams MA, 'What is a Barrier to Entry?' (2004) 94 AmEconRev 461

McCarthy T, 'Practical Discourse: On the Relation of Morality to Politics' in Calhoun C (ed.), *Habermas and the Public Sphere* (MIT 1992), 51

McDonnell A, *A Review of Forty Years of Community Law: Legal Developments in the European Communities and European Union* (Kluwer 2005)

McGrady B, 'Necessity Exceptions in WTO Law: Retreaded Tyres, Regulatory Purpose and Cumulative Regulatory Measures' (2009) 12 JIEL 153

Mei APvd, *Free Movement of Persons Within the European Community* (Hart Publishing 2003)

Menéndez AJ, 'The European Democratic Challenge: The Forging of a Supranational Volonté Générale' (2009) 15 ELJ 277

Menon A and Weatherill S, 'Legitimacy, Accountability and Delegation in the European Union' in Arnull A and Wincott D (eds), *Accountability and Legitimacy in the European Union* (OUP 2002), 120–131

Mestmacker E-Jv, 'On the Legitimacy of European Law' (1994) 58 RabelsZ 617

Metzger SD, *Lowering Nontariff Barriers: U.S. Law, Practice, and Negotiating Objectives* (Brookings Institution 1973)

Michelman F, 'The Supreme Court 1985 Term—Foreword: Traces of Self-Government' (1986) 100 HarvLRev 4

Moore M, 'Freedom of Movement and Migrant Workers' Social Security: An Overview of the Case Law' (2002) 39 CML Rev 808

Montesquieu CdS, Carrithers DW and Nugent T, *The Spirit Of Law: A Compendium of the First English Edition* (University of California Press 1977)

Moravcsik A, 'In Defence of the "Democratic Deficit": Reassessing the Legitimacy of the European Union' (2002) 40 JCMS 603

Mortelmans K, 'Article 30 of the EEC Treaty and Legislation Relating to Market Circumstances: Time to Consider a New Definition?' (1991) 28 CML Rev 115

Mortelmans K, 'The Common Market, the Internal Market and the Single Market, What's in a Market?' (1998) 35 CML Rev 101

Mortelmans K, 'Towards Convergence in the Application of the Rules on Free Movement and on Competition?' (2001) 38 CML Rev 613

Möstl M, 'Preconditions and Limits of Mutual Recognition' (2010) 47 CML Rev 405
Müller F, Die Einheit der Verfassung—Kritik des juristischen Holismus (Dunken & Humblot 1979)
Münch Iv, Riba J, and Coderch P, Zur Drittwirkund der Grundrechte (Lang 1998)
Munch W and Séché J-C, 'Les Droits de l'Étranger dans les Communautés Européenes' (1975) 10 CDE 251
Muylle K, 'Angry Farmers and Passive Policemen: Private Conduct and the Free Movement of Goods' [1998] 23 ELRev 467
Neussl P, 'European Citizenship and Human Rights: An Interactive European Concept' (1997) 24 LIEI 47
Neuwahl N and Wheatley S, 'The EU and Democracy—Lawful and Legitimate Intervention in the Domestic Affairs of States?' in Arnull A and Wincott D (eds), *Accountability and Legitimacy in the European Union* (OUP 2002), 223
Nicolaïdis K, 'Mutual Recognition of Regulatory Regimes' [1997] Jean Monnet Working Paper 97/07
Nicolaïdis K, 'Globalization with Human Faces: Managed Mutual Recognition and the Free Movement of Professionals' in Schioppa FKP (ed.), *The Principle of Mutual Recognition in the European Integration Process* (Palgrave Macmillan 2005), 142
Nicolaïdis K, 'Trusting the Poles? Constructing Europe through Mutual Recognition' (2007) 14 JEPP 682
Nicolaïdis K, 'Kir Forever? The Journey of a Political Scientist in the Landscape of Mutual Recognition' in Maduro MP and Azoulai L (eds), *The Past and Future of EU Law: The Classics of EU Law Revisited on the 50th Anniversary of the Rome Treaty* (Hart Publishing 2010), 449
Nino CS, *Introducción al análisis del derecho* (2nd edn, Editorial Astrea 1988)
North DC, *Institutions, Institutional Change and Economic Performance* (Cambridge University Press 1990)
Nourse V and Shaffer G, 'Varieties of New Legal Realism: Can a New World Order Prompt a New Legal Theory?' (2009) 95 Cornell LRev 62
O'Brien C, 'Social Blind Spots and Monocular Policy Making: The ECJ's Migrant Worker Model' (2009) 46 CML Rev 1107
O'Brien M, '*Fidium Finanz* Case Note' (2007) 44 CML Rev 1483
O'Brien M, 'Taxation and the Third Country Dimension of Free Movement of Capital in EU Law: the ECJ's Rulings and Unresolved Issues' (2008) 6 BTR 628
O'Leary S, 'The Relationship between Community Citizenship and the Protection of Fundamental Rights in Community Law' (1995) 32 CML Rev 519
O'Leary S, 'Developing an Ever Closer Union between the Peoples of Europe? A Reappraisal of the Case Law of the Court of Justice on the Free Movement of Persons and EU Citizenship' (2008) 27 YEL 167
O'Neill M, 'Democracy and the EU: Legal Perspectives on the Political Debate' (1995) 4 IrJEurL 48

Obermaier AJ, 'The National Judiciary as Sword of European Court of Justice Rulings: The Example of the Kohll/Decker Jurisprudence' (2008) 6 ELJ 735

Obstfeld M, *Models of Currency Crises with Self-Fulfilling Features* (Centre for Economic Policy Research 1996)

Odudu O, *The Boundaries of EC Competition Law* (OUP 2006)

Odudu O, 'Economic Activity as a Limit to Community Law' in Barnard C and Odudu O (eds), *The Outer Limits of European Union Law* (Hart Publishing 2009), 230–231

Ogus AI, *Regulation: Legal Form and Economic Theory* (Hart 2004)

Ohlin BG, *Interregional and International Trade* (Harvard University Press 1933)

Öhlinger T, *Verfassungsrecht* (8th edn, Facultas 2009)

Oliveira AC, 'Workers and Other Persons: Step-by-Step from Movement to Citizenship—Case-Law 1995–2001' (2002) 39 CML Rev 77

Oliver P, *Free Movement of Goods in the European Union* (5th edn, Sweet and Maxwell 2010)

Oliver P, and Roth W-H, 'The Internal Market and the Four Freedoms' (2004) 41 CML Rev 407

Oliver P, Roth W-H, and Enchelmaier S, 'Free Movement of Goods: Recent Developments in the Case Law' (2007) 44 CML Rev 649

Orlandini G, 'Right to Strike, Transnational Collective Action and European Law: Time to Move On?' [2007] Jean Monnet Working Paper 08/07

Ortino F, 'From "Non-Discrimination" to "Reasonableness": A Paradigm Shift in International Economic Law?' [2005] Jean Monnet Working Paper 01/05

Owren M and Bachorowski J-A, 'The Evolution of Emotional Expression: A "Selfish-Gene" Account of Smiling and Laughter in Early Hominids and Humans' in Mayne T and Bonanno GA (eds), *Emotions: Current Issues and Future Directions* (Guilford Press 2001), 239

Page AC, 'The Scope of Community and National Rules against the Overlapping of Social Security Benefits' (1980) 17 CML Rev 211

Partridge PH, *Consent and Consensus* (Shapiro L ed.) (Pall Mall 1971)

Paskalia V, 'Co-ordination of Social Security in the European Union: An Overview of Recent Case Law' (2009) 46 CML Rev 1177

Paulus A, 'International Adjudication' in Besson S and Tasioulas J (eds), *The Philosophy of International Law* (OUP 2010)

Paunio E and Lindroos-Hovinheimo S, 'Taking Language Seriously: An Analysis of Linguistic Reasoning and Its Implications in EU Law' (2010) 16 ELJ 395

Pelkmans J, 'Mutual Recognition in Goods and Services: An Economic Perspective' in Schioppa FKP (ed.), *The Principle of Mutual Recognition in the European Integration Process* (Palgrave Macmillan 2005), 92

Pelkmans J, 'Mutual Recognition in Goods. On Promises and Disillusions' (2007) 14 JEPP 699

Pelkmans J and Winters, A, *Europe's Domestic Market* (Routledge 1988)

Perju V, 'Reason and Authority in the European Court of Justice' (2009) 42 VaJInt'l L 307

Perisin T, *Free Movement of Goods and Limits of Regulatory Autonomy in the EU and WTO* (TMC Asser Press 2008)

Pescatore P, 'Le recours, dans la jurisprudence de la Cour de justice des Communautés européennes, à des normes déduites de la comparaison des droits des Etats membres' (1980) 32 RIDC 337

Pescatore P, 'Public and Private Aspects of European Community Competition Law' (1986–1987) 10 Fordham Int'l LJ 373

Petersmann E-U, 'European and International Constitutional Law: Time for Promoting "Cosmopolitan Democracy" in the WTO' in Búrca Gd and Scott J (eds), *The EU and the WTO—Legal and Constitutional Issues* (Hart Publishing 2001), 81–82

Petersmann E-U, 'Do Judges Meet their Constitutional Obligation to Settle Disputes in Conformity with 'Principles of Justice and International Law'?' (2007) 1 EJLS 1

Petersmann E-U, 'Judging Judges: From "Principal-Agent" Theory to "Constitutional Justice" in Multilevel "Judicial Governance" of Economic Cooperation Among Citizens' (2008) 11 JIEL 827

Pigou AC, *The Economics of Welfare* (4th edn, Macmillan 1962)

Pocock JGA, 'The Ideal of Citizenship since Classical Times' in Beiner R (ed.), *Theorising Citizenship* (State University of New York 1995), 31

Polanyi M and Sen A, *The Tacit Dimension* (University of Chicago Press 2009)

Post R, 'Theorizing Disagreement: Reconceiving the Relationship between Law and Politics' (2010) 98 CLR 1319

Postema G, '"Protestant" Interpretation and Social Practices' (1987) 72 Law & Phil 283

Postema G, 'Implicit Law' (1994) 13 Law & Phil 361

Prechal S, 'Free Movement and Procedural Requirements: Proportionality Reconsidered' (2008) 35 LIEI 201

Preuss UK, 'Problems of a Concept of European Citizenship' [1995] 1 ELJ 267

Raz J, *The Authority of Law—Essays on Law and Morality* (OUP 1979)

Raz J, *The Morality of Freedom* (OUP 1986)

Raz J, 'The Problem of Authority: Revisiting the Service Conception' (2006) 90 MinnLRev 1003

Raz J, *Human Rights Without Foundations* (SSRN 2007)

Regan DH, 'The Supreme Court and State Protectionism: Making Sense of the Dormant Commerce Clause' (1986) 84 MichLRev 1091

Regan DH, 'Judicial Review of Member-State Regulation of Trade within a Federal or Quasi-Federal System: Protectionism and Balancing, "Da Capo"' (2001) 99 MichLRev 1853

Regan DH, 'The Meaning of "Necessary" in GATT Article XX and GATS Article XIV: the Myth of Cost-Benefit Balancing' (2007) 6 WTR 347

Reich N, 'The "November Revolution" of the European Court of Justice: Keck, Meng and Audi Revisited' (1994) 31 CML Rev 459
Reich N, 'A European Constitution for Citizens' (1997) 3 ELJ 131
Reich N, *Bürgerrechte in der Europäischen Union* (Nomos 1999)
Ritter C, 'Purely Internal Situations, Reverse Discrimination, *Guimont*, *Dzodzi* and Article 234' (2006) 31 ELRev 690
Rivers J, 'Proportionality and Discretion in International and European Law' in Tsagourias N (ed.), *Transnational Constitutionalism* (Cambridge University Press 2007), 107
Rodrigues S, 'Chronique de Jurisprudence Communautaire—Marché intérieur' (2009) 45 CDE 217
Rönnmar M, 'Laval Returns to Sweden: The Final Judgment of the Swedish Labour Court and Swedish Legislative Reforms' (2010) 39 ILJ 280
Rosen A, 'The Normative Fallacy Regarding Law's Authority' in Will Walluchow and Steffan Sciaraffa (eds), *The Nature of Law* (OUP 2013), 75
Roth W-H, 'From *Centros* to *Uberseering*: Free Movement of Companies, Private International, Law and Community Law' (2003) 52 ICLQ 177
Röthel A, 'Grundfreiheiten und Private Normgebung' 36 [2001] EuR 908
Rothschild J, 'Observations on Political Legitimacy in Contemporary Europe' (1977) 92 PolSciQ 487
Rousseau J-J, *Du contrat social, ou, Principes du droit politique* (Bordas 1985)
Rubin EL, 'The New Legal Process, the Synthesis of Discourse, and the Microanalysis of Institutions' (1996) 109 HarvLRev 1393
Russell B, *History of Western Philosophy* (Routledge 2004)
Sabel CF and Gerstenberg O, 'Constitutionalising an Overlapping Consensus: The ECJ and the Emergence of a Coordinate Constitutional Order' (2010) 16 ELJ 511
Sandholtz W and Sweet AS, 'Integration, Supranational Governance, and the Institutionalization of the European Polity' in Sandholtz W and Sweet AS (eds), *European Integration and Supranational Governance* (OUP 1998), 18
Sarmiento D, 'The Silent Lamb and the Deaf Wolves—Constitutional Pluralism, Preliminary References and the Role of Silent Judgments in EU Law' in Avbelj M and Komárek J (eds), *Constitutional Pluralism in the EU and Beyond* (Hart Publishing 2012), 4
Sartori G, 'Democracy' in Sills DL (ed.), International Encyclopaedia of the Social Sciences, vol IV (Macmillan 1968), 112
Saunders C, 'Constitutional Rights and the Common Law' in Sajó A and Uitz R (eds), *The Constitution in Private Relationships* (Eleven International Publishing 2005), 195-199
Sauter W, 'The Economic Constitution of the European Union' (1998) 4 ColumJEurL 27
Sauter W and Schepel H, *State and Market in European Union Law: The Public and Private Spheres of the Internal Market before the EU Courts* (Cambridge University Press 2009)

Schaefer D, *Die unmittelbare Wirkung des Verbot der nichttarifären Handelshemmnisse (Art. 30 EWGV) in den Rechtsbezienhungen zwischen Privaten* (Lang 1987)

Shapiro M, 'Federalism, the Race to the Bottom and the Regulation-Averse Enterpreneur' in Scheiber H (ed.), *North-American and Comparative Federalism* (Institute of Governmental Studies Press 1992), 328

Shapiro M, 'The European Court of Justice' in Craig P and de Burca G (eds), The *Evolution of EU Law* (OUP 1999), 328

Scharpf F, *Governing in Europe: Effective and Democratic?* (OUP 1999)

Scharpf F, 'Legitimacy in the Multi-Level European Polity' in Loughlin M and Dobner P (eds), *The Twilight of Constitutionalism?* (OUP 2010), 93

Schauer F, 'Rules and the Rule of Law' (1991) 14 Harv JL & Pub Pol'y 645

Schauer F, 'The Convergence of Rules and Standards' (2003) NZLRev 303

Schepel H, 'Constitutionalising the Market, Marketising the Constitution, and to Tell the Difference: On the Horizontal Application of the Free Movement provisions in EU Law' (2012) 18 ELJ 177

Schepel H and Wesseling R, 'The Legal Community: Judges, Lawyers, Officials and Clerks in the Writing of Europe' (1997) 3 ELJ 165

Schepel H and Wesseling R, 'Constitutionalising the Market, Marketising the Constitution, and to Tell the Difference: On the Horizontal Application of the Free Movement Provisions in EU Law' (2012) 18 ELJ 177

Scheuing DH, 'Freizügigkeit als Unionsbürgerrecht' 38 (2003) EuR 744

Schillig M, 'The Interpretation of European Private Law in the Light of Market Freedoms and EU Fundamental Rights' (2008) 15 MJ 285

Schiltz C, '*Akrich*: A Clear Delimitation Without Limits' (2005) 12 MJ 241

Schmidt SK, 'Who Cares about Nationality? The Path-Dependent Case Law of the ECJ from Goods to Citizens' (2012) 19 JEPP 8

Schneewind JB, *The Invention of Autonomy: A History of Modern Moral Philosophy* (Cambridge University Press 1998)

Schueler B, 'Methods of Application of the Proportionality Principle in Environmental Law' (2008) 35 LIEI 231

Schütze R, *From Dual to Cooperative Federalism* (Craig P and Búrca Gd eds) (OUP 2009)

Schwartz IE, 'Rechtsangleichung und Rechtswettbewerb im Binnenmarkt—Zum europäischen Modell' 42 (2007) EuR 194

Seabright P, *The Company of Strangers: A Natural History of Economic Life* (Princeton University Press 2010)

Seché J, 'The Revision of Regulations nos. 3 and 4 (Social Security and Migrant Workers) in Light of their Interpretation by the Court of Justice' (1968) 6 CML Rev 170

Séché J-C, 'Quand les juges tirent au but: l'arrêt Bosman' 32 (1996) CDE 355

Segal JA and Spaeth HJ, *The Supreme Court and the Attitudinal Model Revisited* (Cambridge University Press 2002)

Shaffer G, 'A Structural Theory of WTO Dispute Settlement: Why Institutional Choice Lies at the Centre of the GMO Case' (2008) 41 JILP 1
Shaw J, 'Citizenship of the Union: Towards Post-National Membership?' [1997] Jean Monnet Working Paper 06/97
Shuibhne NN, 'Free Movement of Persons and the Wholly Internal Rule: Time to Move On?' (2002) 39 CML Rev 731
Shuibhne NN, 'The Free Movement of Goods and Article 28 EC: An Evolving Framework' (2002) 27 ELRev 408
Shuibhne NN, 'Settling Dust? Reflection on the Judgements in Viking and Laval' (2010) 21 EBLRev 681
Shuibhne NN, 'The Resilience of EU Market Citizenship' [2010] 47 CML Rev 1597
Shuibhne NN, '(Some of) the Kids are All Right: Comment on *McCarthy* and *Dereci*' (2012) 49 CML Rev 349
Siems MM, 'The Impact of the European Company (SE) on Legal Culture' (2005) 28 ELRev 431
Simon H, 'A Behavioral Model of Rational Choice' (1955) Quarterly Journal of Economics 69
Simon H, Models of Thought (Yale University Press 1979)
Sinn H-W, 'The Selection Principle and Market Failure in Systems Competition' (1997) 66 JPE 247
Snell J, *Goods and Services in EC Law: A Study of the Relationship between the Freedoms* (OUP 2002)
Snell J, 'Private Parties and the Free Movement of Goods and Services' in Andenas M and Roth W-H (eds), *Services and Free Movement in EU Law* (OUP 2002), 211–212
Snell J, 'And Then There Were Two: Products and Citizens in Community Law' in Tridimas T (ed.), *European Law for the Twenty-First Century*, vol II (Hart Publishing 2004), 50–67
Snell J, 'Non-Discriminatory Tax Obstacles' (2008) 56 ICLQ 339
Snell J, 'The Notion of Market Access: A Concept or a Slogan?' (2010) 47 CML Rev 437
Somek A, 'Solidarity Decomposed: Being and Time in European Citizenship' (2007) 32 ELRev 787
Somek A, 'The Argument from Transnational Effects I: Representing Outsiders through Freedom of Movement' (2010) 16 ELJ 315
Sousa AFd, 'Company's Cross-Border Transfer of Seat in the EU after Cartesio' [2009] Jean Monnet Working Paper 07/09
Sousa PCd, 'Through Contact Lenses, Darkly: Is Identifying Restrictions to Free Movement Harder than Meets the Eye? Comment on Ker-Optika' (2012) 37 ELRev 79
Sousa PCd, 'Quest for the Holy Grail—Assessing the Normative Overlap between the Market Freedoms and EU Citizenship' (2014) 20 ELJ, 499

Spamann H, 'Choice of Law in a Federal System and an Internal Market' [2001] Jean Monnet Working Paper 8/01
Spaventa E, 'Caixa-Bank Case Note' (2005) 42 CML Rev 1151
Spaventa E, *Free Movement of Persons in the European Union* (Kluwer Law International 2007)
Spaventa E, 'Seeing the Wood Despite the Trees? On the Scope of Union Citizenship and its Constitutional Effects' (2009) 45 CML Rev 13
Stein E, 'Lawyers, Judges and the Making of a Transnational Constitution' (1981) 75 AJIL 1
Steiner J, 'Drawing the Line: Uses and Abuses of Article 30 EEC' (1992) 29 CML Rev 749
Sternberger D, 'Legitimacy' in Sills DL (ed.), *International Encyclopedia of the Social Sciences*, vol IX (Macmillan 1968), 244
Stigler GJ, *The Organization of Industry* (R.D. Irwin 1968)
Stoppel DA, 'Grundfreiheitliche Schutzpflichten der Mitgliedstaaten im Europäischen Gemeinschaftsrecht' (Heinrich-Heine-Universität Düsseldorf 2003)
Streeck W, 'From Market Making to State Building? Reflections on the Political Economy of European Social Policy' in Leibfried S and Pierson P (eds), *European Social Policy—Between Fragmentation and Integration* (The Brookings Institution 1995), 399
Stryber R, 'Legitimacy' in Smelser NJ and Bates PB (eds), *International Encyclopedia of the Social & Behavioural Sciences*, vol XIII (Elsevier 2001), 8700–8701
Suchman MC and Edelman LB, 'Review: Legal Rational Myths: The New Institutionalism and the Law and Society Tradition' (1996) 21 L& SocInquiry 903
Sullivan K, 'Foreword: The Justices of Rules and Standards' (1992) 106 HarvLRev 22
Sun J-M and Pelkmans J, 'Regulatory Competition in the Single Market' (1995) 33 JCMS 67
Sunstein CR, *After the Rights Revolution: Reconceiving the Regulatory State* (Harvard University Press 1990)
Sunstein CR, 'Incommensurability and Valuation in Law' (1994) 92 MichLRev 779
Sunstein CR, *Legal Reasoning and Political Conflict* (OUP 1996)
Sunstein CR, 'State Action is Always Present' (2002) 3 ChiJInt'lL 465
Sunstein CR and Vermeule A, 'Interpretation and Institutions' (2003) 101 Mich L Rev 885
Sweet AS, *The Birth of Judicial Politics in France: The Constitutional Council in Comparative Perspective* (OUP 1992)
Sweet AS, 'Constitutional Courts and Parliamentary Democracy' (2002) 25 West European Politics 77
Sweet AS, 'Why Europe Rejected American Judicial Review and Why It May Not Matter' (2003) 101 MichLRev 2744
Sweet AS, *The Judicial Construction of Europe* (OUP 2004)
Sweet AS, 'The Politics of Constitutional Review in France and Europe' (2007) 5 I•CON 69

Sweet AS and Mathews J, 'Proportionality, Balancing and Global Constitutionalism' (2008) 47 ColumJTransnat'lL 72
Sweet AS and Brunell TL, 'The European Court of Justice, State Noncompliance, and the Politics of Override' (2012) 106 AmPolitSciRev 204
Sweet AS and Caporaso J, 'From Free Trade to Supranational Polity: European Court and Integration' in Sandholtz W and Sweet AS (eds), *European Integration and Supranational Governance* (OUP 1998), 102, 128
Sweet AS and Fligstein N, 'Institutionalizing the Treaty of Rome' in Sweet AS, Sandholtz W and Fligstein N (eds), *The Institutionalization of Europe* (OUP 2001)
Sweet AS, Sandholz w, and Fligstein N, *The Institutionalization of Europe* (OUP 2001)
Sykes AO, 'The (Limited) Role of Regulatory Harmonization in International Goods and Services' (1999) 2 JIEL 49
Sykes AO, 'Regulatory Protectionism and the Law of International Trade' (1999) 66 UChiLRev 1
Syllar R, 'Political Economy of Supplying Money to a Growing Economy: Monetary Regimes and the Search for an Anchor to Stabilize the Value of Money' (2010) 11 TheoInqL 1
Szczekalla P, 'Grundfreiheitliche Schutzpflichten—eine "neue" Function der Grundfreiheiten des Gemeinschaftsrechts' (1998) 113 DVBl 219
Szydlo M, 'Export Restrictions within the Structure of Free Movement of Goods. Reconsideration of an Old Paradigm' (2010) 47 CML Rev 753
Tamanaha B, 'Understanding Legal Realism' (2009) 87 TexLRev 731
Tate CN and Vallinder T, *The Global Expansion of Judicial Power* (New York University Press 1995)
Tiebout C, 'A Pure Theory of Local Expenditures' (1956) 64 Journal of Political Economy 416
Trachtman J, 'Regulatory Competition and Regulatory Jurisdiction' (2000) 3 JIEL 331
Tridimas T, 'The Court of Justice and Judicial Activism' (1996) 21 ELRev 199
Tridimas T, 'Proportionality in Community Law: Searching for the Appropriate Standard of Scrutiny' in Ellis E (ed.), *The Principle of Proportionality in the Laws of Europe* (Hart Publishing 1999), 68
Trivers R, 'The Evolution of Reciprocal Altruism' (1971) 46 Quarterly Review of Biology 35
Trivers R, *Social Evolution* (Benjamin/Cummings 1985)
Tryfonidou A, 'Jia or "Carpenter II": the Edge of Reason' (2007) 32 ELRev 908
Tryfonidou A, 'Reverse Discrimination in Purely Internal Situations: An Incongruity in a Citizen's Europe' (2008) 35 LIEI 43
Tryfonidou A, 'Family Reunification Rights of (Migrant) Union Citizens: Towards a More Liberal Approach' (2009) 15 ELJ 634

Tryfonidou A, 'In Search of the Aim of the EC Free Movement of Persons Provisions: Has the Court of Justice Missed the Point?' (2009) 46 CML Rev 1591
Tryfonidou A, Reverse Discrimination in EC Law (Kluwer Law International 2009)
Tryfonidou A, 'Further Steps on the Road to Convergence among the Market Freedoms' (2010) 35 ELRev 36
Tryfonidou A, 'Resolving the Reverse Discrimination Paradox in the Area of Custom Duties' (2011) 22 EBLRev 311
Tushnet M, 'The Issue of State Action/Horizontal Effect in Comparative Constitutional Law' (2003) I I•CON 79
Tushnet M, 'The Relationship between Judicial Review of Legislation and the Interpretation of Non-Constitutional Law, with Reference to Third Party Effect' in Sajó A and Uitz R (eds), *The Constitution in Private Relationships* (Eleven International Publishing 2005), 170
Usher J, 'Monetary Movements and the Internal Market' in Shuibhne N N (ed.), *Regulating the Internal Market* (Edward Elgar 2006), 193
Vallinder T, 'When the Courts Go Marching In' in Tate CN and Vallinder T (eds), *The Global Expansion of Judicial Power* (New York University Press 1995), 13-15
Verschueren H, 'Reverse Discrimination: An Unsolvable Problem?' in Minderhoud P and Trimikliniotis N (eds), *Rethinking the Free Movement of Workers: The European Challenges Ahead* (Wolf Legal Publishers 2009), 118
Vilaça JLdC and Piçarra N, 'Y a-t-il des Limites Matérièlles à la Revision des Traites Instituant les Communautés Européennes?' [1991] CDE 3
Vossestein G-J, 'Companies' Freedom of Establishment after Sevice' (2006) 4 EBLRev 177
Waal FBMd, *Chimpanzee Politics: Power and Sex Among Apes* (Johns Hopkins University Press 1989)
Waelbroeck M, 'Les rapports entre les règles sur la libre circulation des merchandises et les règles de concurrence applicables aux enterprises dans la CEE' in Capotorti F and others (eds), *Liber Amicorum Pierre Pescatore* (Nomos 1987), 782
Wägenbauer R, 'Free Movement in the Professions: The New EEC Proposal on Professional Qualifications' (1986) 23 CML Rev 91
Waldron J, 'Fake Incomensurability: A Response to Professor Schauer' (1994) 45 Hastings LJ 813
Waldron J, 'The Core of the Case against Judicial Review' (2006) 115 Yale LJ 1346
Waldron J, 'Can There Be a Democratic Jurisprudence?' (2009) 58 Emory LJ 675
Waldron J, 'Representative Lawmaking' (2009) 89 BULRev 335
Walker N, 'The EU and the WTO: Constitutionalism in a New Key' in Burca Gd and Scott J (eds), *The EU and the WTO—Legal and Constitutional Issues* (Hart Publishing 2001), 34-47
Walker N, 'The Idea of Constitutional Pluralism' (2002) 65 MLR 317
Walzer M, 'Citizenship' in Ball T, Farr J, and Hanson RL (eds), *Political Innovation and Conceptual Change* (Cambridge University Press 1989), 211

Wathelet M, 'The Influence of Free Movement of Persons, Services and Capital on National Direct Taxation: Trends in the Case Law of the Court of Justice' (2000) 20 YEL 1

Wattel P, 'The EC Court's Attempts to Reconcile the Treaty Freedoms with International Tax Law' (1996) 33 CML Rev 233

Weatherill S, 'Consumer Safety Legislation in the United Kingdom and Article 30 EEC' (1988) 12 ELRev 87

Weatherill S, 'Discrimination on Grounds of Nationality in Sport' (1989) 9 YEL 55

Weatherill S, 'After Keck: Some Thoughts on How to Clarify the Clarification' (1996) 33 CML Rev 885

Weatherill S, 'Better Competence Monitoring' (2005) 30 ELRev 23

Weber M, *Economy and Society: an Outline of Interpretive Sociology* (Bedminster Press 1968)

Weick KE, *Making Sense of the Organization* (Blackwell Business 2001)

Weiler J, 'The Transformation of Europe' (1991) 1000 Yale LJ 2403

Weiler J, *The Constitution of Europe* (Cambridge University Press 1999)

Weiler J, 'The Constitution of the Common Market Place: Text and Context in the Evolution of the Free Movement of Goods' in Craig P and Búrca GD (eds), *The Evolution of EU Law* (OUP 1999), 349

Weiler J, 'In Defence of the Status Quo: Europe's Constitutional Sonderweg' in Weiler JHH and Wind M (eds), *European Constitutionalism Beyond the State* (Cambridge University Press 2003), 18-22

Weiler J, 'Mutual Recognition, Functional Equivalence and Harmonization in the Evolution of the European Common Market and the WTO' in Schioppa FKP (ed.), *The Principle of Mutual Recognition in the European Integration Process* (Palgrave Macmillan 2005), 25

Werlauff E, 'Cross-Border Transfers of SE Companies' (2004) 1 EurCoL 121

Wernicke S, 'Au Nom de Qui? The European Court of Justice between Member States, Civil Society and Union Citizens' (2007) 13 ELJ 380

White EL, 'In Search of the Limits to Article 30 of the EEC Treaty' (1989) 26 CML Rev 235

White EL, Banks K, and Marenco G, 'Intellectual Property and the Community Rules on Free Movement: Discrimination Unearthed' (1990) 45 ELRev 224

Whish R, *Competition Law* (6th edn, OUP 2009)

Wils WPJ, 'The Search for a Rule in Article 30 EEC: Much Ado About Nothing?' (1993) 18 ELRev 475

Wilsher D, 'Does Keck Discrimination Make any Sense? An Assessment of the Non-Discrimination Principle Within the European Single Market' (2008) 33 ELRev 3

Wollenschläger F, 'A New Fundamental Freedom beyond Market Integration: Union Citizenship and its Dynamics for Shifting the Economic Paradigm of European Integration' (2011) 17 ELJ 1

Woods L, *Free Movement of Goods and Services within the European Community* (Ashgate 2004)

Wouters J, 'Fiscal Barriers to Companies' Cross Border Establishment' (1994) 14 YEL 73

Wouters J, 'European Company Law: Quo Vadis?' (2000) 37 CML Rev 257

Wyatt D, 'The Social Security Rights of Migrant Workers and their Families' (1977) 14 CML Rev 411

Wyatt D, 'Horizontal Effect of Fundamental Freedoms and the Right to Equality after Viking and Mangold, and the Implications for Community Competence' [2008] CYELP 1

Wymeersch E, 'The Transfer of the Company's Seat in European Community Law' (2003) 40 CML Rev 661

Zagrebelsky G, *Il diritto mite* (Einaudi 1992)

Ziegler K, 'International Law and EU Law: Between Asymmetric Constitutionalisation and Fragmentation' in Orakhelashvili A (ed.), *Research Handbook on the Theory of International Law* (Elgar 2011), 278-279

INDEX

Access to market 87–89, 104–115, 143–146, 170–172, 196
Attitudinal model 16, 229

Balancing 28–32, 45, 47, 49–50, 85, 101–102, 129, 166–169, 174, 206, 221, 226–227

Centralization 120–121, 123–125, 129, 132–136, 168
Citizenship 73–75, 80
Cognitive framework 15, 19–20, 24, 27, 32, 42–43, 51, 133, 145, 173, 212, 229
Collective regulation 201, 211–213
Common market 58–59, 65–66, 68–69, 77, 80, 83, 171, 198, 202, 217, 222
Constitutionalism 2, 3–4, 11, 22, 35–36, 225–226, 230
Contextualism 2, 4, 6, 85–86, 124, 128, 130, 136, 165, 167, 214, 217, 224–229
Cross-border requirement 78, 81, 97, 109, 114, 176–178, 180, 182–183, 185–188, 193–199, 214–215
Custom duties 178, 181
Customs union 59, 65

Democracy 2, 22–23, 25, 35, 37–38
Democratic deficit 35–36, 38
Deregulation 66–67, 121–124, 127–128, 131–136, 146
Direct effect 11–12, 66–67, 87, 88, 141, 201, 203–206, 208, 210–214, 223
  Horizontal 203–206, 208, 210–214, 223
Direct taxation 62, 147–151, 163–164
Discrimination 68, 76, 79, 87–98, 106–109, 112, 114, 138–140, 142–143, 148–151, 153, 170, 182, 184, 194, 203, 212–213, 222–223
Double taxation 147, 150–151

Economic due-process clause 1, 87–88, 98–103, 106, 108–109, 112–114, 127, 138–140, 143, 146, 150, 170
European Citizenship 1, 55, 69–83, 85, 148, 182, 184, 194, 197–198, 200, 203, 208, 215, 217–219, 226
European integration 1, 11, 74, 82, 118, 125, 130, 132–134, 136–137, 145, 164, 166–170, 173–174, 186, 217, 225

Federalism 12, 121
Financial services 66–66
Free movement of capital 58, 65–68, 70, 83, 85, 110, 113, 147–148, 180, 191
Free movement of goods 57–58, 64, 69–70, 85, 87–88, 90–91, 93, 95, 99–102, 104, 107, 109, 114–115, 126, 140, 146, 161–163, 170, 172, 179, 181–185, 190–191, 203, 206–213, 220
Free movement of persons 57, 60–62, 68–71, 76, 79, 81–82, 85, 87, 94, 96, 106, 109, 140, 142, 149, 153–155, 182–185, 197–198, 201, 203, 208–213, 215
Free movement of workers 56, 60, 62, 69, 76, 78, 94, 96, 107–108, 110, 141, 143, 148, 176, 177, 180, 203, 208, 213,
Free provision of services 58, 60, 62, 64, 69, 76, 81, 85, 96, 107–110, 140, 142–143, 148, 180–181, 184, 193, 195
Free trade area 12, 59, 65
Fundamental rights 13–14, 23, 48, 56–57, 69–71, 75, 78–79, 81–83, 182, 184, 197, 199–200, 203–204, 208, 215–217, 226

Harmonization 120, 123–125, 128, 130–133, 135–136, 154, 157, 164
Health-benefits 154–155
Human Rights *see* Fundamental rights

Indirect effect 162, 204–206
Institutional ability 41, 53–54, 169, 216
Institutional change 18–19, 24, 134
Institutional choice 1, 50–51, 118, 168, 171–172, 174, 187, 192, 216, 227
Institutional constraints 5, 14, 41, 50, 53, 86, 165, 192, 223,
Inter-governmentalism 36, 176
Internal market 58–59, 67, 69, 78–79, 83, 85, 87, 89, 111, 113–114, 117, 120, 122, 127, 134, 164, 166, 169, 171, 173–174, 176, 178, 181, 184, 187–188, 198,

Judicial review 11–12, 25, 101, 221, 223
Judicial test 5, 91, 112, 114, 117–118, 133, 135–137, 139, 144–146, 163–164, 169, 171, 173–174

Legitimacy 9, 17, 20–24, 32–41, 45, 47, 49, 51, 53–54, 63, 103, 130, 138, 167, 170
Lock-in 19–20, 43, 54, 145, 164, 198, 212

Majoritarian bias 51
Mandatory requirements 90, 99–100, 119
Market access *see* Access to market
Market equivalence 91–92
Market failures 124, 129–130
Market integration 36, 77, 79, 83, 117, 132, 171, 203
Means of payment 65
Minoritarian bias 51
Mutual recognition 24, 47, 99–101, 107–108, 125–128, 130, 132, 138–142, 150

Negative integration
Non-discrimination *see* Discrimination
Non-ergodicity 19, 43
Non-tariff barriers 105

Ordo-liberalism 36, 102, 104, 131–134, 139

Path-dependence 19, 43, 54, 139, 145, 164–165, 170, 185, 198, 212
Pluralism 13–14, 30, 41, 49, 54, 85, 123–124, 131–133, 136, 227–228
  Constitutional 13–14
  Moral 30, 227
  Regulatory 123–124, 131–133, 136
  Value 30, 49, 54, 85, 228
Precedent 9, 17–20, 43, 50, 52–53, 138, 143, 212, 219, 223
Preliminary reference 11, 62, 179, 186–187, 200
Preliminary ruling *see* Preliminary reference
Primary seat 155–158
Product requirements 90, 92, 103, 105, 126, 146
Production factors 59, 64–65, 67, 122, 129
Proportionality 28, 45–49, 51–52, 57, 63, 67, 83, 103, 118–121, 214, 218, 226
Protectionism 12, 46, 59, 89, 94, 98, 100, 114, 117, 123
  Barriers 12, 114
  Intent 89, 98
  Measures 46, 117, 123
Purely internal situations 75–76, 79, 176–178, 180–187, 194, 219

Quantitative Restriction 88, 105, 161

Race-to-the-bottom 122, 124, 131
Real seat 155–157, 159–160
Regulated profession 141, 142
Regulatory competition 122–125, 127, 129–135
Regulatory equivalence 92, 99, 140–141
Restriction
  On constitutional rights 57
  On economic activity 61, 113,
  On free movement 5, 60, 64, 83, 87, 95, 97, 101–102, 110, 111, 117, 119, 121, 125, 130, 134–139, 144–145, 147, 153, 155, 163–166, 169–171, 173–174, 176, 214, 219, 223, 226
  On the free movement of capital 67, 113
  On the free movement of goods 64, 90, 99–102, 112, 126, 140, 146, 209
  On the free movement of persons 142, 213
  On the free provision of services 64, 96, 107, 140, 142–143
  On the free movement of workers 95, 213
  On market access 114
  On the right of establishment 157, 161
Reverse Discrimination 182–184, 186, 215
Right of establishment 60, 62, 69, 81, 96, 107–108, 110, 141–143, 148, 156, 157–158, 160–161, 180, 209
Rule of reason 79, 101

Selling arrangements 90, 92, 104–105, 109
Separation of powers 1, 3, 25, 46
Social benefits 80, 82, 152–154
Social security 152–154, 163–164, 170, 189
Solidarity 79–80, 189
Sovereignty 12–13, 128, 138, 150, 166, 230
Specific object 206–207
Students 71, 78
Subjective public rights 56, 76
Subsidiarity 120–121, 220
Supranational 2, 12, 225
Supremacy 11–14, 38, 52, 87

Tacit dimension 2, 27
Tax *see* Direct taxation
Tertium comparationis 91, 98, 114, 148–149
Transnationalism 30, 36
Typological approaches 87, 88–89, 103–106, 109–110, 115, 172

The manufacturer's authorised representative in the EU for product safety is Oxford University Press España S.A. of El Parque Empresarial San Fernando de Henares, Avenida de Castilla, 2 - 28830 Madrid (www.oup.es/en or product.safety@oup.com). OUP España S.A. also acts as importer into Spain of products made by the manufacturer.
Printed and bound by CPI Group (UK) Ltd, Croydon, CR0 4YY
14/09/2026
02216305-0008